Thomas Sinclair

The Sinclairs of England

Editions Dedicaces

THE SINCLAIRS OF ENGLAND

Back cover: ROSSLYN CASTLE FROM THE EAST, 1803 by Julius Caesar Ibbetson.

Copyright © 2015 by Editions Dedicaces LLC

All rights reserved. No part of this book may be used or reproduced in any form whatsoever without written permission except in the case of brief quotations embodied in critical articles or reviews.

Published by:
   Editions Dedicaces LLC
   12759 NE Whitaker Way, Suite D833
   Portland, Oregon, 97230
   www.dedicaces.us

Library of Congress Cataloging-in-Publication Data
   Sinclair, Thomas
   The Sinclairs of England / by Thomas Sinclair.
   p. cm.
   ISBN-13: 978-1-77076-560-3 (alk. paper)
   ISBN-10: 1-77076-560-3 (alk. paper)

Thomas Sinclair

The Sinclairs of England

Contents

Foreword 7
Preface 11
Introduction 13

Chapter I - At the Norman Conquest 15
Chapter II - Before the Conquest 19
Chapter III - French Antecedents 23
Chapter IV - The Norman Civilisation 29
Chapter V - Walderne's Sons and Daughter 35
Chapter VI - Tenures of Land 43
Chapter VII - Eudo, Filius Huberti 47
Chapter VIII - Eudo Dapifer's Conquest 55
Chapter IX - The Seneschal as Lord of Colchester 59
Chapter X - Eudo the Founder of Religious Houses 67
Chapter XI - The Dapifer's Latter Years 75
Chapter XII - Eudo's Lineage 81
Chapter XIII - The Lands of Eudo Sinclair 91
Chapter XIV - John, Comes Essexiae 101
Chapter XV - Margaret Sinclair, Countess of Essex 107
Chapter XVI - The Younger Hubert's Line 117
Chapter XVII - The Earl of Nottingham 125
Chapter XVIII - Who was Simon of Senlis ? 135
Chapter XIX - Simon's Sons and Daughter 143
Chapter XX - Simon Sinclair, Third and Last Earl 151
Chapter XXI - Relations 155
Chapter XXII - The Countess of Gloucester 163
Chapter XXIII - William de Sancto Claro 169
Chapter XXIV - The Knight of Rye 175
Chapter XXV - Hamo Dapifer 189
Chapter XXVI - The Archbishop of Canterbury 195
Chapter XXVII - The Earls of Corbeil 199
Chapter XXVIII - The Viscount abd Fee-Farmer of Colchester 213

Chapter XXIX - The Hero of Bridgenorth 219
Chapter XXX - The Two Williams of Longvale...................................225
Chapter XXXI - Commissioner of Domesday Book 231
Chapter XXXII - Hugo de St.Clare..239
Chapter XXXIII - The Descent of the Baron of Aeslingham 247
Chapter XXXIV - Two Walters of Medway 253
Chapter XXXV - King's Chamberlain 263
Chapter XXXVI - Richard of East Anglia 269
Chapter XXXVII - Gereberd, Viscount of Norfolk and Suffolk...........273
Chapter XXXVIII - Two Johns...279
Chapter XXXIX - Vicecomes and Escheator..287
Chapter XL - Cousins..291
Chapter XLI - The Adams Sinclairs..295
Chapter XLII - Three Johns in Succession..299
Chapter XLIII - Sir Philip, Thomas, and Philip....................................309
Chapter XLIV - Sir Philip of Burston and his Sons..............................315
Chapter XLV - Mother and Daughters..323
Chapter XLVI - William, Son of Hugo Pincerna..................................331
Chapter XLVII - Governors of Rochester Castle..................................337
Chapter XLVIII - Robert, Nicolas, and John 345
Chapter XLIX - Coroner of Kent 351
Chapter L - The Essex Men...361
Chapter LI - Wolsey's Appreciator-General and Others 367
Chapter LII - The South-West...379
Chapter LIII - The Somerset Family...385
Chapter LIV - The Devenshire House...393
Chapter LV - The Sinclairs of Cornwall 401

Conclusion...409

Foreword

M. Guy Boulianne, the Editor-in-Chief of Editions Dedicaces, whom I have known for over 20 years and with whom I have shared a common fascination with the Sinclair story, has asked me if I would be prepared to write a foreword for this book. I had a number of reservations about doing so and shared them with M. Boulianne.

Before I deal with those reservations, I think it important to put "The Sinclairs of England" in a proper context. Up to the point where Thomas Sinclair began to write this book, the story of the Sinclairs in what is now the UK, was entirely centred on the Scottish families of the name. And it would not be wrong to say that this is also true for the period after Thomas published his book. Put another way, we are looking at virtually the only attempt to organize the history of the various Sinclair families that existed for nearly 1000 years on the English side of the border. When you think of it this way, you realize that what Thomas Sinclair was attempting to do is massive and that he got it done at all is a tribute to tenacity and a broad reach of historical research and knowledge. It would have broken many a lesser man and that we have it at all is of benefit to historians of any stripe and not just to Sinclairs.

My first reservation about writing a foreword for such a book is that I am neither a researcher nor an historian and in the light of this, it takes some temerity to take on the task. But I will say that I have read much on the subject of the history of the Sinclairs, mostly, it has to be said, as an enthusiast rather than a note-taking scholar looking for concordance amongst sources.

The second reservation has to do with the book itself as well as Thomas Sinclair the writer. This is the way I put it to M. Boulianne: Thomas Sinclair has written a dense and discursive text, but for all we know, he might well have made it all up out of whole cloth. The book is infuriating for not having an index [which makes it hard to go back and find material] but even worse he cites no sources. Finally, he says things that no one else says and the upshot is that people quote him and hence unproven facts if not outright errors are perpetuated. For example Thomas says that 9 St. Clair Knights fought at the battle of Hastings. No one else has ever said or written that except Thomas and of course the subsequent people who quote him. Drives me crazy.

In this vein, and as a an aside, Thomas Sinclair was related to a branch of the Caithness Sinclairs called the Broynach family. In the late 1700's the Broynachs disputed the transfer of the title of Earl of Caithness to the Rattar Family but the Broynachs were deemed ineligible to succeed to the title by act of Parliament because of the illegitimacy of a grandmother. Nevertheless, 100 years later we see Thomas resurrecting the cause of the Broynachs with dubious evidence. This does not speak well of Thomas' interest in factual material presented in a disinterested manner.

I said to M. Boulianne, that if I did write the foreword, I would want to say such things and was M. Boulianne okay with this if I did?

M. Boulianne, to his credit, replied that the truth was paramount in book publishing. So I here I am.

I have consulted others on the matter of the Sinclairs of England and Thomas Sinclair. The first is Gerald Sinclair of Australia co-author of the recently published and acclaimed book "The Enigmatic Sinclairs" which is an attempt to separate out factually provable parts of early Sinclair history from conjecture and outright confabulation. The second person I have consulted is Captain Craig Sinclair of north Yorkshire in the UK who has spent some time with Thomas and the Sinclairs of England. He agrees with much of what I have said above about Thomas' unreliability but goes on to say that that not all of it should be jettisoned for, as the popular saying goes, we would be guilty of throwing the baby out with the bathwater.

First off, although Thomas is the only one to put a number to the St Clair Knights at Battle of Hastings, there is no evidence to say nine. But there could have been; there just isn't any contemporary evidence to support it. The Norman poet Wace reports as follows In his chronicle, The Roman de Rou, written between 1160 and 1170:

>   Normant a pie e a cheual
>   Les assaillment comme uassal
>   Donc poinst Hue de Mortemer,
>   Od lui li sire d'Auuiler,
>   Cil d'Onebac e de Saint Cler;
>   Engleis firent mult enuerser.

Translated to English -

> The Normans attacked them courageously on foot and on horse. Then Hugh of Mortemer spurred his horse; he had with him the lord of Auvilliers, and the lords of Les Oubeaux and of Saint-Clair. They overthrew many Englishmen. (translation Wace, p. 188)

Captain Sinclair goes on to say "I call some of the chaps like Thomas Sinclair as the 'chocolate fireguard' historians of antiquity.

Thomas Sinclair's errors? Well, I describe the book as a glorious mess. Glorious because there are things within this book which are absolute gold, and can be backed up with solid primary source evidence. However, there are equally, moments where his assumptions are veering toward and beyond some of those awful "history" programmes I see on the History Channel."

I know what the Captain means. Such programmes begin with the following script: 'If we assume that A might have been in [name a place] and that he had read [name a document], he might have taken the road to the north end [of the named place] to meet B who we are pretty sure was not there but might have been and A then might have said to B [such and so].

I have read the Sinclairs of England but I have to say it was not an easy read and it seemed at times unfocussed and all over the place. Captain Sinclair puts it this way: "I've spent the last 10 years working through Thomas' tortuous book. I have a callus on my forehead from banging it so much! But you just can't leave it alone. So please don't dismiss it completely as pure fabrication. It is that, but it isn't also."

I think that is as well as it can be put.

With all this in mind, you can now read the book and mine for the gold and discard the dross.

RORY A. P. SINCLAIR
Past President,
Clan Sinclair Association of Canada

Preface

If the purpose of this work had been merely genealogical, it would have followed the usual course of publication by subscription at high price, for the delight of collectors of county histories, family records, and curiosities of antiquarian literature.

It is hoped that the contents will be of decided interest to lovers of English antiquities, but the direct appeal is to the large public who accept with appreciation any real contribution to the history of their country. To get at the spirit of past periods through tracing the action of particular families, is a new historical method; and the immense mass of personal materials which is now open to research in England, makes the field one of the most promising. A view of facts from the side of the ruled rather than from the usual monarchical standpoint of historians, must have its practical use; and it ought to be especially grateful to a time when democracy has learnt rights, and is dimly seeing duties.

The pedigree mania, with which even America is smitten, has little to do with the inquiry; substantial showing of the lives of a line in the press of national growth, being the intention. With the Romans a Fabian or Julian stock was an inspiration to the simplest member of the populus; and because the width of a remarkable family's connections causes an inevitable democratic feeling, there is no danger of that exclusiveness which is at once the nemesis and cause of ridicule to higher position, however nobly gained. No country has been more generous than this in receiving worth into its best grades.

To contemporary republicanism there is somewhat of wonder when it realises how free to persistent ability all offices and honours in England have been and still are. It was thought that the days of science would bring men to a dead level socially; and the evolutionary hypothesis which reduced, or threatened to reduce, mankind to brotherhood with the ape in the first place, and with the whole animal world ultimately, was considered to be the most effective destroyer of all pride of race and position. But human nature returns; and the doctrine of survival of the fittest would create, if left to itself, an aristocracy which for iron exclusiveness and the worst vices of selection, might surpass all domination that the world has yet seen. The poor and the miserable, below a certain point, would be exterminated; and the fittest must lord it over the earth, as prime monkeys, to an extent beyond conception.

An easier way of social existence which left chances to such broken lives as those of Shakespeare, Pope, Scott, Byron, and many others lame of body, is to be preferred to that of the so-called reign of law (for law is as unrealisable as everything else in the eternally limited province of human science); and nothing in our history is more comforting than the knowledge that some field was allowed at all times for the rise of every talent to its rights. There was nepotism enough, but in this there has been at least political safety, for the presumption is usually in favour of experienced stocks having the most natural aptitude for ruling position, though it has never been forgotten that to this law there are brilliant exceptions, who must have their places.

No democracy can ever get free from some form of aristocracy, but the wisdom is to keep the best men and women as healthy as possible by continual mixture with the elect of the people.

It is an ethnological fact that marriage of those too near of kin is as dangerous as of those too distant in blood, cousins to cousins, northerns to southerns, Swiss villagers to Swiss villagers, Desdemonas to Othelloes; and social unions in a country have similar dangers.

But it is the insight that is to be got as to the formation of the nation, from the Norman Conquest downwards, individually rather than collectively, that was the attraction of the toil expended on this subject; and if others also realise something of the inner life of the past through these gatherings, the object will be attained.

A word of detail is that the varied spelling of certain places and names is followed because of peculiar light thus thrown on changes of historical value.

London, 1887

The Sinclairs of England

Introduction

Novelty and originality are great aids to all narration.

There has been for the last two hundred years so little written or known of the English branch of the Sinclair family, that what were simply taken from the various records, authentic and available, ought to have much of those desirable qualities. The Scottish house has had for many centuries the full light of fame over it. The Danish Sinclairs, of whom Sir Andrew, ambassador to James First of England from the king of Denmark, is a prominent figure; the Swedish, known most by Count Malcolm's tragic death returning from his embassy to the Porte during the Czarina Catherine's reign, in the violent time of the "hats and caps", - Major Sinclair of Carlyle's Frederick the Great; the Norwegian, Russian, and German, remarkable by their literary, civil, and military positions of substance and honour: these are all better to the front than the forgotten Englishmen.

With the Romans it was piety not to neglect the ashes of the fathers. In real generosity of feeling dwellers in these happy islands of the west cannot but be their successful rivals. The dark clouds of antiquity are over many of our brave actions as a race; but we have not been disrespectful of the past, and the world of writings in our national keeping are unique for their quantity and equality.

There is a notable Irish family of the last two centuries upwards, of whom the Rev. John, girt, with sword and pistols at the siege of Derry, is the hero; and the History of Belfast and Froude's English in Ireland give knowledge of a family of civic and political importance in Ulster's chief town. Recent American, African, and Australian offshoots show the old ability and courage.

Of this, in some respects, too cosmopolitan, though never numerous name, the English representatives can well bear now all the publicity which can be given to them. For the general mind, Sir Walter Scott has done much with regard to those lords of Roslin, who were the princes of

Orkney and Shetland, earls of Caithness, dukes of Oldenburgh, and chief nobles of Norway. His verses in The Lay of the Last Minstrel, and his notes to them, about what he well called "the lordly line of high St.Clair", are of almost over-frequent reference, however much backed by chivalrous and splendid deeds. Even of chains of diamonds the fitful souls would get tired, if too much used.

With a direction to Sir Bernard Burke's no doubt well-grounded enthusiasm about the Scottish family's noble and royal claims and traditions, especially under "Lord Sinclair", they may be left out of notice. His books alone, if there were not the libraries which are, could keep their memories green. The Vicissitudes of Families may be mentioned in particular as of easy reading and reference.

John Fordun, the old monk of Aberdeen, never felt easy in his mind with a genealogy till he got it to Noah; George Buchanan, the historian, went back through endless paths of Gaelic darkness with his Scot kings; the ingenious and useful, if too superstitious, Matthew Paris, had to get his Henries of England traced somewhere near the flood: our standard authority on peerage, baronetage, and all other rank, has almost laid himself open to the quiz of similar monastic scholasticism in his generous and perhaps scientific reckoning of Sinclair relationship through Scottish, Irish, Norman, Norwegian, and other blood, noble and royal, to the mythological Odin, god, king, and father to all the Dacians.

Of the English Sinclairs he has only a word or two, though they are closely knit with that great Burgh lineage to which he attaches, with evident interest, the northern family on slenderer grounds. Some related families, like the viscounts Gage of Firle Place, Sussex, know that there existed people here of the name; and the antiquaries have a vague suspicion of certain dark figures so yclept moving in the back-chambers of their wonderfully-made memories: but, practically, this is breaking entirely new ground; and with the special interest of such work, there cannot but be the accompanying imperfections.

The strongest arm in art, historic or other, is limited by thousands of chances. Human effort is at its best when sincerity is a sleepless watchman over what ability may come into exercise. To give the proper limits to the imagination where facts are broken and sparse, and also to preserve artistic unity, are a difficult enterprise.

Chapter I
At the Norman Conquest

Of those lithe athletic figures in armour on horseback around William, duke of Normandy, on that famous October day of 1066 near Hastings, nine at least were Sinclairs. With the Greek-like ease familiar from fine expression in tapestry, they moved in the inmost circles of his gallant surrounding. Hubert Sinclair, earl of Rye, was still in the strength of manhood, though he had near him his four sons in the flower of warriorhood. Radulph was the eldest, Hubert second, Adam third, and Eudo the youngest. The earl of St.Clare, Walderne, the brother of the earl of Rye, was also there, with his three sons, Richard, Britel, and William. It is not improbable that the earl of Senlis, though then a French and not a Norman subject, also added with his sons to the roll of "De Sancto Claro" in the decisive contest for England's sovereignty. Of him, however, there is no record existing with this established. The others are discernible in wonderful distinctness through those more than eight hundred succeeding years. Many of them, no doubt, did doughty feats at Senlac.

One is immortalised; and, considering how events suffer under the tooth of time, several more have been very kindly rescued from oblivion by the fates of the chances. In Wace's Roman de Rou, written within hearsay memory of living witnesses of the Norman Conquest, there is this passage in an admittedly very faithful description of the battle of Hastings, the chief event in his history of Rollo's line:

> "'Dunc puinst Hue de Mortimer,
> Od li Sire d'Anvilier;
> Cil d Onebac e de Saint Cler
> Engleiz tirent mult enverser'"

It was at a critical point of the fight that this Sinclair, Richard, the son of Walderne, "'overthrew many of the Angles'".

Angles they were, and not for a moment "English", as we now understand the word. To dub the Normans with the name of Frenchmen, and so to gain sympathy for the supposed patriotic side, was hardly ingenuous procedure on the part of some late fanatical historians. We have as much honour now from the deeds of the brilliant conquerors as of the brave conquered of that memorable field. It may not be granted to some writers that the majority of present names is Norman, but we have all the fame of every gallant deed on both sides. It is not an enviable distinction, to have given an evil twist to the facts of this finest chapter in the growth of a great people, when Normannic united with Celtic and Saxon blood to form what Americans and others, with conscious meaning, call the Britisher. If there was patriotism it went on a false scent, and judicious treatment of history was left in the background.

Our Freemans and our Froudes are passionate pleaders to contemporisms when they might be aspirants to immortality in their line of art. It has been said of William of Malmesbury that his account of the grossness of the Angles or Saxons and of the refinement of the Normans, was probably true, because he had the blood of both in his veins; one could almost think that the historian special of the Conquest had discovered in his honest enough researches, that he was a descendant of some Saxon bondman, and felt therefore bound to see nothing good in what like the chronic Irishman he assails as the oppressor. There is a subtle truth in the saying that Herewald was the last of the English. He was the wake of the brave but brutal Angles; and it is reason for thankfulness that too much of the Teutonic, partially Tartaric, grating grit, is not conspicuous in our national composition.

At the warriors' table on the night of the battle, spread among the dead, where forsworn presumptuous Harold's standard all day had stood, these Sinclairs were; and there they also slept the sleep in mankind's estimation perhaps the most dignified possible on earth, that of conquerors after victory. On that very spot, Battle Abbey was to rise, as if to guard their memories for ever with its shelter; and it has not been altogether unsuccessful. Its roll of heroes, broken, and perhaps fuller also than it should be, still keeps the "lord of St.Cler" as one. The head of the then great family, Walderne, earl of St.Clare, had his name on the memorable list, the representative of all. It is true that "Richard de Saint Clair" is expressly mentioned in the roll in the church of Dives, Normandy, of the companions of the Conqueror in 1066; but this does not conflict, seeing that the warriors had then only first names, and were designated after some one or other of their estates. Huberts and Walters of various localities occur in the list. Through the advance to coronation and complete possession of the country, the family followed worthily their great chief; and their services are well seen by the offices they filled.

Dark gaps come in the history of kings themselves so far away in time; it is not wonder that there are clouds often over their noblest supporters. The sons of Hubert Sinclair, earl of Rye, can, however, be followed.

Radulph was sent with troops northward to secure the heart of England, and he was made castellan and earl of Nottingham. To him the castle of Nottingham was given to keep, and keep it well he did.

Another Radulph, of another strain, a semi-Saxon, had got the tower of Norwich to guard; but he was the worst traitor of the marriage-feast which cost Waltheof his head in 1075. After this Radulph of Waer took to flight, the young Hubert Sinclair was sent to take and hold it.

His cousin Richard, the hero of Hastings, went with him; and Domesday has its account of the pain and blood it cost to restore all the disorder. The lands of the rebellious burghers knew the necessary fire and sword. Hubert became the governor with the hand of iron, and Richard had gifts of land and house in the district where the soldiers had done soldiers' duty. Richard also was to the front among the high war and court officers of the time.

Adam got lands in Kent. He is known as "of Campes" there. His possessions were large; but all men were warriors who followed the duke of Normandy, and only the oblivion of time and the frequency of the military heroes, hide him in this character also. When troubles began in 1066 in Normandy, King William had sent him and his two brothers, afterwards the castellan of Nottingham and the governor of Norwich Tower, with their father Hubert, to quell the Cenomannic region, the most refractory part of the dukedom.

In the battle of Hastings itself, the rebellious spirit appeared, in the person of one of the Cenomannic nobles; and it needed good counsel and prompt hands to deal with them, their duke away in England. The work had been thoroughly done, and the sons returned to this side of the Channel. Adam was one of the able commissioners who compiled that wonder of the world, as to state record, The Domesday Book. It was the civil capacity of such born rulers that put the right finish to their valour and skill in war. The first opportunities which peace gave, were always eagerly taken advantage of, to shape things into beautiful civil polity.

When the father and three brothers went thus back to Normandy on that weighty enterprise, Eudo the youngest remained with the king, and of them all he was destined to become the greatest. He was in the king's immediate service, and his history is as remarkable as it is full.

Britel Sinclair was sent to Devonshire. In the fighting around Exeter he bore his share; and, when quiet came, he settled in Somersetshire and Cornwall.

What became of William, the youngest son of Walderne, is perhaps the most interesting, as it is at all events the most celebrated, of all the narratives of the Sancto de Claro family, whose representatives thus surrounded and followed their duke and their relation, when he conquered, with most masculine vigour, the malcontents of his plighted kingdom of England.

Chapter II
Before the Conquest

Far distant as 1066 is, there are previous and pleasing records of their doings too romantic and readable to be missed. In the early struggles of Duke William against the rebellious earls of Normandy, supercilious exceedingly as to his love-birth by Arlotta, the daughter of the tanner of Falaise, Hubert Sinclair, earl of Rye, figures, with these same sons of his, afterwards so famous, as the most loyal of vassals, according to his oath to Duke Robert, saint and devil, father of the brave boy.

In 1047 it was only by the watchfulness of his fool that William's life was saved from conspirators who at opportunity would not do things by halves. Both Freeman and Cohen have described that terrible midnight gallop and pursuit. Though taken from Wace's Roman du Rou, they give full credence to the narrative; such rhyme being then the trustworthy and almost only medium of history. Cohen, better known as Sir Francis Palgrave, refers to the Voie du Duc as present geographical corroboration of the truth of the duke's ride. He also shows that the tale, in its best parts, could only have been told by William himself. The escape from Valognes, in the Cotentin, after the sudden alarum by the court-fool, has been digested by Freeman.

"'The duke arose, half dressed in haste, leaped on his horse, seemingly alone, and rode for his life all that night. A bright moon guided him, and he pressed on till he reached the estuary formed by the rivers Ouve and Vire. There the ebbing tide supplied a ford, which was afterwards known as the Duke's Way. William crossed in safety, and landed in the district of Bayeux, near the church of Saint Clement. He entered the building and prayed for God's help on his way."

His natural course would now have been to strike for Bayeux, but the city was in the hands of his enemies; he determined therefore to keep the line between Bayeux and the sea, and thus to take his chance of reaching the loyal districts. As the sun rose he drew near to the church and castle of Rye, the dwelling-place of a faithful vassal named Hubert. The lord of Rye was standing at his own gate between the church and the mound on which his castle was raised. William was still urging on his foaming horse past the gate, but Hubert knew and stopped his sovereign, and asked the cause of this headlong ride. He heard that the duke was flying for his life before his enemies. He welcomed his prince to his house, he set him on a fresh horse, he bade his three sons ride by his side and never leave him till he was safely lodged in his own castle of Falaise. The command of their father was faithfully executed by his loyal sons. We are not surprised to hear that the house of Rye rose high in William's favour.'

In the ancient rhymes the tale is told with poetic fulness of question, answer, and narrative. Dramatic as well as historic interest, makes the several pages which the story occupies, to nearly a couple of hundred lines, full of colour, and well worth special reading, the old French in which they are written being easy enough to understand. A modest recent biography of William the Conqueror by Lamb, not "Elia", gives much pictorial detail of this dangerous personal conspiracy in favour of Guy for duke, his aunt's son. Hubert himself, after the birds have flown, gets on horseback to guide the pursuers, leads them all roads but the right one, and saves his prince. The duke triumphed over these deadly enemies of his then, and Hubert had such favour with him that before the invasion of England he had promised to make him dapifer or seneschal of that kingdom, when it should come into his possession.

But this adventure was not the only cause of Hubert's popularity. In the difficulties of choosing his successor, Edward the Confessor thought often of William, his cousin of Normandy. Secretly he sent him a message by Goscelin of Winchester, an English merchant accustomed to traveling on the Continent. William must appoint his most trustworthy and capable subject to come to England to receive the king's mandates and the symbols of bequeathing the kingdom. A council of the earls was held, and no one could be induced to risk his life in such an embassy to what they all considered a barbarous nation. The cruelties perpetrated at Guildford shortly before, in the seizure and murder by Earl Godwin and his sons of Prince Alfred and the Norman nobles who accompanied him, were unanswerable arguments to all invitations to the high office. It was not fifty years yet since its guests the Danes were massacred on St.Brice's dreadful day.

Hubert Sinclair offered his services; and, with prophecies of tragedy, there was universal applause for his gallantry. He was appointed ambassador and executor between the princes. To impress the barbaric nation, he had a specially magnificent following. There is a highly picturesque description in monkish Latin, of the great equipage, grand pomp, horses housed brilliantly, "terrible with foaming", and men in parti-coloured and attractive garments. The result followed that the embassy was received in special honour by the people and the king. The mission, further, was wholly successful, and Hubert brought back to Normandy all the mandates as well as the peculiar symbols which made his master heir to the crown of England. Some relics of the saints, a golden hunting-horn, and a stag's head, were the peculiar signs of possession to come. It is said that it was on his return from his successful visit that he had the appropriate promise of the dapifership of England.

Such transaction explains the sympathy of the pope and the religious world with William's expedition in 1066, to secure his rights from the usurping private nobleman, Harold, who had rebel blood in him enough to lead a stronger mind than his astray. The blessing of the Norman banner, a kind of earliest oriflamme, could have been no inconsiderate act, as giddy pleaders seem to hint. The world was always as far as possible ruled by fact, and no time was more honestly sincere in polity or religion than those centuries. The duke himself was as religiously inclined always as he was a cultivator of refined morality. Whether the story of Harold's oath is true or fable, he was out of account except as a king by violence, and, even for England then, law and order had some existence.

Of the reality of this mission of Hubert's there is the illustrative fact that Edward the Confessor, a well-known favourer of Normans, gave him a perpetual grant of the estate called Esce in The Domesday Book, now Ashe in Hampshire, says Freeman. In the time of King Edward the Confessor it is noted as having been held under Earl Harold. If not the very first land possessed by a Sinclair in England of which there is record, it is perhaps the most generally interesting by its historic association. As shall appear, there are indications of even earlier connection, but Ashe has very particular interest in respect to this kind of antiquity.

Hubert was not wanting either, in generosity on his part. He left at least one substantial mark of his visit. If he did not altogether establish the church of St.Mary, West-Cheap, London, he gave it great gifts. He had the advowson of it, and his family after him. That it was ordinarily in the Conqueror's time called New Church, is corroborative proof that he was the founder of it. Religious munificence was the highest type of honour then next to bravery and counsel.

It may have been that his lands in England brought him often there; and such strong sympathy with London's religious condition as is implied by this ecclesiastical connection, would seem to point to some continued presence. Few have been so fortunate as to have even so much of their good deeds chronicled for posterity as Hubert of Rye has had, but there is not further mention of him after his return to Normandy to quell the Cenomannic rising. He did not hold the dapifership he had been promised, but it is more than probable that he lived to see his youngest son Eudo enjoying the fruits of their loyal deeds towards the king, in this the position next to royalty itself.

The Rye family was a branch of the Sinclairs, lords of the castle of St.Lo, which Palgrave says gradually gathered around it the well-known town of that name in the Cotentin. They again had come to reside there from St.Clare, whence the local name, upon that historic river Epte which flows into the Seine not far from Rouen. There Rollo got his dukedom acknowledged by the king of France. The earls of Senlis to the east, in the direction of Paris, had gained great possessions; other members traceable from this castle of St.Clare, which the Germans would call the "Schloss Stamm" of the kin.

Chapter III
French Antecedents

It never was, nor shall it ever be, easy to fish substantial facts from that muddy pool of French history when it was difficult to know which was the king and which was the noble. What records there were the English took in battle and destroyed. To risk already the saying that the Sinclairs were equivalent connetables in those times when lords did what was right in their own eyes, with little or no reference to the sham royalty always claiming allegiance so helplessly, would not be judicious. But it is right to say, at all events at this stage of search, that dim lines of evidence seem to point to their Frankish rather than Norse origin in the male line.

That they speedily recognised the advantage of marriage with the Neustrian dynasty founded by Rollo is pretty well established. There may be more French blood in them than was usual among the Normans of the eleventh century, and their intellectual characteristics do not much combat the idea. That they were strangers from Kent in England some time before the ninth century may also allow some Celtic blood. The prevailing theory of the extermination of the Celts by the Saxons has nowhere more absolute living contradiction than in the bodily frames and mental peculiarities of the genuine Kentishmen.

It is to be gathered from Holinshed's Chronicles that the mother of William Longsword, the second duke of Normandy, was probably a Sinclair [Poppa de Valois]. His wife, Sprota, daughter of the famous, and specially generous if we may trust Palgrave, Hubert, earl of Senlis, there can be even less doubt about. To none more than to this Hubert were both Rollo and his son indebted for high acceptance among the French nobility, the most exclusive and turbulent men then alive. Palgrave says that Popee, Rollo's Neustrian wife, was the half-sister of a Bernard, and that Bernard took heartily to Rollo and his family. He gives Dudon de Saint Quentin as his authority. Rollo's line, he thinks, would have failed but for this Frenchman, Bernard of Senlis, who, "trusted and worthy of Trust", fought well for the strangers he so much loved. He had his reward too, becoming lord of Coucy, and always a prime counsellor in times of danger.

So many have claimed false relationship to the dynasty of William the Conqueror, that it is neither safe nor at all assuring to those who know the state of things, to make much of such historical notices. The insuperable difficulty, that the use of first names was then and long after all but universal, is at once trap for the unwary and open door for the impostors. The luck of assuming a surname early belongs more perhaps to the Sinclairs themselves than to most European families. They also have suffered extremely, and particularly in England, as will soon appear, by that peculiar pride in first name which was effective contemporaneously but disastrous for posterity. Who, for example, in his senses could contend about the rights of a Welsh genealogy ? And there were features in those Gilberts and Fitz-Gilberts, Odoes and sons of Odo, that make problems of early Norman descent even more inscrutable. The threads sometimes can be scientifically unravelled, and one bit of success in this way is worth thousands of attempts, not to say falsifications.

Glimpses from fixed facts can be had back into the comparative darkness of Duke Richard's reign, the grandson of Rollo. He was married to Gunnora, a princess of the Danish line, and her female relations are by marriage closely related to this and other English notable names. Indeed, the comparative equality then between princes and their nobility goes far to excuse, if not explain, the ties so often found to exist by the heralds, of undoubtedly obscure persons with the line of the Conqueror. Accumulation of record and history puts the Sinclair family within the ducal circle, and for centuries. The rest, as the Gauls say, goes without saying.

It is not overshooting the mark to hint that, in the tenth century, the Norse dukes had the better side of the bargain in the alliances by marriage. It was England that widened the distinction of royalty and nobility to what has since prevailed. Father Hay, the Augustine friar, who was son to the widow of the last Sinclair baron of Roslin, and who had full access to the charters in the castle, says that the wife of Walderne, earl of St.Clare, was daughter to Duke Richard of Normandy. The friar wrote about the end of the seventeenth century.

Alexander Nisbet, an Edinburgh antiquarian, writing in 1722, quotes Jacob van Bassan's M.S., a foreigner who lived long at Roslin Castle, to the effect that "Wolderne, Compte de St.Clare", was married to Helena, daughter to the duke of Normandy. [The Duke's daughter Helena/Eleanor was married to Baldwin of Flanders]. William, his second son, who went to Scotland and became steward to Queen Margaret Atheling there, marrying, Agnes Dunbar, daughter of Patrick, first earl of March, he shows to have been cousin-german to William the Conqueror. Holinshed says that Duke Richard had no issue; but he means merely that he had no sons, the writer's purpose being dynastic. Even if he did state this with the full meaning, his authority is both weaker and later than that of the Roslin investigators, having access as they had to the carefully preserved documents of, as one writer has it, "the magnates of Scotland during the reigns up to the fourth James".

Nisbet says of Henry of this line, that he "married to Florentia, daughter of the king of Denmark, with whom he got a great estate in Norway"; of his son William, that he "married the fair Egidia" Douglas, granddaughter of Robert II, king of Scotland; and that their son William was "the greatest subject by far of all others of his time". He shows how they got the principality of Zetland and Orkney under the king of Norway, and the dukedom of Oldenburgh in Denmark. This nobleman's offices and titles, some one has said, would have "even pleased a Spaniard".

Writing of the earl of Douglas and James II of Scotland, when Edward IV reigned over England, Rapin says of James, "'At the same time he gave the administration of affairs to the earl of Orcades, mortal enemy of Douglas'". Tindal gives the note to this, "William Sinclare". But northern history is full of their deeds. The records of such a public family are as trustworthy documents as history can have; and what is true of the relationship of the first William, son of Walderne, to the Conqueror, is applicable also to Richard and Britel, his brothers, who remained in England.

There is no necessity to plead the case, because affinity will appear, sufficient for the gravest purpose, incidentally, as the English fortunes are described. In a chapter of antecedents, likelihoods are nearly as appropriate as what can thus be proved by recognised evidence. To give breathing-room, it may be said that the element of uncertainty is continually present in all genealogical and historic details. After this, the closeness of grasp upon facts is the test of right science. Do we not need our theatrical fool to tell us with hidden wisdom, like the court one in the palaces of ancient kings, that it is a wise bird which knows its own father ? The scientific mind is inclined to be wise over and beyond what is written or really knowable, and the humanest spirits have to save souls alive from the valuable but mechanic machineries of partial truth. The wings of imagination must not be clipped too closely. The creature will die for want of the food to be picked only on the wing. To the present quest also this is pertinent.

Why should not the Clare of Rochester in the county of Kent, who became the famous St.Clare of the ninth century in his hermitage on the banks of the Epte in France, be the progenitor, or, at all events, the earliest relation on record, of all the Sinclairs ? One writer says that it was considered immoral for priests to be unmarried in those centuries, but even if that cannot be admitted, what is more likely than that this saint either had set up his hermitage, the remains of which still exist, and whose well yet gives, it is said, clearer sight to the eyes, on the estate and under the protection of a relation from England, or was himself the first French Sinclair, a monk on his own land ? Rice of Oxford University is the recent authority as to the birthplace of this martyred saint of France, but in the books of the saints he is by the Roman Catholics also accounted an Englishman. His martyrdom by two tools of a lady whose conduct needed and got his thorough criticism, is one of the events consecrated in religion. It is not at all unlikely that the neighbouring castle, then in 894 just taking the name of St.Cler, was the scene of this woman's evil doings. The experience of history shows that virulence and violence of the fiercest kinds have happened among blood relations, love and hate being equally capable of supreme excellence by reason of the narrowness of the sphere.

It cannot be asserted on such slight ground, that the lord of the castle and the monk of the neighbouring lowly hermitage were absolutely of one strain in blood. It is true there are additional probabilities pointing in this direction. The history of the great Clares of England, the first of whom came here in 1066 and the last of whom died on the battlefield of Bannockburn, the earl of Gloucester, is suggestive to the effect that they were somehow a branch of the French house of St.Clare. They gained their best importance on this side of the Channel; but before the death of the martyr the whole family were Clares, and in all probability political exiles from Kent, who found a home in France. The history of Richard Clare, son of Gilbert, the greatest warrior of William's army, will have proved and near relation to the Sinclairs, of a kind other than this legendary. It is noteworthy that he seemed to have a special and, as it would appear, traditional love for England. He exchanged his estate of Brionne, of which he was earl, acre by acre, for land around Tunbridge in Kent; and here he built his famous castle and home, and seemed as if to the manner born of the county. It is true he had many estates elsewhere, but he seems to have further satisfied his likings for England, by getting his property in Suffolk called Clare, from which to become the earl of Clare. It is not improbable that the castle of St.Cler on the Epte was first that of Clare, and that only after the saint became a saint did it and some members of the lineage become St.Clair.

All this is professedly imaginative. The return to somewhat steadier ground is agreeable. Moulins, the Norman historian, says that the Bretons had possession of the ashes of Saint Clare during Rollo's earlier visits to France. He had been the bishop of Nantes, and this explains why the Bretons were so privileged. On one of these terrible comings of the Norse pirates they carried his remains inland for safety to Bourges. There is mention also of similar dealings with the relics of a Saint Maur. These things might show that the two families, the Sinclairs and the Seymours, were of the country, and not new importations from Scandinavia under the banners of Rollo. The Clares and the Maurs were not likely to have been confined to these two priests. Bernard of Senlis has been already noted, as the shrewd welcomer of the Norse Rollo to his native land; and that he was a St.Clare is also a problem amid the general obscurity.

In 912 Charles, king of France, met the Norse prince on the banks of the Epte, near St.Clare Castle, who then got installed in his dukedom of Normandy or Neustria by that remarkable proxy homage which sent Charles on his back in a double sense. "Ne si, bi Got", cried Rollo to the demand of his personal submission. The French kings were long accustomed to ducal home insolence, and this king kept his temper as only sad experience can teach. That at that meeting Sinclairs were fully represented, and perhaps on both sides, could hardly but be. It was not for nothing that the place had so thoroughly fixed and then historic a name. If it is admissible to draw geographical conclusions at all into history and genealogy, this place may be used to the extent of suggesting that it took its name, as is usual, from its proprietors; and that, if so, they were not novi homines, but old patricians of the Gallic land.

Between this period and the conquest of England many changes must have been with the family. Walderne, the earl of St.Clare, resided, not at the castle whence his name and title came, but at the castle of St.Lo in the Cotentin, when Duke William got his and his sons' services in 1066; and for generations that must have been the chief home. The commune of St.Clair there is proof modern of this. Border troubles were continually prevalent near Rouen; but it is very probable that as Caen, Bayeux, and St.Lo became the more recognised centres of Norman policy and civilisation, the reason of the new home was to have the benefit of the presence of what was best in the dukedom. It is very plain, but quite substantial, politics, that absence from court is not good for the most legitimate of ambitions. Duke William was of Lower Normandy by birth, breeding, and heart.

The castle of St.Lo, Palgrave says, was built in the time of Charlemagne against the Danes. It became municipal, the town growing around it gradually, and taking its name. There is no evidence to show how early the Sinclairs had it in possession. Sir Andrew Malet, one of our ambassadors to European countries of this century, and an authority on Norman questions, said that the site of the castle was observable in his time, and that the English Sinclairs were of that stock. The aid to their prince was collected at St.Lo, and it is to this quarter of the Cotentin that it must be looked, for the right information as to the kind of men its culture made them, before the settlements were made in their new, or, it may be, former or first land.

The earl of Rye and his family were offshoots from St.Lo; and there are indications of yet other branches, which played considerable part in the Norman period of English history. The earls of Senlis, for example, with their previous strong ducal ties, by marriage and political valuable mutual aid, seem somewhat apart from the Conqueror's doings till the latter period of his reign; and their interests being within purely French territory at Senlis, it may be guessed that they had lost sight of Normandy for, as they no doubt judged, the wider field of the politics which had Paris for centre. When the western expedition drew the eyes of all Europe upon this island, the Sinclairs of Senlis freshened their memories, and came to their great relation fortune-hunting, and with much success. But these Sinclair earls of Senlis may have been the successors merely of the Bernard of Neustrian early history.

The mythological period, with families as with nations, being indication rather than any realised fact, cannot bear too much handling. Mythology, all the same, has its own particular charm; and it undoubtedly carries its very valuable offering of truth to the eyes and hearts which know its right worthy message.

Chapter IV
The Norman Civilisation

That strip of intricate needlework, nineteen inches broad and two hundred and ten feet eleven inches in length, called the Bayeux tapestry, which hung long in the cathedral there, is one of the worlds greatest historical monuments. Its art is only second to the high burden of history it carries. Those graceful Norman warriors in armour have no sufficient counterparts except among the sculptures of the ancient Greeks. There is the same fine masterful spirit in the whole composition. Straining after passing effect is completely absent, which is one of the best tests of the immortality of any art. The whole tale of the union of England with Normandy goes on, picture after picture, with a clear unconsciousness as of the free processions on the frieze of a Greek temple. Harold's visit, his aid in war, the oath, the embarkation, the landing, the battle: what history in words has ever excelled this work of fair ladies' hands in suggestiveness as to what is beautiful in woman or noble in man ? Were there absolutely nothing further extant as to the kind of people the Normans were, the proof should stand complete in this, of the existence of one of the world's polished nations. And such confidence in woman as is implied by committing the celebration of their fame to female wit, shows that those warriors couki bear what is considered the last test of manly culture, the wise devotion to woman which brings her up to choicest womanhood, as it does the man to his best manhood.

No raid of Gothic savages was it of which William was the successful leader. Rather had England the unspeakable good fortune of being taken into hand, for high training, by a nation of cultivated masters of the best life then existent. This country would, but for the Normans, probably now be little in advance of Russia or Sweden. It is only when one goes fairly within the records of our law and politics that he can dream of what we owe to the high civilisation planted so fortunately here by the accident of a disputed succession. And this island was not the only part of the world benefited by these same true ladies and gentlemen. Even the seemingly indifferent fact, that the conquerors of Hastings were shaven like priests, has its suggestive analogy with the habit at Rome in the height of its civilisation. But there are clearer or less subtle indications of the artistic condition of this people. Whence did the admired Gothic architecture come except from their genius. The arch, which is allowed to them, was the origin of all that is distinctive in the Christian form of building. Their manly curve rose into the pointed, rather effeminate arch; their powerfully barred window developed into the floral; their dignified column sprang into the spiritual but spasmodic buttress. If the Doric holds its own among the Greek modes, the Norman is equally stubborn in its claim on rational admiration. Corinthian luxuriance and Christian superfluity of form and decoration, if splendid arrivals, were sure indications that decay had begun. Let there be, however, no depreciation of the several stages of any art; for, like all other growths, they must rise, blossom, and fall. It is of importance to remember that, as with discoveries generally, most honour belongs to the planting of such trees of life for man. Had there been marble rather than freestone quarries near Caen, as Athens had, there certainly should have been new births in sculpture as well as architecture.

The Norman needed only scope to excel in whatever he tried. History is full of what action was open to him in those centuries. He had far more than his share of all that was being done greatest in the world then. To sing new chansons, to form chivalries and literatures, to shape kingdoms out of Anglo-Saxon or Pelasgian mobs, to lay new foundations in art, to make manhood and womanhood glories of leadership and reverent devotional following, who has been than he a better master? The art of life is the finish of all other arts, which are but its handmaidens; and he would be a presumptuous modern who might risk thinking that of this, the divine art, he knows more than did the elect of Normandy in the eleventh century.

Religion was there in its best strength before it began the downward path of sensual monasticism and clerical wealth and sloth. The historians are afflicted with spiritual blindness who are not affected by the frightful contrast, on that decisive battlefield, of men preparing for death or victory under the sublime influence and regulated awe of a cultivated worship, to men howling like beasts over what intoxicating liquors they could secure to hide their own barbarity from themselves, and to give them some false hope and courage against the bright army of intellect arrayed in front of them, under all the sanctions of religion and the rights of men and states. It would have been England's loss beyond words that her Saxons had gained that day. The sleep of intellect would have continued for centuries, and the ghouls of barbarism and all the gluttonies should have had their new lease of prolonged wassail.

Like all other human things, the Norman civilisation only went too swiftly and far when some of its paths to excellence opened, and its best aid, religion, became its greatest snare. Where did the Christian world look for its perfect crusaders when the madness seized entire Europe that the Mohammedans ought to be exterminated? Over-wrought by the high honour they paid to culture and worship in their own country, the Normans were only too ready for the wild cry of Peter the Hermit. Their natural bravery and love of adventure, added to their great devotion to refinement of which the church was then chief or next to chief embodiment, made Normandy for centuries the arsenal of men, money, and weapons in the gallant but false and fatal expeditions which a fanatical state of church culture began, and a scheming condition of ecclesiastical rule found it policy to continue.

Enough is gained for present purpose if the homeland where these Sinclairs who settled in England had their training, is recognised as being in the eleventh century the noblest heart-centre of the world. The dullest men thence could not but aid by their mere presence most nations, if only they brought with them the outward ordinary manners of that land. To get souls from it as bright as ever stepped on its soil, was the luck that statesmen covet for the countries they hold dear. Not nothi were these chief strangers, like many of the Conqueror's followers who have since achieved distinction here, but souls who knew, as long lines of ancestors did before them, the best secrets of the civilisation of their times. What Thucydides said of Greece before the Peloponnesian war could not be said of Normandy then: "Greatness was not in it, neither as to wars nor other things". If the determined missionaries it sent to our island were of another temper than the modern ones of persuasive ineffective smile in a political world of moral suasion, this has been all the better for England. It will take a long and difficult process to make the ordinary mind understand that nothing best is got except through struggle of bitter but, to noble natures, ennobling kind. It is irritating to read some of the old chroniclers, of Saxon blood, maundering about the tyranny of these genuine rulers, as if the fault of unreasoning violence had not to be continually met by skill and energy, even to the correspondent severity of punishment proper to command.

That historians living in these days of science and maturer judgment can be found who join in those wails of ignorant slothful monks, and of the men whose eternal type of character is symbolled by praise of good old times which never existed, and abuse of the present which always calls for them to be up and doing, is one of the inexplicable phenomena which appear amid very general mental advance. What better good can man do than drill, at whatever cost, his disorganised and therefore savage or helpless fellows into such shape as will save them from being continually devoured, in respect of their substance and lives, by any accidental hordes that have gained first elements of unity ? As a calculation of spilt blood, it is probable that a visit to these unprotected shores, in the Celtic and Saxon periods, of the war-vessels laden with the sea-kings and their pirate soldiers, was more destructive than several of the pitched battles which the sullen unreasonableness of the Angles made necessary. This great difference must also never be lost sight of, that Norman battle was against men in arms, while by invasions of a shapeless country the defenceless and the weak suffer.

If they suffered at Norman hands, as in the Yorkshire destruction by fire and sword, historians (as chroniclers and the unthinking multitude cannot be expected to see things from the right point of view) should recognise, for themselves in the first place, and then show those whom they address, how rulers, to be rulers at all, could not escape the heavy burdens of ordering such punishment and preparation to be made in the face of the actual problem. Danes and Scots to the north in their many thousands, rebels behind without any right ground of rebellion, Normandy seething with aristocratic ambitions; what with these and hundreds of other elements only fully experienced or realisable by and to those who are at the centres of such combinations, the terrible but necessary wasting of Yorkshire had in it more of the nature of calamities which occur in the material world than those of man's doing. It should never be overlooked that even kings must do the best they can, and that the game of all life is one of success or failure. The charge of inhumanity so foolishly cast about without appreciation of the stern necessity and logic of facts, is not the best sign of thorough intellectual culture and ability. It is venial that those low on the steps of training should clamour about tyrannies and injustices; for thus, in their shortness of vision and hand-to-mouth living, wise rule and essential justice often, indeed almost always, appear to them. The philosophic historians, like the statesmen, should address themselves to the inmost facts of their problems when they mean to influence the strong minds.

It was at Caen, and around it, that the most characteristic culture of the dukedom existed. Rouen, the other lung as it were of the country, had political life more active than the artistic and religious. Not far from the borders, it had acquired a French spirit to considerable extent. It was in Basse-Normandie that the richest state of feeling and action had its cradle and home. The district of the Cotentin supplied almost all the names of which our aristocracy are proud. The largest sharers in the partition of England were the neighbours of the duke at his castle of Falaise.

Geoffrey, bishop of Coustance, who celebrated mass on the field of Hastings before the battle, was one of the luckiest of his followers in securing lands. The castle of St.Lo was in his diocese, and it is easy to understand that there was frequent communication all round among those leaders who were in the royal compass of Caen. In 890 history shows this castle besieged by Rollo, and the then bishop of Coustance was slain, the Norsemen gaining the place by cutting off the water. It would be valuable to know if it was in the possession of the family who held it in the eleventh century, and that all this time they had the benefit of the very best surroundings of the country's excellence in government, art, and religion; or if they were of the conquerors, and therefore later. A visit to Caen and its companion towns gives sufficient indication of the superiority the humanities reached at the early periods.

The conquest of England was misfortune in the end for Normandy. Its annexation to France killed the originality and vigour of its artistic as well as political life; and it is one of the many things which ask mourning, why so promising a sphere of possible new and perfected production should have been blotted out, so to speak, by crass political necessities and troubles. Take Normandy away from France, and where, even as things went, are you to look in it for excellences that can be called European, not to say worldwide ? But enough. Let the way now be considered clearer to follow some of the Sinclairs after they have added England to the land of their birth as another sphere for energy.

Chapter V
Walderne's Sons and Daughter

Richard, Britel, and Agnes spent their lives after 1066 mostly if not altogether on English soil.

William for some unexplained reason espoused the cause of the Athelings, and was one of the emigrants who took refuge with Malcolm of Scotland. Motives of love, hope, or justice may have separated him from the interests of his Norman chief. He was not singular, for he was only one of a considerable company who set sail for the purpose of reaching Hungary with Margaret Atheling in their charge.

Their ship was driven on the coast of Scotland by stress of weather, and it was the destiny of royal Margaret to become King Malcolm's loved wife, as it was that of William Sinclair to remain there as her steward or dapifer. He had all kinds of honours, and his personal popularity is well enough indicated by the phrase which his fine proportions, features, and yellow hair gained him, "The seemly St.Clair".

The William "le blond" in the roll in the church of Dives, Normandy, of the companions of William I in the conquest of England, appears to be Sir Walter Scott's favourite in his notes to The Lay of the Last Minstrel. He is in these called the "'second son of Walderne, count de St.Clair, and Margaret, daughter to Richard, duke of Normandy'"; but his mother was Duke Richard's daughter Helen. There is a theory mooted of his lineage and consequent motives that deeper historic study might establish, though present evidence only points in the direction.

It would seem that the introduction of Norman styles at the Scottish court began with the advent of Queen Margaret Atheling, and that her dapifer or steward became dapifer of Scotland, the same office from which the royal Stuarts took their name. Now this highest position, next to the monarch, was always hereditary; and was not this "seemly St.Clair" therefore the direct fore-father of the Stuarts who by marriage

35

with the Bruces became kings of Scotland and afterwards of the United Kingdom?

Robert Crawfurd in his History of the Royal and Illustrious Family of the Stuarts gives an origin to them that might be made to agree with this curious likelihood. He says the Banquo of whom Shakespeare writes in Macbeth was the son of Ferquhard of Lochaber, a scion of the royal house of Scotland. Banquo was killed in 1050 by the usurper Macbeth, but his son Fleance escaped to Wales and married Nesta, the daughter of Griffith, the son of Llewellyn. Their son was Walter or Walderne. In charters he is Walter, "senescallus domus", or dapifer, to Malcolm III of Scotland. It is supposed that he is the same with Walter, earl of St.Clair in Normandy, and that his marriage there with the duke of Normandy's daughter gave him the lands of St.Clair.

It is recorded in history that he sent his second son William to the Scottish court before the Norman conquest of England, as if to be his substitute. The tale has it briefly that he sent him to see how affairs were going in Scotland. William's second arrival with Queen Margaret may have been simply returning to his hereditary rights as dapifer. There is a common similarity in the first names that aids these inquiries, Allan and Walter being the prevalent ones.

The stewards of Scotland had Paisley with its abbey and the neighbouring district of Kyle for their chief patrimony, and the chartulary throws considerable light on the family after the first three or four. From 1160 the lineage is clear, but the previous hundred years is almost a blank. The earliest notice of a Sinclair after William, the dapifer, is of an Allan in some land charters of Haddingtonshire, given before the "stewards" got the Renfrewshire and West of Scotland properties. What the real blood of the royal Stuarts is, has not yet been settled, though they have been also as Alans referred to Normandy.

But these questions may have thorough treatment in a discussion of the descendants of this "seemly St.Clair", the ancestor of all the Scottish kin of the name. The theory of a longer residence in Normandy of the family previous to the Conquest is the more accepted. But William's espousal of the cause of the Athelings is a considerable difficulty.

Wodrow in his useful reminiscences says that the chief secretary of Scotland, Sir Robert Spottiswoode, son of Archbishop Spottiswoode, got the MSS. of the famous Black Book of Paisley, the headquarters of the Stewarts, from Sir William Sinclair of Roslin, who was married to his only sister. The charter-room of Roslin Castle had many secrets to tell before an unfortunate fire reduced its records. That Sir William should about 1638 have the Paisley writings in his possession is at least suggestive, however unlikely that it may throw desirable light on the early Stuart history. If these references should lead to inquiry, what is too much of digression on mere probability may not be fruitless.

It is quite possible that the cup-bearer of Queen Margaret has his hereditary representative in the Henry Sinclair, panitarius, or steward of the household, who is mentioned in the famous letter to the pope in the time of Edward I, where another Henry is mentioned as pennander or bannerman of Scotland, the equivalent to the office of the custodian of the French oriflamme. For the present the subject must be left entirely open, and the more that it is somewhat out of the straight course of progress.

It is a puzzle why William De Sancto Claro should have left him he fought for at Hastings. Great bitterness arose between the Conqueror and some of his best nobles. The division of offices and lands would of all things be of the character to raise heart-burnings, and it is proverbial that the amour-propre of his followers was particularly keen. King William had no more determined enemy at the Scottish court than this namesake and relation of his. They met more than once in the many fights of William's reign on the borders of the kingdom, and in one battle at least the former subject was successful against his king. Married to the daughter of Cospatric, the Saxon earl, to whom the Conqueror had acted capriciously because of the capricious character of this his most northern count, and because of the difficulties of the period, this was additional cause of vexation between the two Williams. Sinclair, as warden of the marches, lost his life fighting bravely against King William and his lieutenant, Robert Fitz-Hamo, the earl of Gloucester. It is doubtful whether the course he took, brilliant career though his descendants have had, was as hopeful as if he had stayed with his brothers and sister. The indications are that his line of action had some limiting effect on their fortunes.

How could their monarch be sure that the others also would not go away and leave him ? Richard, the hero of Hastings, had the highest claims on his generosity in the share of lands and offices. In the absence of sufficiently distinct documents, it would hardly be right to state that he was comparatively forgotten. As the sons of Walderne, earl of St.Cler, and the nephews of Hubert, earl of Rye, both he and Britel were well entitled to large notice, even if they had no personal relationship to the king.

It is established that nothing irritated the Conqueror to anything like the same degree, as did the presence of the emigrants at the Scottish court. Their continual appeals to the Danish king, to come and help them to drive "the bastard" out of the island, were as annoying as they were dangerous to his very existence. That the relations of perhaps the most active and formidable of all these malcontents, the steward of Queen Margaret Atheling, sister of the Edgar whose claim to the crown which the Conqueror then wore was formally perhaps better than his who bore it, suffered from the state of things, at least in the negative way of neglect, seems somewhat apparent.

Were it not that jealousies against each other are very exceptional in the history of Sinclairs wherever they have been, it might be possible that the influence of Eudo Sinclair at court was not exercised much or at all in favour of his cousins. His character, certainly, from his youth upwards was of gallant type, and something must have been barrier to larger favour of Richard and Britel with a master so profuse of gift to himself. Had we writings earlier than The Domesday Book, which was drawn up during the six years from 1080 to 1086, we might however find both of them in high office, and in possession of wider lands than this record shows. They may have been involved with the rebellions which occurred so frequently during the reign, and have suffered the usual stripping from them of all or most they had. There can be no doubt about the difficulty there was of ruling such men.

It was William's dying words to his son to hold the hardest possible hand upon the lords of Normandy, and it is not likely their tempers suddenly sweetened in this island's climate under the invidious difficulties connected with the sharing of great offices and wide possessions. It is more than possible that there should be thankfulness for the lands Domesday Book does show as being in their possession. If they, like many of the best of his followers, were among those who fain would have cast off his rule, especially after his nature seems to have grown embittered, against Saxon and Norman almost equally, they may not at all have had reason to wonder at limited prosperity under William I. It would be a great mistake, and possibly a sheer injustice to the king, who was of most manly, and to his relations most forgiving, nature, not to remember that the entries in the renowned two volumes of his survey take little account of surnames.

The name Richard occurs with lands in every county, and it is quite probable that this son of Walderne, earl of St.Clare, is hidden under the frequency of its appearances. The fact that his full name is twice entered, while it has very special interest, is also cause of embarrassment. It seems to limit his property to where his surname has been written, though this cannot be fixed either for a moment, the habits of naming being different in the special counties, and the survey itself the labour of several independent commissioners, whose styles of work are quite distinguishable from each other. The wisest course is not to fix any quarrel at all between the great captain of his age, either personal or family, and his heroic warrior of Senlac battlefield. He could not possibly be the only Richard who got lands, even if Richard of Tunbridge, Fitz-Gilbert as he was called, is kept apart. On the whole, he must have had part of the lands mentioned simply under "Richard", and this is all that the state of the facts will allow or demand. Whether luckily or not is very doubtful, but there can be absolute security of his possession of lands in two counties. If it could be shown that these were all he ever had, then, in comparing his rewards with those of others, inferiors in rank and distinction, he would have deep reason to grumble. It was common among these four hundred chief Norman followers to have pluralities in the way of estates by dozens, nay, by hundreds, and it is almost absolute that Richard fared likewise; but this kind of facts cannot be supported except on documentary evidence, and it is scanty in all such antiquities as are being discussed. There would hardly be excuse for wishing that so unique a boon to descendants as Domesday Book had been fuller or more consistent throughout with regard to its Richards, were it not itself the cause of thus whetting the curiosity.

From its Suffolk part this comes: "'Hartsmere hundred: Richard de St.Clair holds Wortham from the king'". In Norfolk county he appears with Hugh Bigod, earl of Norfolk, and with William of Noies, as to lands etc. confiscated from the burghers of Norwich because of their rebellion. His entry in Norwich is "1 house Ric'ard de sencler"; and underlordship as his, he takes one of the runaway burgesses, who nearly all filed out of Norwich, where Richard probably resided in his own house there often. Blomfield's History of Norfolk has several valuable references to Richard, and he finds also that Hubert Sinclair of Rye, castellan of Norwich, was married to the daughter and heiress of a Domesday Book magnate, Radulph de Bello Sago. But besides his careful search of this record, he finds from the register of the monastery of Castleacre that Richard de Sancto Claro or St.Cleer gave the monks of Castleacre his rights over their monastery as founder, in free alms for ever, for the health of his own and his wife's souls, with those of his ancestors and heirs. Such a survival goes far to prove that Richard was one of the leading men of his time, and evidence may arise further of what he was. Mention has been made of his cousin Hubert's governorship of Norwich Castle. This is the Norwich house with lands Richard got after aiding him in a most trying time, and his Suffolk estates being near the borders of Norfolk gave him opportunity to be further useful should it be necessary. No greater hotbed of disaffection was there than in the district around Norwich, and it might not be assuming too much to hazard the statement that Richard was both put there as a faithful vassal of special ability in war, and that could we see through the millstone that so many Richards make for the eyes, he would be found as great a favourite as most of the select courtiers of the king.

Much the same difficulties arise about Britel. In this, the Exchequer Domesday Book, there are many Britels, particularly in the districts which we know from other sources to have been the spheres of his action. In the south-western counties a Britel holds numerous lands under the earl of Moreton, brother of the Conqueror, and the greatest sharer of his bounty. It is, from relationship and position and name, a likely theory that this was Britel, the third son of Walderne, earl of St.Clair. In the charter of the foundation of the priorate of Montacute, near the castle of the earl of Moreton, and of his successors, the Montacutes, who became earls of Salisbury and princes of the Isle of Man, three signatures among several other Somersetshire ones are remarkable, namely, Britel de Sancto Claro, Jordanis de Barnavilla, and Robert de Bruis.

But before showing the reason why, it is best to substantiate Britel in what locality it is still possible to discover. With his surname, he is not to be found in the great Exchequer Domesday Book, like his brother; but in the Exon Domesday Book, which was brought to light at Exeter from among ancient gatherings in the famous city, and which is, from the number of Anglo-Saxon names in it supposed to be earlier than the other, the name and surname, the latter in its best known documentary form, authenticate him as steadily as record can. In the hundred of Bolestane, Somersetshire, he held land. The translation is, "And from the half hide which Britel de St.Clare holds the king has no tax". Those who work in old records know the pleasure of finding seemingly so small and unimportant an entry as this, but there is often wonderful fruitfulness in the shortest, where darkness may be said to be the rule and not the exception. If we take Hallam's guess as fairly accurate, here are only sixty acres of land as a possession, but they are arable, and these only were counted at that time. They are truly "representative" acres. The same writer has valuable remarks as to the extraordinarily small portions in culture on the manors then the largest in the country. As for Britel, it is not even possible that this could have been all the land he possessed. The Britel of the great The Domesday Book is only not to be fixed by reason of the same misfortune of naming whose trouble meets us at every turn. That he shares there largely, both as holding in capite, or directly from the king, and by under-tenantship to some of the great earls, is as certain as anything can well be that is not absolutely registered. This will appear the more when his descendants, especially those among the Cornishmen, come to have their stories told.

But it is suitable to take up again the question of the three signatures which awaited discussion. That of Britel de Sancto Claro substantiates, by the proximity of one of his homes to Montacute in Somerset, the Exon Domesday Book; though this is, perhaps, painting the lily and gilding refined gold. It is notable that the Jordans were a Devonshire family, and afterwards, it will be seen, they entered into afiinities with Devonshire Sinclairs, who are of the Britel descent.

Robert de Bruis is one of the great Norman family who became of high account in England and Wales, before they reached the royalty of Scotland. Bramber in Sussex and Brecknock with its castle in Wales were their earliest homes in this island, and it is to them it must be looked for this Robert Bruce. To him Agnes Sinclair the sister of Richard and Britel married some writers say; and this has its hints with regard to signature thus in common at Montacute. It does not go far, for there is nothing more noticeable than the width between the various estates then of the same man, and the consequent visits which must have been constantly kept up from one of them to another. The inference of knowledge of each other is certainly implied, and such a tie by marriage explains a good deal.

This account of Agnes, however, is not the only one. All agree that she was married to the head of the Bruces then in England. Collins in his Peerage says that "'Agnes, the daughter of Waldron, earl of St.Clare, was married to Philip Bruce, the grandson and heir of William, lord of Breos, Normandy, and of Bramber, Sussex'". If so, it was not her husband who signed the charter; and this would show at that early period additional intimacy of Bruces and Sinclairs. They were friends, it is more than likely, in their native land before they reached their Canaan. This William was also husband to one of these Sinclair ladies, the daughter and rich heiress of Johel Sinclair of Totness and Barnstaple, for which Jones in his History of Brecknock is authority, Johel being, as shall be seen later, brother of Walter of Medway.

Any account of the Bruces which forgets their Welsh and western history cannot but be deficient. In England they were best known by their quarrel with King John. The wife of a William de Bruce refused to give her sons as hostages to, as she said, the murderer of his own nephew, and the troubles of the English Bruces began. They were not wiped out; they had too much skill and determination for that; and they gradually struggled back into importance, chiefly through marriage ties with the great Clares, those earls of Pembroke, Hertford, and Gloucester, to whose fame and lineage, by the mother, William Marshall the greatest earl of Pembroke succeeded.

But this in closing what has to be said of Agnes, whom we may leave as the lady of Bramber, Sussex, or, if it should so be proved, that of Brecknock Castle, Wales, or of both. Philip Bruce of Sussex has the name of being the most subtle man of his time. To be the chosen companion of one of those Bruces was distinction, even to her, who was their superior in rank, traditions, and blood.

Chapter VI
Tenures of Land

England and Normandy to this day are remarkable for nothing as much as their inveterate love of law business. It may be a tribute to their intellectual capacity that they have the most innate relish for the intricacies which to uninitiated minds seem the tortures of the region of nightmare. The stability from this conservative love of the past, and of its dicta as sacred, it is to be feared ready writers are not thankful enough for. Precedent is the cue-word to get at the secret of the whole time-enlaced system. Our courts of exchequer, king's bench, and so on with variety of titles, though to the weaker consideration they seem each as self-creative and self-existent at least as the sun, can be traced back, step by step, till we are in the presence of William the Conqueror and his dapifer in one room, who have swallowed up in their own powerful persons wigs, gowns, general paraphernalia, and the very judges themselves that are so awful to the popular eye. Justice, civil or criminal, was administered more simply and readily by the king or his vicar from his own bench or in his own counting-room, but on the very same principles as still hold. Lord chancellor downwards to barrister and attorney, are fair copies of what division of duties a sovereign had to do in simpler times, when a king's court did not mean merely a thing of exuberant feathers, low dresses, tight uniform, and futile ceremonial business, but the place where action was strongest, wisest, and of the kind we still associate with the word, where now no royal foot enters except on idle curiosity. This simple watching of the actual development of regal surroundings into universal legal rule through the country by substitutes, is fruitful of clear seeing also in respect to the chief interest about which law is engaged. Let land now be bound by ten times as many green or old withes as Samson was, there is a way of cutting through the knots, at least for the understanding. It is more than probable that violent actual dealing with tenures might be as dangerous to the body politic as unscientific surgery would be among the veins of the strongest human being. To see the inmost anatomy of the land system, in most countries, is the study of long lives; and in this country the extended, varied, and on the whole extra-ordinarily prosperous history of the nation makes the quest almost a hopeless one. In the earlier reigns there is perhaps most light to be found, the further process being mostly evolutionary.

Here it will he sufficient to draw such general lines of indication as may keep minds awake to the drift of what is meant by possessions in land. The feudal system, which essentially is that which exists, because legal action works still in its grooves, had three chief forms of tenure, not including the absolute possession of the sovereign or rather of the crown. The highest way of holding for a subject was called in capite, because none stood between the head of the state and him; all duties connected with the land being finally settled between them, with no interference except by free choice. That for long these duties were chiefly military, as the supplying and supporting so many soldiers for certain periods correspondent to the size of the feed or property, does not, as has been supposed, give special military colour to the principle of land tenures. In every sense the system is equally applicable to the civil duties of peace. As matter of fact, surely the dullest will see that the greater portion of the eight centuries since 1066 were devoted, not to the necessities of wars, but to the common course of national existence. Sweeping reforms are ignorant ones, as a rule; for the very things they are apt to abolish have to be set up again, and nearly always in a maimed and less healthy state.

At first the earls, who were not merely ornamental lord-lieutenants of counties, actually did justiciary business, now relegated to paid sheriffs; and it was to them the tenure in capite was given. The inevitable growth of claimants for office and title gradually usurped upon the privileged earls. Barons, who grew from various accidents of state, and particularly of royal service, became suitors. At one period, their importance in comparison with earls was calculated, somewhat arbitrarily of necessity, at the numbers 13.5 to 20. If this were right, it could have only been by miracle, and for but a moment. The growth of society in any of its ranks will not wait for the pedants. Barons became holders in capite; they secured rulerships of counties; if the ability were there, they could take the cakes from the very teeth of the fiercest earl that ever concussed a county into his own brave image. So afterwards with the knights, who were a still more difficult because more numerous section to keep out of the privileged fields. Sheriffships and coronerships opened ultimately even to the untitled, the new check discovered being merely the now well-worn one of money qualification. Land in capite grew as common as the commoners themselves, and the word "esquire" was invented to keep off the last degree of bareness.

The second form of tenure belongs almost by necessity to all periods of national growth. Under-tenantship, though its honourableness varies considerably, on the whole keeps a middle position of steady dignity. It swings between all but absolute proprietorship and the tenure of a farmer by lease. For the necessities of war or peace it was responsible to the earls as they in like manner were to the sovereign. There is nothing particular to be said of a state of life which cannot but be with much the same conditions while man's nature is as it is.

The varieties of freemen, socmen, villains, belong rather to folk-lore than state arrangements by law. It may be otherwise with the system of bondsmen, which was long so prominent a feature of English society. The troubles which it caused of wild rebellions and wide destruction of life, even in the select ranks, may have been necessary lessons to slothful statesmen. But the question has become for us merely an antiquarianism, having nothing to do with our actual conduct of life. The seething masses of slaves, however, which were always at the bottom of early English political difficulties, must never be forgotten as an actual element at work. To be food for the sword under leadership of ambitious nobles was their commonest experience; but their use thus, as a terrible instrument when organised, was only one of many ways in which they affected the life and morality of their fellows of other degrees.

The most distinctive of all the forms of tenure was that by serjeanty. Particular bravery in the field, favour at court, royal visit, and generally royal will and pleasure, gave in capite holding, and other serjeanty special privileges besides, to men of title or of none, to old men or to young; and for mere system-mongers this made a chaos of what they foolishly dub the feudal system, thinking they have got something real by calling names thus very loudly at the facts, which, being living things, are always metamorphosing for new necessities and requirements. No wise politician nails his colours to such a mast. Changes ? Yes, and welcome, if in the actual spirit of the facts; not otherwise. The royal ladies would seem also to have had privilege of conferring serjeanty. In law there came to be a whole department of business from this institution, though survival of the all but extinct legal title "Serjeant" is the most that is current of the much-desired system of tenure. There was something too poetic and free about it, and perhaps this is the right reason of its decline. To have an estate for the service of holding a towel before even the most dignified lady on state or religious occasion, savoured too much of Spanish chivalry and donism for our rational, and really more sentimental, because more sincere, natures. Anything that tends to being maudlin, cannot boast always, with impunity, in the slow but surely demolishing English presence. It needs precedents for everything; but it has faith in the honesty of the fathers, that they have somewhere met and dealt with just such unreal phenomena. Serjeanty, or romantic service, grand and petit, need not be depreciated; it was the natural appendage to the spirit of chivalry, which also did its valuable work, and then metamorphosed as speedily as it could into other form of fact.

Only the imbeciles hunt after the ghosts, which cannot but walk, after the life has found a new body. For a time the cannon's report must reverberate, but the work has been done long before the echoes are over. Appropriations, alienations, mortgagings, conveyancings, processes of kinds as numerous as men's wits are quick to make varieties when acuteness and suppleness are at market and high price, fill the limbo of legal history to overflowing. For present use, the main lines on which land has been and still is possessed, are quite enough. To show that the most intricate transactions are soluble by this historical method would be possible. If fair guidance bo given to make the labyrinth not wholly a maze the object is attained.

Chapter VII
Eudo, Filius Huberti

In 1047 when Eudo's father at the castle gate of Rye gave the command,
> "'Fait sei Hubert: "Dreit a Faleise",'"

to his three brave eldest sons, to whom he had entrusted the safety of their prince in extreme personal danger, it may be guessed how Eudo mourned his youthfulness, like another David.

He could not have been more than ten or twelve, and he does not count in the passage from the Chronique des Ducs de Normandie,

> "'Le vavassors aveit treis fils,
> Chevaliers bons, proz, e hardiz'".

Radulph, Hubert, and Adam were the vigorous youths who swore that their equally vigorous and youthful duke should reach his castle of Falaise if it cost them their lives a thousand times, or, more rational possibility, if it cost the lives of as many of his deadly pursuers. Perhaps Eudo got his farewell kiss from Duke William before mounting the fresh horse which his faithful vavasseur had provided for him. The memory is keen with regard to the incidents of a dangerous time; and the ruddy cheek, no doubt wet with a tear of sorrow that he was too young to help, of the boy destined for a noble future, may have long and effectually haunted the mind of his gallant sovereign. Sure it is that the tale of the midnight ride was hallowed by a breathless repetition in the presence of, and it may be by, the youngest of these four sons. There are numbers fresh enough of heart to picture the yellow-haired lad near his anxious but shrewd father, watching the swift departure of those four chevaliers bons, proz, e hardiz, with his heart almost bursting because he also is not stretched at their soldierly gallop. His admiration of his father's skill in, not long after, putting the foam-covered cavalier conspirators on the wrong road for their purpose, may also be imagined. The intellect of the man he became, we may be certain was already well open; and if he had keener troubles than a duller boy might have, the joys were exquisite proportionately. It is easy to go too far, however, with probabilities; and it may be quite enough to imagine that Duke William then first saw and liked the future greatest subject of Normandy and England.

The usual knightly training was his, within among the ladies, and without among the soldiers and nobles, of the castle of Rye. Of this period of his life nothing perhaps has survived. It is at the court of William in Normandy that we get note of him. No personal danger to the duke then gave chances of distinction; he had wholly triumphed over his own and perhaps still more his mother's foes. Eudo got the usual knightly place of sons of favoured vassals, and it is possible had relish of life and enjoyment too strong in him to be greedy yet for office and fame. His first great stroke of fortune, which it may well be called, seems to have sought him rather than he it.

William Fitz-Osborn was then dapifer of Normandy, an office which included the duties and honours of seneschal and constable. The Chronique des Ducs de Normandie has defined it once for all by saying that the dapifer was in all things next the king. The civilisation of that period also, like ours, seems to have held dining to be one of cultivated man's most distinguished actions. So far was this carried then that none but gentlemen of nobility could serve as much as a spoon to a sovereign. The duke of Normandy was a stickler for perfection in this kind. William Fitz-Osborn, as highest authority, was responsible that all should be right for prince and for guests, from whatever lands. He was neglectful, and no doubt repeatedly.

The crisis came. A special festal day had to be enjoyed. The dapifer, who had his greatest of offices, like royalty itself in this, from hereditary succession, of his Bretulensian forefathers, failed in his supervision. The flesh of an uncooked bird, in such a state , was placed before the very king, and easily guessing how the others were being served he utterly lost his temper. Fitz-Osborn had position of honour near him, and Eudo Sinclair, by favour, or less possibly only by chance, was also beside him. The king struck at the dapifer, but Eudo had more than his father Hubert's wit to be equal to occasions, and he saved his master, and as it will appear his personal friend Fitz-Osborn, from a chance that could not but have with such men fatal consequences, if years should have to pass first. He received the blow, and if the tear put on his cheek in childhood has no historical foundation, the chronicler of his manhood in this trying scene makes tears fall freely, though the record also takes care to state unwillingly. If during the height of Greek periods of gallantry it was considered no virtue, as with moderns and the Red Indians, to bridle too much nature's impulses, so it may have been with the chivalrous

Normans. It is more probable, however, that both the physical pain from the angry hand of him whose bow no one but himself could bend, and the rush of charged feeling at the sight of his friends engaging in what was tragical beyond measure, both as to that moment and the future, were the causes of Eudo's generous weakness.

His stern history is none the worse of this bit of early tenderness. Lachrymosity has not been put to the account of the Normans by the most depreciatory of their virulent critics. Matters could not with men of such proud stomach be arranged. The king was thankful exceedingly for Eudo's presence of mind, but William Fitz-Osborn could never stand again his right-hand man. His hereditary claims availed nothing with the iron will of him who was every inch a king; he was stripped of his office without appeal. But the best of the tale appears in the special and pressing message of the fallen Fitz-Osborn, that the young Eudo, and none else, if it please the duke, be appointed in his room. The loyalty of Hubert, the father of Eudo, and the promises to him, may have made it easy for the prince to make his selection; but it can safely be inferred, from the favours of other kind which came afterwards to the erring but leal major domus regiae, that his recommendation had decisive influence.

Henceforth Eudo was mayor of the palace. For him also the dapifership of Normandy was made hereditary, which his family history will afterwards exhibit. No faux pas of uncooked goose or swan, it maybe easily asserted, occurred under his able rule of the roast, or it should certainly have been chronicled; and from management of the national exchequer to executing justice to all men, even the meanest, his action in Normandy was of similar soundness. The conquest of England, its greatest good fortune, was probably accomplished by Eudo Dapifer and the duke's lieutenants like the brave Fitz-Osborn, before the Conqueror did it, who has and well deserves the fame of it. The preparation of those sixty thousand warriors, gathered from wide Europe, and their embarkation in perfect equipment, were the victory. It is possible that the supplanting of Fitz-Osborn may have taken place after the conquest, at one of the several periods in which King William had returned to Normandy, and the credit of the collection of such a splendid army in that case belongs to his fame.

In favour of this it may be urged that not only was he a chief leader at Hastings, but that he was the first earl the king made in England. As earl of Hereford, on William's early return to Normandy, he got with Odo, earl of Kent, the king's half-brother, the entire rule of England to hold for their generous sovereign. He does not seem to have been born to succeed, and his son Roger went still farther wide of the mark, rebel and exile being his invited fate. That it was Eudo Sinclair who was at the helm of affairs, practically second only to his soldierly prince, agrees best with the character of the two dapifers. But rivalry not being at all between them in the full friendship that preferred one before another, their claims to this success of all time need not be discussed. It is undoubted that either of them might be, and one of them was by the fact, equal to the glorious necessity of 1066. This, too, was no single, though the greatest, piece of energy required in that masterful period. If Eudo's power came after, he had infinite opportunity of using it; and the pacification of two kingdoms into one, both fiercely troublesome, is abundant proof of his great civil ability. His wisdom and life-long success would suggest that the army led by the pope's consecrated banner of religion was the result of his steadier head rather than the work of the far less politic and skilful William Fitz-Osborn, known in English history as the violent and, certainly with the Anglo-Saxons, unpopular earl of Hereford.

There is a theory quite possible to be hold from the scantiness of historic facts, that Eudo was only dapifer of Normandy under the Conqueror, and thus obliquely the duke's promise to Hubert of Rye had its fulfilment, that himself was to be dapifer of England when in possession. The possibility of the Normandy hereditary officer getting supplanted by any chance whatever, could not have been imagined then, and the earl of Rye must have been more than satisfied by the position his son had gained so honourably. Indeed, it is to be said, that the refinement and fame of the French dukedom, if not the wealth and influence also, altogether outshone the comparative barbarism of the turbulent kingdom of the Angles.

Madox in his History of the Exchequer, which is in substance the history of the division of the duties of king and dapifer, has his mind greatly exercised by the fact that there seemed to be two contemporary dapifers, namely, this Eudo and a Hamo. He risked the guess of another writer: Eudo was dapifer of Normandy as Hamo was that of England. He is right.

But even as late as Domesday Book three dapifers, all of unmistakable highest rank, appear; and the word being also applied to county, hundred, and even abbey officers, more than a dozen dapifers altogether appear there as landholders. There can be no mistake as to the comparative insignificance of all except the three, and their positions are quite fixable.

Goderic Dapifer was a Saxon whom the Conqueror so far recognised that he gave him the sheriffship of several of the eastern counties as a compensating sphere of rule for what he lost. Of all the Anglo-Saxons, he retained most steadily and safely the wide lands of which the "good King Edward", as they invidiously were apt to call him, left them possessed.

Who Hamo Dapifer was is a much more difficult inquiry. That he held the rule of England under William I, and for considerable period, is quite certain, but by what condition is not fixed. It may be rash, but there are grounds for supposing that he was dapifer-substitute, so to put it, for Eudo, whose presence was required alternately in both divisions of the kingdom.

An accumulation of facts, not altogether decisive yet, but extremely assuring, goes to show that Hamo was also a Sinclair; and as the chief dapifer's relation, nepotism being then no terror, even if Eudo and not the king made the appointment, he was the right person for the intimate duties of such a position. Contiguity of their properties in Domesday Book is evidence not quite to be cast aside. The recurrence of the name Hamo, at a near period, in a family of Sinclairs related to Eudo, about which later national records give absolute statement, is at least suggestive. The circumstances of what Palgrave calls "the bourgade of Rye", in Sussex, almost make the pleading good, that Hamo Sinclair, the reputed dapifer of England, was in reality the near relation and under-dapifer of Eudo of Normandy and England, William's vicar in the full sense, as he by stricter record was so under the two succeeding kings. Hamo, a scion of Hubert's house of Rye on the Norman shore of the Channel, would be the natural founder of a Rye on this English side. He could quite well have been the cousin of Eudo.

Again and again it will be noticed that Sinclairs, like most chief Normans, were as careful to erect religious houses as they were to have defensive castles. In Rye the ancient chapel of St.Clare testifies more to the existence of such a family once there, than to memorial devotion to the well enough known religieuse, St.Clare, who was foil to the ecstatic St.Francis. She was revered first at Assisi and then throughout the Christian world more or less to this day. The frequent naming of churches and chapels from the neighbouring lords is a thing stamped on the very soil of the island.

Sussex had in the twelfth and thirteenth centuries, and later, Sinclairs very difficult to recognise now through the few relics left by the storms of civil and other war, and by the usual wasting of time. Arms of the dimmest kind belonging to the name in such churches as Eckingham of this county, do not give but the slightest clue. In records, which are a far more fruitful field however sparse, Sinclairs appear; but it is as difficult to know whence they have come as whither like ghosts they have gone. Hamo of Rye, dapifer, had no children, else that might explain several of such mysterious wanderers on this southern shore who once were its gallant lords. Little has been discovered about him, says Palgrave, except that he was a kinsman of the Conqueror, and followed him here. It is quite a probable way of things that he owes some obscurity to the greatness of his relative Eudo. To take account of a great man's friends is often unwisely considered to be quite as needless as lighting candles in sunshine. Perhaps this delusion accounts for the over-prevalent saying that geniuses never have geniuses for sons or relations.

We know of Hamo's brother. He was the Robert, "knight of Rye", who got much favour from William Rufus. Eudo in this reign was in full power, and with him chief at court it could be understood how the "knight of Rye" became lord of Glamorgan and Montgomery, and also had the earldom of Gloucester, so much coveted and so famous afterwards. Most of this was granted by the Conqueror to Matilda his queen. Henry, his youngest son, to whom he had only given £5000, contended bitterly for his mother's lands and their titles with his brother Rufus and Robert Fitz-Hamo, "knight of Rye", but the strife ended very happily.

There is a pedigree of Robert Fitz-Hamo among the Cottonian MSS. which gives him daughters, one being the heiress Maud, Sinclair inferentially. She marries Robert Consul, a natural son of Henry I; the earl of Gloucester who built Bristol Castle and fought gallantly for his sister the Empress Matilda against Stephen. Their son is William Consul. This William's eldest daughter, whose mother was daughter of the earl of Leicester, became queen of England, but was divorced on the plea of consanguinity by King John. She afterwards married a Mandeville earl of Essex, who will appear again in these researches, and lastly Hubert de Burgh, earl of Kent. His second married Gilbert, earl of Clare, who, through her, there being no brother, ultimately became the first earl of Gloucester of the descendants of the Conqueror's greatest warrior, Richard of Tunbridge and Clare. This Gilbert was followed by Gilbert; Richard; the Gilbert who added Hereford to the other earldoms; Gilbert, the husband of Joan Plantagenet, sister of Edward I; Gilbert; and, last of his race, the gallant young Gilbert (heir to such traditions as the conquest of Ireland and many another civil and military success) who, fighting against the son of one of the ladies Clare, King Robert Bruce, his own near relation, on the battlefield of Strivelinge, as the MS. calls Bannockburn, put the period by his death there in 1314 to perhaps the noblest race of men England's soil has yet borne.

But returning to Hamo of Rye, all that can be said yet is that his prosperity may have attracted collateral relations to Sussex, which might account for the isolated later appearances of the name. The records of Seaford, near Rye, have entries of struggles between the burghers and Sinclair lords of the soil as to rights. Fishings were at all periods, on both coasts, a valuable interest, and about property of this and other kinds disputing is not to be avoided always by any skill. Nothing can be much made out of such references to a long-extinct name in Sussex helpful to the proof that Hamo Dapifer was Hamo Sinclair. With these probabilities the question may be left for further, and not too hopeful, investigation, considering the darkness eight hundred years can draw over the most distinguished persons and facts. The two contemporaneous dapifers of William the Conqueror's reign, if not later also, is an acknowledged difficulty with the antiquarians and historians.

Contributions to the discussion, if not successful wholly in themselves, ought to have frank welcome when ingenuity gives chance of resolving what has been always interesting to those who have toiled in these first pages of our real history.

Chapter VIIII
Eudo Dapifer's Conquest

Writers great and small have excelled themselves in describing and moralising over the death and burial, or want of burial, of William the Conqueror. His corpulence; the fatal stumble of his horse, in a city's ashes; the king's hurt; the deathbed, with its repentance of crimes, as the weak souls call his inherent religious manliness of confession according to the best ritual of his period; the division of his kingdom and treasures; his advices, sage as his own practice had been, as to ruling the two peoples; the supposed shameful neglect by his courtiers, and his own very sons, of his corpse: all these are the commonplace themes of varied and mostly silly comment. It is plebeian rather than aristocratic virtue, to cry, and keep crying, over spilt milk, even if that noblest of all lost liquids, or gases, or higher essences, a truly regal soul. No mistake, on the part of historian or parochial superstitious moralist, is greater than reckoning the ways of rulers by common tables, fitted only for the multitude. The subject has been worn threadbare. There is only the necessity now, to protest inexorably against the miserable carping and maudlin superstition that are the stock of the great majority of those who have, with the daring of fools, not with the awe of angels certainly, attempted to expound the final chapter of the great king's life, and the opening one of his son's reign in England.

If any scandal, as this is understood in court circles, occurred before or after that scene of scenes, where the dying monarch did his dying duties as royally as he had lived, in the presence of his three sons and his greatest offices, Eudo Sinclair as being his first deserves all the blame. Had any wrong been really done, was it possible that he could have prospered afterwards as he did ? Let the dead bury their dead, is an aphorism always clearly known by the greatest men. The state is before the highest man, its king when alive. Departed, Vive le roi, is the true sentiment of the deepest statesman. Normans cling to fact too well, to be lost, and to lose others, especially the tender and young, in Eastern ghoulish howls of lamentation or in modern exuberance of undertakers' feathers. Shows for the mobs, and welcome, as they teach something to those who are essentially unshapely; but the art of rule needs masterly strokes, and the sternest design.

Possibly no more difficult problem was ever given to a man, to solve by skill of head and heart, than Eudo got from his sovereign; and the Conqueror, if he could have risen from the grave to give his approval, would, in the spirit of all his own splendid actions as a king, give that dapifer according to his own heart his best tribute for loyalty of pursuing his will. William Rufus, his second and most faithful soldierly son, must be king of England at any expense of exertion, not to say of lifeless ceremonial. His mind was fixed on this. Let the less dutiful Robert, the eldest, have Normandy, let Henry get large treasure, but William Rufus for England.

Says Palgrave:"'Eudo Fitz-Hubert, more usually called Eudo Dapifer, from the office which he held placing him in immediate relation to the royal person, earnestly moved Rufus to the enterprise. It was the tradition in Eudo's family that he thus exerted himself in pursuance of the Conqueror's instructions. Nor would this be otherwise than consistent with William's experience and feelings. In one sense he owed the crown to Hubert's promptness and adroitness, and these qualities had descended to Hubert's son'". The historian takes the "Herbert" form of spelling the name, it is correct but hardly very material to add.

Scarcely had the life left the body of the monarch, as the croakers grumble and disparage, when the fierce necessity of the case compelled the leading personages into action. Bishop Odo, the too renowned earl of Kent, and brother of the Conqueror, took also the side of Rufus; a fact quite sufficient of itself to answer the cavillings at funereal neglect.

"'These two supporting Rufus, formed the nucleus of his party. Eudo Dapifer was first in action, wisely not before the castle or in the open field, but assailing the heart of the empire. All the treasure amassed by the Conqueror was deposited in the vaults of Winchester. Whither Eudo proceeded, and treating with William de Ponte-Arche (equally accommodating in the next reign) induced him to surrender the keys. Hence the high steward proceeded rapidly along the coast. Dover, Pevensey, Hastings, and the other principal castles on the seaboard were visited by him. His known station constituted his letter of credence. He boldly quoted Rufus as "the king", and the garrisons promised obedience and allegiance to the soldier's friend, the Conqueror's favoured son '".

This account by Palgrave, if a little deduction be made for the absence of the English idiom, and also for the want of literary sanity in the Jewish nature, as is shown by his over-graphical splay enthusiasm, is as explanatory as true.

That it was thus Rufus got possession of England is the received narrative of historians, and Freeman also raises no real obstacle to the fame of Eudo. Indeed, the highest tribute of all comes to him from this quarter, because of the extremely little love lost in every other Norman's case with the barrister for the Anglo-Saxons. Speaking of "the house of Rye", he says, "'We can hardly grudge them their share in the lands of England, when we find that Eudes, the son of Hubert, the king's dapifer, and sheriff of Essex, was not only the founder of the great house of Saint John at Colchester, but won a purer fame as one of the very few Normans in high authority who knew how to win the love and confidence of the conquered English'".

In other more characteristic passages the same personal esteem for Eudo is to be seen. "'Among those to whose grasp the lands and homes of Englishmen were thus handed over, we come across many names familiar to us in our Norman history, to some of whom we should not grudge any amount of wealth and honour in their own land. The men whose exploits we could follow with delight below the steep of Arques, or among the burning streets of Mortemer, now meet us again in a less pleasing form, as intruders in the shire which gave birth to Alfred, William of Eu, Ralph of Toesny, etc. ....'"

"'Here we see the lands which Eudo of Rye, Eudo of Colchester, the worthy son of the faithful Hubert, received as the reward of his own and his father's loyalty....'"

Carte, in his able History of England, has this passage, "'In the meantime his friend Eudo, son of Hubert of Rie, and steward to the Conqueror, had visited William de Pontedelarche and all the governors of castles and fortresses in Kent and Sussex, and having engaged these in favour of Rufus, came to Winchester'".

Rapin says, "'Eudo, high-treasurer, and Lanfranc, archbishop of Canterbury, were very serviceable to young William on this occasion. The first had secured Dover, Winchester, Pevensey, Hastings, and other places on the south coast. Moreover, he delivered to him the late king's treasures, which amounted to sixty thousand pounds in money, besides plate and jewels of a much greater value'".

For this The Bromton Chronicle is given as authority.

Tindal makes the doubtful correction that Eudo was not the high-treasurer, but steward. Dapifer included both offices.

It is in the Monasticon by Sir William Dugdale, the valued and famous collection of papers and charters connected with the monasteries and churches of the Anglican province of Roman Catholicism before the Reformation, that the fullest account of this peculiar but effective conquest of England by Eudo's political skill is to be found in print. The Latin MS. whence he copied is in good preservation in the old monkish print-like hand at the British Museum among the collection Cottoniana, and it boasts of not only a pictorial headpiece, but of side illuminations, with the names of the abbots of Colchester Abbey included within them.

The gist of the story has been given from Palgrave, but here are some additions to the narrative. With the king dying apud Cadomum, in Normandy, the Latin goes on to say, Eudo, getting authority from his sovereign, embraced the opportunity of pressing William Rufus, juniorem, to master the situation. Then Eudo, having crossed into England, and having reached Winchester, gained over William of Ponte-Arce so far that he gave him possession of the keys of the treasury of Winchester, of which William was keeper.

Next, Eudo speedily made for the castle of Dover, and bound the garrison by their honour and oath to deliver the keys of their fortified position to no one except at his direction. The very same thing he did at Pevensey Castle, at Hastings Castle, and at all the other maritime castles, allowing it to be understood that the king, requiring to make some delay for state reasons in Normandy, wished to have special security as to all the fortifications of England, and that being seneschal he was the right person in absence of royalty to receive such assurance. Entirely successful in this swift revolution of affairs, he returned to Winchester, and openly proclaimed William Rufus, who had arrived there, the new king of England.

The Latin account finishes with this pregnant sentence: "'So, while the rest of the nobles are disputing in Normandy, about the succession to the kingdom, meanwhile, by the zeal and actions of Eudo, William the younger is elected, consecrated, and confirmed as king, in England'". Thus bloodless a coup d'etat in so military if not violent a period, is one of the greatest triumphs the world has known of statecraft, in the noblest sense of the word, as the system of finest art by which a people is ruled to its greatest possible happiness according to its circumstances and political growth.

Chapter IX
The Seneschal as Lord of Colchester

Next to London, Colchester was the most important town in England. The royal residence at Winchester, as well as its history as being capital of a Saxon kingdom, gave it prominence; and Exeter, which was fully described by its soubriquet of Little London, claimed the attention of the cultivated, the military, and also the mercantile minds; but the city in "the eastern part of Britain", as the Cottonian MS. localises it, from its very ancient foundation, its well fortified yet pleasant situation, its connection with the most distinguished persons and events of British experience, and its comparative nearness to Westminster, already at this period the place of highest state sanctions, took a position before the distinguished south-western cities. Under the Roman sway London itself was second to it; if not perhaps in population, certainly in state importance.

Camalodunum was to the emperors what Calcutta is to us. Nor did its fame begin with its fortification into a permanent inhabited castra, and arrangement into an imperial civitas by the conquerors of the earth. Virgil's line occurs,

"'Romanes, rerum dominos, gentemque togatam'"

though it is probable that the early Briton, the "Kelt", had more acquaintance with them in the kilt and the practised perfect use of the skean dhu or short sword than in their state drag. In Colchester's antiquities there are abundant proofs of the full arrival of all the refinements of that great civilisation, in the civil and legal aspects as well as the military; and if any soil in this island has a monopoly of distinction from the Latin humanities of the first centuries, it is the site of Camalodunum. Streams everywhere, a sufficient river and harbour, healthy air, made its pleasantness equal to its fame.

Here the British king, Coel, from whom it takes its present name, lived an actual historical personage, though some ribald rhymes give an unreal tone to his existence. His palace was the centre to such a Celtic town as

Caesar describes that of Cassibelaunus his antagonist to have been; and with the very strong walls of Roman style built around, it still remained an object of veneration, and not improbably of somewhat imposing architecture. The three years' siege which Colchester endured, when King Coel rebelled against the lords of the world, is not, but perhaps ought to be, as famous as that of Troy for ten. The Helen of the English is quite as reputable a heroine as she of the Asiatic fortress, unless, as is thought, Ilium was really, for all the prying persevering Schliemanns and Gladstones, situated in nubibus. Comparison would then vanish.

Like the favourite novel, the historical three years' siege ends, A.D. 264, with a marriage, though comedy was the less general ending of the tragic panoply of war led by such imperatores as Constantius. It was probably a most desirable solution of the political difficulty for him personally, that by marrying Helen, the king's daughter, all would not only be well but as he pleased. Constantine the Great, the first Christian emperor, was the son of this romantic match; and Anglican clericalism claims with pride for Britain, the Celtic mother of him who gave the coup de grace to what they call the pagan cults. King Coel is said to have been educated himself long and carefully at Rome; and Helen undoubtedly would, in addition to that of her own race, have also all the culture of the aliens.

The gloom of oblivion is considerably around, in Colchester's Celtic and Roman periods. When the Saxon chiefs and Norse pirates secure their dreadful days of mastery, the darkness can be felt. As a chief if not the richest city, siege after siege, plundering, sacking, piracies, depopulation, what of human misfortunes did it not suffer ? Some records and monuments of its long sufferings exist, but time and savage hands have left too little of the history of a place which would have been largely England's history if the fire of trial through which it had to pass were less severe. Not till the middle of the seventeenth century, in the time of Cromwell, 1648, did it see the last of the bitter experiences of war. So late as days of the royalist cavaliers its fair maids, not to mention the ruin of memories of the past always inevitable under the rough-shod foot of war, had cause to rue the attraction their city was for men of the sword, officers hardly less brutal than their dogs of violence and wrong.

But Colchester got also its good times. When William Rufus was thoroughly established on his throne, its citizens put in their ardent petitions to him that he would be pleased to allow his great seneschal, Eudo Sinclair, to become their protecting feudal lord. They had already some experience of him of most pleasant kind. It was not because of his recent fame they came to do him and themselves honour. He held property among them, and at intervals they previously enjoyed his personal presence, busy as he was on both sides of the Channel. In a time of popular distress, when hands to help were rare, had he not kept many of them alive when they should have died of hunger ? He was rich, but was he not generous ? He brought untaxed corn from over the sea, by shiploads, to relieve them: what luck better in such times of trouble with the Angles, when property declined suddenly to half its value, under the effects of transition to undoubtedly better rule, than to have the care of such a lord, who not only possessed most power in the kingdom, but whose heart they experienced was as powerful for action as his head? The king was nothing loth to promote any interests of his first and able servant and subject.

His gratitude for services, made him grant their petition; and Eudo, considering the advantage of vicinity to where royalty and its affairs did most frequent, and bound further in various ways of property and kindness, took the position of lord of Colchester. It was not in him to make a sinecure of any office. At intervals (and one seems to have been of some lengthened period, either through family sorrows, personal exhaustion, or temporary delegation of the duties of dapifer to Hamo) he resided at Colchester, and paid considerable attention to its monied and other interests. He heard cases, relieved the oppressed, put down the oppressing; and, what had a specially endearing effect, he was not unwilling to re-instate, as far as he could, all in their original possessions who had lost them by the storms and injustices of a transition time. While without sympathy for the weak and turbulent Anglian cry for the laws and times of the "good King Edward", he was far more attentive to the actual wrongs of Saxons than most of his fellow-ruling Normans; and he has by this alone gained with them a kind of canonisation for his name.

For Colechestrians to this day he is a state idol. To say, a municipal idol, would not savour enough of the proper antique. But one of his reforms deserves particular note. The people had to pay, by any method of collection they pleased, the taxes, not only of their own holdings, but also of all those who had been condemned as criminals, outlawed, or evicted at fault; and this, without being allowed to put or keep in cultivation the land which the trespassers occupied. Such frank-pledge grew intolerable, and all the more by reason of the difficulties of the time creating unusual quantity of crime. No one could suggest a remedy for a grievance which was fast binding each of them as with chains for their worldly ruin. Eudo came to the rescue with a plan as original as effective. By hook and crook he got all those wasting lands into his own sole possession, no doubt giving double their value for them; and, paying the whole of the taxes himself always, universal Colchester was freed from the irritating burden.

Such things dwell in the popular memory, and deservedly, though there may be no reason to think that he lost even pecuniarily in the end by the transaction. Thomas Cromwell in his History of Colchester makes "the powerful and wealthy Norman", Eudo Dapifer, the builder of the Moot Hall, where such questions of law were settled in the most orderly way, and has some account of various other ruins of houses associated with his traditions; but to him that hath, is given, in the antiquarian as in other worlds, and Colchester has no hero equal or second to Eudo.

Thus he dealt as judge and protector of his and their own special, choosing and chosen, city; but a dozen years before, he had appeared in this very scene under quite a different character. To the Anglo-Saxon populace he must, in 1076, have seemed the worst possible, because the most powerful, incarnation of Norman tyranny, when he came to build, exactly on the site of King Coel's palace, the most powerful of the strongholds by which William the Conqueror put all Anglo-Saxondom into manacles and fetters. Colchester Castle, whose ruins are among the most venerable and imposing within our borders, was built by Eudo Dapifer in that year; and there is no better tribute to the genial power of his strong character, than the fact that he both gained, and kept, the respect, and even the love, of the Colchestrians, while employed at such a piece of work. Every stone laid was another knell of remembrance to them, that the wild liberty of semi-savagery, which Saxons clung to so rancorously, was inexorably passing away, and that only by law, and according to the refined manners of the civilised man, was it henceforth possible to live without punishment. Most human creatures, it is to be feared, have a natural dread of being washed; cold water which is, on the whole, the best for them and for the neighbours, in a thousand ways of health and good humour, is a sore trespass on such freemen as these. Other populaces everywhere too generally, are of the same mind.

The Conqueror and his companions were rulers, and acted according to their nature; but few of them tempered severity with kindness so well as Eudo. In a dozen years after thus putting the iron hand in the silk glove over them, their warmest cry was, "'Come you, and none else, to rule over us; for in you we, though blind and stiff-necked enough, have found more happiness than is, as we can now see, the prevailing lot not only of Saxons but of men'".

There may be some shading or illuminating by imagination in these picturings of the past; but to those who wish corroboration, Morant's

History of the Antiquities of Essex and especially his History of Colchester are ample and the best authority. Indeed, he had access to some ancient Latin documents, of which his quotations are now in all probability the only remnants. In the present connection, while giving the biography, marriage, and relationships of Eudo, this stands four-square. Qui construxit castrum Colecestriae. There are dozens of references to him as the builder of the great pile, which had at the beginning and subsequently so large a place in English story.

As a Norman building, it is still its own evidence, and even if we had not a vestige left, there are prints enough of it in the British Museum to enable it to tell its tale, with a fullness only limited by the spectator's knowledge of events and of military architecture. It is built on arches, and there is said to be no example of the use of the arch in this country before 1066, when it came from Normandy. The square tall ranges of walls, averaging twelve feet of thickness, the substantial pilasters at widish intervals, the small and somewhat irregular windows, placed for inside convenience rather than external show, the loopholes, the magnificent general massiveness which speaks such volumes for the powerful and grave characters and conceptions of the rulers, appear exceptionally marked in these drawings; and the earlier ones as taking the castle in less decay are particularly instructive. No wonder one of the writing natives speaks of it as the glory of his birthplace, set on its moderate height in the centre of the town's rather dissonant modern structures. Some of the prints, indeed, suggest the pathos of ruin with almost a comic pungency. What kind of human brain must it have been which found satisfaction, at some not very ancient period, in building a contemporary toy of a house, with quite the usual shape of roof and walls, on the high ridge of this giant structure of a stronger day ? It was its proprietor, Gray, who put what he called a dome somewhere about the middle of it, of the proportion of a small pot on a large church without a steeple. But time has swept away these insults, and nothing less appropriate than whistling grasses and twigs, to that manner born, decorate the later elevations of this venerable pile, which teaches the grandest lesson man can and, in some degree, must learn, namely, the necessity of ruling and being ruled.

Whether Eudo held the governorship of it in the military character, either personally or by substitute, those twelve years upwards between the erection of it and his creation as lord of Colchester, is difficult to substantiate. He was so much with the Conqueror in Normandy that in any case his presence here could have only been at intervals. The story of his sympathy with the people is proof of his responsibility to some extent as well as of his natural generosity.

His marriage took place the year after the accession of Rufus, 1088; so that it cannot be said that his celebrated wife from the Clare family needed an English home during those years. One supposed first wife would have felt the home in France more suitable for many reasons than this fortress among the incensed Angles. Light may fall back on this as advance is made. The probability is that not long after Colchester Castle was built, he became a regretted stranger for most part during the latter years of the Conqueror's reign. That though often absent he did not forget, nor did they, is one of the precious and authenticated passages of history which show that humane natures can rise, at their best, above Norman and Saxon and other phenomenal faction.

But when, by his doing, England was separated from Normandy, he needed a home, and with his lady of ladies he took possession of and resided in this princely home of Colchester, where they were blessed with a family, and with all other things which make life desirable. Again he had assumed the full weight of his office as dapifer of England; but henceforth Colchester was the centre whence all his action came and where his heart always was, whithersoever his duties and interests might summon him.

King-maker as he was, with the aid and countenance of Lanfranc from the monastery of Bee till he died in 1089, Eudo had at the beginning of Rufus's reign the healthiest influence over the king. Odo, the bishop of Bayeaux and earl of Kent, who soon proved faithless to the nephew, as he had done to the nephew's father, had been thoroughly crushed, with his followers discontented to rebellion, by the siege and taking of Rochester Castle; and Eudo's retirement, from whatever cause, to the comparative quiet of the duties of his recent lordship of Colchester must have occurred shortly after. The early signs of a coming storm between clerical and secular, especially monarchical, rule, were already beginning to appear in various parts of Europe; and the sensual but energetic and brave Rufus was not a likely king to escape the quarrel. Anselm had come from Bee to fill the place of the dead Lanfranc; but there was a new light in William's court, probably not an agreeable one naturally, but distasteful to the clergy as if a brand from the hottest place.

We hear nothing of Hamo Dapifer, who does not seem to have been of the mould his probable relation was. A Ralph Flambard was the bete noir on which the Jupiter and satellites of the holy catholic church would fain, if they dared, have rained their thunderbolts to his speedy extermination. The Norman king felt that his side was Ralph's; and without venturing to oppose the church then, a herculean impossibility even to kings, he secretly approved of Flambard's plan of delaying actual inductions, from archbishop downwards, and turning the proceeds of the benefices meanwhile into the royal coffers. It should be remembered that this was less mercenary than politic; the question of money being always the vulnerable part of clerisy, if otherwise armed cap-a-pie.

Anselm, a mild man by nature, but bitter as only clerical office can make one, had his wrong, that he was defrauded of the fruits of his archbishopric of Canterbury for several years, while waiting the abandonment of the king's proposed final appointment by giving of the crozier, as in similar way with the sword he made his political officers. Symbolism meant a great deal then, and the pope could not and would not vail his prerogative for a moment in favour of royalty. The terror, and perhaps superstitious dread, of having defied the clergy, which his extraordinary illness caused him, gave the game back into the church's hands, and promises and appointments were made freely, as vows for possible recovery. He did save life; and it is probable that Eudo, before this, had come back to be helpful in such storms at his old place.

Palgrave, on what authority is not clear, makes both Eudo and Hamo staunch supporters of kingly prerogative in this bodeful first trial of strength; but, with the deepest of all loyalty, it is more likely, from his subsequent history, that Eudo calmed a quarrel for which even William's energy was not yet fit. The same writer pictures the two dapifers as amicably, at once and together, moving about the duties of high steward, especially in festal scenes, without questioning as to whether two such were possible, when there was only the king of the one kingdom. He thus escapes the puzzle which seems to have much troubled the learned and very patient author of The History of the Exchequer.

Eudo the sewar of Normandy and Hamo of England, is Madox's last guess; but Palgrave, with a brilliancy as charming as original, attacks the subject freely, and as sprightlily leaves it for imaginative consideration. Madox, on the means of investigation then open, is worthy of more trust, though dull compared with the knight who, as a Jew, was deputy-keeper of the English records. The Jews are apt to see us too much as Israel; but this Cohen is bright and good of his kind, had he only been in the right place. As it is, he deserves the Englishman's best wishes, seeing the field is so wild and untilled yet. He is juster to the highest humanity of the time than "Anglish" Freeman.

But who with the right birth, training, and ability is to sift from the earth the gold that certainly exists in the codexes and books of such collections as the Bodleian and British Museum libraries, not to hint at the Paris, Rouen, or Vatican bibliothecas, with regard to these valuable facts of English, and indeed European and world history ? What will occur now of research comes from our national collections both in the state paper offices, Fetter Lane, and the Museum at Bloomsbury, London; but even these would take a lifetime of fine leisure and practised ability to do them fullest justice.

Whatever the means, whether by Eudo's grave influence or not, the fierce struggle between church and king was passed on for the solution of future but not very distant years. The dapifer saw no more of it, but spent the remainder of his life in as successful union with the religious cult of his time as he had done with the interests of the two able Williams of England, I and II. Henry I was for periods by no means his friend so absolutely, but Eudo died in peace with him. The civitas, with its pertinents, of Colchester, given him by Rufus, had as good reason in sacred as in justiciary and political matters to be proud of its lord.

Chapter X
Eudo the Founder of Religious Houses

The first crusade began in 1096, and the church had a new lease of ascendency. That year, Eudo Dapifer, on the fourth of the kalends of September, had the site fixed and the work measured out, in the presence of Maurice, bishop of London, of his weightiest religious enterprise, namely, the building from his own resources of the famous abbey of St.John the Baptist.

Says Weever, in his Funeral Monuments: "'Without the walls of Colchester, stood a large and stately monastery, which Eudo, sewar to King Harry I, founded and consecrated to the honour of Christ and St.John Baptist, wherein he placed black monks'".

Tanner in his Monasteries gives the information that the abbey was of the order of St.Benedict, But it is in Dugdale's Monasticon, as might be expected, that fullest details are to be found. Besides the account of the foundation, it has the Latin charter by which the founder endowed, with lands and other properties, this abbey which he built to preserve his memory, and, in the words of undoubtedly the monastic writer, suae animae suffragia aeterna preparare.

There is the usual miraculous "business", without which a monk would no more think of narrating than Livy could forego his prodigies. On a little hill to the south-east, where Siricus the presbyter dwelt, there was a wooden church, consecrated to St.John the Evangelist. Here in the darkness of the nights, and they were apt to be very dark then without the gates of walled cities, lights were seen to shine mysteriously, and voices praised God inside of the wooden structure, seemingly without human or monastic agency. It was distinction to places to have direct communication from above, and St.John's became one of the lions to frighten all the unbelievers. But this was not its best honour in thaumaturgy.

Peter, Paul, and many others, in favoured times and localities, had supernatural interference in their favour, in the way of sudden freedom from chains and prisons. A man here, whom the record does not credit with any particular saintliness, experienced what was sufficiently similar, in a desirous scene, to be reckoned miraculous.

"'Quidam vir, qui jussu regis erat compeditus et vicissim alebatur a civibus, dum quodam die festo Sancti Johannis adesset ibidem cum multis, subito dum missa celebraretur pessulus boiarum ultra quartum vel quintum assistentum exilivit, et boiae cum, sonitu fractae sunt, et homo solutus astitit.'"

The whole civitas, it seems, exulted in this miracle. But more than enough of such introductory flourish.

Eudo might not as a politic mind object to fame of that kind, but it was his delight in the amenity of the situation which made him build his abbey on the site of this highly-favoured shrine. It was 1097 before the foundation stones were ready to be laid in grand state. Through the multitudes usual to great occasions, a procession of nobles and their ladies made their way to the place where the symbolic, and some actual, work was to be done. Eudo himself placed the first stone of the edifice; Rohesia his wife the next; Count Gilbert of Tunbridge and Clare, the brother of Rohesia, the third. These proper ceremonies completed, the work began to show its proportions, but it was not till 1104 that the pile was finished.

During the years of building this sister abbey to Westminster, he had grave political troubles; but something must now be said of the peculiarly irritating ones he met with in arranging proper clerical service for the foundation on which he was expending so much of his mind and means. His particular friend, Gundulph, bishop of Rochester, first came to his aid by sending him two monks. These Eudo treated too kindly, admitting them to the luxuries and delight of his daily routine and personal presence. "'Jeshurun hath grown fat and kicketh'". The monks soon began to grumble, even at the Norman's cooks, and weariness and departure inevitably ended the absurdity. Several others were sent to fill their place, with an energetic and religious leader, by name Radulph.

He after some time began to press Eudo, who had been very friendly with him, as to the inconvenience of the monks being supported by the laics. Though then, so to speak, in political chains, Eudo did what he could to take away this reproach. He gave the fruits of ten churches on different parts of his estates; but, by reason of the distance from the various counties in which they lay, and more likely by the extravagance and improvidence of the collectors, very little leached the abbey. The result of this and other things was that Radulph and his party also left. The actual building was lagging through these private as much as Eudo's public difficulties. He began to consider that at least he could get rid of this voluntary tax on his spirits. But the abbot of York came to the rescue. He sent Stephen, a monk, with twelve others, and the services were kept up.

Eudo also, at this time, induced a relation, of his own temper, William Sinclair, a priest, to oversee the workmen; and he spared no means or pains till the last touch was put to the splendid edifice. Its first abbot, Hugo, was consecrated by Maurice, bishop of London, in 1104; and the founder's joy and special munificence, on the occasion of the first full services, are especially remarked upon by the chronicler. He gave various lands and tenths, and had the further satisfaction of seeing his example liberally followed. There was a grievance of the townspeople that some of their land was seized by the authorities of the abbey; he sent money directly from his own treasury, and satisfied them all. The final dedication was made on the fourth of the Ides of January, "with the great glorying and the deep devotion and praise of the populace". The religieux, from York soon after joined Abbot Hugo, Walter senior and Osmund senior, who in the happy circumstances would be able only too speedily to form a staff. But not yet were the dapifer's annoyances over. His approved abbot, Hugo, got timid about the hot questions between Eudo and King Henry, and retired to York again, leaving the Parthian arrow of a formal deed of cure of this cenobium, the heart-work so long of the founder, to the king. No doubt in the circumstances it was the safe thing for himself to do, and it is probable Eudo knew humanity too well to blame the weakness.

He did not lose faith in religion for all his disappointments. The secular storms passed away from his noble life, and his devotion and liberality to sacred causes still increased from year to year, as he went towards the end of his earthly course.

The substance of his chief charter may be given. "Charter of Eudo Dapifer concerning the foundation of the church of Saint John of Colchester", is its heading in the Monasticon. It begins, "'Eudo, the dapifer of my lord the king of the whole Anglican kingdom, to all the faithful of God, now and for ever, salvation. Since by the overflowing clemency of the divine mercy, He has gifted me in this life with many benefits, though undeserving; and, created out of nothing, He has enriched me with the amplest honours, with lands, and with abundance of riches; mindful from such great beneficence why I should very specially offer to the Lord, the King of kings, for all the things which He has granted to me, I considered frequently in the most watchful mind.

Opportunely the helpmeet of my pious devotion, with zeal from above, insinuated that piety in this matter would be acceptable for her, and of saving influence for me, if showing to the Lord, the King of kings, for His goodnesses and gifts, zeal for religion, I should offer a monument of piety'", etc.

It is possible this is enough of what may have been rather the usual legal form of such institution rather than an expression of the peculiar character and sanctity of the present donor. There is a temptation to give him the benefit of the judicious gravity and serene thoughtfulness of such introduction, but it might not be honest to do so, however consonant the sentiments are with his known character. This passage has at least as much of him in it: "'I have built a church near Colchester in my fee, by God's help, and I have placed in it men, religious after monasterial ritual, and with my most pious lord, Henry, king of the English [Anglorum inclusive of Normans then], permitting it, I will grant lands and other returns for the salvation of my same lord, King Henry, and of Matilda his queen, and for the peace and stability of this kingdom, nor not also for the redemption of the souls of his antecedent rulers, of his father and his mother, the great King William, and Matilda, queen of the same, besides for the saving of the soul of King William, his brother and predecessor, for me myself in addition, for my wife Rohesia, and for all our ancestors and descendants. In all devoutness I have offered these'".

Next follows the list of his gifts. "'The four manors of Willege, Brichling, Mundovor, and Picheford he gave whole, except the fee of a Radulph in Picheford, and the portion of Ailwin, a socman. He gave the marsh of Lillecherche which afterwards went with Picheford and Hallingbery, with all its pertinents. In his Colchester fee he gave two carucates of land, one dwelling-house, two vivaria, one mill, one wood, and money to feast the people four days at the birthday of Saint John. The rest are the whole fee of Turstin Wiscard; the land of Ranulph de Broc; in Turncrust the church of that town; one hide of the land of Esse (probably the Ashe of Hampshire, which his father Hubert of Rye, the first Sinclair proprietor on English record, got) and also the tenth of its cheese, wool, and wood; of Lillecherche the tenths of the mills and cheese and wool; two parts of the tenths of Berton and Sandford; of Etonia the half tenths and the whole tenths of the mills; the tenth of the swine food of all his groves and parks on the Essex side of the Thames; of Standeie two parts of the tenths; and of Hamerton and Estune, ditto; of Nieveseles the church; of Walden the tenths of the mill and of wool; two parts of the tenths of Hallingbery; the third part of the tenths of Sabricheworth; of Takelee two parts of the tenths; Royages all the tenths; Waltham three parts of the tenths; Witham two of tenths; Cresswell,

Estanweya, Lereden, the same; Grinstede all the tenths; in any one of those manors a croft of two acres free from all secular or feudal services, except in the three manors around Colchester, and Witham, Waltham, Sabricheforth, Waledene; the whole tenth of Eudo's swine-feeding and brood-mares and mills; the church of St.Helen and the fourteen acres belonging to it; the church of St.Mary, Westcheap, London, which was then called New Church, with the concurrence of Ailward Gros, the priest, who had the presentation of the living from Hubert Sinclair of Rye, Basse Normandie, the father of the dapifer; the church of St.Stephen above Walebroch; Eudo's stone-built house, probably his town mansion near New Church, with its appendages, and six acres of land which was that of the woman Alveva, a widow; all the fruits of all the chapels in his manors on the Colchester side of the Thames, and particularly the offerings on principal feast days of those serving God, the monks there to transmit the same.'"

This is the tale of his gifts at that time, and he closes the charter with perhaps a usual form also. "'These portions and returns of my fee and barony, I have granted freely to God and His most blessed forerunner John. If anyone add to them, may God add good days to his, and eternal life; if anyone take from them, or rob, or damage, etc., let his life be shortened, and let him have his portion with Judas, Dathan, and Abiram, unless he make amends to God and Saint John.'"

But perhaps enough of what is rather heavy legal reading. Of his other foundations, little of the documentary kind can have survived; and it may be as well, for he might become too much a quarry for inane, professional, or antiquarian struggling, as to the exact meaning of Latin terms to things which are as changeful in their substance as almost the words themselves. Fortunate abbey of which the above is only one specimen of many grants. But for it also time has been too strong.

Like the gorgeous palaces which leave not a wrack behind, all of it was out of being in 1724, except its beautiful gate, of which there is a print extant, of that period. Much either way cannot be taken as to its earlier wealth from the valuation in 26 Henry VIII (1535) of its annual income at £523, 17s. Always in one of the hottest political and clerical districts, its fortunes would be as varying as those of the great families, for most part, who lived and died within its range.

Morant, the best Essex authority, has noted the important fact that both a William and a Hubert de Sancto Claro were also markworthy benefactors of this monastery, certainly members of the name subsequent to the founder. He had a list of all the benefactors of the abbey given him, after his book was written, by Lord _, which he inserts as an appendix of great value. Greenstead manor is there granted by Hubert de Sancto Claro, and also Lexden mill, while Stokes manor is the gift of Hamo de Sancto Claro. Morant's own research discovered William Sinclair as one of the donors of the monastery.

Other houses, churches, and chapels there are still some fragmentary evidences to prove that Eudo either built, or aided to build, but his religious fame now is eternally associated with the abbey of St.John Baptist at Colchester. He is among those who gave charters to Glastonbury Abbey, and Ordericus Vitalis makes him one of the founders of Lessay Abbey, but this has been challenged as confusion of Eudo Dapifer with Eudo an Chapeau, though the challenger does not seem competent enough to condemn so established authority. Tanner in his Notitia Monastica for fair example of really unsatisfactory scraps, queries whether the pillory of Cluniac monks of Reydon St.Peter's, Wangford, Suffolk, said by Leland the antiquary to have been founded by Doudo Afini, steward to the king's household, was not one of Eudo Dapifer's foundations. Bishop Herbert gave a charter to Norwich in the reign of Henry I, where Eudo's signature stands immediately after that of Roger Bigod, earl of Norfolk, the founder of Thetford; and out of respect to him, Tanner theorises that the dapifer might have given that priory to this monastery. Perhaps such probabilities are worse than worthless; at all events, in illustrating the character of a man whose actions can be measured on authenticated facts. Matthew of Westminster, in his Flores Historiae, recounting the monasteries built in Normandy before the Conquest, has, "'But Eudo built the church of the Holy Trinity, with the chapel, at Exaqueum'". His work was not confined to England in this kind.

Nor did he limit himself to religious foundations. The hospital for the sick has in France sometimes, if not always, the beautifully appropriate name of "Hotel de Dieu", or "house of God". Such a house Eudo established during the reign of Henry I, and with his special sanction, for people infected with the contagious disease of leprosy, which, from whatever cause, not improbably from Saxon filth or excess with its alternating poverty, must have been common then here. To save Saxonic feeling, it is quite possible to suppose that Easterns, even in the army of Hastings, said to have been widely gathered in one at least of its wings, or Westerns themselves who had been crusading in the East, were the bringers of this frightful disease of humanity. Froude has suggested want of vegetables. Institutions imply something indigenous rather than passing or exotic, as to this English leprosy; but in any case the question is one of peculiar social interest to those who are devotees of ethnologic and related science.

The building was dedicated to St.Mary Magdalene. It was without the town, and ruled by a master, probably leprous like his unhappy companions. In 28 Henry VIII (1537) its endowments gave an income of only £11 a-year; but though this is a far larger sum for the practical buying of food and clothes and medicine than all but experts can now imagine, there is little doubt that the place was kept up, as some of our similar houses are, by voluntary contributions. A satisfactory way of explaining the possible dwindling down of its income to such a sum would be by discovering that the better blood and habits of the true Englishman, of as well-mixed a race as his thorough-bred nonpareil horse, had banished the loathsome disease to its native or chronic regions, and that the building was dying of having nothing more to do.

There is a statement that Eudo had to build it as a punishment for the political quarrels between himself and the commanding, unforgiving, sullen, but able Henry. If so, a better method of making peace could not be invented; for it was work not penible, but we well know wholly according to the man's heart. Independently or by regal command the foundation is equally a tribute to him as a great soul. The hospital of St.Mary Magdalene at Colchester, for leprous persons, stands as an early beacon in England of the medical sanitary science and humanity which have made the poorest of lives worth living, if the present and the past could only be well compared.

Chapter XI
The Dapifer's Latter Years

Prince William, the only son of Henry I, and the whole company of the White Ship with its noble passengers, sank in the English Channel, Berold the Rouen butcher alone surviving to tell the dreadest tale of 1120. From Normandy in great gaiety they were coming, and when the crashing rock split their vessel into pieces, the gallant prince in vain efforts to save the life of his natural sister, the Countess of Perche, was drowned, to the consternation of England and the inconsolable grief of a souless king.

In that same year, during the spring, and before the disaster of 25th November, which ended the male succession of that Norman dynasty that he had served so long and loyally, the dapifer also died.

It was a saddest of times to the whole people; for Henry had courted and gained the affection of the Angles, more than he had perhaps kept that of his own race, by his charters, his return to the laws of Edward the Confessor, his administration of justice by circuits and all good means, and by his marriage to Matilda, the grandchild of Edgar Atheling, the fated prince's high-born mother.

To Eudo the tragedy would have been, were he alive, a greater grief than to all other men, the king alone excepted. Had he not been first servant and subject to three of these great descendants of Rollo, the kings who were his own relations ? and had he not looked forward to the reign of a fourth, with whose person and education he had been so long conversant ? This young brave William would have well kept up and advanced the traditions of the Williams to whom Eudo owed so much, and for whom he had toiled so watchfully.

The twenty years from the accession of Henry, though successful for Eudo, had been troubled and dangerous. When on the death of his own King Rufus in 1100, doubts began to spread as to whether England and Normandy had not better be united under the elder Robert, the dapifer's state became fluctuating. His adherence to Henry was less ardent than the revengeful Beauclerc thought loyal to him. Some of the best of the Normans longed to have one ruler over their various estates in the two countries, for all reasons of policy and comfort. Robert de Belesme was the leader, and his failure was as bitter as the slighted Henry was unrelenting, to the utter ruin of his brother's party.

Fortune smiled everywhere on the Conqueror's youngest son, and in 1106 he himself had secured the very union many wished, by Curthose's defeat at Tenchbrai and subsequent imprisonment for life.

Eudo's full cup was never nearer spilling than in the trying crisis, and that he weathered such storms, shows sagacity of an extra-ordinary kind.

It came, however, to this point with the suspicious Henry, that Eudo's wife, Rohaise Clare; her uncle, Walter Giffard, bishop of Winchester; and Peter of Valoniis, or Peter de Valence, ancestor of the royal earls of Pembroke - a son of one of Eudo's sisters and of the Petrus de Valoniis who as sheriff of Hertford appears, with Geffrey de Mandeville, sheriff of Essex, and Ralph Barnard of Middlesex, in William the Conqueror's charter separating the temporal and spiritual courts (see Ancient Laws and Institutes); had to use their powers of intervention to bring matters into peace. Count Gilbert of Tunbridge, and earl of Clare, her brother, had gained great position by his support of Henry, and Rohaise dreaded his ambition, or that of some other of the successful party, for the supplanting of her husband from his hereditary office. Stripped of this, he might be stripped of more.

But she being of that very noble chief of Normans, to wit, Richard who was the son of Count Gilbert, Eudo was not dispossessed, says the chronicler, "for his wife's sake". This Richard Fitz-Gilbert was the Conqueror's greatest captain, and justice of England. He had married Rose Giffard, daughter of Walter Giffard, of whom afterwards in discussions of lineage. It is to be presumed that Eudo's politic hand was in the balancing of the sister's interest against the brother's probable ambition, founded on high services to Henry; and these two Clares at this crisis preserved their traditional nobility of action. Count Gilbert and more of her brothers and relations were all gained over; and the placing of the foundation of a new prosperity for the dapifer was made.

The Harleian MS., 312, has saved extracts from the monasterial register of his abbey of Colchester, and one of them is the remission of all grudges by Henry I against his minister, the confirmation to him of the feudal lordship of Colchester, and the possession of its castle and tower. Both words are mentioned, and this might explain the discussion about the date "1090" in part of a modern building, on the site of which tradition says was Eudo's private Colchester residence. It is not improbable that the remnant of ancient wall thus preserved was part of the turris mentioned in the manuscript. There does not seem any other notice of two fortified places, and it is hardly likely that legal tautology is the explanation. That he lived in a private residence, separate from the castle, is against all the ways of his rank and time; and his occupation of the tower part of the whole lordship may be the popular authentic tradition of "Eudo's house".

The signatures to this remission and confirmation are extremely useful. His power rose higher than it had ever been. Under the Conqueror he may have been dapifer of England and Normandy; under Rufus his own policy gave him only the stewardship of England; in Henry's reign he was full minister for the then united kingdom. The shortest and clearest proofs of this last fact are contained in the charter to his own abbey at Colchester, "Eudo, dapifer of my lord the king of all the Anglican kingdom", and in the record of one of his relations getting the dapifership of Normandy at a subsequent period by the claim of its hereditary tenure in Eudo Sinclair's family. Unfortunately there does not seem to be a, date to the charter, and as the abbey was finished and consecrated in 1104, it may have been given before Henry I had possession of Normandy. The proof would have been doubly complete, had its date been subsequent to 1106; no long time for the monastery to wait for its founder's endowment. On the evidence given, it is proved that in Henry's time he held both dapiferships.

Nothing is more an axiom in court and political experience than that *nil desperandum* is the sagacious motto of the born statesman. Wolsey's is pulpit sentiment that when a man falls he must fail "like Lucifer, never to hope again". Eudo was not the man likely to

"Fall into the compass of a praemunire"

either of hierarchical or political nature; or, if he did, he would not sit down and lick his chains but use his power and break them. Only monastic tempers get weary of the real world, and his vigour continues in those twenty years of Henry's reign as full as though he had not the weight of dignified and venerable age upon him. He came into, and kept, the strong grace and favour of the king, who was as stubborn in his likings as he was fell in his hate.

The details of Eudo's political and social doings, by their very success, have not left much record; but it is noticeable that religious devotion grew on him as he neared the end of the continued sovereignty, rather than pilgrimage, of his rich life. It was not in England, but in his native Normandy, that he breathed his last. He died a brilliant example of a good man who lived according to the Christian ritual of his time. Around his deathbed in his castle of Preaux, France, stood, with the reverence or interest that could alone bring such personages there, Henry, king of England and Normandy, Geoffrey, bishop of Rouen, and Turstan, archbishop of York. In their presence he did the duties of a dying man. To all whom he owed anything, either for their service or whatever else, he directed payment to be made. His last days were passed in continual penitence and sorrow for sin, in confession again and again, in absolution, and in penance severe even then, according to the directions of these high dignitaries of the Galilean and Anglican churches. With the king's sanction, and their witness, he divided all his fortune as his practised wisdom and clear mind dictated. When this was done, he made his surrounding relations, and his personal following, give their solemn word, that by all they owed to him they would take his body to his own abbey which he had built at Colchester. Says the chronicle, "'Ita Eudo uti bonus Christianus, poenitens, pectus tundens, et Dei invocans misericordiam, ultimum efflavit spiritum'". His noble wife was still beside him in this, the dark shadow, as she had been his faithful companion in all the life difficulties of the thirty-two years of their devoted partnership, Bonquet quotes, in a note, a writer in Latin, that Eudo was "'an old man and blind'".

Rose Clare, one of England's earliest and greatest ladies, could not be too much honoured by volumes written in her praise. When it grew certain that he was not to rise again in health, her continual prayer to God was that with His will she might not survive a whole year "'so dear and so noble a man'", (Cott. MS.) It was a great grief to her that the pride of her brothers, the Clares, and of her relations, who were then securing her claim to be a queen, prevented the wish of her heart to accompany her husband Eudo's remains herself to the loved abbey of Colchester. She would have been made queen, too, had she not been the prophetess of her own desired fate. Within the year she died, to the keen disappointment of her ambitious friends; and not an aged woman, for though so long the wife of Eudo, she had married him when under age. Her last directions also, were to be laid in the abbey of Colchester, beside him whom she loved so deeply; but by her brothers, who had lost their secular game, and did not care for spiritual things, she was buried instead at the famous monastery of Bee. It is perhaps gratuitous of the chronicler to add that they did this to save expense.

While she was alive such a compromise could not happen to her husband's remains. She took care that it reached England. When it arrived, and, as it appears, having gone by way of London, it was met coming from the west by all the monks a mile from the coenobium, or monastery, with a large accompanying crowd, not only of the townspeople but from distant places. When they reached the abbey, a miracle of a kind the whole world apart from the frequent, too frequent, monastic ones, astounded the multitude. Another solemn procession had just come, like this great one from the west, from the north, and, grief added to grief, it was found that Walter Sinclair, the nephew of Eudo, was being brought to the same family resting-place, by accidental if not miraculous concurrence. Under one monument the uncle and nephew wore laid, with the highest honours of sepulture, "'die pridie Kalend. Martiarum, anno Domini,1120'". His tenderness for his loved Colchestrians appeared even then; for, that they should not be burdened with the expense of this celebration, he had willed for the purpose the manor of Bryht Lyngeseia, and a hundred librae denariorum, besides his gold ring with a signet of precious topaz. His cup ornamented with plates of gold, within and without, of fine workmanship, was given to the abbey. The abbot, however, Gilbert, a monk from the Bee monastery, who took the place of Hugo, gave it to King Henry, asking in return the royal approval of Eudo's grant of the manor and gifts which were kept. It is possible that the Dapifer's cup may be still somewhere among the royal precious vessels of the kingdom, most probably, however, in other shape.

Nor did his wife Rose Claie forget to send similar last gifts to their own abbey. She sent four phylacteries, two serica pallica, one silver calix, and one silver censer. She gave, like her husband, a final gift of land, Tholi in Halyngeberia. It was not her fault that some of the yet unborn King Richards took violent possession of it from the abbey. As much as woman could be such a man, she was Eudo. Besides building with him, she built and ornamented other religious houses. Near Rouen she built a xenodochium at her own expense. She was truly a woman known in all the churches; for not only were her presents of gold, of silver, and of that needlework in which Norman-English ladies excelled so much, to be seen among the ornaments of home churches, but of those beyond sea. The finest, because most womanly part of all her delightful character, can close a chapter that may well linger if dearness of subject is excuse for delay.

It was shortly after Eudo had been the means of establishing William Rufus on the throne of England, himself then a great, the greatest, statesman and officer in the land, that he was so human as to be caught by especially the beauty of the eyes of this dear Rose, then a girl of fourteen, in her father's halls at Tunbridge Castle, Kent. His admiration she returned with an enthusiasm told by the fact they were married before she was fifteen. If ever two became one they did. Who could wonder at Rufus's pleasure in giving Colchester Castle to the young wife with her husband, as a fully compensating home for her father Earl Richard's fort and palace united, as was the mode of the chief Norman homes, the greatest warrior of Hastings field. She loved her husband as he well deserved. The Latin word is, she "'worshipped him, and with wonderful zeal, with wonderful affection' Rose Clare and Eudo St.Clare were the living poem of their period."

Chapter XII
Eudo's Lineage

In his Introduction to Domesday Book, with regard to which he is one of the authorities. Sir Henry Ellis has an easy task in showing that Eudo the son of Hubert is Eudo the dapifer. It lies patent on the surface of the great record. His statement, however, is so clear and short, that it may serve for finish to this first step towards the recognition of the man.

"'Terra Eudonis filius Huberti'" stands as a title to Eudo's lands in Berks., Herts., Cambs., Hunts., and Beds., but the entire entries themselves uniformly begin "'Eudo Dapifer tenet de Rege'". That this Hubert was Hubert of Rye, Freeman, Palgrave, and all the writers assert on the support of worlds of evidence.

To give proof that Hubert was Hubert Sinclair is the only thing after this necessary for the complete identification of Eudo's line. The succession of others of the name in positions and places of close relation to him and his history, might be quite legitimately used in the way of cumulative evidence. Indeed, in the case of reigning royal stocks, what with the ravages of time and the varied accidents of lives, such sidelight is often the only thing available. The extraordinarily chequered course of the history of the "Sancto de Claro" kin in England, the heights to which they reached at intervals, the mad pride of new local surnaming, and the seemingly sudden extinction of important branches, with various special experiences, which will gradually appear, make it something of a miracle that they should have had the fortune to be known thus at all.

Continuity and permanence of blood, with steady and considerable wealth, are the best conditions of the preservation of family record through such periods as eight or nine hundred years. Where gaps of centuries occur, when if any representatives at all exist, they are what is well called out of the world, it is only a chapter of accidents which rescues the facts of even their greatest men and women. The ashes of the fathers are blown away with the common ruin. When the sons are dead, or as good as dead, how can there be the piety of the natural and noblest affections ? The daughters are frail reeds in the storm of decay; for is it not their mission to find new names and interests to decorate with their beauty and effort ? It may be the cure of a dangerous exclusiveness that they are ever unconsciously busy in merging a high race among their fellow- mortals in plainer ranks, through the subtractions by dowries, and, above all, by the accidents of being heiresses.

However it has happened, considerable and authentic details have survived of the Sinclairs. Many are still to be discovered of the Norman period. Among the state MSS., among the codices of the Oxford Bodleian and other English libraries, it cannot be doubted that much additional knowledge will yet be found. It is not so likely that France has such documents, the early periods of that country, by loss in battle of their records, having far less illustration than ours; but the Normans before 1066 were learned and literary beyond all peoples, and there are indirect and perhaps undiscovered direct gleanings from French archives, for the future. Bouquet's twenty-four immense volumes, Historiens de la France, are themselves a rich store, though made up considerably of other than French writers.

The present purpose is abundantly served by what has been selected from such a rich garnering as the Cottonian and Harleian MSS. in the British Museum, One manuscript in particular, should by the lovers of England's royalties and best nobilities, of the older periods, be brought, if possible, to the full light of fame which it so well deserves. Praising it is one thing, but the sincere form of admiration would be to print it, for publicity and for the safer preservation. Filling about a hundred leaves of thick antique, but porous and therefore ink-blurring, yellow paper. No. 154 of the Harleian collection has more, and, by all the checks of cross comparison for authenticity, more accurate, information on early pedigrees than perhaps is to be found anywhere else in the same extent of writing. Its date is easily fixable from the distance it brings down the accounts, circa 1640 certainly. The handwriting is slightly difHcult, like the usual survivals from that period. The well-known signature of Shakespeare may give an idea of it. The scribe, however, was of the artistic nature, and his MS. is as beautiful to look at as the writing of his time admits, with its Germanic sweeps and knots of the letters. These externals are of importance, but the contents are such as to be grateful for, whether on genealogical or historical grounds. The value of the MS. is of national as well as wide family interest, all parts of the kingdom, in royal and noble descents, having some connection with its details, which are full where the more modern works are, by ignorance and sometimes by design, weakest, namely, during the rule of the Norman dynasty and the early Plantaganets.

What gives the greater weight to its account of the family of Eudo, the dapifer, is the consideration that there were no high titled and rich Sinclairs here, except those hidden under local and other new names, when the account was drawn up so carefully. Cases have been known of admiration of great living personages affecting their contemporary genealogists to untrustworthiness. Beyond mere record from materials, then much more plentiful than now, genealogy being the chief literary subject of all writers previously, it is not likely that a fraction of sentiment would go to aid of this pedigree. To forget to say so would be injustice to its so much the higher value and accuracy. The contrary possibility, that the family were so far out of sight and mind that there may be carelessness in the record, gets a double negative. Their ancient distinction was at all times akin to a national boast, and no greater insult could be thrown at a genealogist of the times when books and manuscripts were few and careful exceedingly, than to say he undervalued or overlooked anything he could possibly know of his subject. Genealogy was long the only held for the exercise of that spirit of exact science which has been lately engaged so heroically in conquering the world, and with considerable effect as to England.

Both the Cottonian and Harleian collections are wealthy in pedigrees, some by Glover, of the time of Queen Elizabeth, being remarkably beautiful and scientific. He was the Somerset herald at that time, when heraldry was the subject of subjects, Ralph Brooke, the York herald, turns up also, of these professionals. Ordinary enthusiasts are frequent. Of them all, however, amateur or otherwise, the unknown author of this somewhat late volume deserves attention for fine work. He makes reference to previous workers of the professional order, with the tone which gives the feeling that not only did he feel himself their equal, by such experience and training, but their superior, from stronger knowledge gained by later writing, with such a rich spoil of previous lore at his disposal. More than enough may have been said of a MS. that has been extremely useful, yet it would not have been just to it, nor fair to the general exposition, to pass lightly over its peculiarities. Confidence has to be gained for facts from the general obscurity of the past, though it may be said that there are few who are fully aware of the seas and lands of such literature of historical matter which exist in shapely or rugged state. To explorers of experience the nearer centuries seem barer, if the newspaper one be excepted, of the serviceable materials of history, than those stretching their steps out of England back into Normandy. The want of surnames is the sole cause why we cannot know of the men of the time then as well as of those now.

On the page where Eudo Dapifer's lineage appears the arms of the Sinclairs are given, the shield with a thick upright cross of gold dividing the quarters, three of which are gules or red. There are other antiquated heraldic distinctions describing the border. Under this "Hubert de Sancto Claro" begins the pedigree. His son is "Eudo Dapifer, Norman, lord of Colchester, who came in with the Conqueror".

Hubert, who is Hubert of Rye, has a daughter Muriel, Eudo's sister, who married Geffrey Mandeville, as his second wife. She had a son Osberne, who had a descendant Walyein. Osberne was the ancestor of the De Caillis of Normandy, and of the Cayleys of Norfolk and Yorkshire, now represented by Sir Digby Cayley, bart. An immediate descent from Rollo is claimed for them by Burke, on the probability that they are descended from William Fitz-Osborn, the first Norman earl of Hertford, cousin to the Conqueror. The claim is made only as he says on supposition.

The truth is shown by inference drawn from part of his account of the Caillis in Normandy, coupled with facts that are well known by record and otherwise. "'Osberne de Cailli appears to have been in possession of that barony either immediately before or immediately subsequent to the Conquest, probably father of Humphrey and of William Fitz-Osberne. Osberne, son of Osberne de Cailly, obtained the honour [barony] of Preaux (Pratella). He calls himself, in a deed of gift to L'Abbaye de la Trinite, Queen Matilda's foundation at Caen, "Ego Osbernus de Pratellis, filius Osberni de Cailleio". From him descended the noble and distinguished family Des Preaux in France. John des Preaux was a favourite minister of Richard I and John. His brother, Sir William des Preaux, saved the life of Richard in Palestine. Osberne de Cailly married Maud de Baudemont, and his son Roger married Petronilla de Vere.'"

The castle of Preaux and its barony belonged to Eudo Dapifer. It was there he died, and it is clear that his sister's son, Osberne of Cailli, really a younger son of Geffrey Mandeville of 1066, received it, the Mandevilles getting Eudo's Norman estates. This Sinclair lady's descendants are thus of high distinction. But Sinclairs have more to do with the descendants by his first wife of Geffrey, who, the pedigree says, "came into England with the Conqueror, who gave him all the land which Aesgarus Stallere, earl in Essex, had".

He was made sheriff or viscount of Middlesex, Essex, and Hertford. He had a son by his first wife (Ethelarda, buried at Westminster, the lands of which, to the fourth part, was her husband's), William de Mandeville (Magna Villa), who got the title of earl of Essex the first of this family. How, will appear hereafter. He simplified the paternal arms by making the coat plain and leaving out the carbuncle which Geffrey wore. This hint as to his character need not be lost, though it is possible his wife or others may have had something to do with so curious a change, recorded here.

Eudo is given as married to Roesia, filia. She is therefore the daughter of Rose Giffard, the wife of Richard Fitz-Gilbert of Tunbridge and Clare. The Monasticon in one place mistakes the mother for the daughter, both being Roses, probably in all senses, and makes Eudo marry Rose Giffard as a widow, and not his real wife, the Rose Clare of fourteen. It corrects itself in its Genealogia et Historia Eudonis Majoris Domus regiae in Angliae Regno, which Dugdale and Bouquet have printed in their collections Ex MS. codice in Bibliotheca Cottoniana, sub effigie Neronis D.8, ad calcem. It was to be expected that this more elaborate account should be the right one, but it is none the less pleasant to have it corroborated by the Harleian authority. Morant quoted the wrong passage in the Monasticon with regard to the relationship of Eudo St.Clare with the Clares, though both accounts keep them as near as marriage can bring families.

If the dapifer was the first man next to the king, his wife's father, Richard Clare, was the acknowledged greatest fighting captain, possessor of, if not the widest, the best lands, of all the Normans, and justice of England besides. The love match was as wise as it was fortunate. She had too many brothers to bring chance of heirship to her husband and his family. Gilbert succeeded his father; Roger got the estates in Normandy of Brionne and others; Walter had Welsh and western lands; there was a Robert; and, besides herself, a daughter married to Roger of Tillieres. The mercenary thought then could not have been present, but only the high honourable, in gazing so effectively at youthful Rose's famous eyes.

Monks are monks, or their colour also had been celebrated. William Gemeticensis, a monk, however, tells us that the brother Gilbert, earl of Clare, had a daughter Rose, and we ought to be grateful for his giving a third Rose to this fine family of the castle of Tunbridge. Each of the generations had its Rose, and Eudo plucked the fairest flower in all the gardens of his period.

His descendants will illustrate his lineage further, but it is by the record of his father, Hubert of Rye, as "Hubert de Sancto Claro" at that time, 1640, when there was no motive whatever to create a lineage, as has sometimes, though perhaps seldom, in the older periods at all events, been done, that success of tracing the family is assured. The chances were all that Eudo Dapifer should have been lost in the crowd of first men with first names only, as a very powerful Norman, had not the Harleian MS. saved thus what is a brilliant addition to the roll of England's great names in the very highest rank of political activity. It is, however, quite possible that other, but it cannot be better, evidence may be gathered of this same fact, now that the darkness, even of Domesday Book, has been thoroughly cleared away as to who "Eudo filius Huberti" or "Eudo Dapiferus" really was in blood.

Some of the findings of Robert Glover, the Somerset herald, may be referred to in this inquiry of lineage. Smith, the Rouge-dragon in 1600, transcribed in red and black ink, very beautifully, a volume of his pedigrees, and which forms MS. 245 of the Harleian collection. The connection of Hamo Dapifer and Eudo Dapifer has had general treatment already in the chapter "Eudo Huberti Filius", but Glover's tree of Hamo is too suggestive not to notice. He begins with Richard, duke of Normandy after William Longsword, and husband to the famous Princess Gunnora. Their third son, Mauger, was archbishop of Rouen and earl of Corbeil, and Glover makes him the ancestor of the Robert Fitz-Hamo and Hamo Dapifer family. The son of the archbishop was Hamo, called Dentatus, the Earl of Corbeil. His son was Hamo, the lord of Torigion or Thorigny, in Normandy. This Hamo's two sons were Robert Fitz-Hamo and Hamo the dapifer and viscount.

One Cottonian MS., which must be much older than Glover's time, Sir Robert Cotton, the heir of the last of the English Bruces, living in the sixteenth century, is much more limited, beginning with Hamo, father of Robert, calling him a kinsman of the Conqueror. The connections with the Consuls, descended from Henry First and a princess of Wales, Tudor, are fully given, and agree with the usual accounts. Sir Henry Ellis says no one has made a guess at the Hamoes' lineage except one writer, who thought they might be Crevecoeurs. There are relationships, at all events affinities, between later Sinclairs and these Crevecoeurs; and as their name is only a Norman soubriquet, it is within the bounds of possibility that this thought may be corroborative of the Hamo lineage, for which the proofs are being sought, Palgrave is incautious in his sweeping statement that nothing is hardly known of even this dapifer's father. The view that the family was of male line of the dukes of Normandy, and also Sinclairs, conflicts with the theory given previously. Marriages early and frequent did connect them. Glover, an expert, can hardly but be correct, the connections of the family being soon semi-royal.

Robert Fitz-Hamo was the famous "knight of Rye", in Sussex, who fought so well for Rufus at Rochester against his uncle Odo, and in Normandy against his two brothers, Duke Robert and Henry. In pity for his landlessness, but also for cash down, £3000 to moneyless Curthose, Henry had the province of Coustance to govern. Rufus got everything his own way. Henry at one period was so weak and stripped that he had only five attendants, and these of the peaceful clerical and serving orders, going from place to place as he could find hosts. His fierce struggling with his nobles all through his reign, but most at first, is explained by the early bitterness of life he had. The character of the man must have been bad, though he was so undoubtedly able a king. The monks have carefully chronicled his thirteen illegitimate children.

Describing the beginning of his reign Brady, in his History of England published 1685, shows how if it were not for Archbishop Anselm, the German, he would probably not have reigned. William of Breteuil, son of William Fitz-Osborn, the fallen dapifer, who got the earldom of Hereford, the Isle of Wight, and the half-governorship of England from the Conqueror, when the death of Rufus in the New Forest was known, proposed at once to Henry to fulfil his vow of allegiance and theirs by going directly to Robert his brother and acknowledging him as king of England and Normandy. William of Breteuil bravely kept up the controversy which Henry's refusal to submit himself caused. William of Malmesbury says that only four nobles clung to Henry: Robert Fitz-Hamo, his former bitter enemy, in whose favour Rufus had dispossessed him of the lands of his mother; Roger Bigod; Robert, the earl of Mellent; and Richard de Redvors, Robert de Belesme, who was a Montgomery, Walter Giffard, Eudo Dapifer's wife's uncle, and William de Warenne, the earl of Surrey, began in 1101 the fighting in England and Normandy that made Henry's reign so dangerous a time, especially for leading men.

It has been seen how difficult Eudo himself found it to keep his position in so fierce and uncertain light as played then around the throne. The ruin of great men is the notorious feature of the reign. Surrey's appeal as exiled loser of his lands, worth £1000 annually, is suggestively described by Brady.

But it is of Robert Fitz-Hamo and his brother the inquiry now is. Robert married first a daughter of Tudor ap Rhees, prince of South Wales, and afterwards the daughter of Roger Montgomery, count of Arundel. His daughter Matilda became Henry I's daughter-in-law, by marrying his son Robert Consul, earl of Gloucester, the greatest noble of his time. When he died in 1146, after his brave struggling for his sister, Matilda, the empress, and for her son Henry Second, his wife married another husband, Nigel of Mowbray, son of Roger of Albeni. Robert Fitz-Hamo had three other daughters. Amicia was married to the earl of Brittany. Two were abbesses, Hawisa, of Shaftesbury, and Cecilia, of Wilton.

Hamo the dapifer's personal history, Robert Fitz-Hamo's brother, is extremely short in point of lineage. He had no children, Glover says. Sir Henry Ellis shows that he is the same as the "Hamo Vicecomes" of Domesday Book. It is a possible theory to maintain, that as he was viscount of Kent, and as viscounts, whose chief duties were to settle cases like sheriffs, walk with twelve men any disputed marches, and so forth, were often called dapifers, he may have only got called dapifer of England as being that of the leading county in England. The viscountship Kanciae, was easily situated to Rye, in Sussex, and the younger brother had claim and opportunity there. But the relationship by blood to Eudo Dapifer is the best explanation of his services, both as dapifer of England and viscount of Kent. The substitute-dapifership was high appointment for the "vicecome", and the necessary absences of Eudo in Normandy, for the great duties there of his seneschalship, gave Hamo practically the dapifership of England. His want of heirs would also satisfy the hereditary nature of the appointment. That it was an arrangement of consanguinity is implied by the fact that in the roll in the church of Dives, Normandy, of the companions of William in the conquest of England, the names of both appear, as "Eude le Senechal" and "Hamon le Senechal".

Perhaps one of the strongest arguments that Hamo and Robert Fitz-Hamo, with his four brilliant and religious daughters, were Sinclairs, and nearly related to Eudo Sinclair, the dapifer, is to be found in the tenacity with which hereditary right to this office was always maintained. When Hamo and Eudo were registered in Domesday Book as dapifers, Eudo was in high favour with the Conqueror, and no encroachment could have occurred upon his rights. Eudo's brother, Adam of Campes, in Kent, was one of the commissioners in 1080-86; his wife's uncle, Walter Giffard, earl of Buckingham, was another; Ferrers, earl of Derby, was the third; and Remigius, bishop of Lincoln, the fourth: his rights would probably be well upheld by them; and if they have not entered his name as dapifer of England and Normandy in words, it is because Eudo Dapifer meant dapifer as wide as the king's rule was. Dapifer, in the small sense, it has been shown, occurs often.

There is nothing to be gained in the way of male lineage subsequent to Robert Fitz-Hamo and Hamo Dapifer, both of them, unless Robert Fitz-Hamo be found to have had sons by his first wife, dying without successors to whatever name they had, Sinclair or other. Such accumulation of coincidences does all but fix them as of the line of Hubert of Ryes, of whom Eudo was son, Eudo de Sancto Clare. Dr. Brady says, "He was son to Hubert de Rie, privado to both Edward the Confessor and William the Conqueror, and envoy in the greatest and most private matters that passed between them"; and in another place he has, "Eudo being his fourth son". The date of the great embassy is given as 1065. Besides the sister married to Geffrey Mandeville, first of the name in England, he had another sister married to the lord of Valoniis, whose son Petrus was one of the intercessors for this uncle Eudo with King Henry I.

It is not yet satisfactory wholly, the discussion of relationship of Robert Fitz-Hamo and Hamo Dapifer to Sinclairs, but the likelihoods recur in so many ways that the question could hardly be escaped. Eudo's family, the Clares, the Consuls, the Giffards, the Hamoes, are inextricably woven together; and perhaps this is the wise way now of leaving the question of fixing the past for the house of Rye, to which Eudo was so great an ornament, of whose surname there is, by the Harleian MS., absolute surety. The relationships of his own children to the Mandeville earls of Essex, the Bigod earls of Norfolk, the Vere earls of Oxford, the Beauchamp earls of Warwick, the Bohun earls of Oxford, Hereford, Essex, and Northampton, and to the lords Saye, Buckland, and Ludgershall, are accurately and artistically displayed on its pedigree page, the evidences taking the other side of the leaf.

Chapter XIII
The Lands of Eudo Sinclair

It does not seem possible to discover what the possessions of Eudo were in Normandy, except indirectly and generally. The Doudo whom Bishop Tanner makes complimentary to Roger Bigod, founder of Thetford, the date of whose death in the same year, 1107, with Robert Fitz-Hamo, has been preserved in his remarkable Latin epitaph, may have had a Norman property called Afini, that steward of the household being so designated; but nothing has been found to establish this. Matthew of Westminster's notice of him as founder of the church of Holy Trinity at Exaqueum may imply that as part of his land.

Ordericus Vitalis, who, with Matthew Paris, is the great ecclesiastical and historical authority of the earliest periods, has most satisfactory reference to his position as land-holder in Normandy. He describes Eudo thus: - "'The dapifer of the Norman duke, who, in the province of Constance, excelled among the nobles of Normandy by his riches and authority'". Those who are acquainted with the brevity and nonchalance with which the greatest persons and events are treated in such writers, will understand the importance of Orderic's words.

It is known that the castle of Preaux, Praels, or Pratelli was his chief residence in Normandy, and had he no more than the wide demesnes which followed it, he would have been of first rank. Duncan, author of The Dukes of Normandy says: "'Preaux is in the arrondissement of Rouen. In 1070 its castle belonged to Odo, called dapifer, son of Hubert of Rye; not Rye in Sussex but Rye in Normandy, three leagues to the north-east of Bayeux'". It was in his castle of Preaux that he died in 1120. A younger branch of the English lords De Cailly, and related to the royal families of England and France, took its name from Preaux, but it is difficult to discover how they succeeded Eudo, whether by consanguinity, affinity, or ducal favour.

If something is added as to his offices, sufficient insight will be gained as to the seneschal's lands across the Channel. Madox, in his

History of the Exchequer, has great difficulty in separating the offices of dapifer, seneschal, lord chief justice, and others, to different persons in England after the Conquest. As matter of fact they only separated in the reign of Henry I, our modern forms of courts of law and parliament then taking shape, to the disgust, as it may easily be believed, of the conservatives and beneficiaries of the Grand Customs of Normandy. It was the Saxon necessities, and the reintroduction of the laws of Edward the Confessor, which divided the great office of seneschal or dapifer into so many smaller offices, responsible no longer to the dapifer but to the king, and in due time to the parliaments. Under Duke William in Normandy there was not yet an inkling of subtraction from the power of his mayor of the palace. The history of Mayor Pepin, the father of Charlemagne and of the Capets, illustrates the position.

The dapifers were often more powerful than their kings, and supplanted them in more countries than France. First, second, third, and every lord of the treasury seem incarnated in this prime minister and prime subject. Brady and Hallam explain his powers with something like enthusiasm. The former says that "'he might do in all things as he thought most expedient'". The Grande Customier of Normandy is the best source of information, and it says that "'a certain superior justice, called the prince's seneschal, travelled and passed through Normandy, corrected inferior justices, looked after the prince's lands and rights, and, after the laws of Normandy, rectified what was done wrong in the bailliwicks and in the forests'". Once every three years he visited all the bailliwicks or provinces, redressed criminal wrongs, considered questions of treasure-trove and wrecks, saw to it that the highways were in right condition, and in a thousand other modes kept the kingdom in its best order. There were seven bailliwicks in all Normandy, the bailiffs occupying a position like the comites or county ruling earls of subsequent England, and the triennial visit of the dapifer would be to them the event of events.

Brady says that this seneschal or dapifer could remove all the inferior justiciaries from office without any appeal. He adds to his exposition, and he has paid great attention to his subject by consultation of very numerous and the best authorities, that "'This great officer was also general viceroy and guardian of the kingdom in the king's absence, and sometimes made peace and war by the advice of the chief nobility'".

To such a man the extent of his fief could be practically as wide as he might care to make it. His was a despotism only limited by the king's will; but that this was a great and effective limitation so far as the Rollo dynasty was concerned, has appeared already by the fall of William Fitz-

Osborn as suddenly as that of the chief ruler of a Persian monarch, or the vizier of a Turkish sultan. It is true, the immense difference, even in the case of such a determined will as was that of Duke William, is to be seen in the fact that he could not afford to degrade his officer to real ruin, the European kings being always but a best among equals.

The honours and lands of Fitz-Osborn afterwards in England, were the politic healing of perhaps the Conqueror's most daring step. He knew his Norman peers well; they would have no such irresponsible powers in any hands. The dapifer was their safeguard from kingly despotism, and their vigour never feared that if the viceroy should wish to be tyrannical they could not meet him. Such a mode of checks was as original to this curious system as it was effective for good government, so long as the king was not a faineant; and even then, as Charlemagne's case, and more pointedly as his father Pepin's shows, who had transformed himself from dapifership to kingship, a tyrant was not the inevitable, if probable result. Responsibility of the ministry in modern phrase, is the exact equivalent to dapifership in this aspect.

But the object is gained of showing that Eudo was actually, as well as proportionally, a greater landholder in Normandy than we know by record that he was afterwards in England. When he so faithfully toiled for the fulfilment of his master's last will and testament, in securing the English crown for Rufus, the Conqueror's second son, it would be injustice to his great-hearted character, not to remember that he jeopardised the confiscation of all his Norman lands and wealth, as well as his hereditary office of dapifer of Normandy. Had Robert the will of his father, it is probable that Eudo might have been wholly stripped of all he had in his kingdom; but the indications are, probably from the duke's awe of Eudo's fellow-nobles, and the great respect among his whole people for the sacredness of law, that he neither lost his lands nor the office, even though not occupying either. Probably the needy Robert received the fruits for years, but when Rufus so thoroughly brought him and their brother Henry to terms, and got earldoms of Ou and others for himself in Normandy, it may be safely assumed that his English dapifer's rights in Normandy would be restored, if indeed they had ever been seized.

It is probable that Robert had a steward of the household during the reign of Rufus in England, but the curious appeal of William of Breteuil, the great Fitz-Osborn's son, to Henry in 1100, that he should complete his vow of loyalty to Robert, gives the idea that the latter clung with Norman pertinacity to the laws and customs of his country, and while Rufus reigned it must have been with his brother protesting usurpation.

In this light he would always keep both the lands and hereditary office of Eudo open to the time of his restoration to his full kingdom. The imagination must not go too far in these directions; but we know that an English Mandeville, long after this, got the Norman dapifership solely through his relationship to Eudo, and respect for law being characteristic of the country, surely its chief officer's rights may have weathered through even the dreadful fraternal storms of that angry season. When he passed the greatest danger of his life, the temptation, and perhaps one encouraged by Norman respect for his rights in most difficult circumstances, to go with all the nobles of England, except four, to put its crown at the feet of Robert; and when Henry I received him fully into the royal favour that, rightly speaking, he never had foregone, being advocate only for the just, like the son of his first great friend, the dapifer Fitz-Osborn, his union of the two offices of dapifer of England and Normandy again occurred, if they had been separated in fact or in form or in both.

His beginning to build the great abbey of Colchester at his own expense, in September of 1106, the very year in which the battle of Tenchbrai put both countries wholly into his master's hands, Henry I, is no slight indication that his fortune got great and free enlargement then; and the tradition of Henry putting tasks upon him, in his favourite amusement and devotion of great architectural building, further suggests ideas as to his princely wealth. Nor must it be forgotten, that this astute and, like all his dynasty, money-loving king, was at Eudo's deathbed, with purposes no doubt quite other than those of holy counsel.

Waltheof's possessions, it has been said, were in the reign of the Conqueror his greatest enemies, and the inference is that they lost him his head. The saying is probably a Saxon prejudice; for compare William's conquest and rule of England for twenty-two years of stern struggle during cardinal political transition, and only this one decapitation for state reasons, with a dozen years out of Henry VIII's reign. Battle is civilisation beside the use of the block and its two-handed engine. But it may not be scrupled saying that Henry was with the noblest man by birth perhaps, as certainly by his life, of his kingdom, for reasons of property, which may appear by-and-bye. It is probable that if this king needed it, the blind old man, his faculties not impaired for all his busy powerful life, as wisely an-anged for that as his Genealogia shows him to have done with the other things which occupy last hours. The church had prospered well at his hands, and his monarch represented himself now with the valuable result. Henry indulged strong likings, but his memory was long and unforgiving; the ablest, the bitterest, and the most selfish, even in his loves, of the three king brothers of the dynasty.

It is to England and to its Domesday Book that attention must be turned for accuracy as to any of Eudo's lands. What he had in Normandy must always remain a svibject of inference, and however absolute that may be, general knowledge cannot compare with such as Adam Sinclair of Campes in Kent, his next elder brother, and the three fellow-commissioners gave in this monvimental record, not only to England but to the world, and for all ages. An immortality such as Adam's in connection with this large but not ponderous book of two volumes, one very much thinner than the other, is more to be envied than most of the immortalities, royal, noble, military, and literary that could be named. To copy out all the entries of Eudo's lands, not to say translate and explain them, would be work not in keeping with narrative. The technicality would weary.

There is abundant material for a volume of this special character. One example, and a description of the others, must be enough. It is taken because of its being very short, and because of its historic interest. When Hubert of Rye, bis father, as privador between William, duke of Normandy, and Edward the Confessor, successfully accomplished his embassy in 1065, he had a grant from the king of England of Ashe in Hampshire. It is situated near the source of the Tees, which falls into Southampton harbour, and is at nearly equal distances from Basingstoke, Kingsclere, and Andover. In No. XXX of the Domesday survey of this county, this son is found possessor of it.

'Terra Eudoñ Filii Huḃti. In Ovretvne Hď.
Eudo filĩ Huḃti. teñ Esse de rege. Æluuacre
comite
tenuit de Heraldo. Tc̃ se defď p. viii. hiď. modo p. iii. hiď.
Tr̃a ẽ. viii. car̃. In dñio sunt ii. ⁊ iiii. uiłłi ⁊ x. borď
cũ. iii. car̃. In aeccła ⁊ x. serui. ⁊ iii. ac̃ p̃ti.
T.R.E. uałb. vii. lib. ⁊ post ⁊ modo. vi. łb ⁊ x. soliď.
⁊ hoc p dimiď hida quae miñ ẽ p Hugoñẽ uicecomitẽ.'

Translated from the abbreviated Latin of records, this would run more simply: 'TERRA EUDONIS FILII HUBERTI.   IN OVERTUNE HUNDREDO. *Eudo filius Huberti tenet Esse de rege. Alwacre tenuit de comite Heraldo. Tunc, se defendebat pro 8 hidis ; modo, pro 3 hidis. Terra est 8 carucatce. In dominio sunt 2, et 4 villani et 10 bordarii cum 3 carucis. In aecclesia et 10 servi et 3 acrae prati. Tempore Regis Edwardi valebat 7 libras ; et post, et modo, 6 libras, et 10 solidos ; et hoc pro dimidia hida quae minus est per Hugonem vicecomitem.'*   Its English is clear as to language.   "'The land of Eudo, the son of Hubert. In Overton hundred. Eudo, the son of Hubert, holds Ashe from the king. Alwacre held it from Earl Harold. It was then assessed at 8 hides; now at 3 hides. The arable is 8 ploughlands. In demesne are 2 ploughlands and 4 villagers, and 10 borderers employ 3 ploughs. To the church also belong 10 slaves and 3 acres of meadow. It was worth in the time of King Edward 7 pounds, and afterwards and now 6 pounds and 10 shillings. This diminution is because of the half hide which is in the possession of Hugo, the viscount '".

It might give a wrong impression to direct much attention to this, one of the smallest parts of Eudo's English property, but it is of use to remember that a hide was 120 acres. The Black Book of Westminster, last chapter, liber i., says, "'Hyda a primitiva institutione ex centum acris constat'". It was written under Norman auspices, and therefore its 100 are equal to 120 English acres. A ploughland varied in size according to the kind of agriculture and district vigour of the men and cattle, 60, 70, 80, and even 100 acres, as well as much smaller portions, getting the name in the survey. The demesne was the part of an estate cultivated for the proprietor or for the manor-house. The villagers were his feudal tenants, giving their personal services on the demesne, or wherever their lord directed. Borderers were cottars whose chief subsistence was in labouring for the villagers. They were under the feudal protection of the lord, but had only the lowest duties to perform from him. It is probable that the slaves on and in the manor were their superiors practically, for if executioners were required the borderers got the employment. They had opportunity, however, of making money, and becoming villagers or villani. The servi were slaves, and nothing more or less, though some interpreters try to give the idea of service and not slavery. They were bought and sold; their children were born slaves; differences in their position were solely at the will of their individual masters. The church, too, accepted, as even here appears, the state of things without question.

The scale of money value may be understood from two somewhat contemporary statements: first, that William Warenne, earl of Surrey, when he lost all his very wide English estates, and got Robert, duke of Normandy, to intercede for his pardon with his brother, stated that they were worth nearly; £1000 annually; and, second, that the famous Hubert de Burgh took from Henry III; £50 a year, as equivalent to his third part of the returns from perhaps the richest county, Kent, of which he was then ruling earl. It is interesting to know that Harold, the Conqueror's antagonist, once held Ashe. Hugo, the sheriff or viscount, was a Norman frequent in the survey: the sheriff's office, one of great dignity, being to attend to all the king's concerns in a county; his lands, castles, their rents, and whatever royalty business required to be done. The viscount was the natural chock upon the count or earl, when the latter was not ornamental but useful, and remunerated for his services like the sheriff.

Of the lands Eudo held in capite or directly from the king, there is only one other entry as short as this. His property in "the shire which gave birth to Alfred", the Saxon king, Berkshire, Kipplesmere hundred, takes but four lines, though those commissioners certainly knew how to put a great deal into little bulk of writing. The Hertfordshire estates fill fifty-three lines; those in Huntingdon, nine; those in Northampton, fourteen; those in Cambridgeshire, forty-two; those in Bedfordshire a hundred lines; while those of Essex fill three great pages of Domesday Book. Nor do these at all exhaust the list. He holds very much land by under-tenantship in Berks., Beds., Suffolk, and especially in Essex. It would almost appear that he had liking or policy for this mode of tenure, and probably his popularity with the Saxons may have been owing not a little to his moderation in that, as in most other respects where his action is seen. To be anxious to exhaust this subject were needless, because the original record, with its clearest of showings, remains for the benefit of an illimitable future of those interested and inquiring. No substitute is sufficient for its unique pages. If the dapifer's lands were to be all extracted from it, and dealt with in a way corresponding to the gravity of Domesday Book, the work would have to be both independent and wholly scientific.

Here one other thing from it may be added, which is more in the stream of purpose, that both in Norfolk and Suffolk this Sinclair family held land before the Conquest, in the time of Edward the Confessor. Already, notice was drawn to the gifts of Hubert to New Church, West Cheap, London, if he did not also found it; and it is a commonplace how favourably the Confessor looked upon the Normans. In the Chronicon Johannis Bromton the second reason which the chronicler gives for William the Conqueror's enmity to Harold was - "'Because he had ingeniously driven from England the archbishop, Robert, a Norman by race, and Odo, his consul, and all the French'". If this is Eudo Sinclair, Odo and Eudo being often the same name with the chroniclers, though ultimately distinct, it is capital addition to his biography, that he was a consul or ruler of several counties or bailliwicks before he was dapifer. Consul was also applied in the sense of lieutenant, and he may have been at the court of Edward in this capacity for Duke William. This would explain his holding land then in Suffolk and Norfolk. The first and probably most instigating reason of hatred to Harold is given, because Earl Godwin his father, with himself and his brothers, killed William's relation Alfred so barbarously, and his retinue of Norman nobles, at Guildford; and this is the event which made Hubert of Rye's bravery so conspicuous to his fellows when all but he refused to take the embassy to receive the Confessor's last will and testament in favour of the duke. It was no carpet errand, with Godwin's unscrupulous and murderous sons striving for their own hands.

One cannot but think that Hubert, with his gallant and polished sons no doubt at his side, knew England well, and had skilfully calculated the chances. His extraordinary preparations made to gain the Saxon populace, an equipage somewhat foreshadowing a lord mayor's show, were grounded on knowledge of their character. Probably he and his four boys and their sisters formed "great Part" of that continual grumble which Earl Godwin found it convenient, for his evil usurping purposes, to keep up through Edward's reign against the Frenchmen, as he took care they should be without qualification considered. If Eudo,the consul, were driven away from England previously, he must have lost his lands here; and Hubert's determination to take the embassy may have been aided by chance of recovering these to Eudo, and probably other lands which he and his sons, Ralph, Hubert, and Adam, may have had. It was shown, how he got the entirely new grant of Ashe; and what his family had would perhaps also be as much given back as the difficult period allowed. The duke's historical silent rage for most of a day, when he heard of Harold's making himself king, can be better understood that Hubert's successful mission in 1065, added to Harold's own sacred oath, made it all but a certainty that the English kingdom awaited him without a stroke. It is easy also to imagine with what indignation, and with what hope and courage also, Hubert and his sons prepared for, and energised in, the conquest of, or more truly the suppression of, soi-disant King Harold and his rebels. If they had possessions once in England, it agrees with the whole previous and subsequent history of Norman nobles, that they would never rest till they had their rights. Determined persistency is the note of their characters, though gracefulness and honour were always awake.

But a word or two must be said of Eudo's position in Essex. Here his largest landed and other interests lay. Of this county he has always been a chief hero till the present time; and while Colchester has existence, it is probable that its great lord, Eudo, who ruled it so well, built so much of its famous stones, left so full a share of his wealth to its best purposes, cannot be forgotten. Besides Domesday Book, his charter to his abbey gives good idea of the lands he held there. Colchester was feudatory to the castle till Elizabeth's reign, and Eudo had the income of quit-rents and the 170 arable acres of land which followed it, perhaps more for the conveniences a manor-house usually had, of home produce, than at all as a measure or even aid of his feudal office. He had also the great fee of the district. By his position as governor he was both the steward and bailiff of Tendring hundred, and that he had sufficient municipal sympathies is shown by the register of him having five houses within the walls. He had 40 acres of land which belonged to the burgesses in King Edward's time, and which probably lay very near the city. It is of genealogical interest also that Hamo Dapifer, who has been claimed as near relation to Eudo, held one house, one court or hall, one hide of land, and 15 slave-burgesses in Colchester. A nice question, it would be, to fix his usual home at this justice-giving hall, so near Eudo Sinclair of the castle and tower of Colchester. Eudo and Hamo, the dapifers, cross each other so agreably, and so often, that relationship seems the enforced explanation.

For quick reference as to Eudo's standing, Sir Henry Ellis, in his Introduction, is good guide. He says Eudo's lands in capite were in Hertfordshire, Lincolnshire, Norfolk, Suffolk, Hants., Berks., Cambs., Hunts., Beds., and Essex; and he is, if Domesday Book itself be not available, sufficient authority also for the statement that he held lands both in Norfolk and Suffolk, in the time of King Edward before the Conquest. Morant, the historian of Essex, and of Colchester particularly, in the middle of the eighteenth century, took the trouble to count Eudo's lands in some counties, and found that he had 25 lordships in Essex, 7 in Hertfordshire, 1 in Berks., 12 in Bedfordshire, 9 in Norfolk, and 10 in Suffolk.

Essex's historian, Wright, of our century may be further referred to in this and in other lines of Eudo's biography; and with the advantage that he tells of many things which have not been able to find any place here. His description of the castle is very full and interesting. The interminable vaults of it aid the view that there was underground tunnelling to a large extent, and that there was a tower as well as a castle. He mentions another church, and other foundations, ascribed to the dapifer. Of the castle, his book has a suggestive illustration, the absurd dome, it may be said, not looking its very worst. Altogether, his picturing in words of Colchester, and of Essex generally, is of a kind most helpful to a reader, though not so useful to a writer. The town he notes to be 120 feet above the Colne. It certainly commands wide prospects, and for this as well as other reasons has long had distinction, antiquarian, civil, and military, among the chief cities of the land.

It would not be safe to say that Eudo's English income far surpassed that of the earl of Surrey with his £1000 a-year, though his office making him first subject of England it might be supposed that he could be the richest also; but when, as addition, we take into account his Norman office and property, to which Orderic has given considerable clue, it would be probably difficult to find a man altogether so wealthy at that period, not only in England but in Europe. There are apparently larger landholders than he in Domesday Book although he is one of first magnitude, even in appearance of entries; but his sagacity and favour with the crown probably were the causes in the metaphorical sense of the goodness of the soil where he pitched his various camps, and of their proximity to great English centres, and especially to the ultimate centre of London. When calculating results in value from the survey, such considerations must never be forgotten. Hughs of Chester may get provinces, if they please, where the wild men run; Mortimers may have large portions of Welsh hills, and even strips of English border; Saxon Goderics and treasonable or coward Anglian Ralph Waers may keep eastern sheriffships and consulships of Anglia, the prey of pirates; Danish Waltheofs may be left, if they will only be sleeping bears, in their northern earldoms; but we must have our faithful Eudoes, Huberts, Adams, Richards, FitzGilberts, Geffrey Mandevilles, and Walter Giflards, near our hearts as sure bucklers. They shall not want, where the royal conquering face shines, and shines not proudly, but as that of comes among his comites. Charles the Great and his paladins are a type that never dies, but which is always working to repeat itself. The Conqueror only of his rebels, and rightful king of all that were best in England, had, and deserved, worthy peers and cousins. The lands of Eudo Sinclair were wide, and richer than they were wide; but his offices, and how nobly he filled them, whether those of the individual who gets love and reverence and needs to give them back also, or those of the man of state who is as wide as his sphere, and that practically the widest, are the true subjects of exultation to any one who, having a soul, recognises a rightly great and, as it were, universal man.

Chapter XIV
John, Comes Essexiae

The first Norman earl of Essex was John Sinclair, son of Eudo Dapifer, the lord of Colchester. His father dying in 1120, if no interruptions occurred, he would have had fifteen years of the hereditary dapiferships of England and Normandy under Henry I.

The Harleian MS., 154, is the authority for the creation of John as comes or count of Essex. Dugdale, who gets most of his facts from the Bodleian, Harleian, and Cottonian codices, missed this, and runs to the conclusion that Eudo's daughter Margaret was his sole child and heir. So far from that being the case, we know of a third, a William who, Madox, a most trustworthy and learned writer, says was crucified, or more likely cruciatus, tortured, before being killed. This occurred in the reign of William Rufus, 1087-1100; and it has been thought that it was the cause to Eudo his father of withdrawing, as much as his offices would allow, from the court of the king whom he had so successfully helped to the throne. If it was his son, as there does not seem reason to doubt, Eudo's position must have been somewhat parallel to Brutus with his sons. William was in conspiracy against Rufus.

In Collections for Hampshire, by D.Y., and edited by Richard Warner, there is further knowledge. William, earl of Ou, was accused by Geoffrey Baynard, of that Baynard's Castle near where the office of the Times, on the banks of the Thames, London, now is, that he was conspiring against the king, and offered his wager of battle on the point. William of Ou was worsted, and Rufus condemned him to be mutilated and have his eyes put out. His relation, William Dapifer, engaging in the same conspiracy, was hanged. D.Y. gives the reference for this, Annales Waver, apud Gale, vol. ii., p.140. Why death overtook the younger and not the other relation it is hard to see now. It was the conspiracy of 1095 by Mowbray, earl of Northumberland.

Brady says that Rufus had afterwards for his bitterest enemies Robert of Ou, as natural affection might well prompt; Stephen of

Albemarle; Gerard of Gournay on the Epte, it is thought, also a relation of William Dapifer; Ralph of Conchis; Richard deCurcey; Walter Giffard; and Philip de Braiosa or Bruce, Agnes Sinclair's husband, the daughter of Walderne, earl of St.Clare. In this quarrel the name and its closest relations seem divided much, but Eudo kept loyal to his own king. The death of his son, already a man of position, if dapifer meant anything further than attachment to his father's title to him as heir presumptive, must have been the severest of blows to his father. He was the eldest son, and it is perhaps the best explanation of matters that, before 1095, the real cause of his father being so much at leisure, in his great fee of Colchester, was that William had assumed fully the hereditary duties of dapifer in his room. This would explain the special severity of his punishment, as being able to do most mischief, having most power.

Eudo at the time of the revolt must have been nearly sixty; and some years before, he might well have thought it time to retire for the religious life he loved so much. Madox says that this William, the son of Eudo, was the king's aunt's son. If this is true Eudo must have married, before he married his faithful Rose Clare, a daughter of Baldwin, earl of Flanders, sister to William the Conqueror's wife Matilda. Such connections are apt to make men conspirators, as subsequent English history illustrates only too well; but the evidence is not yet svifficient to reach conclusions as to this unfortunate William. If he was Eudo's son, as Madox says, he was certainly not a son of Rose Clare, for she had married at fourteen, only seven years previously. That his mother may have been one of the sisters or half-sisters of William the Conqueror is a possibility which could clear matters.

Eudo's son John, this first earl of Essex, must have been very much younger than William. He was a child of a few years in 1095, and there is no reason why it could not be supposed that he was not born then. We know from the MS. that he lived within the reign of Henry II, which began 1154. The signs are very apparent that he led a chequered life, though the materials to judge by are scanty. He must have lost the hereditary dapifership, in new legal and state arrangements of Henry I; and it is not unlikely that the division of offices which the increasing population and wealth of the country may have required, disgusted him altogether with dapifership. It is quite possible that his abilities may not have been equal to the position, no family having a continuous monopoly of talent. Certain it is that William Bigod, who was drowned in the White Ship, and Hugh Bigod were dapifers towards the end of the reign, as well as Fitz-Eustace and Robert Clare, "Fitz-Richard of Tunbridge"; and probably this was part of King Henry's business at dying Eudo Sinclair's bedside. That John took the estates and dapifership in Normandy may have been the case for some years after his father's death; but we know that his sister Margaret's rights gave them to her son Geffrey Mandeville, the third Norman earl of Essex, long before the date of John Sinclair the first earl's death.

The theory that would best fit John's life is that, like Robert, duke of Normandy, and many another of the chief men of that time, he was carried away with the crusading enthusiasm. A John de St.Clare, knight-bachelor of France, appears in historic lists of crusaders, but the time is too indefinite to say that this was he. It would be quite against all that is known of the respect for relationship and hereditary law of Normans to suppose that his king did violence to his rights; and so inspired were many in warring against the infidel for the cross of Christ, that worldly duties and titles weighed nothing in the balance. The son of a father so devoted to the church's highest interests might well be expected to take the cross, and devote his whole life to that; though he never had the able and equally religious mother that it was fortune to have in Rose Clare. In any case he seems out of the political throng around the royalties, feminine or usurping, after Henry I; and if ever he returned to Colchester from the East, it must have been to die, and not to assert any rights, at the beginning of the reign of Henry II. It was not at all an uncommon thing among the Norman nobles then to retire in manhood, or even early life, to a monastery, and oftenest the one they themselves founded. Sir Richard Luci, chief justice of England, and the repeller of the invasion of the earl of Boulogne in Henry II's reign, is an example, with his abbey of Lesnes. All these things, however, being problematical must be left so. In such times of religious madness and political, not to say personal, ambitions, a thousand explanations could be suggested as to the short record that seems to have survived of John Sinclair, the first Norman earl of Essex.

Of him and his elder brother, as the last of Eudo's male line, it would be interesting to know much; but their stories are equally broken. Madox speaks of William, filius Eudonis, as paying 20/- to the king's treasury for recovery of some land from the earl of Brittany, and his account of him may have been taken from Stow's Annals, published in 1631. "'In a councell holden at Salisbury, William de Owe was accused to the king of treason, who whiles hee provoked his accuser to fight with him in combate, by the king's commandment his eyes were plucked out ... Many innocent men were also accused, of which number was William de Aluerie a man of goodly personage, godfather to the king, his auntes Sonne, and his sewar, yet the king commanded him to bee hanged: which William making his confession to Osmond, bishoppe of Salisbury, was first whipped throughout by all the churches of the cittie, who dealing his garments to the poore, went naked to hanging, bloodying his flesh with often kneeling upon the stones: and at the place of execution, hee satisfied the bishop and people, saying, So GOD helpe my soule and deliver it from evil, as I am guiltlesse of the thing that I am accused of: and after the bishop had commended him to God, he was hanged'".

Stow calls it "Cruelty of Wm. Rufus" at the side of his text, and gives 1095 for date. Some of this cannot possibly apply to a son William of Eudo Dapifer, though the main facts may. He could not have been godfather to William Rufus, as both were of similar age; but even the "industrious" Stow may have nodded in his desire to give too many circumstances to this tale of all the chroniclers and historians. William Sinclair he probably was, and a man in his prime. It is possible that Madox may be right after all, though there might be sufficient satisfaction and to spare in accepting Eudo Dapifer as the husband of one wife, and that one such a treasure.

There is an explanation of Stow's account which would resolve all the difficulties, and give this turn also to Eudo's married life as with Rose only. The king's sister's son was Stephen, the usurper of the crown, and William Sinclair could quite well be his godfather, and the "man of goodly personage" also, who was sewar or high steward to Rufus. What Madox extracts of him in connection with the king is filius amitae illius, which is a phrase that occurs in ancient Latin more than once about Stephen. It is possible that extracts have been mixed when quoted, but nothing substantial can depend on such a chance.

The passage in the Annals, however, can bear without straining yet another interpretation, which will establish all that is required, making the facts consistent throughout. "Godfather to the king his aunte's sonne" is the archaic way of saying that William Dapifer was godfather to the son of the king's aunt. Rufus had such female relations, so that it is quite fair to accept this as the final version. One of the two sisters of the Conqueror was married to Walter de St.Valery, the other to an earl. Radulph de Diceto's chronicle seems one of the origins of these details, and after describing the punishment of William de Auco, or more usually, William of Ou, his words continue - "'And his dapifer, William of Alderi, son of his aunt, the king ordered to be Hung'". The language in itself is as ambiguous as one of the Delphic oracles, since he also, so far as the words go, might be both dapifer and aunt's son to William, earl of Ou.

Alured of Beverley, after describing William, earl of Ou's punishment, continues, "Et dapiferum illius Willielmum filium amitae illius tradicionis conscium jussit rex suspendi". This has the addition that the dapifer "knew of the treason", and it goes also to show that he was the dapifer of the earl of Ou if it shows anything at all.

Some of the chroniclers copy predecessors wholesale. It is hardly likely that William of Ou's dapifer could be godfather to a king.

Blomfield in his History of Norfolk, in describing Grimston manor there, which belonged for many generations to the Sancto Claro family, Gereberd, John, and Guy being men of national importance in later centuries, speaks of Warin and Drogo, sons of William, the sewar, as holding it about 1100. The Montacutes, which is a local name only, had Drogoes, and the Warrens of Surrey were related consanguineously to Eudo's line; but it is difficult to tell where Blomfield got this knowledge, and neither is it also remarkable for its definiteness, however suggestive and confirmatory.

Both William Dapifer, who had what seems a martyrdom even if he had been undoubtedly guilty, and his brother John, earl of Essex, are shadowy, like so many past figures who may have been unusually substantial in their day. What is heroism itself without its poet or historian ? Where good men are numerous, the chances of immortality are not always the clearest, even for the able.

With their only sister, and the ultimate heir of their father Eudo, and of themselves, there is firm footing. Record is plentiful as to what things and persons affected her life and state.

Chapter XV
Margaret Sinclair, Countess of Essex

It would be easy to write pictorially about the early years of Margaret, Eudo Dapifer and Rose Clare's only daughter. In the grand military surroundings of Colchester Castle, half palace, half garrison of control over hostile, repressed, but brave Saxons, the elements were at work which go to form one of the high types of men and women. Courage, drill, beauty of order among soldiers, from governor to plainest warder; high spirit, decorative ability, and the inspiration which comes only from love and danger and great wealth united, among the ladies, from the thoroughbred infant to the chivalric grandmother of many heroic tales: such a home was the right scene for the upbringing of the mother of the "great Geffrey Mandeville". The clank of armour was continual music in her ears, and special occasions of assembling of the panoply of successful war were ninnorous, in this castle fifty miles from London, where danger had its visually quite regular threatenings of revolt, or of invasion from France or from Saxony to its Norwegian limits.

Her grandfather from Tunbridge Castle, Richard Fitz-Gibert, earl of Clare, the Conqueror's greatest captain and the justice of England, would be a frequent figure in Eudo's genial home, and her four brave uncles would probably be as often with their sister Rose's family as their military and civil duties permitted. All that was high and inspiring in civil or military life had a popular centre where the dapifer held his private and popular court; and nowhere else in the country could, and did, royalty more freely take its ease from state care. Dim those far days are, but not dark. There is sufficient fact to guide a careful imagination to full realisation of the splendid vigorous time which, more than all other periods, has gone to the making of this nation of the nations. It is perhaps a matter most for private musing. Progress calls now for the hand to plainer but quite as satisfactory work.

Margaret must, after no doubt one of the best educations that human chance has, first appear historically as the wife of William Mandeville, the second earl of Essex. The husband was worthy of her, though it was by the right of her and her family he became earl. His father was Geffrey Mandeville, or, as they said then, Geffrey of Magna Villa, his land near Valognes or Valence, in Normandy. He came to England with the Conqueror, and was one of his brave warriors of Hastings. He got more than a hundred lordships or estates here in different counties. His king's largest gift was the land which Aesgar Stallere, the Saxon earl of Essex, had, though he did not add the title. Instead of this he was made sheriff or viscount of Middlesex, Essex, and Hertfordshire, which was probably as good in the way of wealth as the third part of the taxes which was the following of the title of earl then.

Geffrey was twice married. His first wife was Athelaise, buried at Westminster, of which land her husband had the fourth. She was mother of William Mandeville. Geffrey's second wife, Dugdale says, was Leceline, though some have her name as Muriel. All are agreed that she was the sister of Eudo Dapifer; and that she had some of his spirit, is evident by the fact that she was the foundress of Hurley monastery in Berkshire. She had a son Osberne, as has been already noted, who had descendants, probably altogether lost in the rich stream of English ordinary life. One of them was Walyaine, but for the present their history is not wanted.

This Norman, Geffrey, was the first constable of the tower of London, and was one of the earliest to wear armorial distinctions, a carbuncle for remarkable part of them. Freeman has interesting notices of him, founded on study of Domesday Book. This, for example: "'One grant of lands recorded in Domesday (ii. 59) would seem to belong to the very first days of William's reign. Lands in Essex which had belonged to a certain Leofsuna, appear as the property of Geffrey of Mandeville, with the comment Hoc manerium dedit Rex G. quando remansit Londoniae.'" But it must be said that the grasping character, as he thinks, of the Mandevilles does not find favour in his prejudiced sight. He is right enough that they took as much as they could get, but that was the order of the day; and it testifies to their courage and ability that they succeeded well in the stormiest of times.

Margaret Sinclair's husband, William, would please this historian better, both from the mildness of his own character and his relationship to Eudo Dapifer, Freeman's only favourite among the haughty persevering Normans. One thing is particularly remarkable of him. Though titular earl of Essex, as well as substantial earl, he does not seem of so ostentatious a temper as his father. The coat of arms he changed to plain, and the prominent carbuncle was put aside altogether. It is not likely that the countess had most to say to this, for her son Geffrey, and sons are in such matters often of one mind with their mothers, restored the carbuncle, and probably improved on his grandfather's general displaying. She had a daughter, Beatrice, and her history is as remarkable in a womanly way as her only brother Geffrey's was as the first man of his times.

The son Geffrey's doings are a notable part of English history. The chronicles are full of him and his deeds. He lived in the time when Matilda, the empress, daughter of Henry I, and Stephen were so bitterly striving for the crown. Hugh Bigod, dapifer at the death of Henry, came over from Normandy with his tale that the dying king had there disinherited his daughter, and he imitated, somewhat successfully as imitations go, the political feat of Eudo as king-maker, by getting Stephen crowned by the archbishop of Canterbury on the strength of his report. He had his reward by being made the earl of Norfolk, first of his family, getting the third penny and other usual returns of that county. He gained Geffrey Mandeville, then earl of Essex, constable of the tower, and who was the superior of London, much against the municipal will, then even beginning to wake. It was owing to this accession of strength more than to any other circumstance, that Stephen's standing was not like that of Harold, merely a few fighting days.

Geffrey got all kinds of honours and promises heaped upon him, and what seemed to please him most of all, he, as lord of the tower, got the citizens of London wholly put into his hands. He and they were the bitterest of enemies, though it is difficult to discover the cause. He calls them, in some of the records, his enemies, with peculiar determination of temper. The most probable explanation is that the quarrel between Norman supremacy by the rule of strength, and the Anglo-Saxon aspiration to not only self-rule but some kind of revengeful assertion, was hottest where the two powers were at their greatest central strength. Geffrey Mandeville, Margaret Sinclair's son, chief in the tower, which he strengthened and made much more formidable than even it previously was, and the boiling strength of Saxon manliness surging outside, storm of the strongest force kept running. Were it not that the dynastic struggle gave other objects to divert attention, London-at-the-Tower would then have been the scene of feudal and municipal bloodshed till the strongest hand prevailed. He had a new charter of the earldom of Essex from Stephen, of which the witnesses were William of Iypres; Henry of Essex, the standard bearer of England; John, the son of Robert Fitz-Walter, a Clare; Robert Newburgh; William de St.Clare, of whom by-and-bye; William de Dammartin; Richard Fitz-Urse; and William of Ou.

Whatever were the reasons, Geffrey did not hold by Stephen. He may have been jealous of Bigod, as dapifer and new earl of Norfolk. Through his mother, the daughter of Eudo Dapifer, he must have had a better claim to the office than the Bigods, who had it immediately on the death of Eudo in 1120. Geffrey might not then have been of age to claim his rights, and the Bigods were related certainly through marriage to Eudo. Stephen could not possibly dispossess him to whom he owed his crown, even if Geffrey might show his superior rights. In any case, Bigod's good fortune boded ill for Mandeville, and should there be no other politic reasons of self-preservation, not to say aggrandisement, the espousal of Matilda's cause was wise on his part.

The earl of Gloucester, Robert Consul, her brother and champion, being married to a Sinclair, as will appear yet more fully, the interest of the countess of Essex's family would be on the side of Henry I's daughter; and this might also say most for their civilisation and sense of justice. Matilda gave Geffrey her charter to his earldom of Essex when he came over to her. He grew thoroughly awake to the trick that had been put upon England by Bigod, the dapifer, for Stephen's election. The charter is of antiquarian interest, as well as historic and biographic, because it is one of the very earliest writings by which nobility was created, tenure being the rule previously, and most in practice afterwards. Matilda calls herself "domina Anglorum" in it, after the style of her father's ordinary charters of foundation and grant, and the creation reads in its chief part - "'I give and grant to Geffrey Mandeville for his own use and for his heirs after him hereditarily, that he may be the earl of Essex, and may have the third penny of the taxes of the county as the earl is accustomed to have in his county'".

It would hardly be evidence of the two previous earls' occupancy of this title and office, to put forward the use and wont character of the end of this extract, but it may be allowed as favouring such a state of things. General legal reference it may be, though the Normans were not wasters of words in the kind of work. But this was only part of Geffrey's favours from Matilda. He seems to have got whatever he wished, and the nature of the man was to wish a great deal. Consciousness of strength is certainly as good an explanation of such search as ambition. She gave him the constableship of the tower of London, with the authority over the citizens which he had contended long for; and if he used his power, he does not appear to have abused it, though there never was any love lost between him and those in his lordship, unlike in this to his grandfather Eudo with the Colchestrians.

Perhaps the great awakening of London to its future importance accounts best for the warfare. It would have then two or three hundred thousand inhabitants, and the public spirit of such a number would be galled by the Norman ability to rule, if no other way were possible, by the strong head and the strong hand. He was also made hereditary sheriff or viscount, of London in particular, as also of Middlesex and Hertfordshire like his grandfather Geffrey, the Conqueror's captain. He paid £300 for the Middlesex and £60 for the Hertfordshire sheriffship, which were large sums as money then went: so that the empress could drive bargain well enough with her best favourites, the necessities of war being always clamant. His father, William, the second earl of Essex, does not seem to have been of the active, but of the amiable temper, and may not have had these offices.

Perhaps Geffrey owed his energy most to his mother. Her hand may be expected to have been at work in the next advance her son had. Whoever had them till now, Matilda granted him all the lands in Normandy of his mother's father, Eudo Dapifer, with Eudo Sinclair's office also of dapifer or steward of Normandy; and these are mentioned as being "his rightful inheritance". The information comes from the best state sources, "From the great register in the office of the duchy of Lancaster".

This was not all. Not only did he get these grants, but one of Matilda's charters adds that, if she and the earl of Anjou her husband should think fit, Geffrey must get all the lands in England whereof the same Eudo died possessed; and no doubt this would also gain for him the dapifership of England. She mentions at the same time £100 lands, and also twenty knights' fees of land which she had recently given him. His eldest son Ernulph received £100 lands and ten knights' fees of land, £100 land in addition to be taken from escheated manors. If she got Castle Stortford in the fighting, it was to be his and his heirs for ever. Through all her long struggle she kept favouring Geffrey for the very good reason that he was so powerful to help her cause. His family castle was Walden, but he was allowed to build Plessy Castle, Wye Castle, and at the peace of London she gave him special permission to build another, pledging her brother, Robert, earl of Gloucester, Henry Curcy, her steward, and Henry of Essex, the standard-bearer of England, of whom Carlyle makes perhaps too much fun in Past and Present as a Saxon runaway whom Norman bravery prevented doing the worst of all military harm. She seems also to have completed her grant to him of Eudo's lands in England, without proviso, the completion being made at Westminster.

That he well deserved all this from his rightful queen, Henry of Huntingdon's chronicle is ample proof. In the same year, says Henry, in which Stephen assaulted Lincoln unsuccessfully, the ninth of his usurpation (1144), "'the earl or consul, Geffrey Mandeville, powerfully harassed the king, and, eminent over all, shone strongly'". His seizure by Stephen in open meeting of king and barons at St.Albans, is one of the great events of English history around which much discussion of personal rights has always been held. The king never attempted to justify the proceeding, except by necessity. If he did not seize Geffrey, his power and favour with Matilda would lose Stephen his crown; and he had stretched so many points already for this, that a new injustice could not seem to have quite its proper nature to him. Geffrey was stripped of the tower of London, and of his castles of Walden, Plessy, and the rest. He was kept in prison for some time, and when it was safe to liberate him, Stephen, Henry of Huntingdon says, "'restored to him the tower of London and the castle of Walden and that of Plaisseiz'". His lands were, however, not to be got again; and this made the ablest man in England the most desperate.

He seems to have cast away these remnants of his power altogether, and Radulph Niger, the chronicler of the Cottonian MSS., says that, in 1143, "'Geffrey Mandeville by violence entered into Ramsey [abbey] and drove out the monks'". No subject of the time has had half the fulness of treatment that this one received from the historians of the period, mostly monks themselves. Miracles innumerable occurred to punish the dreadful invasion of the sacred monastery of Huntingdonshire. The walls were seen to drip with blood, is one of the mildest of them. Geffrey's sorrows and those of his posterity, to their smallest ache, were all caused by this.

William of Newburgh has two pages of the opposite of encomium of this earl who made the monastery a den of robbers. Even in Stephen's wild time the terrors from the landless man were wholly of their own kind. His lieutenant, by another miracle, was pulled off his horse, and his brain "effused", apparently in accident of playfulness. Much of useless tale there is, but the bitterest writer puts this down as his final conclusion with regard to Geffrey, and it does not read very dreadfully to us who appreciate Roman Catholic clerisy at that period. "'He was of the highest probity, but of the greatest obstinacy against God; of much diligence in worldly things, of great carelessness towards God'". The only thing that has to be added to this is, that master minds do not worship the same God at all as monastic ones. The certificate, properly read, is one of high if not the highest quality. But the monks were ungrateful the moment he trod the slightest on their extremely tender toes. Was it carelessness of

God that made him build, in 1136 Weaver says, the magnificent abbey of Walden ? That he also endowed it liberally goes without saying. Such souls cannot go tamely into the monastic habit when misfortune has overtaken them, like Henry of Essex, the Saxon, of Reading notoriety.

The last three or four years of his life were indeed very miserable, but the man was noble-souled to his last breath, and those who knew him best, kept their faith in him wholly unchanged. His son Ernulph in particular held by him, and gets his share of monastic blessing. Geffrey was excommunicated, with all the severities and ceremonies possible, by the church; but even this, the weightiest curse that then could fall on man, did not crush him. His valorous heart and hand were wanted when brave work had to be done, and it was while engaged in one of the many inexplicable expeditions of private warfare in England's dreadest reign, or, rather, no reign, that he got his fitful but vigorous personal drama closed.

He was besieging the castle of Burwell in Cambridgeshire, when an arrow out of a loophole struck him in the arm. He made light of it, but from the carelessness of a brave heart the wound was neglected, and he died in a few days, still under excommunication. How could a scratch not be fatal to a soldier in that state, was the universal monastic moral. Did not the grass wither for ever on the spots where the excommunicated lord lay to rest him a little. The 14th of September 1144, was his last day. Roger of Hoveden, the famous chronicler, gives the details of his death, and many of his deeds. But this is suggestive as to how he could be loved.

Says Camden out of the Register Book of Walden, "'The Knights Templar came and put red cross on him, and put him in a coffin of lead, and hung him in the orchard of the Temple, London, 1144'". They durst not bury him, being excommunicated, but it is said that the pope ultimately rescinded excommunication, and that they buried him in the New Temple. His "enemies", as he had often called the stubborn Saxon Londoners, probably thought they had their revenge in having their tyrant thus hung in dishonour; and yet it was in the greatest of all honour, the esteem of those who knew his personality best. The impression, besides, need not be left, that there continued special enmity between him and the citizens, the quarrel being rather that of development of public liberty under needed limitation than of the individual kind. Says another writer of the small-souled character, "'A violent invader he was of other men's lands and possessions, and therefore justly incurred the world's censure and church's doom'". Different criticism from this will be his or hers who reads well the gallant and able Geffrey's life, and the materials are not scanty, in the main stream of England's growth. Henry of Huntingdon's account of his death is of antiquarian interest because of

Leland's abbreviation of it in his Collectaneum of about 1550 - "'Similarly Geffrey, the consul or earl, in the thickest of the line of his men, was alone pierced with an arrow from a certain commonest foot-soldier; and himself laughing at the wound, after some days, however, being excommunicated, died of that very wound'". Leland runs, "'Geffrey Mandeville, earl of Essex, by a certain commonest foot-soldier was wounded with an arrow, from which not long after he died'".

One abbreviation he has which is too suggestive to pass over: "'Ernulph, the son of Geffrey, bewails him at Magna Villa'". Ernulph had fled from England before his father's death for this best of reasons, namely, to keep together the Norman possessions to which he was heir. He remained always at the original home of Magna Villa, and does not appear further in English record. It is also said that it was he who was killed while being one of the so-called robbers, in the time when the king himself was an arch-robber, at Ramsey monastery, and that he lies buried there, though Leland's quotation has the ring of most likelihood in it. In either case he is out of English history before his father. And he is so also, if the account that he was taken and banished be true.

The second son, a Geffrey when Henry II came to the throne, for whom the Mandevilles had suffered so much, got back the earldom, and most if not all of the lands. A man of great talents, it is enough to say that he became justiciar of England, and died without issue in 1165. The third brother, William, succeeded him, and by marrying Hawise its heiress added the earldom of Albemarle to Essex; but he was also without family, and died in 1189. This was the last of the Mandevilles in fact, but not in name. The Fitz-Piers de Lutgershall, earls of Essex, subsequently took the name of Mandeville, from marriage of the heiress.

Eudo Sinclair, the dapifer, had another sister than she who was married to the first Mandeville. Her name was Albreda, and she married Petrus of Valognes, the father of the Petrus who helped with William Giffard, chancellor, the bishop of Winchester, and others, to make peace between Eudo and Henry I, Eudo's nephew. Their homes were Hertford Castle, Herts., and Orford Castle, Suffolk. Albreda Sinclair's husband, ancestor of the Valence earls of Pembroke, so famous in English history and royal relationship, had got more than fifty lordships at the beginning of the Conqueror's reign. It was from the Valences' part of Normandy, that the duke before he was the Conqueror was fleeing when Hubert of Rye succoured him. How Albreda Sinclair, Hubert's daughter, met Peter of Valoignes is not difficult to understand, if the ride of a cavalier for some hours covered the distance between the castles of Valoignes or Valence and of Rye.

It must be returned to the relationships of Geffrey and his mother, Margaret Sinclair, countess of Essex, Albreda's niece. Geffrey was twice married, but there is difference about the marriages among genealogists. Most of them make the mother of his three sons to have been Rose de Vere, daughter of Aubrey de Vere, earl of Oxford, and chief justice of England. Weever in his Funeral Monuments gives this, and Sir William Dugdale also in his Baronage. They add further that she had a second marriage to Pain Beauchamp of the earl of Warwick family. Dugdale gives him another wife, but he cannot tell who she was. Their daughter Alicia was, he says, the mother of John de Laci, constable of Chester Castle.

The connection of Margaret Sinclair's only son Geffrey with the De Veres and Beauchamps, is also given in another way; and it is not less likely to be true because of one connection which might be thought to have something of stain. Geffrey's only wife was Rose, the daughter of the unfortunate standard-bearer of England, Henry of Essex, grandson of Swain, the Saxon lord by tenure in Essex of the time of the Conquest. Her mother was a daughter of Roger Bigod, the earliest of that great name in England. Her sister Adeliza, or, as is said now, Alice, was the wife of Albery de Vere, earl of Oxford, and mother of the two subsequent earls, Albery and Robert. It was Rose of Essex, wife of Geffrey, the great earl of Essex, who afterwards married Pain Beauchamp and was mother of Roger.

It is probable that the wholesale confiscation from their father of his estate for the unfortunate accident, or false impression, as Stow shows it to have been, and not cowardice, of letting fall the standard in the Welsh war, to the danger of King Henry II's life, and of the lives of his army, came back to the daughters and their husbands. He was one of the richest and in every way greatest men of many years of his time, and to secure alliance with him was object to any family then existing. But the mistake of a moment spoilt the brilliancy of his own life for ever, and still dims the lives connected with him. Carlyle's mockery, however, is ridiculous, as against himself, to those who really know the men and circumstances of that period. There was no such puppetry as he makes of the matter, and Henry of Essex would not be the man to miss meeting him or another in any personal trial of courage. It is too much of the ephemeral order of criticism of a man, to suppose that once he judges wrongly he is for ever out of court.

It may be true that Henry was not of the fiercest build of nature or he would not join, even if condemned to it, the Reading monks; but the facts do not at all go to prove that he was deficient in personal valour, however limited in judgment at critical moments. His daughters must have had keen personal sorrow through the misfortune which came to their father; but it was thirteen years after her Geffrey Mandeville was dead, and Rose, if it were she who was his wife, and not Rose de Vere, would then have Pain Beauchamp to help her to make the most of affairs. Probably Geffrey's great power in the wars of Matilda and Robert, earl of Gloucester, with Stephen, was owing partly to this then all but highest connection in England. His wife Rose, whoever she was, founded the monastery of Royston, and was buried at Euge in Normandy; the latter fact rather going to prove Dugdale's finding, that she was Rose de Vere.

But something has to be said of the only daughter of Margaret Sinclair, Beatrice Mandeville. Through Geffrey's instigation she got a divorce from her first husband, William Talbot, a nobleman of Normandy, who had displeased him; and she then married William Saye of the baronial Kent and Sussex family long celebrated. They had a son who married a sister of a William Mandeville. Sir Francis Nicolas, in his Synopsis of the Peerage, says that Beatrice Mandeville had a son, William Saye, whose daughter Beatrice Saye married the Geffrey Fitz-Piers who changed his name to Mandeville and was made earl of Essex, after many difficulties, by King John on his own coronation day, 26 June 1199. If so, Beatrice Mandeville lived to see it, for she died in 1200 at a very venerable age. Dugdale says 1207 is the date, and that she died at her house at Rikelings, and was buried with great honour in the abbey of Walden, founded by her noble-hearted, powerful, but unfortunate brother about seventy years previously. It was well the part of the monks there to do all honour to "old Beatrix de Saye", sister to Geffrey de Mandeville, earl of Essex; for she had been always their special friend, which chiefly means land-grants, but gifts of all kinds as well.

If Margaret Sinclair, countess of Essex, was the last of Eudo Dapifers line, she had a son and a daughter to be proud of exceedingly. She had her last resting-place also in Walden Abbey, with them both; for Geffrey's corpse was ultimately taken from the tree in the garden of his loving fellow Knights Templar on the banks of the Thames, and laid in the abbey of Walden, of his own foundation, near the family home of Walden Castle, Essex.

Chapter XVI
The Younger Hubert's Line

Eudo Dapifer's brothers were by no means lost in the glow of fame and honour which surrounded the youngest of them at the courts of the kings. The Cenomannic tumults shortly after the battle of Hastings quelled, the treis fils, chevaliers bons, of the ambassador, Hubert of Rye, came back to England; and all of them distinguished themselves. When Roger Fitz-Osborn, earl of Hereford, and son of William Fitz-Osborn, once dapifer of Normandy, and governor of England with Odo, earl of Kent, married his daughter to Ralph Waer, earl of Norfolk, against King William's expressed will, the marriage-feast of conspiracy so celebrated in history took place. The oath to dethrone the Conqueror, sworn over their cups in Norwich Castle, proved as useless as all other traitorous proceedings against the able monarch.

Waltheof, the Saxon earl of Nottingham, who received many favours from him, and had even his niece Judith in marriage, to bind more to his interests, proved faithless with the rest. He had been once pardoned before for something very like treason, but this time his repentance could not be accepted, and he was beheaded at Winchester in 1075, the only nobleman of that terribly tried reign who suffered death by law. To those who falsely confuse the Anglo-Saxons with the English as they now are, he is one of the martyrs of Norman tyranny. Not to answer such prejudice, but to calm its outcry, reference may be given in this respect to subsequent reigns, in times of supposed higher national development, such as those of Henry VIII, Mary, or even Elizabeth. The necessities of death in war are beyond the power of a monarch, but legal sentences are valuable indications of his temper and character.

Hubert Sinclair was, under the governor of the kingdom, Bishop Odo, the means of scattering this detestable conspiracy finally; and he took the place of the semi-Saxon, semi-Celtic earl of Norfolk, who fled from England in 1074, and died in the Holy Land, his companion, the earl of Hereford, being taken, and deservedly imprisoned for life. Eudo Dapifer's brother was made governor of Norwich Castle; and though record is scanty, he enjoyed the full rights and benefits of the earldom of Norfolk, which the traitor had forfeited. It is he who, before these honours were got, was Dugdale's "Hubert de Rye (a great man in Lincolnshire)", who married Agnes Todenei, the daughter of Robert Todenei of Belvoir Castle, the father of the William who is so well known to record by the surnames Albini and Brito, the hero of Tenchbrai.

The earls of Arundel, also Albinis, were of the same stock, descended from the uncle of Rollo. The latter were butlers of coronation-day, and had surname from this of Pincerna. It was one of them who was married to Adeliza, Henry I's widow. He and she received Matilda, the empress, and her brother, Robert of Gloucester, in Sussex, for their first contest with Stephen. Such relationship as this of Hubert's explains the names appearing in court-given charters so frequently. Eudo Dapifer and Albini were related thus and otherwise.

A daughter of the Raoul de Bello Sago of Domesday Book was married either to Hubert or one of his sons, and she brought West Lexham as dowry. In Rymer's Foedera Alured de Todenei is one of the witnesses to Henry I's charter to the city of London, and must have been the brother of Agnes. Alured at a later period is a noted first name for Sinclairs of the Midlands. But the same document has as witness Hubert, regis camerarias, or king's chamberlain, and if he is either son or father, as is certain, this branch of the house of Rye was in as high favour as any. Hubert, the father, castellan of Norwich, son of Hubert Sinclair, the ambassador, is established to have been, with his other duties, dapifer of the Conqueror's half-brother, the earl of Mortaine, and time would favour his son for being king's chamberlain to Henry Beauclerc.

In 1147 Pope Eugenius gave a letter of protection to the church "within the walls" near Aldgate, London, beside the convent of St.Clare. It is preserved in Rymer's Foedera. Ten years before, Pope Innocent II had given a similar letter to the same monks. The popes specify the lands and gifts, such as two parts of the returns of Exeter, the land of Lexton, church returns of Bix and Tottenham, tenths of Heham, church of Soresdich [the modern Shoreditch], land of Scelgham, lands in Brachingis, from Stephen and his queen.

What is of present purpose is that part of this last property was De dono Huberti camerarii in eadem villa. Several of these names are associated with his lineage, but the suggestive fact is that there was given also - "'Land from Tela by the liberality of the same'". The lords of Tela, of whom Jones writes in his History of Brecknock as chief Englishmen, are remarkable as late as the reign of Edward Third; for that king confirmed a grant by his heroic queen, Philippa, to her maid of honour, Mary Sinclair, of lands which were those of William of Teye, in Havering-at-Bower, Essex. This will occur again with other purpose more fully, but it aids here towards proof that - "'Hubert, king's chamberlain'", was of the same blood with Mary, and one of the Norwich branch. His family were mostly on the side of Matilda, against King Stephen, at the latter's accession to or seizure of the crown; and in 1135 Hugh Bigod, the dapifer, was created earl of Norfolk.

After this period fortunes and titles went into the inextricable disorder which civil wars and changing dynasties alone account for. During sixty years, however, it will be found that this family were the rulers not only indisputably of Norwich and its famous castle, but also, as the Cottonian MSS. state, of the county of Norfolk, receiving the thirds, and doing the relative duties of its earldom.

Dugdale gives good account of these Norwich Sinclairs. Hubert, the brother of the dapifer, he makes the governor; but Nicolas is mistaken when he says that this same man was governor of the castle of Norwich, 1 Stephen (1135) and was alive so late as 1146. This must have been a second Hubert, and probably the last earl of Norfolk of his family. There was a third Hubert, the son and heir of him whose position Hugo Bigod, the dapifer, seems to have secured by Stephen's help. He was known in Henry II's reign as the baron of Hengham, in Norfolkshire, and died in 1172 without male issue. That there were enough of male heirs is suggested by Dugdale's notice of a Henry who, 11 Stephen (1146) gave a manor to monks of Kent.

The early Huberts must have had large property, for this third one, after the twenty years' struggle of Stephen's reign, in which they do not seem to have been fortunate, on assessment for marrying Henry II's daughters, 1162 and 1164, had thirty-five knights' fees, an amount of land which at once suggests more than the governorship, great as this office was, of Norwich Castle. In 18 Henry II (1172), he paid £35 as his share of the scutage raised at that time for Ireland, which was being then finally conquered by England. He died in this year. His fees were in Suffolk as well as Norfolk.

In the reign of King John a Hubert held the very same number of fees, so that it may be supposed that he was the heir of the baron of Hengham by all the property as well as title. In the state records of King John, 1199, Robert Fitz-Roger gives three hundred marks to the treasury, for sanction to marry to his nephew the younger daughter of this Hubert, who had no sons. Dugdale says Fitz-Roger was "a great baron in

Northumberland". This nephew of his is Roger de Cressi, who married Isabella Sinclair. He was one of the barons who, Matthew Paris says, came in 1215 to London to compel the laws of Edward the Confessor and other privileges from King John, for which John took his revenge in 1216 by ravaging his Norfolk and Suffolk estates; and that he was thoroughly in earnest against the reigning family is further shown by the fact that he was one of the barons who invited and supported Louis, the dauphin of France, in his extraordinary attempt to become king of England. He was taken prisoner in 1217, at the frightful massacre of the French in "Lincoln Fair" battle; but he has possession of his lands some years after, so that he cannot have been far wrong. Dugdale says his wife Isabella was first married to Hugh de Lacy, constable of Chester, of the family known well as earls of Ulster and Lincoln.

The other daughter and co-heir of this last Hubert of the Norwich line was Aliva, and she married John Marescal, who, with his four brothers, had their name from being holders of the marshalships of England and Ireland hereditarily. He was brother of William Marshall, the earl of Pembroke who had, by his mother, the rights and titles of "Strongbow", or Richard Striguil, the conqueror of Ireland. He and this brother were barons on the king's side at the signing of Magna Charta. They appear in Matthew Paris's list. In the original copy of the Great Charter, preserved in the Cottonian library, William Marescall, earl of Pembroke, and John Marescall are of the sixteen nobilium virorum whose names begin the document as the king's advisers. They were also both at the coronation of King Henry III at Gloucester in 1216, their efforts saving England from the misery of a foreign conquest of an almost ridiculous character. Earl William as regent is one of the historic personages of his country, and John Marescal, his brother, ably seconds him in his strenuous deeds for the boy-king Henry III, though in John's reign the earl marshal had favoured the French attempt, like Roger de Cressi. The last earl of these Marshalls died in 1245, when the branch became extinct. Five brothers being earls marshal, and only three generations of them altogether, John must have been also a short liver. The extraordinary doings of the Marshalls all through Henry III's reign are a large subject. Roger de Cressi and John, earl marshal, were notable men of the time, and these Sinclair ladies had reason to be proud of their position. In the Temple Church, London, the monuments of these lords marshal, as crusaders with crossed legs, as well as of the lords Ros, descendants of Richard de St.Clair, of battle of Hastings fame, are still to be seen. At the Crystal Palace there are copies in clay, as of the noblest men England has had, side by side with those of her kings and queens. They had each with their wives seventeen and a half knights' fees of lands. Hubert died before 1213, because in paying the scutage of wars with Scotland in 13 John (1212) it was these two husbands who appeared in accounts. In 6 Henry III (1221) they again stand with exactly the thirty-five fees at which the family are so often assessed. Marshall scions survive in Devon.

It seems the rule with Norman families of the early periods to come quickly to their male conclusion; and Hubert, the gallant governor of Norwich, had not many direct descendants to keep up his name and fame. Daughters had privileges stronger than masculine representatives, or the line, like many others, might still be represented. In 48 Henry III (1264) a John fought well on the side of the barons struggling for liberties, and he was one of the prisoners at Northampton, but in 53 Henry III (1269) pardon came. In 5 & 6 Edward I (1276-7), a Nicholas of these Sinclairs was sheriff or viscount of the county of Lincoln, and in 9 of Edward's reign (1280) Ranulph figures in the same district, Blomfield's History of Norfolk under "Hingham" as heading, gives suggestive knowledge. Hingham contained 43 parishes, and King Stephen farmed it to Henry Sinclair, a son of Hubert, the castellan. In 1195 Cardo de Freschaville had the barony by the same form of tenure from Richard I. This town, Blomfield asserts, was always reputed the head of the barony of Rye ever since its first grant to Henry of Rye aforesaid, and uniformly acknowledged as such by those who farmed it.

After the death of Henry of Rye, Hubert of Rye had the barony, he adds; but the manor then belonged to Hugh de Gournay, captain of Castle Galliard, in Normandy. John Marshall got the barony in 1207 and the manor in 1210, as being the husband of Alice, daughter of Hubert de Rye, baron de Rye in Norfolk. He also had the hundred of Forehoe. His second and final confirmation was expressly given him by the king to cut off all claims that the heirs of Cardo Freshville could make. The Freshvilles stood nearest male heirs to Hubert, and were undoubtedly of the same blood male, descended from Ralph Sinclair, governor of Nottingham Castle, as Sir Henry Ellis and others have shown, and only the partibility of fees and the heirship by daughters prevented them keeping up there Hubert's line and surname. Dugdale also testifies that John Marshall, married to Hubert of Rye's daughter Alice, got from King John, 1214, the manor of Hengham, "part of the possessions of Cardo de Freshanvill".

Sir Francis Nicolas, in his Extinct Peerage, makes Ralph de Frescheville receive a writ to parliament as a baron, 25 Edward I (1297) and on this Baron Freshville of Stavely, co. Derby, had the creation renewed in his favour in 1664. Lord Freshville of Derbyshire died in 1682, and the proper male line became then extinct. That Hugh of

Gournay appears as lord of Hengham, is of great interest, because the Gournays and Sinclairs are frequently in close relationship, both in Normandy and England. An earlier Hugh, as having the district of the French and Norman Vexin, in which the historic St.Clair village on the Epte river was whence the name came, appears prominently in treaties between the English and French kings, and he almost holds princely position in the negotiations. The three fees which these great Norman-French Gournays held in England, according to Domesday Book, 1080-86, were in Eudo Dapifer's district at Colchester.

They were Fordham, Listen, and Ardley, quite close to that city, Liston being the Lexden afterwards the property of the governor of Colchester Castle, Hubert de Sancto Claro. What is suggestive also is that Geffrey Talbot, related to Eudo Dapifer, and leaving many knights' fees to Walter Sinclair of Medway, held Lexden as under-tenant from the Gournays, whose small portions then (for by marriage with Warennes and others of first rank, they afterwards increased lands largely in England) are explained by the fact that they were powerful marchers on both sides of the Epte, under the French and English kings, both jealous of their power. It is too obscure to try to discover how they got the lands there which once was part of territories of the St.Clares, whether by marriage or otherwise.

Much general light, and finely true Norman appreciation as against the Saxon grumbling of some prejudiced chroniclers and one or more as prejudiced recent historians, appear in a book by James Hannay, Three Hundred Years of a Norman House. It is founded on a MS. history of the Gournays from the Rouen public library, but the whole spirit of the too graphic work is sufficiently true and illustrative of those earlier centuries to make it a valuable aid to knowledge of them and their chief figures.

It is probable that a great deal is yet to be discovered about the doings of Hubert Sinclair, son of the duke of Normandy's ambassador to Edward the Confessor, and of his descendants. Enough has appeared to show that he was a brother worthy of Eudo Dapifer. Whether, like him, he had lands also over the Channel, and was a great builder of castles and monasteries, are questions hardly needing discussion.

In the work of building, Mrs. Harriet Beecher Stowe says Sinclairs were adepts; and the high philosophies of freemasonry were no doubt considerably of their manufacture. In Sunny Memories, page 87, after indulging in quotation from The Lay of the Last Minstrel, and celebration of the William St.Clair in 1446, "'prince of Orkney, duke of Oldenburgh, lord of Roslin, earl of Caithness and Strathearn, and so on ad infinitum'", as "the seemly St.Clair" of tradition, who he was not, though of whatsoever "noble deportment and elegant manners", she adds two paragraphs on good enough authority"'. It appears by certain documents that this high and mighty house of St.Clair were in a particular manner patrons of the masonic craft. It is known that the trade of masonry was then in the hands of a secret and mysterious order from whom probably our modern masons have descended'". She continues, "'The St.Clair family, it appears, were at the head of this order, with power to appoint officers and places of meeting, to punish transgressors, and otherwise to have the superintendence of all their affairs'". This fact may account for such a perfect geyser of architectural ingenuity as has been poured out upon their family chapel [Roslin] which was designed for a chef d'oeuvre, a concentration of the best that could be done to the honour of their patron's family.

The documents which authenticate this statement are described in Billings' Baronial Antiquities. So much for "the lordly line of high St.Clair". And so much for the democratic mushroom that spreads its fragrance. But it is good tribute from the American mind, so barren of the glow and glory of antiquity, that in spite of all its training to flat ephemeral usefulness, the dignity of true because able and artistic nobility, compels its mede of justice and admiration. The appreciation, however, may have been aided by the secret memory of her own characters in Uncle Tom's Cabin: the planter of the southern states, and his darling daughter, Eva St.Clair, whom the gods loved.

To hold that Hubert, if he did not altogether found Norwich Castle, enlarged its warlike dimensions equal to the pressing necessities then, not only of defence, but of mastery over the entire north, would not be quixotic. No position required more military and engineering ability than this; and the ultimate success along the whole line of the Conqueror's efforts, had its efficient aid from Hubert Sinclair's lieutenancy in an historically troublesome but withal brave part of the kingdom. It would be pleasant to accumulate incident of his lordship of the city and governorship of the castle, and industry could find its reward in the work.

Other things and other men now, however, call for fair share of attention. "The house of Rye rose high in William's favour", says Freeman, who does not grudge them their honours and lands; and were not such men as this Hubert worthy of all honour, so loyal, brave, and capable ? Their skill of pacification by giving justice and showing courtesy to the exasperated Saxons, was the finest feature in their rule, though it has the effect of keeping them less on historic page (which generally loves tyrannies and sensations for its best attraction) than if of the harsh temper and nothing besides. That other conspiracies in the north-east never came to much or anything, must be attributed to the ability and geniality of Hubert and his descendants.

In Domesday Book's pages "Hubertus, filius Huberti", holds much in capite and as under-tenant. What has been said of his brother Eudo in this respect will apply to him, their lands being of similar extent. Hubert held in Sussex, Berkshire, Dorsetshire, Devon, Warwickshire, Essex, Staffordshire, Norfolk, and Suffolk, filling leaves of the Conqueror's record.

Chapter XVII
The Earl of Nottingham

Radulph Sinclair was the eldest son of Hubert, the ambassador, and the eldest brother of Hubert of Norwich, Adam of Kent, and Eudo Dapifer. To him was committed the custody of the splendid castle of Nottingham, the home and fort of Waltheof, the traitorous Saxon earl of Nottingham. Ralph also got the earldom of the county, when William I had in 1074 secured this nobleman, to whom he had married his own niece Judith.

There is general abuse of the lady among the chroniclers, who are chiefly Saxons, for her pretended eagerness to get Waltheof beheaded. Love of another was an easy tale to invent. A lady with two or three daughters at or near womanhood was not of such temper. The more likely theory is that she was a true Norman at heart, and detested with her whole soul the dishonourable scheming that was certainly going on. Her life could well become a burden to her, living it in the midst of such deceit as was around, and if she gave her uncle the king the benefit of her advice, which is not proved, justification might be found for her.

The political game then playing was no matter of three-volume sentiment, and ladies with the fine training of Normandy were more than clinging chattels. They had to be treated on grounds of equality. They founded religious houses, heired wide fortunes, judged effects of dynasties and alliances with the wisdom and decision born only of actual experience; and if Waltheof or his admirers of his own race forgot that to a Norman lady right and honour were first, and protection of evil-doing husbands of very secondary consideration, they deserved justly all the consequences of the crude mistake.

Her uncle afterwards offered her marriage to one of his choice, but she did not seem to have eagerness for another married life; and if this caused her misfortunes, and ultimately, as her enemies say, poverty and vagabondage, for all her high titles and wealth, their gratuitous story of her love of a lover does not appear to have much or any ground. In the freedom of poverty, if it ever did arrive at all, there would have been no political or other bar. But it is a Saxon libel on Judith, countess of Nottingham, to which the unavoidable difficulty with her uncle, the king, gave only too much ease of colour for the complacent fabulists who love a moral more than facts.

It is not easy to realise how dangerous a man this Waltheof was, not only for William, but for the whole Norman nobility and soldiers. He was the son of Siward, the second, certainly not the only son, if Shakespeare in Macbeth had the right version when he makes young Siward fall by Macbeth's sword before the Scottish castle of Dunsinane. In the time of Edward the Confessor, "Old Siward, with ten thousand warlike men", was a power needing politic treatment; and Waltheof his son not only heired the earldom of Northumberland, which itself could raise such an army, but with his wife had got also the earldoms of Huntingdon, Northampton, and Nottingham. They were descended from Ursus, the Dane; and, hereditarily brave, Waltheof had given example of his courage, if not ferocity, by his famous stand at one of the gates of York, where he chopped off the heads of Norman soldiers, then his enemies, as they came, to a number sufficient to make him the most notorious sword-wielder in England. The Conqueror's prizes given to him were politic as much as generous, but when such a man had shown his mind, and by the ability of such leaders as Bishop Odo, Richard Fitz-Gilbert, Hubert, and Ralph, had fallen into William's hands, there was little course open to the king. It was simply a balancing of blood for blood, life for life. Those who know human nature act accordingly, and William's only death for state reasons is capable of defence, if any such doings are at all to be treated as other than the work of fate's necessity. Outside of Winchester at early morning Waltheof was executed, and his body was taken some time afterwards for burial to Croyland Abbey, Lincolnshire. The bishop of Northumberland, Walcher, got the rule of Northumbria; the earldoms of Northampton and Huntingdon remained in Judith's hands, who had three daughters, the children of Waltheof; and Ralph Sinclair had the earldom of Nottingham given to him, together with the governorship of Nottingham Castle, one of the finest structures of the kind in the kingdom.

It has been said that Waltheof 's possessions were his greatest enemies, implying that the Norman nobles were hungering after them. The right sense in which to take the saying is, that the immense width of his lands, and his power of raising thousands of soldiers, gave William no choice of risking again and again the traitorous changes of disposition of the powerful and fickle Dane. His mother, or, as some say, his step-mother, was Elfrida, daughter of Aldred, count of Northumbria, by whom Siward got his northern wide district. Of these counts there had been Utred, Waldesus, and Aldred previously known to record. Her uncle was Cospatric, the lord of Raby, the ancestor of all the Nevilles, and father-in-law of William Sinclair, Queen Margaret Atheling of Scotland's dapifer. There was no preternatural hurry to share the spoil. In Domesday Book the Countess Judith holds the lands, and that was five years at the least after the death of her husband.

If Ralph Sinclair had early possession of Nottingham, it was absolutely necessary for the security of his sovereign's rule. King William knew where the foot must be planted, prepared for attack or defence; but there is no evidence that hungry seizure was at work. Of all Eudo Dapifer's brothers, Ralph needed least to be enterprising in this way, as being the eldest son, and heir to large property in Normandy. With Hubert of Rye deceased, he would be expected to keep up the French home in its old and added splendour. The military and loyal aspect of the affairs of the chief central and northern counties was the matter of first importance to him. It was only accidental, that he and Hubert secured the best things out of the terrible but deserved fall of Ralph, earl of Norfolk, or, as has been said, consul of East Anglia, meaning Cambridge, Norfolk, and Suffolk; of Roger Fitz-Osborn, earl of Hereford; and of Waltheof, a son greater than his father Siward, who could 'wake Northumberland', and lead ten thousand men to the aid of a Scottish prince, or more if need required.

A passage from Duncan's List of the Norman Barons who fought at Hastings, the information of which is chiefly derived from the local and other antiquarian careful research of Auguste le Provost, has valuable reference not only to Ralph or Raoul, as the French write the name, but to other members of his lineage. "'Haie-du-Puits is in the arrondissement of Coutances. The lord of this barony, at the date of the Conquest, was Raoul, seneschal of the earl of Mortain, and brother of Robert de la Haie, a contemporary of Henry I. Raoul seems to have been the son of Hubert of Rye, to whom was entrusted the castle of Nottingham, and the governorship of that county; he is frequently mentioned in The Domesday Book. It is certain that Robert de la Haie was nephew to Odo Dapifer, another son of Hubert of Rye. This Odo Dapifer has been frequently confounded with Odo au Chapeau, son of Turstin Halduc, or Haldup, one of the founders of the abbey of Lessay. This error may be traced back even to Ordericus Vitalis, who wrote in the twelfth century. In addition to other grants, Robert de la Haie received the lordship of Halnac, in Sussex, in the reign of Henry I, and founded the priory of Boxgrave, a dependency on the abbey of Lessay. The name of his wife was Muriel. They had two sons, Richard and Raoul; the former had an only daughter, who carried the estates into the family of Saint-John. In the war between Stephen and Geoffrey Plantagenet, Richard de la Haie, who commanded at Cherbourg, for the king of England, was seized by pirates, and his brother, Raoul, was compelled to surrender the castles in the Cotentin to the earl of Anjou. These events belong to the years 1141 and 1142. Richard de la Haie, son of Raoul, founded the abbey of Blanchelande in Normandy.'"

There is a correction to this, namely, that the same Robert de la Haie could not be the brother of Ralph and the nephew of Eudo Dapifer. If there was only a single individual of the name, he was certainly the nephew of both. The earl of Mortain was the half-brother of the Conqueror, and like his other half-brother, Odo, bishop of Bayeux, he shared largely in the division of lands at the Conquest. They got more than any else of William's following, the earl of Mortain being first in the number of his lordships, nearly 800 in 18 counties, and Odo first in the value of the possessions secured. It speaks of relationship of some close kind, for this is the chief clue to transactions of the period, that, as Ralph Sinclair was seneschal to the earl of Mortain, so Adam Sinclair was seneschal to the bishop, Odo, earl of Kent. Such connection of double brothers could not be accidental.

The fortunes and misfortunes of Arlotta's two sons, had the strongest relation to those of Ralph and Adam. The whole state of matters throws peculiar colour over the conquering duke of Normandy's domestic affairs, and these played large part in the drama of his English years.

More direct knowledge of Adam's stewardship to Odo is attainable, from The Domesday Book and other sources, than of Ralph's to Robert, earl of Mortain and of Cornwall, chiefly because the bishop was a livelier actor in history than his brother. Robert's son William fell into as final misfortune as his uncle, the unfortunate and troubling Odo; though the great Hubert de Burgh and William Fitz-Aldelm, king's dapifer and viceroy of Ireland, restored or regained fortune for this line from Arlotta, the mother of the Conqueror. Such favour as Ralph must have had in these circumstances, substantiates the statement that he had the governorship or earldom of Nottinghamshire, though the fact is settled otherwise by records. It is curious to note that Eudo, the third brother, was high steward to the third and greatest brother of Arlotta's sons, the king of England and duke of Normandy.

The house of Rye was the most successful of the time, and Freeman does not grudge them their successes, wonderful to be said. On the relationship of Robert de la Haie to it, information is to be got in Burke's

Peerage, under "Viscount Bolingbroke and St.John". Roger de St.John, of Stanton St.John, co. Oxon., married Ciceley Sinclair, daughter and heiress of Robert of Haya, lord of the manor of Halnac, co. Suffolk, as Burke finds; and their daughter Muriel, ancestress of the celebrated Viscount Bolingbroke of Battersea and Wandsworth, Pope's friend, seems to have been named after her mother or grandmother. What is of great importance, amounting to positive proof, if Burke's information be correct, is, that he states that Robert Sinclair of Haya was "a kinsman of Henry I". Robert's son-in-law, Roger St.John, further, was the son of the John de St.John who was "'one of the twelve knights that accompanied Robert Fitz-Hamon, earl of Gloucester, in a warlike expedition against the Welsh'", and who got the castle of Faumont, Glamorgan, "for his great services". The connection of Eudo, Fitz-Hamo, and the lords of Haya, can be discerned here, for various inferential reasons. That Ciceley Sinclair's sister-in-law married Sir Bernard de St.Valery, a relation of the Conqueror by the mother's side, is also indication of the "set". The able Tregozes appear in family charters of these families, for they were St.Johns of the Adam de Port line male, to whom Lydiard Tregoze, in Wiltshire, came by a marriage with a Beauchamp. Burke shows that the Scottish Hays, represented by the marquis of Tweeddale, the earl of Errol, and by four baronets, are of Norman origin, the first remarkable one being William de Haya royal butler to Malcolm IV and William the Lion. It is suggestive that the ancient seat of one branch was called Huntingdon, in East Lothian. Was it an English memory ? The earls of Errol were high constables, and such offices were only given to royal blood.

But perhaps the most instructive information in connection with the subject is that given by the famous "Giraldus Cambrends", a churchman of the Barry lineage so remarkable in Irish history, and a contemporary of Henry II. He says that Nesta, the Welsh princess, concubine of Henry I, had seven sons to different Normans, which was gay even for Welsh morality. They were the progenitors of nearly all the leading chiefs in the conquest of Ireland, 1172. One of the seven was William Hay, and Girald Cambrensis says that in the division of Nesta's Welsh properties he got Sanctum Clarum. His father was certainly a Sinclair of Hay. The half-brothers of this William were the Fitz-Gerald, Fitz-Stephen, the Maurice, &c, who figured in the Irish Conquest. One of her daughters was married to the lord of Ros. Girald mentions a Robert and a Richard Hay as constables of Lincoln before the Lacis; and they were probably descendants of Ralph Sinclair, castellan of Nottingham. The Lincoln Hays are well known by charters as well as in the records of the interesting northern ancient city. The true home of this branch of Sinclair blood is to be found on the beautiful banks of the Wye, Herefordshire. Haia Castle was built by Maud, married to one of the Brecknock Bruces, the female Samson or Guy of Warwick of the Welsh border. It is there that the Sinclair, Hay, and Bruce famines get so interknit after the Norman Conquest, that they seem of the same blood, as must have been, if going to Normandy were profitable. Wales has played a most productive part in giving historical Norman figures to the two islands. Jones in his History of Brecknock has varied incidental information as to these families' close union by marriage and otherwise. To one of the Devonshire Sinclairs the William Bruce of Bramber in The Domesday Book was married, and again and again the lines are meeting, the Bruces not being then the greater.

It can be more easily understood how Eudo Dapifer, as Dugdale says in speaking of William Rufus, could "well be accounted the chief instrument in raising him to the royal throne", when it is remembered that he had only the governors of the southern castles to gain over; his two brothers, Ralph, earl of Nottingham, and Hubert, earl of Norfolk, or possibly consul of East Anglia, having such castles as Nottingham and Norwich in their powerful hands. A knowledge of this would aid decision on the part of William de Ponte-Arce to give up the keys of the treasury at Winchester, and on the part of the governors of Dover Castle, Pevensey, Hastings, and other sea-board castles, to swear, in Eudo the seneschal's favour, for Rufus as king.

There is a statement by Nicolas as to the claimed possession of the earldom of Nottingham by the Peverells at some period. He says that no earl was created till 1377, when Baron Mowbray got the title, but he is discussing the times after that reign of Stephen so destructive of previous doings, and difiicult of itself to master. There is record that Ralph had the custody of the castle and county of Nottingham, afterwhich there can be no room for difficulties of formal creation, which also is probably implied in this account. The Ferrers, later, put in a female claim, but without success.

Earl Ralph had a son Ralph who figured in the empress's wars with Stephen, he may or may not have been actually earl, though it is probable he was so at intervals, having followed the fortunes of Stephen. Matthew Paris, William of Malmesbury, and others, have much to say of him. He was a "fierce man and a great plunderer". It is likely these were the virtues of that time. Evidently he had the king's trust as one of his best warriors. He surprised the castle of Devises in Wiltshire by a skilful stratagem, and the chroniclers say he then boasted that with this stronghold for base he would conquer for Stephen all the country between Winchester and London. That he had great wealth is shown by the fact that he sent on his own account for soldiers out of Flanders to put his schemes to their full execution. But unfortunately this biter was himself bit. John, the subtle captain of Marlborough Castle, put his own science into use, and in some way got him taken prisoner. Kidnapping was in accordance with the chivalry of that civil war. He was taken to the empress, Matilda, flighty, sometimes capable, always persistent, sometimes timid (as when she got into a coffin to escape after one of her battles), and often cruel. Earl Ralph she asked to deliver up the castle of Devises on peril of his life. That it was still held by his men shows that the subtle governor John had taken unfair advantage of his gallant enemy, the captain of Devises Castle. It was not Devises he had taken, but its lord, who was probably enjoying an outside walk or gallop unattended. He would not betray the castle to Matilda. He must die then, was the alternative. There was no shrinking, even though the indignity was further threatened that she would have him hung. This was the mode of the execution of thieves, and nothing more bitter could be invented against the chivalrous soul of a Norman; but his honour kept him firm as a rock, and he died the shameful death. His family could not recover in England from the state of matters into which this and other things put them in the reign of Matilda's son. They lived and succeeded most in Normandy.

As early as Henry I's reign Ralph is noticeable as giving gifts to the Knights Templar. His son Hubert, called Hubert Fitz-Ralph, though liberal to the monks of Derley in particular, declined largely from the former estate. He is taxed for only 20 fees; and, what is suggestive of the want of royal sunshine and other advantages contemporaneous, they are all of old enfeoffment. He had a sister, however, who brought 10 knights' fees of dowry to a Norman lord, Henry de Cotentin. The main line seems to have become soon extinct, in England, for in 6 Henry III (1222) a Juliana, the daughter of a Hubert, his heiress, appears for her son, then in wardship. A collateral line through Mary, co-heiress of Ralph Fitz-Ralph of Middleham, Yorkshire, gave this seat to the Nevilles, of which semi-royal line the earl of Salisbury, heir of the Montacutes, and Warwick, king-maker, were chiefs.

When the dauntless "Coeur de Lion", after great successes and in sight of Jerusalem as crusader, was deserted by his European allies, Tindal says, "'Philip of France, immediately after his return to his dominions loaded King Richard with calumnies, and had a conference, January 22, 1192, between Gisors and Trie, wherein he demanded of William Fitz-Ralph, seneschal of Normandy, his royal sister Alice; but the seneschal refused to send her, though Philip showed him the convention made between King Richard and him at Messina. After that the king of France gathered a large army, and would have invaded Normandy; but the great men of his kingdom would not let him.'"

This useful light on the family is taken from Hoveden's Chronicle and the Bromton Chronicle; and it suggests that the Norwich branch claimed, and got, the hereditary rights of Eudo, the seneschal. It is the more likely because in Rymer's Foedera, William Fitz-Ralph, seneschal of Normandy, is witness with Robert of Tregoz and with Peter of Pratellis, Eudo's chief estate and castle in Normandy, to a charter of Richard I for their favoured Rochester. The same authority implies that his father Ralph was also seneschal. In 1226 a Ralph, the son of Nicolas, was "our seneschal", but the reference may be too far afield. There is no doubt of the Gerold, son of Ralph, who was one of the commissioners sent in 1170 by Henry II to the counties to reform the administration of justice, and through him the true descent of the Irish Fitz-Geralds is probably to be found. That this William Sinclair founded a Norman branch is open for inquiry; but enough is said to show that he was of the stock in blood and spirit, and it is to England attention is chiefly necessary. In 1170, after Henry II's four years' stay in France, he found the administration of justice shamefully neglected, and Gervas, the chronicler, names Gerold Fitz-Ralph as one of the commissioners sent into the counties with full powers of inquiry and punishment as to the doings of the magistrates. But Earl Ralph's most remarkable descendants were the lords Freshville of Derbyshire, whose claims to heir the last Hubert of Norfolk have been noticed. They played their part in the best English life till the reign of Charles II, when they became extinct, the last males distinctly traceable from this first Norman earl of Nottingham.

Cooper's discovery of a member of the Rye family is interesting, as showing that they did not limit their efforts to military and feudal courses, but were capable as well at sea and in commerce. "'On 21st July, 1212, the ship of Geffrey, son of Michael de Ria, was at Winchelsea with 120 tuns of wine belonging to the merchants of Iypres and Ghent'". Probably Geffrey was one of the sons expected to provide for himself, and the question arises, was this Michael the son of one of the Sinclairs earls of Nottingham, and also, it is to be expected, lords of Rye in Normandy ? Meantime, it must also be said that Michael of Rye may have been of the next port to Winchelsea in England. If so, it will add further to the large accumulation of facts pointing to Rye in Sussex as companion home of Sinclairs with the famous Rye of Normandy. Another discussion will still further treat this subject. That Michael of Rye was grandson or great-grandson of Ralph Sinclair, governor of magnificent Nottingham Castle, and earl of the county of which it was the powerful centre, there are not known facts to show.

Amid the embroglio which the pride of first names and of lands creates, it is difficult to follow accurately enough some trains of facts.

Says Hallam, "'The authors of Nouveau Traité de Diplomatique trace the use of surnames in a few instances even to the beginning of the tenth century; but they did not become general, according to them, till the thirteenth'". Surnames from the place where the mansion or castle was built, were at first the only distinction; and these were of some use certainly, but not of so much to present search as might be thought. The Sinclairs seem to have early found the value of having a surname in addition to that of their places. Like the Romans they knew their gens. This, however, was cherished at some cost to feudal pride. The same English writer says somewhere that the use of such a general family surname made a man be considered a simple gentleman instead of a lord by tenure. It is great reason for thankfulness, in toiling now, that so many of the name cling to the clear though less demonstrative name. When it occurs, as it does in a remarkable number of earliest records, almost single to itself, there is no shadow of doubt as to what "tribe", as one antiquarian says, its bearer belongs. The house of Rye has been thus absolutely fixed by record, and the modesty or skill may work perhaps equally well for other branches of it than have yet been followed. If it can also help in the next enquiry, which is undoubtedly both difficult and admitting of debate, there need be no reason to regret the frequent signature of the general surname.

Ralph Sinclair in The Domesday Book holds, as "Radulphuis filius Huberti", wide lands in Leicester, Stafford, Derby, Nottingham, Lincoln shires, in capite; and there is one entry in Derbyshire as undertenant. He has 10 manors in Nottinghamshire, and 11 houses in Nottingham itself. In Derby he had 37 lordships, of which Crichc was one; in Lincolnshire he had Gunnebi; and in Leicester, Dalby.

Chapter XVIII
Who was Simon of Senlis ?

On the Paris side of Rouen, the town of Senlis was of importance at the time of the Conquest. Randulph or Ralph le Riche, a Norse soubriquet, was its feudal chief. He had two sons, who came to England in the Conqueror's reign, Simon and the Warner le Riche who was the ancestor of Englishmen of the surname Rich. It is, however, of Simon inquiry is being made. If his lineage were discovered, his brother's will easily be followed, even if with a different surname. He does not seem to have been at the battle of Hastings, as far as can be discovered; but he had, when he first appeared in English history, a renowned name as a soldier of the first rank. Immediately after the Norwich marriage and conspiracy, he begins to be a figure of weight and infiuence. He was a veteran then, and war had lamed him in one leg; but he was still young, and very vigorous of mind and body. He was with Ralph and Hubert Sinclair in putting clown the conspiracy headed in open civil war by Roger Fitz-Osborn, the earl of Hereford; and it is likely he was one of the chief commanders of the proceedings which ended as has been seen.

Considerable time after this, King William proposed that his own niece Judith, the widow of Waltheof, should marry the brave soldier. It was 1075 when the Saxon was beheaded, and the proposal, from what appears in The Domesday Book, could not have at all events been urged as strongly as it eventually was, before 1080. Simon had not only built Northampton Castle, as Ingulphus shows, before this, but lived and ruled there as its governor. It may be that Huntingdon Castle, so much struggled for in English and Scottish history, had him, if not as founder, as governor then; and this would go to explain his wish, from much personal neighbouring knowledge of her, to join their fortunes. Huntingdon Castle was the home of the widowed countess, Judith; and Northampton Castle, which Simon himself built from its foundations, was in feudal proximity. The lady had no heart for marriage, and could not look at matters in the convenient or political way. Her uncle's will was strong; but rather than marry Simon, she and her three daughters fled from their castle for shelter among the fens and fen-people of Ely.

Her enemies give her another lover, as the cause of this escape and personal misery; but the fact that her maiden daughters fled with her is of itself enough to silence all such evil and essentially rebellious libel. She had had enough of marriages and conspiracies, and would rather be a beggar than to live where life and death were continually meeting under dreadest aspect. Simon pursued his purpose with a steadiness explainable to his advantage on the supposition that he really loved the lady, the greatest then in England next to the royal family, of which indeed she herself was a member. That she had immense estate may or may not be read to his credit. Nothing appears to prove that he stretched a point in the matter. It rather became a feud of honour between her and her uncle, the Conqueror. He had chosen Waltheof before for her, and woman's nature might well be capable of saying, "If I meant to marry again at all, at years when I have three daughters women by my side, I would choose this time for myself". William had got somewhat morose then, and no doubt looked on all things, love also, as but instruments of political usefulness.

Simon, it may be guessed, was with all his scars and his halting on one foot more presentable than a blackamoor Othello; and did not he win Desdemona, the fair European in her teens, by the glamour of his soldier's training and history? The Frenchman from Senlis found means to gain the affection of Matilda, the eldest daughter of Judith and Waltheof; and probably Judith was nothing loth to have the difficulty thus solved. On their flight William had at once seized the castle and honour of Huntingdon. The town of Northampton and the whole hundred of Falkely he granted before this seizure to Simon "for shoes for his horses", a phrase that may have a personal innuendo in the contest. Simon's marriage to Matilda, "the lady of Daventry", coheiress and eldest daughter of Waltheof and Judith, gave him the earldoms of Northampton and Huntingdon, as well as claim to that of Northumbria, if events should favour its change from Walcher the bishop's stewardship.

But the clue to his real lineage must be given. Langebek's Scriptores Rerum Danicorum is authority as to some things: in this passage, for example, describing the marriage of one of the daughters of Judith, Waltheof's countess - "'to a certain French-born knight by name Simon Sylvanectensis or Seint-Liz; the name of his father, however, Ralph the Rich'". St.Liz is plainly another way of writing the name of his native town in France. As there were Hubert of Rye, William of Ipres, Eustace of Bouillon, and so forth, there was Simon de Senliz or St.Liz. The change of spelling might be made equally, in the cases of the town, or of those who thus hailed from it, by the usual local surnaming then. What has nearly lost Simon to the genealogy of a family, is the similarity between the sound of St.Liz and of St.Cleere, the midland mode of spelling and sounding Sinclair. Simon was Simon of Senlis by local surnaming, and he was Simon Sinclair by the more modern and far more valuable fashion of family lineage. But if this was all that could be said on the subject, there might well be endless controversy, for nothing is so subtle as such questions of writing and pronouncing words. There cannot be too much care in giving them their exact weight in discussion, and neither more nor less. No judicious inquirer would debar them on the mere diffusiveness or elasticity of all etymologising; but they are, of themselves, decidedly insufficient evidence. They come in usefully as support to weightier things.

It is to Leland, the antiquary of the sixteenth century, that there is indebtedness for the right clue; and it is none the less valuable that it leaves the question an open one for some debate. His notes are as short often as they are always quaint and almost innocently honest. He began his famous Itinerary on 5th May 1542, and he presented it a finished book to Henry VII for a birthday present. When he came to Northampton, he wrote his findings, and one of them is especially interesting. "'St.John's Hospitalle was originally founded by one William Sancte Clere, archdiacon of Northampton and brother to one of the Simon Sainctcleres, as sum of St.John's name them; but as I have redde alway they were caulid Saincteliz and not S.Clere'". This might be safely left to have its own effect, but the full value of these few words would be lessened, if attention were not drawn to some circumstances of persons, place, and time. It were sacrilege to say a depreciatory word of a good sincere antiquary like Leland, to whom so many owe much real gratitude for the glimpses he gives of the past. His character, however, is not at all of the judicial order, although he is faithful in observing and noting his observations. As between him, an itinerant stranger at Northampton in 1542, and those who not only had the traditions then of the place, but actually lived by bounty of the archdeacon, William Sinclair, there can be little doubt as to whose story is the true one. Indeed, the similarity of St.Liz and St.Cleere or St.Cleeres in sound, of itself explains Leland's doubt. No weigher of evidence would hesitate to take the actual local tradition, thus and then delivered by monks or monkish mendicants of literate peculiarities, in preference to the passing impression of any antiquary, not to say one of Leland's guileless, exceedingly pleasant, but rather easy nature. His register of the tradition of Northampton is so valuable, that there would fain be escape from criticism of this most useful of all the itinerants, even to the extent of saying that reasoning is not his strongest point. The tradition is of the honest wholesale kind that testifies most in favour of itself. Not only was William a Sinclair, but he was the brother of the Simon Sinclairs who were the earls of the ground they stood on and of much beside.

Such magnates as they had been were not likely to be lost in this point of lineage, in a town where men could point to their religious, hospital, and other foundations as numerous, and at that period still in existence. Who were better keepers of genealogical details than monks ? and the monks indebted for their subsistence to these Simons for centuries, had been all but as thick in Northampton as the leaves of Vallombrosa. Either nothing at all might be expected to survive of so great benefactors, through the destruction of documents by time and other enemies of record, or what would remain would for very gratitude be truth. The other side is open to those who may take it, but considering the comparative darkness of most historic facts of so far a past, this note of Leland's gives surely Avhat may be called daylight. Other things still will corroborate the fact that William the Conqueror's lame favourite warrior was Simon Sinclair; but in the further narrative he will be wholly accepted as such, the case being already far clearer than is usually possible for such inquiries to be with the greatest perseverance. It is not asserted that here, without additional incidents, the proof of lineage is absolute; though not only tradition but remnants of actual monastic records in the foundations of the Simon Sainct-cleres must have existed in 1542, had the plan of Leland's journey, with its notes wholly trustworthy as far as his information went, allowed him more than the few hours he spent investigating the antiquities of Northampton. To a man who had to do as much of England as possible, the specialties of this town would not have close enough appeal for the thorough search necessary to a decision. In the circumstances the local and learned tradition is supremely valuable, and it will find indirect suggestive corroboration by every step in the history of this family and of their relations.

The characteristic Norman addition to the high military spirit, of religious devotion, showed itself early in Simon. He built the castle of Northampton, Dugdale says, in 1084, and at the same time the priory of St.Andrew's near his castle. It had hierarchical subordination to the abbey of our Lady of Charity in France, which was on his father's, and ultimately his own, French properties. To this also Leland has a valuable note."'St.Andrews the late Monastery of Black Monks stood yn the North Parte of the Toune hard by the North Gate. Simon Saincteliz [Beyng the first in Burton] the first beyng Erle of Northampton and Huntendene made this House; but he is not buried there; for he died in Fraunce and there buried'".

He was earlier than his relation Eudo Dapifer in this field of religious English foundation. It is noticeable that among the descendants of William Sinclair, the son of Walderne, earl of St.Clare, to the smallest and latest proprietors of them, the necessity to their spiritual imagination of communication in things above the material world, with all its pomps and vanities, kept asserting itself in the form of sacred building and provision for the intellect and emotions. It was not so specially remarkable in times when it was the fashion to make such offerings under Roman Catholic rule, though it is true that no name has been more liberal in this way so long as real religious imagination showed itself at actual work. Neglect of the religious necessities for the limited and purely secular political ones, is no attribute of mastery, but the reverse; and a people wisely, or, indeed, instinctively shuns the leaders or higher classes who trust to the raw logic of facts, which are really not true facts till lit by the glow of disciplined imagination.

Simon was one of those Knights Templar who so romantically united the secular and religious. Kennet in his Parochial Antiquities shows that he gave them the manor of Merton, in Oxfordshire; and that he took personal part in their doings is shown by the fact that he went to the Holy Land, where he had probably been often before, in the last year of his life. It was on his returning for England that he died at his French home in 1115, and was buried there in his dearly loved abbey, De Caritate. But his gifts were not limited to these institutions. There is record of him giving the fruits of the church of Pidington to the priory of St.Fridiswidde in Oxford; and, to the priory of Daventry, the produce of several of his churches. These are only accidental survivals of record, and but indicate much other similar grant. His endowment of his own monastery of St.Andrews, built wholly to his mind, was of the same extensive kind as that of St.John's Abbey at Colchester. One item is sufliciently suggestive of the whole. He gave by his first charter the third part of the annual produce of his land jure uxoris, of Daventria, and various tithes besides of that extensive district. The full charter is in existence and the giving of it had national importance, as can be seen from the signatures.

It was in 8 Henry I,(1108) two years after Eudo Dapifer had begun to build at Colchester that a second carta Simonis comitis was granted for St.Andrews, Northampton The names attached are, Henry king of the Engish; Matilda, the queen; Anselm, archbishop; Robert, bishop of Lincoln; Robert, bishop of Chester; John bishop of Lys; Samson, bishop; John, bishop of Bayeux, in Normandy; Gundulph, the architectural bishop of Rochester; Maurice bishop of London; Ranulp, the chancellor; Henry, count of Warwick; William, count of Warenne; Nigell of Oily, the magnate if Oxfordshire; Robert of Ferrers, that of Derby; Eudo Dapifer: William of Aubeney, the bravest warrior of Tenchbrai battle, and son-m-law of Simon Sinclair; William of Curcy Robert, count de Mellent; and David of Scotland brother of the queen. The whole of Stoberiam was part of this second charter. It would only be about generous and very mportant work that such a list of England's best could be engaged, and there is no need to illustrate his religious doings further.

He was one of Henry I's chief nobles, and was a witness to the monarch's charter of public liberties given at the beginning of his reign. Henry addressed it to Hugh de Boclande, then vicecomes or sheriff of Hereford, whom he loved and promoted greatly afterwards. There is a copy of it in Matthew Paris's history. In Baker's History of Northamptonshire there are many facts collected about Simon, and one of his writings, without a date, has equally political and religious interest. It was testified by it that Robert de Pinkeney in Simon's presence at Northampton, granted to the church and monks of St.Andrews all the fee which Godfrey and Gero held of him in Sulgrave by service of one knight; and the earl addresses it, "To all my faithful men of Northamptonshire and Huntingdonshire". High feudal spirit shows well through these words.

The civil condition of things was founded on the obedience and loyalty which make an army the perfect instrument for its work. Fortunately or unfortunately, the existence of women and children is chronically antagonistic to such a system of civil drill, and only at intervals can there be approach to the esprit du corps of men of war among a population. It is not without its beauty when seen, and speaks considerably in favour of the ruling and ruled of the period. Weak idealists alone keep dreaming of armies of factory men and factory girls under captains of industry conquering the ills of life successfully. The direction of effort by order is of greatest value, but mere martinetcy is never more out of place than in such a field. Necessities of soul and body are better guides than any captains of industry, though all personal high action, if it is anything other than pretence and imposture, deserves honour, but not suicidal worship. The system of things and humanity was made according to no high-pressure theories of hysterical and, in practice, fitful and inefficient labour, but in accordance with the suffering and doing as they can, which are, and have been, and always shall be, the chequered lot of men. No one will choose to die young of famine, for the tragic beauty of the business; and even to die so is nothing so unknown to human experiences that we are to madden ourselves into frantic dervishes about the matter.

This great feudal lord, "Simon Sylvanectensis", as Leland in his Collectanea himself calls him, thus answering his own statement that his name was Saincteliz, lived one of the splendid, active, and religious lives of his time; and his faithful men of Northamptonshire and Huntingdonshire have descendants who are still proud of him and of his many deeds. In the Collectanea Lelandi, edited by Thomas Hearne, the antiquary, one hundred years ago from the MS. in the Bodleian library at Oxford, there are even explanations that St.Liz was only the name of the town from which Simon came to England, and not a true surname. Leland makes the abbreviation from a history of Normandy which he had met - "'The St.Liz or Senlian city is in Normandy'". The word originally may have meant the wood-encircled place, though the saintly fashion of crusading times had taken it past Senlis to Saincteliz and to the best-known form in English genealogies, St.Liz. Leland himself, if he had thought of it long enough, would probably find himself agreeing with the Northamptonians of the sixteenth century, that this was the local surname of the feudal Normandy, and that the family surname was, as they had told him on the best authority for such matters, Sinclair, Sancto Claro, St.Cleere, St.Clare, or other of the many forms of the racial surname.

Chapter XIX
Simon's Sons and Daughter

Simon, Waltheof, Henry, William, and Matilda were the family of him of whom the Magna Britannia (a kind of supplement to Camden's Britannia, edited by Cox and others) says that he was one of the Conqueror's captains who came with him out of Normandy, the first Earl Simon. His devotion to the church brought its fruits. Waltheof, named after his brave but unfortunate maternal grandfather of Saxo-Danish lineage, became a priest, and ended as the head of that monastery which, to be seen, must be visited by moonlight, with Sir Walter Scott as guide. The

>"'Slender shafts of shapely stone,
> By foliage tracery combined'",

which has made Melrose Abbey one of the jewels of, particularly the literary imagination, may not have then been in existence. It is supposed that the Culdees, or "worshippers of God", had their divine house near there; and with the passion, and probably freemason privilege, of Sinclairs for architectural beauties, this Waltheof, abbot of Melrose, in the twelfth century, is responsible for some if not all of the Gothic features of the most lovely remnant of the great and greatly genuine church. If so, he can easily be forgiven for forsaking the warlike traditions of his race on both sides, and clinging to the houses of God. They are, or were, the homes of peace, civilisation, and art, where the hardest of all battle ought continually to be waged against the hordes of what is essentially ugly and unholy. He is known in the Roman Catholic calendar as St.Waltheof, and takes a high place among the saints as the second abbot of Melrose. The Acta Sanctorum of the Bolandists, under his day, the third of August, gives much biographical detail, as also do the annals of the Cistercian order of monks, he being the most ascetic of this devoted part of the clergy. Butler's Lives of the Saints may have attention. In old Fordun's Scotichronicon there are many references to this high clerical Sinclair, whose lineage had in it the double Saxon royal alliance which caused Stephen to oppose his election to the archbishopric of York. Billings says that the reason of the opposition (and it was

143

successful) came from the danger that his promotion would give influence to the rival house.

It was in 1148 that Waltheof was transferred from Rievalle to Melrose; and the abbey, being founded in 1136 by King David, "'the sore saint for the crown'", it must have been still in the process of building under the rule of Abbot Waltheof. The Norman features which puzzle architects owe their origin to him. He wrought many miracles, if the religious chapbooks may be believed. He ordered a priest who shuddered to drink the wine with a spider in the cup to gulp all, and some days after, the father being ill of the experiment, he took the spider out at his thumb, to monastic and popular general admiration, if not worship. In a time of famine he fed all the inhabitants of Tweeddale miraculously. It is possible that his English relations, and powerful Scottish ones also, "semi-royal", as Billings calls them, thought otherwise. Last of all, in hagiographic art - "'Incorruption of the holy body and health restored to many sick people at the sepulchre of the saint'". Several times his remains were raised for the spiritual refreshment got from the sweet odours which exhaled, but a jealous successor, as is said, shut up the mortuary chapel. It was the age of Thomas Becket. Vide his list of miracles, and judge softly of human intellect.

The Chronica de Mailros, which ought to be the best authority, has - "'In the year 1148 Waltheof, the brother of Henry, earl of the Northumbrians, and of Simon, earl of Northampton, was made abbot of Melrose'". Another passage is - "'In the year 1159 died Waltheof of pious memory, the second abbot of Melrose, on the third of the nones of August, who was the uncle of the king, Malcolm'". Of the brother Henry much could be found, but this of itself gives him something of a history. How he held the earldom of Northumberland must have been through his mother's rights, as heiress of Siward and of the great Waltheof beheaded in the Conqueror's reign. Whether Henry founded a family is in some respects doubtful because of the succession of the Mowbrays and Percies or Louvaines to the northern dignity.

William, whose sonship to the first Simon is not so directly authenticated, was the archdeacon of Northampton whom Leland calls "the brother to one of the Simon Saincteclcres", and who, he says, was the original founder of St.John's Hospital there, still existing in 1542. What fixes or seems to fix him as the brother of the second Simon, is that it was to William, archdeacon of Northampton, Stephen once ordered Geffrey Mandeville to deliver up the tower of London on the penalties. The clergy were entrapped into crowning Stephen king, by Hugh Bigod Dapifer's tale from Henry I's deathbed, and the religious bonds of this family would compel them to hold by the performed public act of the archbishop of Canterbury. Their ties of lineage enlisted them on the side of Matilda, if the church interest had not been so powerful. That the archdeacon was of the right metal, too, may be understood from his ability, and no doubt desire, to take the command of London for Stephen's side. Archbishops, as for example the Conqueror's brother Odo, earl of Kent, and others of high clerical dignity, were then versed not only in secretarial state business but in actual military commands, and Archdeacon Sinclair had evidently the strong hand equal to the able head. Dugdale says that it was William, archdeacon of Huntingdon, in the reign of King John, who was ordered to receive the tower of London, and from one of the later Mandevilles. If so, then William, archdeacon of Northampton, must rest on the laurels of being the founder of St.John's Hospital, and of being the Sinclair of Leland's reference, nothing further being found of him as yet. The brother or nephew of men so high in state and church, himself also high in the latter, must have had considerable public connections could they be discovered. The late John Sinclair, archdeacon of Middlesex, was kinsman to this ancient churchman, but by the princely Scottish line.

History is at best so tantalising that it only gives glimpses of those we should wish to see fully, and what "George Eliot" has supposed one of her characters as thinking of this science, is often not very wide of the mark: "It is an ingenious process of guessing". Let any one read our recognised and really able historians like Macaulay,Froude, Freeman, Buckle, or Bishop Stubbs, and then go and bury himself for some year or two, or ten, among the original records, and he will come back with a shining and somewhat contented face, and probably with an exclamation something after the form of Solomon's celebrated one, "Poetry of poetries, all is poetry !" This is said, not to discredit history and historians, for they are good, and sometimes great, but to give confidence to timid worshippers in the shrine of fact and imagination, which are inextricably mixed, that they also may enjoy savingly the freedoms of all truly spiritual lands. Let pedants shake their heads off. There need be no anathematising of the most laborious plodders, who are often of infinite even when accidental service; but, referring all things to human head and heart which God has given, let us trust what such oracle tells finally in historical and all other subjects of hell, earth, or heaven. Those who do not like the style have wide field elsewhere, and waste enough for ears short or long. As the Melrose Abbey inscription put it:

> "'The earth builds on the earth castles and towers;
> The earth says to the earth, "All shall be ours"'"

But while we inhabit our tabernacle of earth or clay, castles and towers and their inhabitants will always have their interest to us, however small and insufficient the glimpses got through crevice or loophole of stone or flesh; and let no man browbeat us with his specially skilful microscopic or telescopic success of inspection, when the matter is all of degree, and small degree. The finest scholastic weapons are useless, if there is really no seeing eye behind them, and a deep heart into which to convey its ever partial but inspiring messages.

Simon, the eldest, was the heir to his father's titles, and to much of his estate; and of Stephen he was one of the most faithful and consistent supporters. There were reasons for his adherence, besides the sympathy for the church's engagements through its chief officers. He had been most roughly used by Henry I, or, to be more accurate, by his queen, Matilda, and her Scottish brother David, afterwards king of Scotland. As a boy, Simon had been sent to France to finish his education, according to the beautiful ceremonies of chivalry. His mother Matilda, the widow of the first Earl Simon, had married this brother of Henry's queen, and had possession of the earldoms while the youth was in nonage. When the time came that the young Simon was about to claim his rights, an excuse was needed to keep him out of them. One of England's best nobles had been banished by Henry, and happened to have a son going through the chivalrous curriculum of page aspirant for knighthood in the same home with Simon. Warnings are said to have been given to the heir of Northampton and Huntingdon, not to take his knighthood in usual public form with the offending noble's son. Whether they reached him, or never were sent, he kept friendly with his young comrade; and not only did they take the feudal degree together, but immediately afterwards went off jousting and performing deeds of derring-do, to the indignation, real or feigned, of the Scottish faction who had Henry in their interest. Young Simon's troubles began, and he may well have cursed that bane of England even so early as then, the mixture of royalty with nobility.

Indeed, if the family nature of English politics, from the arrival of William the Conqueror, is not closely recognised, true ideas cannot be got of the kingdom's history. Nobles were sometimes compelled to be ambitious, if they wished to exist at all. The successor of Malcolm, the husband of Margaret Atheling, was King Alexander of Scotland, their son. This David was his brother, Simon's scheming saintly Tartuffe stepfather. When Alexander died, David became king of Scotland, but matters grew little better for the stepson. The Scotsmen did not lose their liking for the southern pastures. David's son, Henry, was the next competitor against whom Simon had to contend in such troublous times as those of Stephen. This Henry paid homage to Stephen for Huntingdon;

which probably Queen Matilda, the mother of Henry and Simon, thought she, through her father and mother, Waltheof and Judith, had the right to do her will with; and in Stephen the adventurer's time of need, Henry had Doncaster, Carlisle, and other grants made very freely. That it is easy to be generous with what is not one's own, is a proverb; and it was of first importance to secure the aid of the Scottish faction in England, by being liberal to the northern sovereign's relations.

Stephen set Henry on his right hand at one of the early meetings with his lords and the clergy, but this was too much even for them, and Henry had to bear the scorn of at least two, who rose and left the court, viz., William, the archbishop of Canterbury and the earl of Chester. This was the William of Corbeil who was elected amid some difficulties at Gloucester in 1123, and the relation of Sir Robert Fitz-Hamo, the "knight of Rye", whose father was earl of Corbeil in Kormandy. The archbishop had not only general and hierarchical reasons for his contempt of Stephen's flattery, but those of consanguinity, since he knew of the injustice systematically being done to Simon. This Henry of Huntingdon was married to Ada, daughter to William, earl of Warenne, and they had three daughters, Ada married to the earl of Holland, Margaret to Conan, earl of Britanny, and Maud who died young. He had therefore English and French connection as well as Scottish to aid him. His sons were Malcolm and William, successively Scottish kings, and the David, earl of Huntingdon and of Carrick, well known to history as the ancestor of the ladies through whom the claims for the Scottish crown were made by Bruce, Baliol, and others in the time of Edward I. On the death of David's father Henry, Simon the disinherited half-brother got at last his rights in great part, 1152.

He had taken his side in the wars long before. He fought hard for Stephen, at Lincoln in 1141 unsuccessfully, and elsewhere otherwise. One of Leland's abbreviations is, Simon comes Hamptoniensis in eodem bello adhaesit Stephano. Robert, earl of Gloucester, champion of Matilda, his sister, and married to Matilda Sinclair, daughter of the "knight of Rye", said then at Lincoln of Simon, his opponent, that he was forward in promises and slow in performing them. His state of life a continual doubt and difficulty among royalties and their needs and ambitions, may have made this quite true. He never does seem to have acted with sufficient promptitude, or perhaps they might have been more careful of meddling with his proper rights. That he was in culture like the best of his time, however, is shown by his founding the nunnery De La Pree near Northampton, the abbey of Saltrez, Huntingdon, and by giving the church returns of Southwick to the Knights Templar, of whom, like his father, he was one. The hereditary love of castle-building is shown by

Bridges's statement that he built Fotheringay, the scene of the last moments of Mary, queen of Scots.

A contemporary chronicle, extant among the Cottonian MSS., says that David, the queen's brother, was made earl of Huntingdon and Northampton by Henry his brother-in-law, on the death of the first Simon; but Nicolas thinks he was only given Huntingdon, and Baker also follows this version. Undoubtedly most of the quarrelling took place about Huntingdon, and during the life of the second Simon's successor too; but the fact was that David had actual possession of the one earldom by sovereign's gift, and tenure of the other till the sovereign should relent in favour of Simon. That Simon had possession of Northampton early in Stephen's reign, could alone explain his support of the usurper. The death of his stepfather in 1152, restored his inheritance to him, and he took forcible possession of Huntingdon.

He did not long enjoy the double earldom, for he died the next year. When Stephen made the peace with Matilda and her son Henry, by which the latter was to become king after his decease, Dugdale says no man stood more opposite to the treaty than Simon. It is supposed that his anger was so roused at the turn affairs took that he died then and there, of his passion for consistency and battle to the last. He was the first of its founder's family who was buried in St.Andrews, unless the Lady Margaret, whose "Tumbe" Leland says was the wonder of the monastery, had been his aunt, and died before him. She was certainly one of the family, the antiquary shows, and he adds, "'But Erle Simon the secunde and Erle Simon the 3, sunne to the secunde were booth buried in S.Andreas'". Simon the second earl's wife was Isabel Bellamont, daughter of the earl of Leicester. To one of the ladies of this family "Strongbow", the conqueror of Ireland, was married. Simon had such and other strong support, but it is not fair struggle between a subject and sovereigns, even with right on the side of the former. His widow married Gervase Paganell, Baron Someri de Dudley, co. Stafford. In her widowhood she had put herself under the protection of her nephew, Robert, earl of Leicester, with regard to the lands of Bradfield, Botinden, Norfield, and Waltham. It would be interesting to know that this was the Waltham of the Mandevilles, and, if so, how she had got it.

Matilda, this Simon's sister, has to have her story told. She was first married in 1112 to Robert Fitz-Richard Clare, one of the Tunbridge family, of whom Eudo Dapifer's wife was so illustrious a lady. He was the lord of Baynard's Castle, London, on Thames bank at Blackfriars, and baron of Dunmow, Essex, the fifth son of Richard Clare, the justice of England. After Eudo's death in 1120, he got the dapifership from

Henry I, probably because he was brother-in-law to this previous dapifer. The Monasticon shows how greatly favoured Dunmow was by Matilda Sinclair and her husband, Robert Clare Dapifer. He is the ancestor of the celebrated English family of Fitz-Walters, who were really Clares, though also hidden by the unfortunate methods of surnaming. There is a charter where "Robertus filius Richardi" occurs, 1 Stephen (1135), among the codices of Corpus Christi College, Cambridge, as dapiferus. In 11 Stephen, Matilda's second husband, Saher de Quincy, was made lord of Daventry, jure uxoris, and from this marriage came the earls of Winchester. When King John was quarrelling with his barons in 1215, Saher, earl of Winchester, son or grandson of this De Quincy, with the aid of foreigners besieged Colchester Castle, but ultimately had to withdraw and go towards St.Edmonsbury. The castle was defended successfully by William Longueville, the husband of a Sinclair lady, whose tale will be told hereafter.

Dugdale says that the William de Albini (called Brito to distinguish him from William de Albini Pincerna, official butler or cup-bearer of coronation day, and the earl of Arundel) was married to Maude de St.Liz, the widow of Robert Dapifer, and daughter of the first Earl Simon. If so, it was before 11 Stephen, when Saher de Quincy heirs some of her rights as his wife. Like Isabella, countess of Gloucester, afterwards the wife of King John, of Geffrey Mandeville, and, The Baronage says, of the great Hubert de Burgh, Matilda also had three distinguished husbands. It was Albini's personal valour which broke the lines of Duke Robert, and gained the battle of Tenchbrai for his brother Henry, in 1106. The charters of this reign are signed as frequently by him as by Eudo Dapifer, and he probably had an official position at court. This Albini Brito's son was William Meschines, and from him came the earls of Cambridge.

Of his lands Aelard Sinclair held two knights' fees. After the drowning of the royal heir, William, in the White Ship, 1119, Henry I (1127) got his lords to promise their feudal support to his daughter Matilda, In the Black Book of the royal exchequer, Liber Niger scaccarii, the name Adelard de Saincler appears on the carta of promise of Willelmi de Albenni, baron. He is of Leicestershire, and promises to furnish in the usual way the two mililes of his two knights' fees of land in case of war. It is the same Aelard Sinclair who holds under the father and the son, and he was a scion of the house of which Matilda Sinclair, this wife of William de Albini of Belvoir Castle, was so remarkable a daughter. Macaulay has the stirring line in his Armada fragment, "'Till Belvoir's lordly terraces the sign to Lincoln sent'"; which sufficiently localises and characterises her home, to the north of Melton Mowbray on the furthest boundary of Leicestershire, now the seat of the duke of Rutland.

The great Northumbrian, Nigel Mowbray, was son of Roger de Albini, and took the new name when he got the dispossessed earl's lands. It was he who married the countess dowager of Gloucester, Matilda Sinclair, widow of Robert Consul, son of Henry I. The Priory, Fawsley hundred, had much of the other Matilda's patronage. Her steward or seneschal was Hugh, vicecomes of Leicester. This monastery was founded first at Preston Capes, a place that has connection with Sinclairs at much later periods, but Hugh got the consent of the first Earl Simon, the lord of the district, to change it to a site near the parish church. The advowsons of it he gave ultimately to Matilda, and she, patrona et domina, was not sparing in her own gifts of land, ceremonial vessels, priestly dresses, and other similar necessities and ornament. Among the women of her time, she is eminent as a donor of spiritualities.

Daventry priory also got from the family, and from such adherents or relations as Hugh, much property for mortuary benefits, as well as from the general and earlier liberality of founders and their friends. Hugh had many such gifts from the first earl, Matilda's father, as that of Thorp Mandeville, part of which belonged to Farthingo, another more recent Sinclair property, and much of lands so got seems to have been heired by Matilda, or given by them in conjunction, or by arrangement, to the monasteries which they favoured. Washington manor, one of the gifts of Matilda or her father to St.Andrews priory, it might be risked supposing, was the original home of the greatest American president. The present earls of Dartmouth claim to have the right English Washington family arms somewhere on their shields, and the Washingtons of the midlands are meant. The church of Duston of the Peverel fee belonged to the Simon of Henry II's time, and to him the next step is taken.

Chapter XX
Simon Sinclair, Third and Last Earl

To the earldom of Northampton there was immediate succession on death of his father for the third Simon; but Huntingdon, so lately possessed, was again wrenched from the grasp of the true heirs. The politics of the two kingdoms required that Simon should go to the wall; but he was a determined and able man, and fought well this and many another battle, civil and military. Malcolm, now king of Scotland, son of Henry who held the earldom of Huntingdon till his death in 1152, revived the old subject, and in exchange for part of the north of England, which he had overrun, got it, to the exclusion of its protesting right lord. King Malcolm's brother, King William, "The Lion", also held it; but in the reign of Henry II, when his undutiful son rose in rebellion while his father was in Normandy, matters cleared up, after this and the other family storms raised by Eleanor of Aquitaine and their sons against the gallant Harry. The earls of Leicester, Chester, and Derby were against him in England, while his son Richard had his defeat in pitched battle in France. King William of Scotland, like enough to Shakespeare's "weasel", did not fail to try the chance of the scramble. Simon was one of Harry's trusted and tried captains of war. The rebel earls had seized and strengthened Huntingdon Castle with King William's connivance, his brother David playing indefinable and waiting game. The castle was captured from the rebels. It was their chief stay, and the loss demoralised them. Simon had his king's warrant to take possession of it, as the rightful heir.

Benedict, the abbot of Peterborough, who wrote his chronicle of the reigns of Henry II and Richard I contemporarily, says that Richard de Luci, justiciar of the kingdom, delivered it to Count Simon by the mandate of the king: "'Because he had been calumniated in the king's court; the county of Huntingdon ought to be his by hereditary right; and the king granted it to him, if he could obtain it'". William of Scotland was compelled to give up all claims to it, on his own part and on that of his brother David. The striving, however, still went on bitterly between these two grandsons of Matilda, the daughter of Waltheof; and towards the end of his reign, Henry II settled the struggle by razing the noble structure to the ground, for the express purpose of healing one of the poisoned sores of the body politic of his kingdom.

To enter fully into the multitudes of intrigues, royal, noble, and common, which centred around the castle of Huntingdon might make a huge book. The lesson, though a long drawn-out one, is that if right is bravely contended for, it will in the end beat mere might. Till his death without heirs in 1184, Simon enjoyed this dearly gained earldom with his others. William of Scotland was made prisoner at Alnwick by Ranulph de Glanville, and had to pay for his intermeddling with purely English affairs by imprisonment, and a ransom. Stow says, of £4000, then a large sum. The excuse for the interference certainly lies in the alliance of the crowns, by the marriage of Henry I with Matilda of Scotland, the daughter of Margaret Atheling of the Saxon royal line of England. The embroglio of the rights, personal, political, and dynastic, was inextricable to human wit; and tragedies alone could clear such an atmosphere. There were quite new elements also at work in this stirring reign. Matilda's struggles had brought numbers of foreign adventurers, rank and file, into the country, lower types of men than the Normans. Her son Harry, with all his ability, perhaps was not the equal in genuine manhood to his predecessors of rightful claim. The Fulc blood was in him, and the Plantagenets may be well enough reckoned England's kingly diamonds of something less than the first water.

Very shortly before the accession of Henry, a charter was given to the church of Holy Trinity, Tottenham, London, by "Simon, earl of Northampton"; and, though undated, its signatures fix its time, and also give hint as to the kind of people then getting into the court circles. The carta is preserved among the Cottonian MSS. It is written very beautifully, on a piece of parchment seven or eight inches by five, to the extent of seven lines and a half; and some of the witnesses' names are suggestive of the beginning of the new time: Matilda, queen of the English; Custac, her daughter, a name and person perhaps not known out of this charter to record or history, English, French, or German; William of Ipres, the Flemish earl of Kent; Reimo of Dieppe; Richard de Bot; and other such barbarous names. Pet. de Hoo was a name that came to fame afterwards in Sussex, but there is a distinct lack of the finer Norman somids of gallant historic names even then in Matilda's surroundings. England has had some reason to regret the unfortunate close of the kingly house of Rollo, though she boasts of great rulers since.

Simon had made a marriage which helped him the better to fight his case to the successful end. His wife was Alice Gaunt, sole heiress to her father, Gilbert Gaunt, earl of Lincoln. Earl of Northampton and of

Huntingdon, Simon had long been earl of Lincoln also, by the right of his wife. Her property was of splendid proportions. The first Gaunt was a nephew of William the Conqueror, and he had secured from his uncle one hundred and thirteen manors in Lincolnshire, with forty-one in other counties. In 12 Henry II (1166) when Thomas a Becket was figuring, there was an assessment made for the marriage of the king's daughter, and Simon, then only earl of Northampton, had sixty-eight knights' fees of old enfeoffment and twelve of new. If to these two earldoms be added the fees of the castle and honour of Huntingdon, the warlike, brilliant, and able captain of Henry II must be said to have succeeded; and perhaps he even surpassed in wealth and influence his grandfather, the Conqueror's favoured lame warrior. But this was not all his good fortune. He had two sisters, Amicia and Hawise, and though record does not seem to have preserved to whom they were married, they must have had bright and rich lives, because it is known that they were both under the king for feudal marriage. Kings took care to have justice out of their wards, and Henry is well known for his generosity to those who were thus in his custody. The irony of human fortune, however, is powerfully illustrated by the facts that Simon died childless, and that once again the bone of contention, Huntingdon, fell to Scottish royalty. His wife's property, with the earldom of Lincoln, went on her death to her uncle Robert, and Northampton became crown land. The last Earl Simon died in 1184, and was buried in the priory of St.Andrews, Northampton; the foundation of his grandfather, and the favoured monastery of his ancestors.

William, king of Scotland, had in 1174 gone back ransomed to Scotland, and Stow in his Annals has the curious tale that hearing that his nobles would not come to meet him farther than Peebles, twenty miles from the capital, "'he took with him many of the younger sons of noblemen in England that bare him good will, and gave them lands in Scotland, which he took from such as were rebels to him there'". Stow continues, "'The names of those gentlemen were Bayelliol, Brewse, Soully, Moubray, Saintclere, Hay, Giffard, Ramsay, Grame, etc'". It is to be feared that the "industrious" annalist is venturing too far from London, but most of his sayings are accurate.

Under "Lord Sinclair", Burke's Peerage has suggestive discussion of different lines of Scottish Sinclairs, as the Roslin and the Herdmanston, whose common origin cannot be traced to one ancestor on this side of the English Channel. If the Scottish Sinclairs first saw Edinburgh and Roslin then, history and records have been making the greatest mistakes; but it is quite possible that some of the English Sinclairs joined the descendants of Queen Margaret Atheling's dapifer at this period.

153

King William ten years after this got Huntingdon, and immediately gave it to his youngest brother David, whose daughters and their descendants were heirs of the Scottish crown, and the occasion of the Wallace and Bruce wars of independence, or of solution as to what Englishman should have the northern province of the island for which the Norman kings exacted the usual tributary homage. Northampton and afterwards Huntingdon fell into the sovereign's hands. For more than a hundred years the earldom of Northampton was in abeyance, till the Bohuns in 1337, earls of Hereford and Essex, constables of England, justices, and all that was well securable, got possession. They, too, became extinct, after some successions, in the person of a youth whose shoulders bore an unheard-of weight of hereditary and patrimonial honours and wealth.

Nothing is more pathetic than some of the sudden disappearances of English nobility, though it seemed to have all that could aid vitality. Simon's wife, Alice Gaunt, was buried at Bridlington monastery, the foundation of her grandfather Walter, earl of Lincoln. If mention is made that Braybrook manor, Rothwell hundred, was always part of the estates of the Simons, who are such singularly dramatic figures at the very heart of English and even of Scottish history, they may be left with their often chequered but always honourable glory.

Chapter XXI
Relations

A good reference to an ancient and authentic account of these Saincteliz and Sainctecleres is Langebek's Scriptores Rerum Danicarum. A collection of about a score of huge volumes, chiefly monastic Latin, it has one little tract in that language, rescued from antiquity, which gives a short but clear and consistent history of this branch of the Sinclair gens. It is particularly valuable for its attention to the more distant and perhaps external Danish and Saxon relationships. Judith and Waltheof, some say, had two daughters, while others mention three. Leland in his Colledaneum of abbreviations has, "'Primo genitam earum accepit Simon Sylvanectensis; aliam Radulphus de Thoeneio, scilicet Judith; tertiam Robertus filius Richard'". He adds that other writers number two daughters to Judith, Matilda and Alicia, the former married to the first Earl Simon from Senlis, and the latter to Radulph de Toneio. This is his own opinion, for he has, "'Matilda autem Matildae ex Simone filia nupsit Roberto filio Richardi'".

The fifth son of Richard Fitz-Gilbert of Tunbridge Castle has been noticed as the dapifer of England, baron of Dunmow, and married to Matilda Sinclair, sister of the second Simon and of Waltheof, abbot of Melrose, and daughter of the queen of David of Scotland. A valuable Harleian MS., which has a very full scheme of the relationships back to Aldred the Northumbrian and Ursus the Dane, follows the same version of two daughters. Alicia marries Radulph or Ralph Toneio, and they have a son Ralph. It also gives the Norman lineage of Judith herself, as being the daughter of Lambert, count of Lentz, in Artois. Among all the chroniclers it is agreed that she was the Conqueror's niece, being the daughter of his half-sister Maud, countess of Albemarle. Brady says that Roger, the father of Alice's husband, was standard-bearer of Normandy, an office hereditary. It was he who went a gallant young knight to the Spanish wars, and when returned to Normandy, finding Duke William, the son of Arlotta, the tanner's daughter, reigning, cost the young ruler all that sorrow of battle to thoroughly establish himself. Probably Ralph his son had his fortune somewhat limited by this, though there does not appear much sign of it.

He is Ralph of Conchis, in Norman history, and lord of Flamstead, Hampshire, in English; and he figured much in both. Brady says that Hampshire, and Dugdale that Hertfordshire, is the county for Flamstead. To Rufus he was, with Philip Bruce, Richard Courcy, Walter Giffard, Robert of Ou, Stephen of Albemarle, and Gerard of Gournay, bitterest enemy; so that his paternal traditions seem active enough.

But there are other relationships which have more direct bearings. If it had not been for the power of royal claimants, the third Simon might have found a successor of his own lineage. The second earl had a brother of the same name, Simon, who was a man of some importance. He gave land to the nunnery of De la Pree, Northampton, and had descendants. Vincent quotes the Latin charter, and other details of value, in his violent corrections of Yorke, the genealogist.

Simon may not have been legitimate, or the peculiarity of similar name might have occurred from being the son of the first earl by a second wife; but to his own property succeeded also Simon, who appears in the records of King John's reign. He had a quarrel with David, earl of Huntingdon, about a knight's fee, and he appealed to the king's favour by presenting him with a beautiful palfrey. If this can be taken as part of a struggle for imdoubted and legitimate rights of the line, it speaks volumes as to the disorder and injustice rampant about the end of the twelfth century in England. As noble a stock as was within its borders seems to have been sacrificed to political necessity and royal cupidity. The facts which survive are not sufficient to establish this, but it is known that these relations of the great Simon resided in the county Rutland, who probably from disgust, or from weariness and weakness of means to fight the prolonged battle, gave up claims. The earls of Denbigh trace themselves to this family of Rutland, which they say changed its name to Seton. Their ancestor Sir William Fielding married the last of that branch, an heiress, and the claim of being heir-general to the three Simon earls and their honours has been made for this modern house. The following is taken from state records: "'Calendarium Rotulorum Chartarum, Anno 19 Henry III, Simon de Seyntclere et Anna uxor ejus; Seyton boscus quiet de vasto et Regard forestae etc.; Rotel'".

It would be difiicult to say whether this is more valuable as a step for substantiating the Denbigh claim, or for completely proving the lineage of all the Simons to be Sinclair. Simon de Seton is the new local surname from the Rutland woody waste and forest district of which the above is part. The charter is proof of these Sinclairs of Huntingdon, Northampton, Lincoln, and Rutland till 1235. If there were no evidence than that connected with Simon Sinclair of Seyton, Rutlandshire, it is amply sufiicient of itself absolutely to establish the three Simon earls as Sinclairs. It would be an easy brief for a barrister, with which to succeed. The genealogists of the earls of Denbigh give valuable assistance to the present inquiry, and probably were successful about the relation of the Fieldings to these Sinclairs. The family in the beginning of the seventeenth century got their own earldom; and they are also barons St.Liz; in reality, if they did so prove relationship, barons Sinclair. Since 1622 there have been eight or nine of them, and they have figured as lords of the German empire as well as of England. Little can be drawn from the fact that several Senlis of plain rank appear at nearly every period in records, for they had no object in tracing lineage further than the Simons, what business they engage in necessitating the use of this name.

The Fieldings, says an old Peerage of 1710, were originally Germans of the house of Hapsburg, founded by Rodolph, and now represented by the emperor of Austria. The first Fielding here was Geoffrey; the second, Sir John; the third, William, to whom Agnes Seton, by local name, Sinclair by lineage, married. She brought him the lordship of Martinesthorpe in the county of Rutland, her descent in blood being "from those great families of Vaux, Longville, and Sellers, a younger branch of Mowbray".

But a world of speculation opens in discussing these Setons, if they are really Sinclairs. Under "Seton, earl of Winton", Burke writes, "'The first of the great house of Seton established in North Britain was Secher de Say, who had a grant from King David I of lands in East Lothian, which being called "Saytun" ("the dwelling of Say"), gave rise to a name and family which became pre-eminently distinguished in the annals of Scotland'". This is a somewhat lame account of the facts. "Secher de Say" was Sinclair of Seyton, one of the many Englishmen who went then to Edinburgh for fortune, and he brought the Rutland name with him to give it a new existence in Haddington, after the prevailing Norman habit. It is quite possible that Burke's explanation, "the town of Say", may apply to the place in Rutland, and that the Sinclairs may have come into possession of it through afiinity with the Says, with whom they were frequently connected. The present earl of Eglinton is the male representative of Secher de Say ton or Sinclair of Seton. John, brother of the third Lord Seton, "married Sinclair, heiress of Northrig, with whom he got these lands". But this is not the most curious effect of local names hiding true lineage in the present inquiry.

The dukes of Gordon, marquises of Huntly, earls of Sutherland, so celebrated in Scottish history as Gordons, are not Gordons at all, but Setons, and Setons are Sinclairs. The Gordons of Gight, of whom

Byron's mother was one, are of the same blood. The Hon. Robert Gordon of Gordonstown, Bart. of Nova Scotia, gentleman of the privy chamber to James I, the historian of his house, the earls of Sutherland, in the violent rivalry he shows existing between the earls of Caithness and Sutherland, and which he aided with all his power, seems a little ludicrous in his family enthusiasm in the light of the truth, to which he was unconscious, that the so-called Gordons and their enemies of the Roslin, Orkney, and Caithness line, were of exactly the same male stock. The Granville-Leveson-Gowers who are the heirs of the "Gordons" as dukes of Sutherland, have themselves Sinclair blood, by affinity, in them from a famous Devon family of Sinclairs. The "baronet" Gordons of Earlston began their line by marrying Margaret Sinclair, heiress of John Sinclair of Earlston, in 1582, just as the progenitor of the dukes of Argyle, the first MacCallum More of 1270 had a Sinclair lady, the ancestress of the Argyles and of the marquises of Breadalbane. To a Sinclair earl an Argyle Campbell married, and created the latest Scottish feud, which ended in a pitched battle, 1680, on the plains of Caithness. The real Gordons, of whom the slayer of Richard "Coeur de Lion" is supposed to have been one, were extinct about fourteen hundred, and did not take very special position. The earl of Aberdeen is descended from a younger line, and represents that lineage.

The Dunbar earls of March, the Comyns, the lords Ogilvy (earls of Airlie, and earls of Findlater, heirs of Sinclairs of Deskford and Findlater), the Hamiltons, and Douglases, were interknit with the various branches of these Setons in ways that give steady assurance of the great part family blood, names changed, and not, took in all position and power when feudalism was at its game. Christopher Seton, the brother-in-law, by his marriage to Christian Bruce, and the brave companion of Robert Bruce when defeated at the battle of Methven (in which Bruce dismounted Aymer de Valence, and was himself unhorsed by Philip Mowbray), was soon after, Barbour says, betrayed to the English, and executed, as well as his brother John de Seton.

> "'Where's Nigel Bruce? and De La Haye,
> And valiant Seton - where are they ?'"

Says Sir Walter Scott in his notes to The Lord of the Isles: "'There was some peculiarity respecting his punishment because, according to Matthew of Westminster, he was considered not as a Scottish subject, but an Englishman'". Hugh de la Haye, of the same male lineage as Seton, the Hayes likewise seeking and getting fortune in the northern district, was made prisoner, but did not share the fate of the more distinguished Christopher. Matthew of Westminster's notice is of much importance, in itself, and as referring to an early period of the history of the Setons, who afterwards figured prominently as Scottish earls of highest offices and account in the kingdom.

In a history of the castle of Oakham and its manor and pertinents, which appears bound up in the state record called The Hundred Rolls of Edward I's time, though the piece under notice was written in that of Edward III, there appears to have been an heiress Sinclair proprietrix in capite of Oakham Castle. The King had the marriage of her, and she is called in the Latin Domina Sencha when he marries her to his brother, the lord Richard, king of the Romans, earl of Cornwall, circa 1250. If this was one of them, the descendants of the Simons cannot have lost skill of keeping in high rank. But Burke probably gives in the Royal Lineage the right account, that she was the third daughter of Raymond Berenger, the second being married to the brother, Henry III. The personages are too prominent for any mistake to have been made.

It has been with many peoples besides the English a continual popular enterprise to turn the "l" out of languages, and this strange spelling, even if deciphered correctly from the MSS. for the printers, must have suffered in that way. Leland, the antiquary, says her heart was buried in the abbey church of Cirencester, Gloucestershire. It would be risking too much, and quite unnecessarily, to say that such a name as Simon de Segre, who held a fee from William de Clifford, as recorded in the Testa de Nevill, had any genealogical reference at present, being as probably Saker, which is a frequent English name. In Scotland as late as the convention of Stirling, 1544, the signature "Willm Lorde Sanchar", is written for Lord Sinclair. Etymologies must not, however, be encouraged much in this line of inquiry.

There is no doubt about one Simon of the reign of King John. He is Simon de Sencler of Buckinghamshire in state records. This is the same spelling as the hero of Hastings, Richard, has in Domesday, and which his brother Britel, son of Walderne, earl of St.Clare, has in the Exon Domesday. He was not the Simon of Huntingdon who contended with Earl David, the Scot. That he would have been able to contend with some purpose can be gathered from the offices in which the records find him employed. One of the chief duties, as well as the most troublesome, of sheriffs or viscounts was to settle disputes of boundaries between properties. The king used to summon three or four milites or gentlemen of a county where any dispute needed settling, and they were called upon to elect twelve milites, or holders of at least some part of a military fee, to be a jury of arbiters. This scrap of survival does not fix Simon as sheriff or viscount, but it indicates clearly his value and weight as versed in the class of work, and having special authority of some kind. It is of interest to find one of the Northampton house so busy in civil affairs, and it is likely that at such a period he was equally energetic in military.

Aelard de Saincler has been referred to under the second Simon as holding two knights' fees under William of Aubeni Brito in Leicestershire during Henry II's reign. William of Aubeni, descended from the Toenis, was married to Maud Sinclair of the Earl Simon family; and Aelard got thus his property in that county; but he is still better known as of Harpolle, in the Newbottle hundred, Northamptonshire, where several generations of his descendants continued. He also had the manor of Lobenham there, as well as other properties. His father was James de St.Clair, and he had a sister Maud, who was countess of Clare and Hertford, being married to Roger de Clare, earl of Clare and Hertford, the heir of the Tunbridge Castle traditions. Sir Henry Chauncey in his history of Hertfordshire, and Blomfield in that of Norfolk, are authorities for this. Maud was married 12 Henry II (1166) and in the same year Roger gave 149 as the number of his knights' fees, on the taxing for the marriage of the king's daughter. He died in 1173, and was succeeded by their son Richard, who added the earldom of Gloucester to the two earldoms his father held. Says Blomfield, "'In 1182, Maud, daughter of James de St.Hillary, countess of Clare, and widow of Roger, earl of Clare, the founder, gave this preceptory (Great-Carbrook, Norfolk), which was not finished or fully endowed by her husband, to the Knights Hospitallers of St.John of Jerusalem, with the churches of Great and Little Carbrook, and the moiety of the town, on condition they paid 13/4d - yearly to the nuns of Buckland, all which was confirmed by Richard de Clare, earl of Hertford, her son, and King John, in 1199, from which time she was declared foundress of this house'". Bridges, an able and fruitful antiquary, in his history of Northamptonshire, gives the valuable information that the Sinclairs and the St.Hillaries were the same people. This connection of theirs with the Clares, therefore, was but the reviving of many previous similar ties.

In the reign of Henry III another Alard was in possession of Harpole, Lobenham, and the Leicestershire properties; and it is of him Bridges writes. "'This Alard de Seynteler was the ancestor of the family in late records named St.Hilary'". On the carta of William of Albenni, the first Alard has his name spelt "Aelardus de Saincler"; but the "c" gets faint through interchange with Seynt Liz, the alternate name, and is lost gradually. Seynteler grew to be Seynt Eler or Seynt Elerio, and by aspiration ended in "the St.Hilary of later records". It is wise to shun changes of names by local pronunciation as of value, except on the one condition of proof being got otherwise in the first place. They are corroboration, however, in addition to facts, or at least may be allowed to be illustrative. There is no question of discussion at all, the unity of the names being acknowledged. Alard de Seynteler in the reign of Henry III gave to the convent of St.Albans two parts of both the great and small tithes of his manors of Horpol and Lobenham, and one half acre of arable land in Horpol. His successors, Peter, William, and Thomas Sinclair are donors to St.Albans.

One of the quaintest survivals of monasterial life is the abbot of St.Alban's astute recovery of the lands and gifts of these Sinclairs as late as 1427, which had been taken possession of by Dominus William Cheselden, the rector of the district, to the loss of the abbey. There are several pages in the Chronicle of St.Albans describing minutely the whole business in monastic Latin. How the abbot got the dean of arches to dine at St.Albans; and how he skilfully broaclied the subject of his wrong; and how the dean did not resent the mixture of business with pleasure, but directed the abbot to go and consult with the bishop of Durham, in whose diocese Northampton then was; and how month after month for a couple of years, a legal process went on under the favouring and fostering care of the dean; and how finally the monastery of St.Albans and its skilful abbot got their full rights, and perhaps more; are told with an infantile inimitability that is quite out of the power of the modern brain. These Seyntclers or St.Hilaries, or Sinclairs in the right spelling, were in themselves (if they had no connection with the Simon earls of Huntingdon, Lincoln, and Northampton, as also of Cumberland, Westmoreland, and Northumberland, had the earls prosecuted their rights from the jura uxorem they had; or if they had no affinity to the earls of Clare, Hertford, and Gloucester; of remarkable territorial and general distinction.

With the Albennis of Belvoir Castle they are knit many ways. In 24 Edward I (1296), Richard de St.Hilary or Sinclair holds among his other lands a half knight's fee from Comyn, Baliol, and Bruce's rival for a throne in 1291 at Norham, namely, Robert de Bos of his own lineage, who married Isabel, the daughter of William of Albenni, and so became possessed of the honour of Belvoir. Thomas and his wife Maud were in 1 Edward III (1327) to get Upton, but it went instead to Piers Gaveston, the favourite. In 9 Edward II (1316) one of the Sinclairs is noted as holding lands from this honour or barony, and in 6 Edward III (1332) Thomas Sinclair succeeds Edmund de Pinkeney, who had temporary possession of some of his lands. In 20 Edward III (1346) he holds lands from the honour of Belvoir, which in 37 Edward III (1364) John de Sco Claro held. Sir William Vaux and Ralph Hastings succeeded him. The Vauxes will appear hereafter, in the story of the earls of Bath.

This inexhaustible field of inquiry must be ended with drawing attention to the continual recurrence of names connected with the kings of Scotland, through the ties between them and the Earls Simon of the earldom of Huntingdon in particular, about which the Scots strove long, and too successfully for the justice of things. Pinkeney, Hastings, Ros, are names competing for the Scottish crown in Edward I's reign.

The indications are clear enough that families of standing survived the three Simons so well known to history, and reflection of their true lineage comes back in these by no means obscure instances. Without even such suggestive aid as Leland's, they are absolute proof. Let the above be final words with regard to the Sinclairs who with other claims, were the earls of Northampton, Huntingdon, and Lincoln shires, and who probably had Norman and French titles and lands besides, if investigation were made beyond the Channel.

Chapter XXII
The Countess of Gloucester

It may be a more difficult and less successful undertaking to show that Matilda, the wife of Robert, earl of Gloucester, the able son of Henry I, was Sinclair in lineage; but it is impossible to escape the task, if respect ought to be paid to most suggestive and, it may be, wholly settling evidence. The king's son was born out of wedlock, by Nesta, daughter of Rhees ap Tudor, prince of South Wales, the same blood as Queen Elizabeth afterwards. He is one of the familiar figures of history, as the champion of his sister Matilda, the empress, against Stephen, and there was no better man of his period. Fosbrooke, in his History of Gloucester speaks enthusiastically of him as a great and most excellent nobleman. Patron of the useful chronicler, William of Malmesbury, was one of his many distinguishing impersonations. His eulogist writes of him as having "'a character of delicious contemplation'". The Tewkesbury Chronicle says he was born in Normandy, before the death of his grandfather, the Conqueror. When he got earldom or consulatum from his father, he was usually called Robert Consul, but he is also named Robert Melhent.

It is of his countess, however, that description is required. She was the daughter of Robert Fitz-Hamo, the famous "knight of Rye", by his second wife, Sibil de Montgomery, daughter of Roger de Montgomery, earl of Shrewsbury. A Cottonian manuscript says she was their only daughter and heir, but Matilda had three sisters. She and her husband, the king's son, by her right, heired also some of the confiscated property of the fiercest man of the reign, and perhaps one of the worst treated, Robert de Belesme, whose lineage name was Montgomery, she being his niece. This was after the famous forty-five charges drove him to Normandy for his life. The Montgomeries were at the Conquest about the most powerful of the Norman families, having got very large possessions from the Conqueror in all parts of England. The bitterness which ordinary historians ascribe to Henry I with regard to this nobleman, finds its rational, if hardly a delightful explanation, in the relationship thus shown.

William of Jumieges is monastically particular in telling of the thirteen love children whom Beauclerc, the pet monarch of the priests, had to provide about and great necessities excuse many things, possibly covetousness with the other venial sins of royalties. One thing has to be said, that better sons and daughters than they were, fall rarely to the lot of kings, no matter what the hierarchical precautions and training may be. It is something to be thankful about, as saving noble fellow-souls from being broken-spirited outcasts for life, to remember that some of the world's altogether best creatures have first seen light out of the usual fold. Virtue of the deepest kind acknowledges this, while with earnest warning voice at the same time it accepts the facts as the exceptional, to prove at once the rule of restraint and the danger of spiritual pride. A son like Robert, earl of Gloucester, was a joy to a father which only made the grief the keener that he could not hand his sceptre after him to such capable hands. As it was, through paternal favour and his marriage with Matilda Sinclair, he became the richest and most powerful next to the sovereign. The shortest proof of what he gathered is that their son, William, earl of Gloucester, in the aid for marriage of the king's daughter, 12 Henry II (1166), was assessed for 22.5 knights' fees of land in Kent, and 260.5 old with 13.5 new enfeoffment elsewhere. And there are indications that William's generosity was decreasing rather than increasing his parents' wonderfully numerous estates.

But this was not all. With Matilda, Robert also got a great inheritance in Normandy. William Gemeticensis gives a full account of it. He says that Matilda's name was Sibil, and not the name of her mother, who was Mabel Montgomery; but he is wrong. His account, however, seems to have quite confused a host of writers who cannot settle whether Robert Consul's countess was Maud, Sibil, or Mabel, or two, or all of the names. It will be seen that Matilda was her name, and no doubt about it. Describing Beauclerc's love family, he says, "'His father, however, married to Robert, the eldest of them, a certain very noble girl, by name Sibil, the daughter of Robert, the son of Hamo, niece by Mabel, the daughter of Roger de Montgomery, father of Robert of Belesme.'". It has been said that she heired much if not all the English lands of her fierce uncle, Robert of Belesme. The king, he states, conceded to her husband, "'Very large inheritance in Normandy as well as in England, which belonged by hereditary right to this maiden'". He describes the head town on her Norman lands as Torrinneium, on the borders of the consulatus or bailliwicks or counties of Bayeux and the Cotentin, two miles distant from the river Vire. It was extremely populous, he says, though the agricultural produce was not remarkably rich, merchandise being largely the interest of a busy and, to its proprietors, profitable town and country. The chronicler adds also that because it was not right to have so much property without public dignity, the king gave him "'The earldom of Gloucester'". Again and again he gets new additions to his lands through this most extraordinary of heiresses, as her relations die. It is also said that Henry I at his death in 1135, gave him £60,000 directly out of the treasury at Falaise.

Robert, earl of Gloucester, had fought beside his father in the battle of Brenneville, 1119, which, by the defeat of his cousin William, son of Robert Curthose, finally established Henry as king of Normandy and England. He was at the siege of Brionne Castle in 1123. But he gained his high reputation as a warrior in aiding his sister to rescue her father's crown from the usurper Stephen. When he first came to England in 1135 after his father's death, he actually paid homage to Stephen. Nothing else could then be done. But he went to his earldom, and having carefully built Bristol Castle, of stone taken from Caen, he negotiated with Milo, earl of Hereford, the constable of England, and they brought his sister from Anjou in 1138, to be received at Arundel Castle, Sussex, by her stepmother Alice, the countess, formerly the queen of Henry. This was the beginning of chequered struggle till he took Stephen prisoner at Lincoln in 1141.

His famous speech in Joreval is of genealogical as well as historic interest. It has been noticed that he criticised the character of Simon Sinclair, the second earl of the name, then his enemy. The actual speech puts the proper light on the subject. It was not likely he would speak very severely, if he could help it, of his own and his wife's kinsman, nor has he. He addresses the soldiers first about Stephen as a forsworn man, having promised to his father Henry to support Matilda his daughter in her accession to his crown; he then attacks the earl of Mellent, as being deceitful above measure, and equally lazy; next, the earl of Albemarle is pictured as a drunkard, and knowing nothing of soldiering; and lastly, because he was too important not to be named, he describes, in comparatively mild terms, Simon, earl of Northampton, as a man of words only, who never makes performance of his promise. To soldiers in the face of approaching battle something strong had to be said, but it does not appear that Earl Robert lost his good sense on the occasion in the least degree, and the historians are rash who draw too much conclusion as to men from this speech, even if delivered as reported. Stephen he took prisoner to Bristol Castle with him, but the tables were turned again, and Rochester Castle kept Robert in durance. But all that is well known history. His death in 1146 takes him out of the troubled time.

In the transcript of Glover by the Rouge-dragon Smith, MS. 245, Harleian collection. Matilda or Sibilla, as he alternates, marries again, and to Nigel of Mowbray, son of Roger of Albini. Albinis were from Thoeni, uncle to Rollo. Nigel, the famous Neel, was brother to William de Albini Pincerna, the founder of Wymondham Abbey, Norfolk, whose son William, the lion slayer, was that earl of Arundel to whom Queen Alice, of Lorraine or Boulogne, was married, when she received Robert, earl of Gloucester, and his sister, the empress, at Arundel Castle in 1138. The countess of Gloucester's second husband, Nigel, became earl of Northumberland in all except the title, having received the lands of Mowbray, the rebel earl of 1095, from Rufus. He changed his name to Mowbray, such conversions being a kind of passion with the Albinis, the Thoenis of 1066 and previously. At her new home, the splendid warlike castle of Northumbrian Bamborough, historic as any in England, Matilda Sinclair spent the evening of her rich life.

Sir Alexander Malet, Bart., B.A., an ambassador of the present century to European states, and something after the twentieth in direct male line from Malet of the Conqueror's special friendship, says that a William de St.Clair endowed the abbey of Savigny, Normandy, in the reign of Henry I, and he adds, "The English Sinclairs are reported to be of this stock". The passage occurs incidentally in a note to his rhymed translation of Wace, the French chronicler of, among much related history and biography, the battle of Hastings. Malet is an authority on Norman subjects. His words are of value. He also states in the same book that the priory of Villers-Frossard was founded by William Sinclair. In the division of France into departments at the revolution of last century, it is noticeable that St.Clair beside St.Lowas made a commune, and Villers-Frossard being in it, the home district of his family was where William founded the priory.

Malet notes further that ladies St.Clare founded religious houses in England. The abbey of nuns in the Minories, at the tower, London, would seem to have been one of these. The church of the nunnery was founded by Matilda, queen of Henry I, in 1108, the burial-place of the earls of Dartmouth and others of much note. In 1797 the ruins of the convent of St.Clare were large and imposing. It has been said that it took its name from its nuns being of the order of St.Clare, the Italian saint who was counterpart and the female friend of St.Francis; but she died as late as 1253, and the nunnery had its title long before her birth from a foundress of the lineage. A striking aid to the proof of this is to be found in the Report of the Historical MSS. Commission. In the St.Bartholomew hospital MSS. John Sinclair of Hardaness, in Kent, is a donor to, and has also much business with others about, a chapel of St.Clare on Hardaness. The usual relations of a lord to his chapel are too well established not to be indicative of the lineage connection; as, for example, the priory of Montacute belonged to the Montacutes in name as in reality.

But this step of proof of Matilda's lineage is not dependent on even Malet's accuracy, as man of position and a Norman of high blood, and therefore of special carefulness as to facts in such field. He may well be trusted as to the dates, wherever he may have found them. There is a beautiful transcript in the public record office, Fetter Lane, London, from Basse-Normandie and Gascony rolls, of the charter given to Savigny abbey. Here Matilda, countess of Gloucester, and William de St.Clair give their lands of Vilers and of Than to the abbey of Savigny. It does not at first sight agree altogether with Malet's note. He says that William Sinclair endowed the abbey in the reign of Henry. The clause that they held the land from the time of Henry I would go to prove that this conjunct endowment was made after that king's death. Malet may be quite right if this, as was usual, is another endowment added to the original one, which his information, however acquired, implies to have been that of William alone.

Duncan in his work, The Dukes of Normandy, has general reference to the foundation of religious houses in Normandy by ladies of the Sinclair lineage. He is aware that the Sinclairs founded houses or "establishments" in England; and this is something in connection with a subject hitherto virgin among writers of the historian class. In his List of the Norman Barons who fought at Hastings a good paragraph occurs. "'Saint-Clair is an arrondissement of Saint-Lo. The remains of the old baronial castle are still visible near to the church. The name of Saint-Clair figures distinctly in the Bromton Chronicle, and though greatly defaced, may be traced in the Battle-Abbey list. William Saint-Clair endowed the abbey of Savigny, in the reign of Henry I. In 1139, the priory of Villers-Frossard was founded by a person of the same name. The Saint-Clairs formed establishments in England, but they are now changed to Sinclair'".

These statements are the more trustworthy because taken from the faithful local researches of Auguste le Prevost, a Frenchman who made Norman antiquities a life study. But to return to the prize of the public record office. The note in French added to the charter is of much later origin than itself, but it is of considerable use: "This charter was sealed with yellow was, and with double hangers, but there remains only the seal of William Sinclair". To parchment charters the seals, sometimes as many as seven or eight, according to the persons interested, were attached by narrow slips, also of parchment, called queues or tails. The seal which survives is as large as a penny. Round the edge, in quaint somewhat irregular capitals, runs "Sigillum Wlelmi De Sco Claro", the beginning and end of the inscription separated by a cross for full stop. The centre is occupied by a crusader on an armoured horse, the warrior armed cap-a-pie, with spear from which hangs a pennon en treble queue, as the describer of the charter would put it, with sword to his side, and an oval shield, having a central device, on his left shoulder. The peculiar saddling, the size of the stirrups and spurs, and the long thin loose look of the knight's boots towards toes and heels, are as characteristic of the time as they are noteworthy for antiquarian purposes. Over the horse's head and neck there are ribbed plates of, no doubt, in the actual field, shining steel. It is easy to draw inference from this remarkable seal that he was in the highest sphere and spirit of his period.

But who are these two granters of the charter ? That they are brother and sister is the probable explanation of all the circumstances. This Matilda is undoubtedly the daughter of Robert Fitz-Hamo, because she was the first countess of Gloucester, through her husband, Robert Consul, Henry I's son. No countess of Gloucester occurs with the same name till Matilda, wife of Richard Clare, in 1230, daughter of the earl of Lincoln. The proof is absolute that it was the wife of Robert Consul and the daughter of Robert Fitz-Hamo who gave this charter conjointly with William Sinclair; and the document answers, besides, the confused difficulties of some chroniclers and genealogists as to whether she was Maud, Sibil, or Mabel. If the history of William will show that he was her brother or near relation complete satisfaction must be the result.

Chapter XXIII
William de Sancto Claro

Robert Fitz-Hamo was married first to a princess, Theodora ap Tudor, daughter of Rhees ap Tudor, prince of South Wales, and sister to Henry I's concubine, the princess Nesta, mother of Robert Consul, earl of Gloucester, and mother by Gerald of Windsor and by Sinclair, father of William of Hay, of the chief heroes of the Irish Conquest. Marriages to the Welsh, even if princesses, were considered low alliances, though these Tudors are said to be the same stock as Henry VIII. But the connections explain Fitz-Hamo's close sympathies with the Conqueror's dynasty; and the high and deserved favour he had is considerably to be attributed to the fact that his first wife was Robert Consul's aunt. Burke says, however, that he was the Conqueror's nephew. The genealogists, from whatever reason, seem to have neglected this marriage. It is not impossible that new evidence of descendants may be discovered. They who refer to the subject at all state the marriage and no more.

Their interest follows quickly to the famous second marriage of the Montgomery heiress of Robert de Belesme's wide English lands; and this is natural, because it has to do with the main stream of history more. It was in Normandy that Henry, the third son of the Conqueror, met Nesta ap Tudor; and there, at the same period, before the reign of Rufus began in 1087, Robert Fitz-Hamo also met her sister Theodora. We know of a son Henry, as well as Robert Consul, whom Nesta bore to Henry, both out of wedlock; and evidence tends to show that the multiplying power of her tribe had in Theodora a sufficient representative. The theory is, and it must end in realised facts before its value is genuine, that William de Sancto Claro was her eldest son. That she had two other sons at least, will be put forward in additional but corroborative connections. It might be thought from the French charter that Matilda, countess of Gloucester, possibly married a William de St.Clair, but the dates at once preclude the possibility. Her husband, the king's son, did not die till 1146, and the French religious houses were conjointly founded by them during his life, 1139 at the latest. Who could stand in such a relation to this married lady but a brother ? Her marriage to Nigel Mowbray, with the evidence of their age, goes to say, that she could not possibly have been married to a Sinclair between the two marriages which all the genealogists and chroniclers tell of, and of none else. Her father, Robert Fitz-Hamo's brother Hamo, the viscount of Kent and dapifer, record shows to have been childless.

We know of the influential position of William from other things than great religious foundation. That he was among the few best men of England is shown by the list of witnesses to Stephen's charter of the earldom of Essex to the second Geffrey Mandeville, the son of Margaret Sinclair, Eudo Dapifer's daughter. The signatures and pledges which the Empress Matilda gave to Geffrey to win him to her cause, and to outweigh this charter and its guaranteers, are wonders of English record. She almost pawned the kingdom, the clergy included, to get the brave Geffrey to her side; and the Sinclair interest was undoubtedly always in her favour when it could get its natural and indeed, as shall be shown, related scope. Stephen's charter to him shortly after 1135, when he usurped the throne, is signed by William of Iypres, afterwards earl of Kent; Henry of Essex, the famous or infamous standard-bearer of England; John Clare, the son of Robert Fitz-Walter of the Tunbridge great family; Robert Newburgh, earl of Warwick; William de St.Clere; William de Damartin, of a famous earldom; Richard Fitz-Urse; and William, earl of Ou, than whom, being ducal with bar sinister, no person was more distinguished in England or Normandy. It cannot be thought curious that William Sinclair is on Stephen's side against the interests of Matilda and Robert Consul, and through them of himself and his own sister. So successful had Bigod Dapifer made the first move of crowning Stephen by the archbishop and the church's full authority, that even the very son of the late king, this Robert Consul himself, had to swear homage to his aunt's usurping son. William was there then simply because of his public importance, and till 1138, when Matilda landed in Sussex, Stephen was indisputable king. Like Geffrey he took his natural place as events righted themselves, and like him he may have suffered.

The indications are, however, that he died at a reasonable age about the middle of the reign, a few years after his foundation of the priory of Villers Frossard in 1139. He was one of the benefactors, according to Morant's histories of Essex and Colchester, published in the eighteenth century, of the abbey of St.John Baptist, Colchester, founded by his kinsman, Eudo Sinclair, dapifer. No more useful or graceful way was there among friends of such rank than thus acknowledging each others' pious deeds of building and endowment, and this of itself is a valuable item to the proof of their identical lineage. The William who was a cleric, and who helped Eudo so thoroughly and successfully in finishing the abbey, despite all state difficulties, "sparing no expense", was probably the William afterwards archdeacon of Northampton, whose building powers on his own account with St.John's Hospital there are well known, the brother of Simon Sinclair, one of the great earls, themselves founders, as Leland has noted. Lay William was too old to have entered much into the fighting of the time, being born about 1080. The date shows that nothing of his English properties can be directly discovered from The Domesday Book, being a child at its production. In the Magnum Rotulum Scaccarii of 31 Henry I (1131) or, as some date it, 5 Stephen (1140), under "'Nova Placentia et Novae Conventiones, Dorseta'", this occurs: "'In pdon bi Willo de Sco Claro'", twice, as paying taxes in this county. His home was in Dorset, and he founded a family there.

Next to London, Winchester and its surroundings were the best scene in the kingdom during centuries after the Conquest. The Chronica of John of Oxenford mentions a descendant, William, who figured in Edward I's Welsh, Scottish, and French wars; and he was as capable in money business as in military. It is in coin connection John writes of him. The bishop of Winchester, the clergy being then the nation's accountants for most part, found his match in William on his own favourite exchequer ground. A Geffrey de Sancto Claro in the neighbouring county of Hampshire held lands near Southampton from the "counts of the island", in 7 Henry III (1222); but the descendant more probably then in the main line was the "Dominus Williamus de Sancto Claro" who appears as witness to a charter given to the abbey of Tichfield, Southampton, in Edward II's reign, (1307-27). He was a baron by tenure so late as this, and may safely be held as representative of William Sinclair, the brother or near relation, as is being argued, of Matilda Sinclair, first countess of Gloucester. In the same state record referred to, he appears twice paying large taxes in Huntingdonshire. The records of the period being yet fragmentary in printed or other really available form, these appearances indicate much wider possessions.

How a supposed son of Robert Fitz-Hamo got large properties in Dorsetshire and Huntingdonshire, however, is a question which, without knowing of other lands he must certainly have had, would have something of answer as to lineage. Ellis in his Introduction to Domesday Book gives no help as to the lands possessed by Robert Fitz-Hamo in particular. He has an immense collection of lands under the name of Robert, and most of them, if not all, were the property of this the greatest of the nobles of three reigns. Robert Consul was only a minor in Domesday time, else it might be doubtful as to the extent of this Fitz-Hamo's lands occurring under the name Robert. Study of Domesday itself is extremely helpful and suggestive, though the indication of

171

lineage through the properties cannot be otherwise than indirect. Indexes to and discussions about the clear and able record are worse often than useless, deterring from the actual reading, for the word "study" hardly requires to be used, of the two volumes. William de Sancto Claro heired property in England and Normandy belonging to Fitz-Hamo, lord of Thorigny. The lands he gave to the religious houses in the latter country, he held in common with his sister or relation; the heiress, by right of her mother, of the Montgomery properties, and of some lands of the proper Hamo line there, through her father.

The relations of the king's son Robert Consul, her husband, to this Sinclair family, are altogether of the most intricate and interesting kind. Through her relationship, as niece, to Robert de Belesme, the arch-rebel of Henry I's reign, he secured the bulk if not all of the immense estates of that intractable Montgomery; and William Gemeticensis, the chronicler, has this, "'The king also gave to him (Robert, his son) the land of Hamo Dapifer, the paternal uncle of his wife'". That this statement can be but very partially true, will be shown on the most unimpeachable authority. She only had her share of her uncle's lands for her able husband. William de Sancto Claro got his share, Hugo de Sancto Claro, whose fame in Kent will appear by and bye, got his share, and Hamo of Colchester and its castle, who is so extraordinarily frequent a name in the papers of his time, got his share, if not the lion's share ultimately, of both Hamo their paternal uncle the Dapifer's lands, and the division of their father's with their half-sister, by different mothers, Matilda Sinclair, countess of Gloucester, and her full sister, Amicia, the countess of Brittany. The two sisters besides, the one Cicely Sinclair, abbess of St.Edward's convent, Shaftesbury, the other Hawise, abbess of Wilton, had also great gifts for the religious houses which they loved so well. There are trite remarks that King Henry made them religieuses because he wished to preserve all the properties from the family of Robert Fitz-Hamo's second wife, by Matilda her daughter's marriage to his son Robert Consul. The fact that the fourth, Amicia, married the earl of Britanny, and had her rights, is answer to such weak inferences. Who had better claim than Robert Consul to have benefits from Robert Fitz-Hamo, the favoured of his royal friends, and the husband of his mother's sister, Theodora ap Tudor ? If he encouraged what was the natural inclination of the Sinclair women, as history again and again has noted, for the high religious life, in favour thus of Robert Consul, this is all that can be said.

It is time, however, to treat these Hamoes on their right footing as of the Sinclair lineage, and in particular Robert Fitz-Hamo and his brother Fitz-Hamo Dapifer. Their sister, too, will be rescued from the obscurity of antiquity's sea as if by the drowning locks. She is a personage quite unknown to the chroniclers and county historians, and her history is as interesting as it is thoroughly fixed by the best of all authority. When return is afterwards made to the brothers, or perhaps the sons, of this William de Sancto Claro, the accumulation of weighty inferences and available evidence will have further effective additions from their thoroughly established and wholly recognised doings. If this brother, at all events, near blood relative of Matilda, countess of Robert Consul, is left now, it is because previous and collateral histories will make the more valuable what has to be said of him when the stories of Hugo de Sancto Claro and Hamo de Sancto Claro of the reigns of Stephen and of Harry II are handled.

Chapter XXIV
The Knight of Rye

So much has already been said of Robert Sinclair, commonly called Fitz-Hamo, in the incidental relations he held with others of the lineage, that many additions cannot be made of entirely new effect. Some there are, however, and of most interesting character. Among English Sinclairs of the subsequent centuries no name appears more frequently in record than "Robert", and it is not any stretch of point to look for the origin of its popularity to this gallant predecessor. Of all the Normans none unless it be "Strongbow", the conqueror of Ireland, has as high fame as the "knight of Rye".

Born in Normandy, at the battle of Hastings he must have been in the flower of his youth. Indeed the Tewkesbury Chronicle expressly mentions that he was a young man, but already the lord of Astremeville beyond the Channel; and he must have done at the Conquest as much as his age could. His father Hamo, earl of Corbeil, did great services, Brady says, for the Conqueror, and seems to have then overshadowed the son's doing, though the latter reaped the benefit of the efforts of both. It looks often as if the charters of such kind as those of Rochester, with Dr. Thorpe's editorship, could prove that this Hamo was dapifer as well as his son, who undoubtedly was Hamo the dapifer and viscount of Kent. Bishop Carileph's charter to Durham, given at London in 1082, is signed by Hamo Dapifer; and it could be either, as far as ages are concerned, but is more likely to have been the younger Hamo, viscount Kanciae. It may be granted that the younger man is the dapifer whose position has puzzled the antiquaries so much, and the sole one of the name.

Robert, the elder son, founded the castle of Rye, or more probably enlarged and fortified it, after his father had chosen his English home there. William Iypres, earl of Kent, added the remarkable tower, which made the place very powerful. The fact that the name Hamo is even still sacred to Rye in Sussex, one of the Cinque Ports, goes to show that to Robert's father the origin of the home there was owing, and that he did the work of making it famous. Many of the surname of Hamon or Hammond in late centuries have claimed to be descended from a

Norman ancestor of Rye. The monks of Fechamp had returns from the district in the eleventh century, but this does not conflict the least with the presence of such an ancestor. Property held in the usual feudal way paid its tithes. In the muniments of Battle Abbey, at no great distance, the name Hamon often occurs.

The Henry of Rye who gave the manor of Diepham to the cathedral church of Canterbury, and who was thereupon admitted a monastic brother in 1146, is one of the English Ryes, as distinguished from their relations who kept up in England the name from the Norman home, Eudo, Hubert, Ralph, and the rest, who possessed chiefly in the east and north of the kingdom. There is a Robert Hamon at Rye in 1314. Of other local indications from the names of persons, the history of Thomas Hamon, six times mayor of Rye, and thrice its representative in parliament, is very suggestive. His tomb still exists. He died in 1607, and had all the honours which civic ingenuities could heap upon him.

To make strange things meet, by an extreme circle, the signature "Alexander Sinclair" is found to the last effort of this once lively nearest ferrying port to France to assert its rights as an independent, and jealous, municipality, having Cinque rights and privileges of the then (1828) musty impossible kind. Could the man be a survival of the old race of Norman Hamoes ? In this century a Sinclair anywhere in England, much more on its southern shore, was rarer than a white elephant. It is almost pathetic, not to say poetic or even tragic, to think of him as the last of such a line. But this is digression, because he may have been an importation or a waif from other shores. The fact is striking, but has nothing further in it. Cooper, the Sussex archaeologist, says the Rye family originated with Robert Fitz-Hamo; and as an accurate and learned district antiquary, he must have had grounds for the statement that there was such a family. This of itself is presumptive proof that Robert's marriage with the Princess Theodora ap Tudor of Wales might have given him sons who were the heirs of his Sussex home with other of his own lineage possessions.

Beyond this marriage, and the general knowledge of his great services as a soldier, which historians like Brady and others describe, there is not much to be said of his doings in the reign of William I. It is in the reign of Rufus that he comes fully to the front. When Eudo Sinclair, the dapifer, came over in 1087 from Normandy, with the Conqueror's dying commission, to help to make his son Rufus king of England, Robert Sinclair, Fitz-Hamo, warmly espoused the cause for which his young relative risked his entire fortunes. Had Eudo's head not been so able, "the knight of Rye" would then have been seen gaining reputation at sword's point. As it was, he was one of the favoured friends at the court of Rufus. Opportunities were not long in arising to test his loyalty for his elect king. Odo, bishop of Bayeux, brother of the Conqueror, formerly earl of Kent and governor of England, had espoused his nephew William's cause, but he soon grew discontented, and with his supporters, "the gallant squires of Kent", fortified Rochester Castle and Pevensey Castle, and schemed and waited for the coming of Robert, duke of Normandy, to take the crown as eldest son.

It is probable that good reasons were not wanting for this rebellion. But at the siege of Rochester, Robert Sinclair was chief military figure, and it was to him the success there was owing. It is said that the Saxon element of the population enjoyed greatly the sight of the Norman nobles led out as prisoners of war, and added sufficient curses in the vernacular to their departure, some of them for ever, from the island. This may be an example of historic imagination. Bishop Odo, the leading proprietor of the county, and a very able man, whether of uncertain temper or not, had perhaps considerable popular sympathy, if only from religious motives. But the last act of the high play he made in this country seems thus to have had its close. It is somewhat of a pity that he did not get his grand scheme carried out of being pope. His imperial-souled brother found the thought hard to brook that he should have to square sentiments with his ruling spiritual father in the person of his own earl of Kent. Undoubtedly Odo was a disappointed man who might have been one of the world's most brilliant stars had the fates been a little more favourable to him. His change against William is a subject that hardly deserves severe if any criticism, for Odo's day was over as to valuable undertakings.

Robert Fitz-Hamo was with King Rufus in his Norman wars against both his brothers, Robert, the duke, and Henry. Henry had bought or some say seized the province of Coustance. Fitz-Hamo gained the highest possible favour from the successful monarch, who in 1091 made what terms he chose at Caen with his brothers. To recount the adventures of that struggle of brothers would take volumes. Rufus had showed his gratitude for Robert Sinclair's services by disseizing his own brother Henry of his mother's lands in England, and giving them to the "knight of Rye", who was thereupon lord of the honour of Gloucester. For years Henry was almost a beggar; but the after events show that he grudged less, though he had the grumbling faculty highly developed, the fortune of Robert, lord of Gloucester, than he would have done that of any other nobleman in England. Probably William Rufus knew this.

The love of Henry and Fitz-Hamo for two sisters gave something of a common interest to them; and, as will appear, real affection existed between the inheritor and the disinherited. The story of these lands is more than romantic. Brictric, a Saxon ambassador from the court of Edward the Confessor, had business at the court of Baldwin, earl of Flanders. The earl's daughter fell in love with him, and had the courage to propose to him. She was disappointed, and nursed her spite. This was the lady who, no doubt soured, said, on William her future husband proposing to her by messengers, that she would not marry a bastard. The stern duke never rested till he horse-whipped her in her father's palace; and so much the better of it was she, that she became soon after suppliant for his grace, and got it. Matilda, queen of England and duchess of Normandy, has a good name, but she could not forgive being slighted. When the Conquest had given her power, she found means of easing her spitefulness. Brictric was seized, with, it is said, the Conqueror's permission, at Hanley, and brought to Winchester. He died there in prison. The Tewkesbury Chronicle says he was childless. At all events, Queen Matilda had her revenge, and the further solace of his very wide lands. When she died in 1083, the Conqueror kept them in his own hand. It may be true that Henry Beauclerc had them only for a short time in Rufus's reign.

They came to the "knight of Rye" with perfectly clean hands, and he enjoyed them till his death in Henry's own reign. The Chronicle distinctly says that Rufus gave them to him on account of many labours with his father. Brady gives an additional item, wherever he got it. The gift, he says, was made because of his own and his father's services. If this is anything but a loose incorrect reading of the Latin, Hamo, earl of Corbeil, and the lord of Torigion or Thorigny, must have been a principal instrument in the subjugation and long and troublesome pacification of the island to its most northerly point. That Robert attached Hamo's to his own has the same lesson. Such a splendid prize as the honour of Gloucester can only be explained on the supposition of special deeds for the crown.

But this was not the highest point of Robert Sinclair's fortune and fame. Nicolas in his Annals of Wales says that Fitz-Hamo's conquest of Glamorgan is allowed on all hands. The tale reads like the adventures of knights of a Round Table in Fairyland rather than the sober history which it actually is. In Powell's translation of the History of Wales there is a full account of "how Glamorgan was won", from which Dugdale has taken his. But there is much literature besides on this spirited subject, and short delay will be enough. He was "knight of the privy chamber" to Rufus, and his lordship over Gloucester as well as his general renown kept him the prominent person on the Welsh border.

In 1091 a quarrel had arisen between Lord Iestin, a Welsh noble, and his prince, Rhees ap Tudor. Lord Iestin, the lord of Glamorgan, as the weaker, sent a secret messenger, Enyon, to the English court to solicit the powerful man of the time, Robert Sinclair, Fitz-Hamo, for help. It is probable that an opportunity of intervention was not unwelcome. Fitz-Hamo got a full commission from the king to enter upon the adventure. He selected twelve knights to accompany him, and they crossed the border. The wild Welsh were not long in meeting the Normans, but they were beaten like foam. Prince Rhees ap Tudor was slain in the battle of Black Hill, and Conan his son shared the same fate. When he fully performed his promises to Lord Iestin, Robert judged that he should have equivalent. Iestin grew haughty, and fate found him soon in pitched battle against his former friends.

Most of South Wales fell like a ripe apple into Fitz-Hamo's hands, and though "he displayed some generosity, a thing quite unusual with his race", as Nicolas, evidently a bitter Celt on this Welsh question, acknowledges, he was not the man to let go his grip of what he had fairly won. He immediately built Cardiff Castle, on the site of the ancient palace of the Welsh prince, Morganiog; and dividing the territories between himself and his twelve knights, he thoroughly established Norman rule. By this position he became lord marcher, a prince in everything but the name, needing no charters of possession, exercising jura regalia, having the power of life and death, and doing all he pleased, but with nominal homage to his king. He had the lordship of Glamorgan and Morgannocke, which, Stow says, was twenty-seven miles by twenty-two; acting like the Saxons, he adds, as to choice of goodness of soil and "best of country and champaign".

The list of the knights, who also each of them built his own castle for the protection of his farms, is given in many places. Tindal notes: "'There is a book written on this subject by Sir Edward Stradling, or Sir Edward Mansel, (for it is ascribed to both), wherein you have the names of the twelve knights. Their names and the lordships each of them had are as follows: "

1. William de Londres had for his share the manor of Ogmor.
2. Sir Richard Granville, that of Neth.
3. Sir Pain Tubervill had Coyty.
4. Sir Robert St.Quintin, Lhan-blethyan.
5. Sir Richard Syward, Talavan.
6. Sir Gilbert Humfrevile, Penmark.
7. Sir Reginald de Sully, Sully.
8. Sir Roger Berkrolles, East Orchard,
9. Sir Peter le Soor, Peterton.
10. Sir John Fleming, St.George.
11. Sir John St.John, Fonmon.
12. Sir William Stradeling, St.Donats'

The antiquary Camden gives the list. Stow has it, and also the later Nicolas in his two-volumed book about Welsh persons and events. The Welsh Chronicle is the authority for these knights. Powel translated and published it in 1580, and it was written in "the British" at least two hundred years previously. Fitz-Hamo and his knights take up several valuable pages of Cambria, as it is named. In his judicious Life of Henry II, Lord Lyttleton gives remarkable prominence to the deeds of these brilliant warriors in the west. "'Robert Fitz-haimon, a gentleman of the king's privy chamber and great baron of the realm, undertook the adventure. Twelve knights of considerable note and distinction were retained to his service, or rather agreed to serve under him, with a large body of forces'".

Nicolas takes care to tell, in an animated way, that, except the Stradlings, the Norman blood has vanished; and he has morals about tyranny that are mere superstition. Caxton in his Introduction to Cato's Distiches (of which book Francis de St.Clair, ne Davenport, was also an editor) says that in his time, the fifteenth century, no one could point out three succeeding generations among the merchants of London. The vitality of Normans, though as with most of the noblest animals production is not superabundant, has been always a subject of astonishment to careful consideration. The frantic nationalists cannot see truth that is still under their eyes every day. Fitz-Hamo had twelve years' possession as lord marcher before his death. He held his monthly court at Cardiff Castle, and of all Normans he was the most popular with the fickle, angry, immoral Welsh, because of his strong hand and generous heart. Enyon, the Welshman who first by his message opened the way to this side of his fortune, he enriched and granted lands to, with characteristic generosity. He built Kensigg Castle, and Cowbridge and other towns.

What is more valuable still in the present inquiry, is that the castle and town of St.Clare are in the district over which he ruled. Again and again the naming of their places by their surname, which, as Hallam has already been quoted to show, was considered beneath dignity to use socially, is to be found with the Sinclair family; and there can be little doubt that the well-known St.Clare of Wales owes its name to Robert Fitz-Hamo, its founder and ruler. In the Brut Y Tywysogion, the chronicle of the Welsh princes, the date of the death of Prince Rhys ap Tudor is given as 1091. He was "'killed by the French (Ffreinc) who inhabited Brecknock, and then fell the kingdom of the Britons'". It tells how the French, who are the Normans really, came into Cardigan and other districts, which they conquered and occupied, fortifying everywhere with castles, of which Pembroke was one of the most remarkable in position of advance. It is

1189 which has first mention of St.Clare. "'That year the Lord Rhys took possession of the castle of St.Clare'".

In King John's reign, 1215, "'Llewellyn son of Iorwath and the Welsh princes in general collected a vast army to Caermarthen; and before the end of five days he obtained the castle and demolished it to the ground. And then they demolished the castles of Llanstephan and Talachur and Seint Cler. And from thence to Cardigan'". It was a few years later that William Rufus, after Fitz-Hamo's success in South Wales, partitioned beforehand North Wales, to be conquered and possessed by Hugh Montgomery, earl of Chester, and others. Montgomery has left his name on part of his conquest, as Fitz-Hamo did his in the St.Clare of Caermarthen, the castle, town, and county of Montgomery being immortal record of this brother of Robert de Belesme, of Mabel Montgomery, the "knight of Rye's" lady, and of Matilda, the wife of Robert, earl of Mortaine, half-brother of William I.

The great border lordship of Nithsdale reaching the Solway south of and including Dumfries, and held by the Sinclair earls of Orkney, had in similar manner its St.Clare for capital or head. In the map of 1732 inserted by Tindal in Rapin's History of England, the ancient divisions of Scotland before counties are given; and Nithsdale has its caput baroniae spelt as "Sanchar", the exact spelling of a Lord William Sinclair's surname to a Stirling document in the reformation struggles.

Thomas Nicholas in his Annals and Antiquities of Wales, published in 1875, knew a little of the Welsh castle, but there is more than his two interesting paragraphs to be found about it. "'At St.Clear's [St.Clare] there was also a Norman castle, about whose fortunes not very much is known, its life having probably been of brief duration as a lord marcher's residence, and distinguished by no extraordinary events. We can measure for it a duration of only about thirty years as a warlike stronghold. It was in existence in the year 1188 when Geraldus de Barri passed that way with Archbishop Baldwin preaching the crusades, for he mentions it as the adjacent castle of St.Clare, giving at the same time rather an amusing account of a method of making evil-doers good servants of the church: - "'On our journey from Caermardyn to the Cistercian monastery called Alba Domus (Whitland), the archbishop was informed of the murder of a young Welshman who was devoutly hastening to meet him, when turning out of a road he ordered the corpse to be covered with the cloak of his almoner, and with a pious supplication commended the soul of the murdered youth to heaven. Twelve archers of the adjacent castle of St.Clare, who had assassinated the young man, were on the following day signed with the cross at Alba Domus as punishment for their crime. So they marched off to fight the infidel'"."

What follows is useful for comparison purpose. "'The next year after this summary conversion of twelve archers of the castle into Christian soldiers, the Lord Rhys visited and took possession of the place. After this Howel Sais became its occupant, who was compelled in the year 1195 to yield it up to the Norman De Breos. In 1214 it was captured and hardly used by Llewellyn ap Iorwarth of North Wales. Not a vestige of the walls is now to be seen; the mound on which it stood and which has partly grown out of its ruins alone remains to mark the spot'". But Gerald de Barri, better known as Giraldus Cambrensis, has already been referred to as giving still earlier knowledge of Saint Clare.

Nesta, the Welsh princess, concubine of Henry I, had a son William Hay to whom he says she left "Sanctum Clarum" as property, and it is certain she got it by one of the Fitz-Hamo connection, from whom the name came. William Hay's father was a Norman of Sinclair lineage. Nesta was the aunt of the then Lord Rhys, so that there is, what with Gerald de Barri being contemporary of Henry II, and other near views, considerably solid ground here in the obscure past. Her husband, Gerald of Windsor, afterwards constable of Pembroke Castle, father of the Irish Fitzgeralds, would seem to be also of the same lineage, from Hugo of Windsor being in Henry II's time the same with the Hugo Pincerna and the Hugo de St.Clare of the historians of the Thomas a Becket controversy. The royal relationships gave the lead to the west, and ultimately to Ireland, as was to have been expected from the feudality of the period.

In records the Welsh town and its pertinents occur as the "barony of St.Clare". The Bruces of Brecknock and Brember had it in the reign of Henry III. William Bruce married Eva, sister of Richard Marshall, earl of Pembroke, and she had eight properties marked out as her dowry, this barony one of them. She had four daughters, Eva married to Cantilupe, the king's steward or dapifer; Isabella to David, prince of Wales; Eleanor to Humphrey de Bohun, earl of three counties; and Maud to Roger Mortimer, the lord of Wigmore. Maud had eight estates as dowry, and among them the barony of St.Clare. But there is later history of it than this. On the death of Roger Mortimer, his son Edmund heired a third part of it. In 11 Edward I (1283) there is a division to three heirs of the town of Sancto Claro, Wall. In Ayloffe's Ancient Charters there is one carta without date: "'Rotuli Walliae: Membrana dorso: De terra Sancto Claro Angey et Pennuliok data Reso filio Mereduci in maritagio cum Auda sorore Johannis Hasting'".

William Montacute, earl of Salisbury, has St.Clare in his feoda in 20 Richard II (1397). The monks of St.Denis, France, writing of the forty-two years ending in 1422, when the great French war was going on, tell of what they call "the strong castle of St.Clare, near Caermarthen", which a body of Welsh and French auxiliaries had tried to storm in the curious invasion of that period. This was of Fitz-Hamo's building, and bore his own surname. In 6 Henry VIII (1515), June 4, there were a confirmation and quit-claim for the Sir Rhesus ap Thomas whose monument is a Welsh "lion". Next to the Tudors then, his was the best family of those originating across the border. He could raise 5000 horse; and his great tournament, and his friendship with Henry, are historic. The confirmation gives him and his heirs the castle and lordship of Trayne March, and the third part of the town of St.Clare, Carmarthen. Fifty years before, St.Clare was mortgaged to John, bishop of St.Davids, and to the Thomases, by Richard, duke of York.

There is one thing to be added to these more modern notes. The name might be traced to Agnes Sinclair, the daughter of Walderne, earl of St.Clare, wife of the first of the English Bruces; but the stern ways of English history plead in favour of a founder and a fighter's title to a strong castle, and to the town which grew under its protection. The best names England ever had, revolve round this remarkable Welsh town; and local tradition, and perhaps record, might be able to put real shape into such subject as the present, with time and perseverance. It is perhaps already made too much of here; but the inferences to be drawn even from the dim knowledge secured, are decidedly useful Further support to Fitz-Hamo's lineage may come from the history of a contiguous Somerset family, in which "Robert" is the favourite name. It may turn out that they are a branch of the family of the Lord Robert of Gloucester and Wales. But this requires separate treatment; for additional related families besides, may still further strengthen the position.

Though so powerful and full of building and ruling energy in the west, he does not forget that he is a courtier. With Rufus he is more influential than any of the time. It was to him, as the chief person, that the monk came, telling the warning dream which Matthew Paris in his Historia Major writes so alarmedly about, as well as others of the chroniclers. On no account was Rufus to hunt in the New Forest that day. Livy is science itself compared with Matthew and the monks generally as to superstition. Fitz-Hamo told the frightful portents to Rufus, and they laughed together over clerical humanity, the king sending a piece of money as the surest way to make the monastic mind easy. The death of Rufus did take place this day, and the death of many another besides; but

Walter Tyrell's arrow was the efficient cause of the miracle, as overeating was that of the monk's dream.

This was a critical period in the life of Fitz-Hamo, and he did not hesitate. His clear sight enabled him to discern the path to still higher place than he had. Relationship by blood, and also by sentiment of love and marriage, probably aided his decision; but he took Henry's side as king for England, against Robert, with a decision and effect which secured the crown for the unpopular but able Beauclerc. Henry is said to have been the sworn feudal man of his brother; and it was on the ground of breaking his oath, more than his being the younger, that Fitz-Osborn, keeper of the treasury at Winchester, so bravely contended there for Robert's rights.

William of Malmesbury, who has the credit of being about the best of the chroniclers, says that only four nobles in all England clung to Henry. They were Robert Fitz-Hamo; Roger Bigod; Robert, earl of Mellent, and Richard de Redvers, ancestor of the Rivers earls of Devonshire. Anselm, archbishop of Canterbury, also, was all the friend he could possibly be to Beauclerc. Robert Montgomery, better known as "of Belesme", a castle in Perch in France, earl of Arundel, Chester, and Salop or Shrewsbury, who had three brothers, Hugh, Ranulph, and Roger, was the greatest opponent. Fitz-Hamo's wife, mentioned as such in 1091, was their sister. Hugh's death in battle in Wales, 1097, gave Robert de Belesme great increase of lands, with these titles of Arundel and Shrewsbury. When the Montgomeries were banished after the fierce struggle with Henry, in right of his wife the nearest heir to these titles and properties was the "knight of Rye". Robert de Belesme had publicly protested that Beauclerc was a usurper, and had fortified his English castles of Shrewsbury, Bridgenorth, Tikhill in Yorkshire, and Arundel in Sussex for a struggle. Henry got up forty-five charges of treason against him, besieged and took his castles; and, before the end of the second year of his reign, had ruined wholly the English prospects of Belesme, that is, Montgomery, and his brothers. Their estates were confiscated, and they had to content themselves with their large possessions in France. Roger had Poitou there.

The violent career of this family in Normandy is notorious. The wife of Fitz-Hamo was their only representative in England, and to her a considerable part of the estates came. Orderic Vitalis gives account of how Robert de Belesme avenged himself in Normandy, by attacking all those who were holders of estates there and at the same time subjects of Henry in England. The disorder of the dukedom came to be beyond human endurance ultimately; and Duke Robert, being slothful and inefficient, Henry was compelled to accept the invitation to create order there, even if against the rights of his brother. Robert Montgomery of Belesme, who had this title or local surname from the possessions he had as a lord under the French sovereign, and who like many other nobles, was so dangerous because of them, would have become duke of Normandy, having thirty-two castles of his own in France, if Henry had not stood in, so great was the supineness of the reigning Robert. The battle of Tenchbrai in 1106 put a period to a frightful time, and Duke Robert his brother, taken prisoner, made Henry ruler of Normandy as well as of England. Fitz-Hamo was at his right hand in all that struggle, and to him as being the most faithful, and perhaps one of the most interested, the captive sovereign was given to be kept in his castle of Cardiff. There the generous crusader, who had refused to be elected king of Jerusalem, the cause to superstition of all his misfortunes, remained in confinement for twenty-six years. He was tenderly treated by Robert Sinclair, Fitz-Hamo, who, dying next year, had the trust only so long. It was under the custody of his son-in-law, Robert Consul, that, after the pitiful attempt to escape on a horse which during the pursuit landed him in a bog, the duke suffered by his brother's orders more severely.

The story of having his eyesight destroyed by the application of a hot brass basin was the invention of the enemies of both Henry I and his able generous son, Robert Consul, earl of Gloucester. Fitz-Hamo in 1107, having some of his Normandy estates attacked, had to go there, and at the siege of Falaise, which was the last effort against Henry by the duke and the Belesme enemies, he was struck on the head by a spear. He died some weeks after, in a kind of physical frenzy, the result of the blow. In 1113 the king got Robert Montgomery, of Belissimo Castle, "the fairest", into his hands, who spent the rest of his life a prisoner in England. His other enemy, the earl of Mortagne, his cousin, was also safe in the tower. It was so teriible a time of every one for his own hand, that blames ought carefully to be weighed before throwing them about.

The great lands of Robert Fitz-Hamo and of his wife Sybil Montgomery, in Normandy, England, and Wales, fell into the keeping of the king, as was then the law, and he did not forget his own interests. It is said that of the four daughters he made two become abbesses, so that Matilda should be sole heir. [Note - Her half-sisters were not Sybil's daughters]. This absurdity, as has been said, is answered by the fact that there was a fourth who married the earl of Brittany. Brady, the historian of 1685, says she got her father's estates in Normandy, but it is at least too wide a statement to risk. The positions of abbesses of Shaftesbury and Wilton were the highest possible for women in England next to being queen. They were baronesses by right of office, as the 28 mitred abbots were lords, and members of the house of peers. Shaftesbury had for abbess about 900 Ethelgiva, the daughter of Alfred the Great; and a century before, Wilton had been founded by Albhura, the sister of Egbert, the first king of England. Ciceley Sinclair, abbess of Shaftesbury, and Hawise, her sister, abbess of Wilton, could have no thought of injustice on the part of the king by the great provision he found for them, their high natures no doubt making them the seekers of their own vocation. That Matilda heired her mother's properties as well as many of her father's, could quite well be a pleasant arrangement for all concerned. In 1109 the king married this ward of his to his own son, Robert Consul, and gave him with the lands in Normandy and England he got by her, the title of earl of Gloucester.

Says Tindal: "'He was son of Nesta, daughter of Rhees, prince of South-Wales. King Henry I his father procured him in marriage Mabel or Maud, rich heir of Robert Fitz-Hamon, lord of Corboil in Normandy, Cardiff in South-Wales, and Tewkesbury in England. By her he had William, earl of Gloucester, after him; Roger, bishop of Worcester; Richard, bishop of Noyon; Hamon; Mabel, wife of Aubrey de Vere; and Matilda of Ranulph, earl of Chester'". Speaking of the year 1110, he further notes, "'This same year King Henry married Robert his natural son to Maud, daughter and heir of Robert Fitz-Haymon, late earl of Gloucester, and then invested him with that earldom'". Tindal may not be entirely accurate, however disinterested. It is a question whether the king's son was not the first earl of the county, though evidence goes most to support Tindal's view.

A great deal could be accumulated from The Domesday Book and other sources about the "knight of Rye" and his properties, but there is the less need for this from the fact that his position, wealth, and biography generally, are plentifully described, and fully valued, by historians. His intimate relations with the kings of the Norman dynasty will always keep his memory green. Account of him may be ended by reference to his foundation of the abbey of St.Mary Tewkesbury. His wife, Sybil Montgomery, and Gerald, prior of Cranbourne, in 1102 got him engaged to found this great house; and not only did he build it, but, with the right liberality, endowed it so as to become one of the greatest of secular saints, in the eyes of the monastic world. His body was brought from Normandy, and buried in his own abbey of Tewkesbury, March 1107; and after some two centuries, 1241, it was, through the gratitude and veneration of the monks, raised by the third abbot, from its original position in the capitulary usual to lords, and placed in the most sacred part of the building, to the right of the priest's reading-desk.

Till the Reformation destroyed the ancient, beautiful, if too loving, and therefore dangerous, ritual, the walls of that English temple heard as regularly as if it were an arrangement of astronomy, a special hymn of mourning and celebration. The great warrior, who was their great religious founder also, was never forgotten. Miserere quesumus Domine, rose in song from the thankful hearts of generation after generation of devout men.

Says the Tewkesbury Chronicle: "'That venerable Robert, the son of Hamo, after the foundation of this famous monastery, and after other deeds strenuously done, died in the days of March of the year of grace 1107, the seventh of Henry I'". If fame is at bottom the desire for men and women's love, it would be difficult to choose between the military and the religious deeds of Robert Sinclair as the more effective towards realisation. The monks of Gloucester Abbey got fine lands from him.

And he did not confine his gifts for the aid of what is noblest in man to the western parts of the island. There is record of his grants in Kent, as probably in other counties. To the monks of Rochester he gave the manor of Merlaw. He had various lands in the county of Kent, and his sympathies on the paternal and fraternal sides were strongly bound up with it, as will be seen from the history of Hamo Dapifer, viscount of Kent, his younger brother.

Chapter XXV
Hamo Dapifer

An examination of the witnesses to charters in the Monasticon or in the Rochester register, will discover no more frequent name than Hamo, unless it be that of Eudo Dapifer. As viscount of Kent sometimes, as dapifer in other places, he appears in all the reigns of the three Norman kings. In their charters he is meus dapiferus, and his signatures occur in Normandy as well as England to royal charters and others. Henry I gives a charter of Aylesford to St.Andrews, Rochester, witnessed there by Eudo Dapifer and Haymo Dapifer alone, and another by William Giffard, Eudo Dapifer, Haymo Dapifer, and William Albini, all relatives by blood or marriage. Gilbert, of Tunbridge Castle, earl of Clare, granted Rethravelda, Sussex, to the monks in the time of Rufus, the witnesses of which were Roger Bigod and Hamo Viscount, at Winchester. Henry often begins his charters, "To Hamo Dapifer and my faithful barons of Kent", as if Hamo's duties or residence had specially to do with that county. One of the earliest of his appearances is in the charter given 1082 by Bishop William Karileph to Durham monastery. It was signed at London by Robert, earl of Moreton; Roger, count of Shrewsbury; Robert, count of Northumbria; Roger Bigod; Hamo Dapifer; and others. In the charter of Simon Sinclair, earl of Northampton and Huntingdon, to St.Andrews, Northampton, 1108, his name does not appear, but Eudo Dapifer's does. He is dead before the end of Henry I's reign, because in 1131 there is an account in state record of him being dead, and of his heirs paying for entry to his possessions.

If "Hamo Dapiferus" and "Hamo Vicecomes" are one, as Sir Henry Ellis and many genealogists state, a great deal can be found about his wide lands in various counties, from The Domesday Book as well as other sources. He was proprietor in capite of lands in Essex, Kent, and Surrey, and as under-tenant in Kent, Surrey, Dorset, Wilts, Cheshire, Devon. Not one of the largest sharers of the Conqueror's gifts, he still held much, and it is known that his land in Normandy was extensive.

William Gemeticensis, after describing the "very great heir-ship" Robert Consul, the king's son, got with Matilda Sinclair, the daughter of Robert Fitz-Hamo, adds, "'The king gave also to him (Robert) the land of Hamo Dapifer, the uncle, by her father's side, of his wife'". He must have meant in Normandy; for, by the state roll of 31 Henry I (1131), Robert de Crepacor or Crevecour or Crepito Corde heirs at least a portion of Hamo's lands. He pays a fine or relief of £156, 13s. 4d. for what he gets of Hamo's lands in Kent alone, which represents, as money then was, large property. It is expressly stated that he only gets part of the dapifer's land. Matilda got her portion and no more. Her brother or near relation William de Sancto Claro likewise shared, it is to be expected.

Hasted, the historian of Kent, is wrong, in supposing that Hamo was a Crevecour; and it is from the fact that Robert Crevecour is part heir to Hamo that he is led to the mistake. In a charter by Robert de Crepito Corde to the canons of Leeds monastery, in the district of Chatham, he describes Hamo Dapifer as meus avunculus. What this shows is that his mother was a sister of Hamo and of Robert Fitz-Hamo of Gloucester, avunculus meaning uncle by the female side. As has been said before, this does not altogether preclude the Crevecours from being themselves Sinclairs; but it proves that Hamo was not a Crevecour, unless the Crevecours recently took their name, being originally Sinclairs. One of them is given by Wace as at the battle of Hastings, and Prevost localises them as from Crevecour-en-Auge, near Lisieux; so that only in Normandy could the lines be traced to any common ancestor, if at all. Philpott the great Kent antiquary is Hasted's authority, and in the third volume of the transactions of the Society of Antiquaries, Hamo Viscount is assumed also by a writer there to be Hamo Crevequer "the lord of Kent" on the same foundation, in connection with a charter discovered freshly, given in the Conqueror's time, where Hamo Vicecomes appears prominently. The fact of the marriage of the sister of the dapifer to Robert Crevecour's father is, in the first degree at least, thoroughly contradictory to Hasted's supposition.

The history of the Crevecours, however, is illustrative of at all events this marriage relationship. Dugdale's Baronage, by the names, Hamo being frequent, and by the places it describes as connected with them, throws sufficient light on a connection that needs no further light for proof than the record. It would have been pleasant to have found something definite as to Robert Crepacor's Sinclair mother. That she was high-souled and religious like many ladies of her family might be inferred from her son's liberality to the church. He founded the priory of Leeds in Kent for canons regular of the order of St.Augustine. His brother Adam (a name suggestive of a great Kent Sinclair, Adam, the commissioner of The Domesday Book), assisted with this foundation, Robert's wife Rose signs a charter for

Leeds. He has a brother and a son Elyas. The Giffards so liberal to Gloucester Abbey, the lords of Brimsfield, have the same strange first names among them. Rose was the favourite name among the Giffard earls of Buckingham, Walter Giffard of whom was also a commissioner of The Domesday Book. Robert Crepacour was heired by Daniel, a name often among the western Giffards.

To draw fixed lines among probabilities, however, is of the nature of making ropes of the salt sea sand. Antiquity will have itself respected by keeping the most eager inquirers sometimes at a distance. There are, however, indications of where and how inquiry might find facts and satisfaction. Hamo's lineage must, beyond this authenticated marriage of his sister to Robert Crevecour's father, be kept apart now from these Crepacours, who by heiring a Kentish baron, Maminot, a name in Domesday, became, Dugdale shows, themselves barons of England. The "barony of Chatham" was their lordship. They cannot on present evidence be claimed as of Hamo's male lineage.

There is a state message from Henry I, preserved in the Reg. Roff. of Dr. Thorpe, to Hamo Dapifer and to Hugh of Bocklande, to preserve most carefully the fishing on the Thames for the monks of Rochester. Who is this Hugh that seems lieutenant or colleague to Hamo's sheriffship of Kent ? Surnames did not begin, Tindal says, till the reign of William the Conqueror, and grew slowly. Bocklande, or Buckland as now written, meant a property for which Hugh or some predecessor had written or book warrant. There is a Bocklande in Kent and one near Farringdon, Berkshire. These Bucklands are, in the genealogical reckonings, relations of Eudo Dapifer by affinity and perhaps by blood. This, however, may have light reflected back upon it from the history of a Hugo de St.Clare, about whom there is nothing problematic.

Madox in his History of the Exchequer has one interesting reference which may be given: "'Concession of King William the Great: William, by the grace of God king of the English, to Hamo Dapifer and all his supporters in the bishopric of Rochester, greeting'". This put with the fact that Hamo was one of the busy persons in the great trial of Archbishop Lanfranc against Odo, bishop of Bayeux and earl of Kent, about Canterbury lands, and is there vicecomes, towards the very last years of the Conqueror's reign, makes his offices almost impossible to separate and distinguish. It has been before suggested that he was substitute dapifer for his relation Eudo, though Spellman's guess may after all be the correct one, that he was that of England alone and Eudo of Normandy alone. But Eudo in Henry's reign was certainly that of England also, and, it may be, after Hamo's death. The puzzle is not made the less because, as probably as not, Hamo was alive after 1119, the date of Eudo's death. One point is certain, that everything shows the two dapifers to have been the most delightful and agreeable of men. Their relations towards each other seem to be entirely without rivalry or jealousy, whatever the explanation.

Hamo, without children, and his estates being apparently well divided among his relations, it is hardly necessary to draw out account of them from The Domesday Book, where they are fully exhibited, under the large capital headings of an in capite holder, and the smaller titles of underholder. In appearance and quantity the estates would be much of a parallel with Eudo Dapifer's, who, except that he had a family, seems another self to Hamo Dapifer. They are as like as brothers in success and abilities on the secular side, but Hamo Dapifer's love of the monks does not much appear, and by this he may be the inferior of the lord of Colchester. An able business man Hamo must have been, without more of the religious faculty in development than "divine manners" and savoir faire. His character, even to the division of his wealth, leaves an impression of sagacity and refinement that cannot be resisted, though antiquity has taken considerable care to make it dim. That he was not neglectful of his soul's welfare, as then considered, a confirmation by the Conqueror of the returns of the church of Tarentford given by him is proof.

"'William by the grace of God king of the Angles, to the very faithful French-born and Angles greeting: Know that I have conceded that donation which Hamo, my dapifer, made to the church of St.Andrew in the town of Rochester, of the chvirch which is in my manor of Tarentford; and the sons of Hamo himself, Robert and Hamo, with me present, have granted the same donation of their father. Witnesses: Robert, count Mellent; Robert, count of Meritolio; and many Others'".

This translation of a charter from the Reg. Roff. would further seem to set at rest the whole difficulty of the dapifers, by making the great earl of Corbeuil who came from Normandy with William the king's dapifer, and his younger son the viscount of Kent. Fitz-Hamo's father seems a more important person for the highest office of the kingdom than his younger brother. If the dapifership were hereditary, surely the "knight of Rye" as the elder were the proper holder of it, after Hamo of Normandy was done with it. But there is another charter in the same collection by Henry, king of the Angles, to Archbishop Anselm, to Hamo Dapifer, and to all the barons and others of Kent, which is witnessed by two names only, at Rochester, Eudo Dapifer and Hamo Dapifer. The ingenious are welcome to the pleasant feat of unravelling these seeming contradictions.

Again, Henry writes about Little Wrotham to Archbishop Anselm and to Hamo Viscount. It may not be impossible to solve this question of identity or difference from the Monasticon and Reg. Roff. alone. With the chief drift now it is not a question of moment, mainly because the younger Hamo, whether never dapifer or dapifer as well as his father, but certainly the viscount of Kent, had no children to perpetuate his name, and give him a place among future Englishmen. He is even as viscount or sheriff an able and interesting figure, but the interest in him dies with the division of his property. Sir Henry Ellis is probably too hasty in assuming that the two great Hamoes of The Domesday Book are one. He is a good but by no means immaculate authority. Adam Sinclair, the commissioner, would have been willing, even if the recorders were different in the various counties, to keep these relations of his clear personalities. The difficulty may be nice rather than particularly useful, though it is a bold or ignorant thing to protest as to what little or great may be useful in investigagations of this nature.

Hamo Dapifer in The Domesday Book, holds in capite in Essex, and as undertenant in Kent, Cheshire, Wiltshire, Dorsetshire, and Devon. The entries under the heading "Hamo Vicecomes" are, in capite, Kent and Surrey, and also various lands in the same counties as undertenant. The account by Thomas Cromwell in his History of Colchester of the entry relating to that city may be added, more for his conjecture and for genealogical aid than perhaps for any biographical weight. "'Hamo, dapifer, or steward of the king's household, had one house and a court or hall (from which it may be conjectured that to him the government of the town had been confided), one hide of land, and fifteen burgesses, holden by his predecessor Thurfern in King Edward's time, all which then paid rent, except the hall: the burgesses still paid so much per head, but nothing for their arable land or the hide they held of Hamo. In the hide there was one carucate or plough-land in King Edward's time, but at the time of this survey none. Hamo had also six acres of meadow. All which in the time of King Edward were worth £4, which was also paid afterwards, but when the survey was made only forty shillings'".

Money values have no present comparison. The burgesses paid sixpence a head by the year for all taxes, rent, and everything; and the exorbitant weight of such taxation caused famines which Eudo Dapifer had to allay with corn from beyond sea. This Thomas Cromwell calls Eudo the dapifer for Normandy, but he is not clear as to the relation between Hamo and Eudo, both being possessors and rulers in Colchester at the same time. The hall or court seems to have been under the castle jurisdiction and lordship of the wealthier Eudo, though it is possible that independent civil cases had their decisions under Hamo. It is of considerable importance for understanding something of a subsequent Hamo, to find this one in official as well as some proprietary position in Colchester.

J.H. Round in the Antiquary of September 1852, discusses Hamo's position, and repudiates Freeman's translation and explanation of the passage in The Domesday Book referring to Colchester. He has in a note the genealogical fact that Hamo was the son of Hamo Dentatus, and with reference to Eudo Dapifer as also there he adds, "Strange to find him by his fellow dapifer, the son of the Conqueror's preserver". Family affairs in the highest circles are often very peculiar; the friend at one period can be the foe of a subsequent, and vice versa, let it be remembered.

Chapter XXVI
The Archbishop of Canterbury

Robert and Hamo were the sons of Hamo, earl of Corboil, Normandy, by the testimony of Brady the faithful historian, Glover the expert herald, and all the authorities. William of Corboil was created archbishop of Canterbury in 1123. Madox says there were difficulties about his creation. He is said to have been the first churchman as apart from statesman appointed to the office. That he was of the Hamo family, and consequently had the royal influence on his side, may be explanatory of the trouble, if it was that he was too young or private a man for the dignity. He figures fully in the clerical records of the prelacy. Enough if what notice he has in some secular histories be discussed now.

Rapin rightly calls him Corbet, and this is the same word which was also spelt Corbie. It was an earldom of Picardy, situated further north than Normandy, and under the king of France, if really at all subject. This externality probably gained William his archbishopric, with other aids which may be noticed. Rapin does not go quite wrong, in his sound and able History of England, when describing the successor of Ralph, the previous archbishop: "'Corbet, abbot of St.Bennet's, was elected by a synod held at Winchester for that purpose'". On this Tindal makes notes, giving his authorities,

1. 'All the historians call him William de Curboil or Curbuil. See Sax. Annals of Huntingdon, p.382. S.Dunelm, p.247. And then he was prior of Chich or St.Osith in Essex, not of St.Bennet's. Hoveden, p.477. R. de Diceto, p.504. Brompt., p.1014'
2. With regard to the place, "'At Gloucester. See Sax. Annals.'"

Homer nods, and Rapin undoubtedly is slightly napping here; for at Gloucester the election certainly took place, as Madox and the moderns, as well as the chroniclers on which they rightly found, state. The connection with St.Osith in Essex, is also of importance for a subsequent inquiry. But English Tindal is wrong when he corrects the Frenchman as to the French local name. "Corbet" it was, and an important town then, near Amiens.

The chroniclers are right also, in the use of the word Corbeuil, Corbeile, or Corboil, because it is only the usual adding of "ville" to the name. Corbet ville, Corbie "villa", or Corbet "town", as easily became Corboil as Magna Villa became Mandeville, and Longue Ville, Langvale. Rapin's foot was on his native soil in the matter, and he has the best of the argument with his interesting and valuable commentator.

There were many Corbets in England's history who might have reminded Tindal. Lord Peter Corbett in 1296 figured in Edward's claims for Scottish homage. Nay, does not Tindal himself note that Reginald, earl of Cornwall, was the son of Henry Beauclerc, the king, by Sibil, the daughter of Sir Robert Corbet of Alcester, in Warwickshire ? She was his own kin, as they both well knew. Burke says of the present baronets of the name that the "'family was founded in England by Corbeau, a noble Norman who accompanied the Conqueror;'" and, in The Domesday Book, Roger holds twenty-four lordships, in Shropshire alone, while his brother Robert has fourteen in that county, and was the lord of Alcester. One of Lord Clive the conqueror of India's ancestors, Richard Clive of Huxley and of Styche, married Margaret, daughter of Sir Richard Corbet of Moreton Corbet and Elizabeth Devereux of the lord Ferrers family.

William Sinclair held the archbishopric till his death in 1136. In church matters he is found in 1127 summoning a council on the burning question then of celibacy, after the faux pas of the notorious Cardinal de Crena, sent by Pope Honorius II to England in 1125 to advocate the cause. William's cure was to put the marrying priests into the king's hand to be dealt with. The plan was good till the king learnt the comfortable addition to his income from dispensations. Rapin says this caused many of the inferior clergy here to be the last in Europe to submit to the pope's decree. One of the great clerical and state troubles of this period, was the power the pope took of sending legates with authority above all the bishops and archbishops of the country. William was the first English archbishop who held at the same time the pope's legateship; and probably this great step gained from the popish thraldom, was somewhat owing to the scandal which the previous legate, the Italian cardinal, created.

The synod met at Westminster where William of Corboil, archbishop and pope's legate, presided. Some of the resolutions carried are suggestive of the period. The third was against money being the way to become monks and nuns. It would seem that there was competition for the idle luxurious religious life. One forbade plurality of archdeaconries, and one that monks should become farmers. The payment of tithes was made sacred by their being considered "the demesnes of the Most High".

But it is on the political side that William Sinclair has most general interest. Henry I had given great favour to his nephews, Stephen, afterwards king, and Henry whom he made abbot of Glastonbury Abbey. They were the third and fourth sons of Adela, Henry Beauclerc's sister, and of the earl of Blois. The eldest was imbecile, and the second took his father's position. Stephen and Henry put heads together to get the rule of England, after Prince William was drowned and Matilda was made heir to the crown. Henry had been made bishop of Winchester, and just before Henry the king's death in 1135, had gained William Sinclair, archbishop of Canterbury, and the wealthy Roger, bishop of Salisbury, to favour his brother Stephen's aspirations to the crown, in preference to Matilda. Rapin's sentences give the clue to the state of matters which made Stephen king of England so unexpectedly. The three prelates secured the whole church; and the lay lords, for all their oaths in favour of Matilda to Henry, were powerless.

"'The archbishop of Canterbury affirmed that the oath taken to Matilda was null and void, as being directly contrary to the customs of the English, who had never suffered a woman to reign over them. The bishop of Salisbury maintained that the oath was not binding, because Matilda was married out of the realm, without the consent of the barons, whose intention was when they swore, not to give themselves a king but of the race of William the Conqueror. In fine, to remove all scruples Hugh Bigod, the late king's steward, swore on the holy evangelists that Henry before he died disinherited Matilda and nominated his nephew Stephen for his successor'".

Twenty-two days after the king's death Stephen was crowned at Westminster by William Sinclair, the archbishop. It is said that his conscience made him let fall the host at the ceremony, but age and weakness are better explanation. He did not live long to support the king of his making; and so much the worse, it is likely, for the king. William's French birth and training made Salique law to him matter of conscience, and he would have used every effort to maintain the position he had taken. Stephen made the immense mistake, on the death of the archbishop in 1136, the year after his accession, when everything was quiet, of seizing not only the revenues of the see of Canterbury, but, as the archbishop died without a will being made, all his effects as the prerogative of the crown. This was against his own express charter of liberties, and the church never forgave him. The mischief of this reign began, and nothing but exhaustion, and Stephen's own giving up of the struggle of fifteen years and more, could end the misery.

It is a possible theory that this is the "Willlamus de Sancto Claro" who endows the abbey of Savigny, and gives the lands of Vilers to it with Matilda, countess of Gloucester; and even so, there would be no contradiction of their common lineage, both being descendants of the earls of Corbeuil. He certainly, as far as time is concerned, could be the William de St.Clare who signs the charter of the earldom of Essex by Stephen to Geffrey de Mandeville, the son of Eudo Sinclair's daughter Margaret. But in all charters of the period the clergy were most particular to put their titles with their names. There is nothing of this in the charter.

Malet's date of the foundation of the abbey of Savigny, 1139, would have to be changed before this William could be its founder and endower. What is most in favour of him being the man is that if he were not Matilda's brother he could as an archbishop appear without indecorum in a conjoint charter of lands gifted. As being a relative also, and having lands in juxtaposition to hers in Normandy, it could quite well be that he was so yoked in a good work. It is right to say thus much, but the vast preponderance of likelihood is the other way. The seal with the warlike crusader is not clerical at all, though it must not be forgotten that civil earldoms and hierarchical office were then quite compatible in one person. On the whole, however, Matilda, covnitess of Gloucester, had another companion than this able and honoured high priest of her lineage, and for him and his affairs further search must be made.

William of Malmesbury in his work The Pontiffs of England, tells of the peculiarly clerical antecedents of this the first wholly-trained monk of the see. His quarrel for supremacy with the stubborn Thurston, archbishop of York, was founded mainly on the want of the invariable political influence; and the monks had great terror lest he should sweep their houses clean, to their personal disadvantage, but the prior of "Cic" was wisely equal to his promotion. The chronicler gives his character pithily, "'He was indeed very religious, somewhat affable, but neither tory nor radical'". The family passion for architecture had in him a good representative. The Magna Britannia says that the cathedral church of Canterbury was rebuilt by him, and that there was a great public consecration of the building in the presence of the king, the queen, David, king of Scots, and the nobles. His work is to be seen to this day at the cathedral which is the centre of England's religious hierarchy; and it might almost be a question whether he was more fortunate in being the primate than in being builder of the revered historic temple.

One other excursion beyond this "island in the sea", this England, with its "happy race of men", and return is made to it for good.

Chapter XXVII
The Earls of Corbeil

Solvitur eundo. The legendary theory of the lineage already risked must be given up, however reluctantly, for the plainer but more satisfactory findings of science. So many names have falsely sought for alliance with the descendants of Duke Rollo, preferring to be sprung from it, through bastards rather than not at all, that it would have been a pleasure and surprise, if the Sinclair name could have been traced to the saint of Rochester, Kent, who went to the cell at the river Epte, in France, and there got, after years of the cup of water and the wooden bowl of holy life and penance, for his honest accusation of an evil woman of rank, the martyrdom which has made him immortal. He is not, nor is any relation of his, the ancestor of the family. He got or took the name St.Cler, and gave it to the place of his dwelling, or others gave it, as populaces do.

It was the fixed name of the locality where Rollo came, after the archbishop of Rouen had been sent to him by the French king, with the offer, if he should become Christian, to give him, as Mathew of Westminster has it, "'The sea-board territories from the river Epte as far as the boundaries of Brittany, with his daughter Gilia'". The archbishop undertook the embassy to the heathen duke, and was received pleasantly. Then this comes, "'On the appointed day at St.Cler the king of the French and Robert, the duke, assemble beyond the Epte river'". Rollo and his people kept the maritime side till the meeting that is so famous occurred, which made him, 912, duke of Neustria or Normandy.

Neither do the old French earls of Senlis who were friendly to the foreign-blooded Rollo and his descendants, turn out to be the Sinclair lineage, and of the same strain as the Simons of Senlis, the English earls, proved to have been of this blood. Every step that has been gone, the scientific findings, or rather the absolute and recognised records, of Glover, the Somerset herald of that sixteenth century so faithful to this department of human knowledge and interest, become from other histories and records more and more impossible to escape. Brady and many such weighty authorities agree with the herald about these earls of Corbeil. The prejudice was all along against his account of the Hamo family, but it is fairly and fully overcome. One can sympathise with the strange ejaculation, in 1704, of the learned Bishop Tanner, "Oh ! the worthy Robert Glover".

Saint Clare's ashes may have been carried about from the Norsemen, even previous to Rollo, as it pleased superstition to do: they were not "the ashes of the fathers" of this English family. The author of the Notitia Monastica and of the Bibliotheca Britannica-Hibernica gives more than such deserved but peculiar exclamatory assurance. In the latter work, published in 1748, he has a notice of the saint which would seem to settle the subject, and the more that he gives for authority Dempster, III., 251. So plain a statement cannot be too clear. "'Saint Clair or Guillermus, Scottish by country, passed the life of a hermit in France, and there at last is crowned with martyrdom. He wrote The Ritual of Divine Duty, one volume. He flourished about 600. He is worshipped on the 17th of July. His memory is preserved in the town of Normandy of that name, on the public road at Rouen'". But the legendary wandering of an early chapter cannot be without its use and its pleasure, mixed as it is with imdoubted facts which may lead to firmer fields. With this acknowledgment, it can fairly hold its place, as at least an imaginative attempt so show an origin; and half of the greatest classics cannot plead more for themselves and their continued existence than this. On the firm solid ground of historic record the steps must now be taken, and if the conclusions may be strange, the facts, and not fancies, are to blame.

The Sinclairs are of the same male blood as William the Conqueror, and their line over and above is free from his bastardy; though in the annals of royalty and nobility the bar sinister is almost as much the rule as the exception. Indeed, the Norse cult, like the German, put not at all the value on legitimacy which Christianity, under papal direction, found right. If there is greater worth in being legally pure and wholly submissive in this respect to the Christian cult, the Sinclair lineage has it. Their connection with the Conqueror is earlier than himself, as will appear now.

The quarrel which separated the sons of Rogenwald, surnamed "The Rich", the favourite of Harold Fairhair, king of Scandinavia, is well-known Danish early history. Rollo "the Ganger", a younger son, went to the Orkneys in first search after a kingdom, when he had to leave his country, which was Norway. Burke's Peerage gives under "Lord Sinclair" detailed account of these early ancestors of the best of the nation. In essential points his historic references are right. The father of Rollo he calls Rogenwald, earl of Maere and Raumdahl, in Norway; and he describes him as getting in 888 a grant of the Orkneys, which meant also as many of the Hebrides as his valour could add to them, from King Harold Harfagr, the student erst at Rome who had to kill a lion set on him as punishment for one of his youthful relapses into barbarism. Rogenwald's son Eynar, Burke makes rightly the permanent prince of the Orkneys, Rollo's hopes stretching to the south very soon. For five centuries his brother's descendants ruled there, while his were conquering Neustrias, Apulias, Sicilies, and Englands. That he spent good part of his youth among those dreamy heroic islands, where in winter it is all tragic bare sea-storm, and in summer always afternoon, is assumed by his better biographers. Torfaeus in his Orcades, seu rerum Orcadiensium Historiae, gives worlds of the earlier genealogy and deeds of this greatest family of the north. Why Rollo was not made permanent count of Orkney was that his father thought he was too brave, and that the principality needed civil administration most, which he knew his second son was not yet ready for. Some historians vary from this account a little.

It is said that Rollo himself was prince of those northern islands of Britain as well as of the parts of Britain next to them, and strangely do extremes meet in history as elsewhere if this could be thoroughly established. To the expeditions and conquests there by Prince Rollo with his dragon vessels of the ninth century, there is almost exact parallel in those by Prince Henry Sinclair, his own genuine full-blooded descendant of the fourteenth century. Says Pinkerton, the Scottish historian, "'In 1380 happened the strange voyage of Nicolo Zeno to Shetland'". Published as the curious tale was, at Venice in 1558, with quaint rough maps of those northern seas and islands, no little book has so much puzzled the learned. The "Frisland" of it is the Faeroe islands, and the Prince Zichmni who is so splendid a hero is Prince Sinclair, well known to Scottish history as Henry, lord of Roslin, Nithsdale (the capital of which district was Sanquhar, after the name so capable of peculiar but quite realisable metamorphoses), Caithness, and Stratherne.

The London Hakluyt Society, named after a clerical compiler of all voyages, have their eager eyes on the little work, *The Voyages of the Venetian Brothers, Nicolas and Antonio Zeno, Navigators*; and they have had influential correspondence and literature between themselves and the Americans, on the necessity of deposing the heroic Columbus of 1492 as the first discoverer of America, in favour of Prince Zichmni of 1380. They are enthusiastic as to the genuineness of the record by the two Zenoes of Venice. These were rich men who equipped two strong ships to navigate for discovery; the descendants, as the book shows, of one of the doges of the mistress of the seas. They were wrecked on Frieslanda, and saved out of the fierce hands of the islanders, getting infinite kindness from Sinclair, who spoke to them in Latin. Being first-class navigators, he got them to command a fleet of thirteen ships of war, besides many supporting vessels, on his expedition to conquer those Faeroe islands, and, it would seem, Iceland. They stayed with him thus many years, and in their account never tire of extolling the generosity, the patience, the courage, the ability of "the great prince", who loved them so much that he could not let them ever get a glimpse of their dear Italy again.

The strangest portion of the narrative to moderns is the brave voyages of the heroic Aeneadic Zichmni. He went along the east coast of America, called "Kerry" there from an Irish colony; the inhabitants rushing along the coast, naked and bearing spears, exactly like South-sea islanders, but fiercer, opposing his landing with everything in their power, barbaric howling included. He does land and fight them at intervals as his voyaging requires.

But the most delightful passages to the literary colonels and admirals of the Hakluyt and American Societies, are those in which the adventures in Greenland and Vinland are related. The men were cannibals, the Zenoes say. Their houses were built round, with a hole at the top. They were naked, and suffered cruelly from the cold, but, the narrative adds, they had not enough of brain to cover themselves even with the skins of animals. Several "cities" or gatherings of people were visited, and Zichmni wished his people to stay with him to found colonies there to add to the Orkneyan and Norwegian princedom. But there was as pitiful complaining of the unheroic, except under such leadership, common men, as was with the Spaniards of Columbus, that they never should see their mothers, sisters, children, or friends any more if they did not get back speedily. There were attempts to build cities, and if the climate and district of America had been more favourable. Prince Zichmni, for all his kindness of heart, would have given full rein to his ambition and intelligence. The narrative is made up of storms, fightings, deaths, sorrows, and braveries that have their counterparts only in such poetry as that of Homer and Virgil. Perhaps the Sagas may be added, as that was the very scene of their strange romance, founded on the genuine action of the brave northern ancestors of Englishmen.

In the discussions about the little book (which is preserved at the British Museum, and in Hakluyt's compilation), these Sinclairs who figured thus in Scotland and Scandinavia, are said to have got the principality of the Orkneys and Shetlands before this, by fighting a cousin, their rival, till he got the worst of it in death. There is knowledge of Spere building a fort at Bressay before Lerwick had existence. The usual account is that they got the principality by marriage to the lady of his surname whose wonderful lineage and claims Burke stands in such admiration at, Odin being the first of the pedigree. Prince Henry Sinclair was in blood as other respects probably as good a match as then lived, the descendant of the Rollo prince of the Orkneys, afterwards the better celebrated duke of Normandy of every one's knowledge.

The Prince Zichmni is one of the world's men. It would be too narrow even to call him an American Sinclair, if the Venetian tale of him and his doings is to be substantiated by literary navigators and lovers of discovery.

The truth of the story of the Italian Zenoes is strongly supported by the findings of the Royal Society of Antiquaries of the North, Copenhagen. In their printed memoirs of the years 1836-1839, Professor Rafn has an able paper on the discoveries of America before Columbus, beginning as early as the tenth century. He found and edited 18 ancient parchment codices, which form quite a literature on the subject. Bjarne Heriulfson in 986 reached Greenland, Leif Ericson in 994 got south as far as Vinland (New England of the United States), Thorwald Ericson in 1004 came to Kialarnes or Cape Cod, Thorfinn followed further, and Florida is thought to have been reached. Bishop Eric of Greenland went south to Vineland in 1121. There seems to have been an Irish colony even then somewhere on the eastern American coast, but it would be difficult to conjecture what became of them. Whether they amalgamated with the Esquimaux, to become the heroic Red Indian, is a question. But "'the last document upon America which exists in the ancient manuscripts, has reference to a voyage from Greenland into Markland (Nova Scotia), undertaken in 1347 by 17 men on the same ship'". It was in 1380 Prince Henry Sinclair made his far more important voyage, evidently with valuable political purpose; and if any man is to have fame out of the ante-Columbian discoveries, he may well be remembered as the first for purpose and enterprise.

The colonisation of North America was, in the end, a history of miseries and sacrifices and wholesale withdrawals from the country, which fact prosperity now all but entirely hides; and Henry broke ground gallantly on the forlorn hope it was, despite its fine climate and the berries which gained the name Vineland for its best part.

Burke's Peerage under "Caithness" gives relevant account of this Roslin Sinclair; and under "Sinclair", baronet of Ulbster, the first paragraph is a condensed history of some of the Roslin family. He says, "'the most powerful and illustrious of the Scottish magnates during the reigns of Robert II, Robert III, and the three first Jameses'". Henry's principality he calls the "princely fief" of Orkney, held by homage to the Norwegian king. It was given him, says Torfaeus, the great Latin historian of the Orkneys (which included the Zetlands), of the Faroe isles, and of Greenland and Vinland, the year before the Zenoes met him. In the chief work of Torfaeus, Orcades, seu Rerum Orcadiensium Historia, published Hauniae 1697, there are copious high-historical Latin pages of the treaties made between him and the king of Norway.

The tale of the Italians referring to war and conquest in 1380, the conditions of homage being settled in 1379, would give the inference that Henry thought these too severe, and thus got his principality made freer and wider. As it reads in Torfaeus, did we not know how particular feudalism was about details afterwards little attended to, the homage was extremely regulated. The scribes of the time dearly loved composition on such occasions, and there is no ground for believing that the prince of the northern isles was the least more bound to the king of Norway than any duke of Normandy was to the French king. The Chronica Regum Manniae et Insularum (especially that published at Perth in 1784 with the additions of the Norwegian account of Olave the Black, the king of Man, and of Haco's expedition to Scotland to resist the invasion of his islands by Alexander III of Scotland) throws the most valuable light on the preponderating importance of the Norwegian kingdom, in the thirteenth century particularly, over all the north. Torfaeus tells of a John Sinclair, lord of Hjaltland, and of a Thomas "Sencler", who both had full ruling powers in those periods over Orkney and Zetland.

But all this belongs more to Norse than English history, though the principality has got divided between the countries as matter of fact, and England has her part yet only as a redeemable pledge. A skilful claimant of the right strain might recover the princedom and its crown. Scotland itself was in exactly similar homage to the English king with that which the Orkneys, Faroes, and the rest gave to the Scandinavian monarch. It was this equality which bred jealousy at Edinburgh against the lords of Roslin, says Burke; and there are only too clear evidences of its base results. There are materials to clear up this chapter of history, and Prince Henry Sinclair and his sailors may yet stand out strongly as some of the world's soundest heroes.

It would, however, be delaying the right progress to say more of him, and Prince Rollo, his ancestor, must now be followed to some extent. It was from this northern principality he fitted his ships and made his voyages of conquest, to England, and ultimately to Normandy, his final home. He died there, 917, leaving behind him his son, William Longsword, who succeeded him as duke of Normandy; a daughter, Gerlotte, who married William, earl of Poitiers; and a son, Robert, earl of Corbueil. This Robert had no issue. Duke William Longsword, who died 948, left Richard, duke of Normandy, who died 960. It is his family to whom it must be looked for the immediate ancestor of all the Sinclairs. His eldest son Richard was duke till his death in 1026, and Robert, earl of Evreux, was the second son, of whom came Raoul, the constable, who fought so gallantly against the king of France for the young son of Arlotta, Malger, earl of Corbueil, was the third son, and the direct founder of the house of Sinclair, the only traceable stock perhaps extant of the legitimate lineage of Rollo. They had two sisters, Hedwiga, married to Geffrey, earl of Brittany, and Emma, queen of England by Ethelred II, and of England and northern Europe by Canute the Great, her second husband. As far as the Rollo male kinsmanship is concerned, this is enough. It may be useful for general purpose to follow the lineage, however, down to the Conqueror.

Duke Richard, Malger Sinclair's brother, had two of his sons dukes after him, Richard who died without issue in 1027, and Robert, the devil and saint, the father of William the Conqueror by Arlotta the tanner's daughter at Falaise, the great illegitimate who has made dishonour into honour. The Conqueror had an uncle Malger, Duke Robert's brother, the archbishop of Rouen, who with William of Arques fought so bitterly against Arlotta's son, William, as not proper heir of the line. He had two aunts, Alix, countess of Burgundy, and Eleanor, married to Baldwin, earl of Flanders, whose daughter Matilda he married, to make her queen of Normandy and England.

It was his grand-uncle, Mauger, earl of Corbeuil, that was the first of the Sinclairs, when the royal direct line is left. According to modern, and even Norman ideas, they have better claim in France or England, apart from conquest, than William had; and when his male dynasty ended in Prince William, son of Henry I, it was the descendants of the earl of Corbeuil, the Hamoes, the Ryes, and the sons of Walderne, who had the rights of the house of Rollo. Had it been a property entailed, and not a matter of intrigue for female relationships, the throne of England (and with the family vigour quite of another character than that of the miserable Fulc, robber, murdering, inefficient Plantagenets, the cruel, displaying, really effeminate, Celtic Tudors, and the degenerate Stewards, probably that of France also) would now be held by one of the genuine and entirely legitimate lineage. Were the monarchy really hereditary, and not the prize of mere adventurers, the heir of William the Conqueror, as of Rollo, would have been the present earl of Caithness, or one of his near kinsmen. There lie also the clearest claims to be inheritors of the fame of the Hamo and Eudo Ryes, he being of one blood with them. It was this that Principal Miller of Madras meant long ago when he wrote that the queen of England's blood from which she holds her kingdom, has its best living representatives in her farthest mainland county.

The Ryes and the Hamoes, from the accident of saving William's life, became his staunch and highly-favoured supporters. Signs, however, are not wanting that they once were among the grumblers against the illegitimacy of their ruler. The earls of St.Clere, as of the archbishop's district, never seem to have acknowledged fully or heartily his right; and this is the explanation of the departure of William Sinclair, cupbearer of Queen Margaret Atheling of Scotland, from England, in 1072 as Scot states in his history, with various others of "the emigrants", as they were called. Tindal supports this as the date, and six years after the Conquest questions had got their fiercest fullest discussion.

The comparatively small estates secured by his brothers Richard and Brito in England are accounted for by the well-known historical fact that the Conqueror systematically slighted his father's family, and feared their claims also. They undoubtedly had made it the hardest possible of struggles for him to get and keep his dukedom. He gave all the honours and property he could to the relations of his despised mother. Odo, bishop of Bayeux and earl of Kent, with Robert, earl of Moreton, the two greatest sharers in England's division, are examples, being his brothers by his mother. The Ryes, Hubert the ambassador and his sons Ralph, Hubert, Eudo, and Adam, with their sister, wife of Peter de Valence, had done so much for him, and had been so loyal, that he could not escape acknowledging their public deeds; but even of them he was jealous. The Hamoes, the Ryes of the English place, in the second instance, had uphill work, with all their gallantry and devotion in his cause. Without study of such family claims and circumstances of legitimacy and its opposite it is not possible to understand that period. If Richard Sinclair, the son of Walter or Walderne, earl of St.Clare, did greatly distinguish himself in the battle of Hastings, probably it was the more reason why his politic relation should neglect him as much as he could safely do. The third son, William, certainly preferred the Athelings as the true successors of the English crown to his own blood relation. It might have been different if the tanner lineage had not mixed with that of the Norse Rollo.

Walter, earl of St.Clare, was married to the Conqueror's aunt by the father's side; so that the young sons were his first cousins, and too dangerously near, by male lineage also, to be over much benefited. The favoured Clares of Tunbridge, earls of Clare, Hertford, and Gloucester were of the same Rollo lineage, but they had the bar sinister like himself over their shield, and it was both safe and sympathetic to give them high place and, what was perhaps more testimony of the monarch's real feelings, wide lands. The Clares and the St.Clares are united in another way than the legendary, and the honour of the connection by blood as also by many marriages, is probably with the first, at least on principles of the Christian cult.

The Cottonian MS., which is a transcript in 1600 by Smith, the Rouge-dragon, of the then dead Glover's MS., Somerset herald, has the clearest possible account of the descent of the Hamo St.Clairs from Malger, earl of Corbeuil. Duke Richard was married to Gunnora, a princess of Norway, and Malger was their third-born son. He is described as not only the earl of Corbeuil but as the first archbishop of Rouen, to distinguish him from his nephew, the second Malger, also archbishop of Rouen, the uncle and bitter enemy of the Conqueror when the young duke of Normandy. The elder Malger's son was Hamo called "Dentatus", and no more powerful baron was there than he in Normandy. Hamo's son was earl of Corbeuil and also lord of Torigion. He was the great Hamo who came to England to aid William the Conqueror. His sons were Robert Fitz-Hamo, the "knight of Rye", and Hamo, viscount of Kent, and, as Glover says, also the dapifer. The roll 31 Henry I (1131) shows that they had a sister, the mother of Robert Crevecour. This finishes to full satisfaction the lineage of the Hamoes, but the question next arises, what were the actual degrees between them, the Rye Sinclairs (as they themselves also were), and the earl of St.Clare's branch of the family ? It could not be expected that full mastery were possible in such inquiry, even with the pedigrees of reigning royalties of much later periods, but sufficient may be gathered to make strong assurance of the unity of the Rye Sinclairs and Walderne's people in very near degrees. More is not wanted for use or ornament.

But before taking this up there is another additional security of the unity of Sinclairs with Rollo's family. No arrival of any of the great lords from the continent in England has been more mysterious, by his seemingly unsupported success, than that of Simon of Senlis. A brave lame soldier, the historians cannot understand how it was that the Conqueror gave him the best he had to give in England as late as about 1076; and he was not, by anything which has been found, even one of the companions at Hastings, to aid his fortune. Waltheof's standing titles and lands were the most important in England, next to the king's own; and it is matter of notoriety how William tried to compel his niece Judith, Waltheof's widow, to marry the unprepossessing, at all events in body through his wounds, warrior, and nothing else, had we no insight beyond the usual accounts of him. He was a son of Warner, surnamed "The Rich", and held under the king of France as well as in Normandy. The Rollo family had the annexation fever in them, and Senlis as well as Corbeil in Picardy were earldoms independent of the dukes of Normandy, though both branches of Rollo's descendants had lands there also, as will be shown. "The Rich" is the oldest substitute for a surname, the Scandinavian method of distinction, of the male blood of William the Conqueror. Rollo's father was Rogenwald "The Rich". When, as Tindal has it, surnames really began in the eleventh century, this gave place to the more fashionable local surnaming from properties, but "Le Riche" survived well, and it is the key and clue to Simon St.Clair of Senlis as the successful relation of William I, and the happy husband of Matilda, Judith's daughter.

The various land possessions, externally to the duchy, of Rollo's descendants, in French dominions, are a virgin subject, which will yet become fruitful in the hands of the able and subtle historian. It is manifest where this set of facts points. Since the Simon earls of Huntingdon, Northampton, and Lincoln, have been proved Sinclairs, and since they are the Riches, of an earlier method of Danish as opposed to the later French system of surnaming, and since the Rollo family, down to Prince William who was drowned in 1120 from the White Ship, were also Riches, the unity of the lineages becomes a certainty. With all those whom history and record note as Sinclairs there can be no further question as to what their blood is. The steps of relationship, however, are as intricate, and often impossible to trace, as they are interesting and suggestive as to what might have been or yet may be. The Senlis Sinclairs were from a distant branch of the Rollo stock, and therefore quite safe to encourage, in comparison with the nearer Walderne, earl of St.Cler, and his sons. Family affection when safe was strong in the Conqueror. Hence the fortune in England of Simon, and also of a brother, Warner le Rich, was princely as compared with that of the relations nearer to the sovereign.

Being of the sons of the archbishop of Rouen, first of the ducal family who held this clerical office there, Walderne at the Conquest was in possession of the neighbouring earldom of which the famous town of St.Cler was the centre; but Sir Andrew Malet says that his habitual residence was the castle of St.Lo at that period, the site of which he asserts is still observable. Sir Francis Palgrave gives Charlemagne as the original builder of it; and of so imposing and numerously-served a character was it, that he adds it created the large town around it. Rollo himself besieged and took it by cutting off the water in his earlier wars. Walderne and the Rye Sinclairs were therefore, in their locality and training, central Normans, Caen being the star of their religious and, as Duke William was near at Falaise, political worship. Rouen at that time was hardly the metropolis had been under previous dukes. The duchy could not breathe at its fullest, so to speak, except near the heart of the territory, and thus is explained the personal, but not proprietary, absence of the Sinclairs of St.Cler, from the district which was destined to give the whole race its name.

The first earl of St.Cler seems to have been a brother or son of Hamo Dentatus, the son of Malger, earl of Corbeil and archbishop of Rouen. The position of Dentatus's son, Hamo, as earl of Corbeuil, but also and especially as the lord of Torignian, is explanatory of the strong connections with the province of the Cotentin which they had. He was lord of Astremerville also, but it is not easy to say whether this was in Normandy, or elsewhere under the French king, as was so common and so much liked by the independent lords who figure on both sides of the Channel about 1066. Fortunately there is a fine Latin description of this town of Torignian by the chronicler William Gemeticensis, which leaves no doubt as to what it was and where it was and whose it was. He is describing the great heritage which Henry I got for his son Robert Consul, earl of Gloucester, by marrying him to Matilda Sinclair, the daughter of Mabel Montgomery, sister of the Robert of Belesme who was earl of Arundel and Shrewsbury, and lord of many places beside in England and Normandy. She brought him, from her father Robert Fitz-Hamo, this Torrinneium, as the Latin has it. It was the head town, the chronicler says, of the lands; and he describes in detail how populous it was, and how thronged with merchandise, though the soil was not so fertile of itself as in many other parts of the duchy. Its site was on the borders of the bailliwicks or counties of Bayeux and Coustance. The feudal castle was near or within it, and stood on a height two miles on what Gemeticensis calls "the hither side" of the river Vire, which is the boundary between the consulatum Bayeux and its neighbour. Where this Vire joins the Ouve was the scene of the historical and romantic story of the assistance of Hubert of Rye to the young duke, William, galloping for his life from Valence, whence his enemies were pursuing him at full speed. The Duke's Way, still preserved there by tradition as the name of the ford, was over the river on which higher up the castle of Torignian stood, as that of Rye was on the Falaise side of the ford. Such juxtaposition of lands cannot be allowed to go for nothing.

The French historian of England, Rapin, has a special claim to be heard on William's enemies. Says he: "'Guy of Burgundy, son of a daughter to Duke Richard II, was the next that appeared on the stage. He had concerted his measures so well, that he was like to have surprised the duke's person who was then at Valognes without any guard, ignorant of what was practising against him. But a certain fool whom the conspirators did not mistrust, hearing their design, travelled all night to give the duke notice, who had but just time to put on his clothes and ride full speed to Falaise. What haste soever he might make, he was so closely pursued that he must have been taken, his horse not being able to carry him thither, had he not been assisted by a gentleman whom he accidentally met on the road'". This "gentleman", according to the sober hue of history, was the lord of Rye Castle, whose tale is told with brighter fire in the rhymed chronicle of the dukes of Normandy, as already noted.

Freeman has written of the incident more picturesquely, though, in the balance, he is light against the honest sobriety of Rapin's account of Hubert Sinclair's needed aid to his distressed relation. Eudo got to be seneschal for this by and bye; and, in passing, it may be noted that he had his name from the husband's family of another sister than this one married to Guy of Burgundy, she who married Geffrey, earl of Brittany. Being the sister of Malger, the direct founder of these Ryes, these Torignians, and the St.Lo Sinclairs, it can be understood how Eudoes and Geffreys were noticeable as names in the families. So much was this the case that it took considerable pains to find that, as to male lineage, the earls of Brittany, of Celtic origin, had nothing to do with the purely Norse Sinclairs. The names are, however, at least another indication of the identity of these families with the ducal house. An attempt will not be made, on the evidence at present secured, to draw the lines between the lords of St.Cler and St.Lo, of Torignian, and of Corbeil, of Rye on the Norman and on the English sides. Torignian, St.Lo, and Rye could well have been families founded by three sons of Hamo Dentatus. Malger, the first archbishop, is still more probable, as being the provider for other two sons, as well as this Hamo Dontatus, about whom Glover's Cottonian codex makes us certain. In those times of the church archbishops as princes were universally family men. Malger being of royal blood had more freedom, if that were at all possible, than even the less high-born prelates.

That the lineage is at last settled, and that all these are worthy and unsullied branches of the family tree of Rollo of Scandinavia, prince of the Orkneys, and the first Norse duke of Normandy, are findings sufficient to satisfy the greatest aspirations after high descent. The much humbler (for could anything be lowlier than a crust and a bowl beside the well still good for the eyes near the Epte ?) origin from the good Saint Clair, who went to that place to which his probably assumed Latin name ever afterwards clung, was something much to be desired. But it could not be. The men who had heraldry as the substitute for all our modern science, cannot be put down on questions which they investigated with what might be called the sorrow and sweat of the brain. His martyrdom was in 894, and this date will in no way assort with facts which cannot be denied, such as French Moulin gives in his History of Normandy. Out of this wood of royalties, and Dantean thrills of joy assail. War of words is tame stuff. Elsewhere than here is that game to be got. Investigation, not pleading cases, is the inspiration that gives sufiicient enthusiasm to arrive through journeyings by night and day of obscurity and sunshine at conclusion. The road is now on English soil, and the guide-books are wonderfully full, and more wonderfully authentic. The world-thinking Jew that Sir Francis Palgrave was, like the best men of his race, called the state papers of England the admiration of all nations. They are mainstay for what has yet to be said of the English Sinclairs.

Chapter XXVIII
The Viscount abd Fee-Farmer of Colchester

The name and locality of this man, who is frequently mentioned in state rolls of the reigns of Henry I, Stephen, and as late as Henry II, bind the Ryes of England and France still more closely. Hamo de Sancto Claro at Colchester, is a combination which could not be accidental. He appears to have been of the Fitz-Hamo and Hamo Dapifer family, and related at greater distance to Ralph, Hubert, Eudo Dapifer, and to Adam of the Two Camps, Kent. He was probably the brother of William de Sancto Claro, the sons, it may be, though more light is necessary, of Fitz-Hamo by the Welsh princess, Theodora ap Tudor. If so, he was the elder, his properties being much more extensive than those of him of Dorset, he who endowed the abbey of Savigny in conjunction with his sister or near relation Matilda, countess of Gloucester, in 1139. The Great Roll of the Pipe of 31 Henry I (1131) makes Hamo the payer of heavy taxes in Essex, Hertfordshire, Kent, Sussex, Boseham, Norfolk, Suffolk, Durham, Northamptonshire, and Bedfordshire. He ranks among the chief men of the time in this respect, his largest properties being, as to their order of size, in Bedfordshire, Norfolk, and Hertfordshire.

These localities point unmistakably to heirship of Fitz-Hamo's lands in part, and also some of Hamo Dapifer's. Whether it is possible to establish this thoroughly from Domesday without other aid, must be left for specialists in legal business. The records of him and his doings are unimpeachable in their integrity; and it becomes a most interesting inquiry, whether successful or not, how he got all these lands, in the most favoured spots of the kingdom. From the other families no likely person could be chosen to fill the place this Hamo of Colchester does. That he was Fitz-Hamo's eldest and William the second son would satisfy many related events. It will be seen afterwards that there was a third brother, and his family distinguish themselves in history. It might be that Hamo Sinclair of Colchester, as far as time and birth are concerned, could have been a scion of the Hubert of Norwich, or Ralph of Nottingham, families; but the extensive properties, and their situations, shut off the real possibility of such connection, even should there be nothing directive in the name.

213

If he is the son of Fitz-Hamo, he is seven steps from Rollo his ancestor, William the Conqueror being five, as the century nearly between their different dates of births might make right. That Hamo was in close relation to the crown, is indicated by the fact that Henry I gave Colchester and its castle to him, after Eudo Sinclair the dapifer's death, the relation of both. It has been noted that Henry was at the deathbed in Normandy of Eudo; and though Eudo had his son, the first earl of Essex, then alive, and also his daughter, Margaret, the wife of Geffrey Mandeville, earl of Essex in her right, he seems to have given a large part of his lands and property to King Henry. Colchester Castle was in the hands of the king, and much besides of the dapifer's emoluments. It is not improbable that the fee-farm which the crown gave of it and of Colchester, on feudal principle, to Hamo de St.Clair, was of the nature of a compromise as to rights of heirships.

His running accounts with the treasury were of this nature, "'Hamo Sinclair renders an account of the fee-farm of the town of Colchester: In the treasury; £38, 16s. 7d.: and he owes £23 0s. 10d.'". At that time, as every one knows, sums of this kind were more than perhaps twenty times present value. These being current sums, it is difficult to be sure of how much Henry let the returns of Colchester to him at. The burgesses a considerable time afterwards, 32 Henry II (1132), got free from feudal customs to the extent of paying their own rent, which was then £42 per annum. This, however, may have been a much smaller sum than Hamo paid. But as late as 1327 the citizens of London paid only £300 for the fee-farm of London. Morant, the historian of Colchester, says fee-farm is equivalent to rent and perpetuity, so that Hamo's possession had all the nature of property, estates often having perpetual tenure by either some personal service or small sum as acknowledgment of superiority. Tindal gives the same explanation of the term.

The fee-farm of Colchester, nevertheless, was then up to its value, though if the times grew better there would be no rise of rent. It was through him as sheriff or viscount that the taxes came to the crown, of aids, scutages, and tallages. There are frequent entries of such kind as this, "'And the same Hamo Sinclair, king's sheriff, concerning the aid from the town of Colchester: In the treasury; £3, 2s. and 4d.'". So it went on continually, as is usual with public affairs, and Hamo was, in some respects, the equal and right successor of Eudo Sinclair, the more absolute lord of Colchester. The Ruber Liber Scaccarii has Hamo de Sco Claro as one of its familiar names. Morant says there is record that Colchester was in fee-farm in Stephen's reign, and also 9 and 17 Henry II (1109 and 1117); the sheriff of Essex and Hertfordshire, this Hamo de

St.Clair, being the holder at these periods, as no doubt throughout, if all the state accounts were available for examination.

The position of viscount or sheriff was then of high importance, he being the king's manager of counties, checking the doings of the count or earl, who had the charge of, and drew the third penny for, the actual rule of his county. Hamo Dapifer did not think it beneath him, though dapifer or high steward, next in dignity to the sovereign, to be '"sheriff of Kent". This Hamo had a double charge with his two counties; and, without reference to his properties at all, this makes him a man of mark, his district of rule being particularly influential and prominent in his period. His entries in the little book by Hunter extracted from the Roll of the Pipe, 1131, are nearly a dozen; and from this it can be imagined how busy a man he was in civil affairs. The fee-farm of Eudo Dapifer's lands also would take much care of management, '"he renders account with regard to the fee-farm of the land of Eudo Dapifer'".

Vice-count grew to be the later descriptive title recognisable under viscount, shire-reeve or sheriff being the Saxon equivalent to the Franco-Latin word. A recorded tax on his properties ranged in the different counties from 6s up to 38s. It is difficult to take conclusion as to their value from one taxation, there were so many taxes under different names; but it is of use by indicating their localities, which is a hard enquiry when The Domesday Book loses it relevance to the estates of new generations. That he was a buyer and seller of lands, and in this respect perhaps before his times, one of his transactions in Suffolk may example, '"Muriel, the daughter of Ralph of Sanineio, renders an account of £18, 6s., 8d. that she has to pay for land free from all claim from Hamo Sinclair: In the treasury ten marks silver; and she owes , £ 11, 13s. 4d.'". Enough, however, of what easily may become duller than useful. Connected with the king's treasury he may have been, besides holding his sheriffships; as others of his relations were, it will be discovered.

Hamo Dapifer had a hall which had the full privileges of holding court, and he had houses besides in Colchester. This Hamo had one mansion near Chelmsford, and it was called St.Clere Manor. It would be built on one of the properties the rolls refer to in Essex, and would have the nature of a castle, as was usual. Colchester Castle did not make defence of less importance at St.Clere Manor. With Henry II he was in great favour, very likely because then well-stricken in years, after a very active and successful life. Colchester has stories about some of its sheriffs being so rapacious that they tried all they could to get the fee-farm given to the burgesses so as to escape exactions. But giving municipal freedom to cities, formerly under their feudal lords, became the habit of those times, and nothing of slight can specially reach Hamo as one of the oppressors. It is probable that villein-grumbling, town or country, had quick cure from the ruling and necessary vigour of all Norman lords, and Hamo would no doubt be equal to the traditions. Possibly Eudo Sinclair with his kindness spoiled the Colchestrians a little, and made them feel small burdens as if they were great. But there need be no injustice to them for what is to all appearance only the prattle and easy prejudice of some chronicler or writer while amusing himself with passing the time. Of this sheriff and his family the Colechestrians are nearly as proud as they are of their loved Eudo. To his only daughter, Henry II gave charters of the splendid estates of Stanway manor and of Lexden, in Essex. His only son was instrumental to this liberality by his doings. The father Hamo added to his other works interest in religious things like his predecessor Eudo.

Accounts are extant of his benefits to the abbey of St.John the Baptist, Colchester, the foundation of the dapifer. His name occur's in its Register, part of which is preserved among the Cottonian MSS. in a work of ancient extracts; and the usual habits of men of wealth and birth, make it safe to assume that his gifts, and perhaps his own foundations, were in accordance with what we know of his noted civil energy. It is certainly of more than genealogical interest to find Eudo and this Hamo of the next generation, of one mind as to Colchester's spiritual welfare. "'At the same time was founded the abbey of St.John, Colchester, by Eudo, mayor of the palace to King William'"; and Hamo as governor of Colchester Castle, fee-farmer of the town, proprietor in a dozen counties, sheriff of Essex and Hertfordshire, and endower of his relation's abbey, as probably of other religious houses, was worthy in good degree to follow him. It would be valuable to know how Hamo's prosperity affected Eudo's son, John Sinclair, earl of Essex, and more especially Margaret, his daughter, after the death in 1144 of Geffrey, earl of Essex, her husband; but it will not perhaps be further cleared up, and there is at least this to depend on, that the lineage had good substance and success, though the times were so unsteady when not unjust and oppressive. Stephen's reign ruined noble families for ever, but this line reached better times in some of its members, and has effective English representatives.

If Hamo is not the son of Fitz-Hamo, the nephew of Hamo Dapifer, vicecome of Kent (the brother of Matilda, wife of Robert Consul, Henry I's son, and also brother of William de Sancto Claro of Dorset and other counties), who is he ? There are contemporaries of the name, but account of them hereafter will show the impossibility of his biography agreeing with theirs. The lineage connection with royalty is the best explanation of Henry I, about 1120, giving Hamo de St.Clair the fee-farm of Eudo's lands, and also of his castle and town of Colchester, the royal and Hamo families being further connected by Matilda's marriage ten years previously. If Henry had gained anything at the dapifer's deathbed, it is not likely he would have taken the trouble he evidently has, to let the main fruits pass out of his own family again. His daughter-in-law's half-brother was a fit and proper person to hold in hand this part of that king's immense possessions. They are still more imposing when reckoning is made of how he provided for his many near relations, his thirteen illegitimate children included. It is granted that there has not yet been found absolute record to make Hamo de St.Clair of Colchester Castle the son of Fitz-Hamo, or the nephew of Hamo Dapifer, but the tendency of what evidence there is points in this direction. Imagination must be kept out of the question, and the relationship accepted above may be open to correction.

Petroburgensis Benedictus abbas, in his chronicle, makes Hamo de Sancto Claro one of the witnesses to King Stephen's second charter to the people of England, and Stubbs in his Select Charters accepts this. But Richard Prior of Hagulstadt, in his chronicle, gives the signature as Hugo de Sancto Claro, whose history as royal cup-bearer will occur subsequently. That Eudo Martel and William de Albini in subscribing the same document are both called pincerna or cup-bearer, would favour Hamo of Colchester's subscription, but further knowledge may arise under Hugo de St.Clare *pincerna*.

Chapter XXIX
The Hero of Bridgenorth

Under the date 1165, Stow in his Annals of England tells this tale. "'In a certain assiege at Bridgenorth against Hugh de Mortimere, when the king was shotte at by one of the enimies, a valiant man, Hubert de Saint Clere, constable of Colchester, did thrust himselfe betwixt the king and the danger of the stroke, and so received death for him, whose onlie daughter the king taking into his custodie, hee gave her in marriage to William de Languale with her father's inheritance, who begote on her a sonne bearing the name and surname of his grandfather'". Lord Lyttleton's History of Henry II has also an appreciative account of this the only son of Hamo Sinclair of Colchester. Henry II was not of the temper to forget such a deed. He had had great contest with his nobles, especially the western ones, who in their powerful castles thought to defy his sovereignty, as the French nobility did so long with their kings. They must reduce their military establishments, was the last word to them of the gallant Harry, and bitter refusals, and sieges of "the most arrogant men alive", as Speed has said of this very Mortimer, ended in the sovereign compelling them to the obedience and duty of subjects. Hubert St.Clere, knighthood being the high ton of the time, had got his; and as Sir Hubert, as well as lord of Colchester and governor of the castle, he had followed his king and relative to the western wars. His career ended in glory that is unique in the history of families; and, a young man, no one of his countrymen can regret so fine an example of English heroism, at the expense of even so distinguished and valiant a life as his was, with no doubt many possible pages to fill by similar action of honour and loyalty.

But accounts vary in different writers. Camden, the antiquary, when describing Shropshire, speaks of Bridgenorth Castle on the Severn, and tells the incident "'At the siege of this castle (as our chronicles tell us), King Henry II had like to have lost his life by an arrow, which being shot at him was intercepted by a truly gallant man and lover of his prince, Hubert de Saint-Clere, who saved the king's life by the loss of his own'".

The Rev. Richard Polwhele in 1797, antiquary and historian of Devonshire, or perhaps better described as commentator upon Sir William Pole's valuable history of the county before 1623, and often not the improver of his predecessor's facts, has the Bridgenorth hero as belonging to the Devonshire and Cornwall family of Sinclairs. He is wrong in this as in others of his reckonings. In the wide sense only Hubert belongs to this branch of the Norman or Norse house. Polwhele's shaping of the tale has its interest, if for nothing else at least as a clerical example of how to improve incident.

When Harry the 2d was besieging the castle of Bridgenorth in the possession of Hugh de Mortimer, Hubert de S. Clere, we are told, a descendant of this family, [the Sinclairs of Tidwell, Devonshire], perceiving the king aimed at from the castle-walls, stepped in before his sovereign, and received the arrow into his own body and expired, "'an act worthy to be recorded in tables of gold with letters of diamond'". In thankful commemoration of this meritorious service, the king not only interred the deceased with all the pomp of funeral honours, but took the young and only daughter of Hubert under his own protection, and when she was marriageable gave her to William de Longville, a man of noble birth and in high favour with the king. With her the inheritance descended from her father, with largo additions, but on these terms, "'that to perpetuate the memory of the faithful Hubert, Longville should bear both the name and surname of her father, and be called Hubert de St.Clere'".

This would seem to be a paraphrase of Camden, and it is certainly wrong if it tends to proving the Sinclairs of Tidwell or Toodvil, Devon, to have been Longvilles in lineage. Nothing but the name must have caused the Rev. Richard to give currency to so haphazard a relationship. Sir Hubert is of Essex by record after record, and he had not an inch of land in the beautiful county. The Cornwall and Devon branch needs no adventitious or supposititious aids to distinction; they have a sufficient history of their own. Another author rightly dogmatises that he was of Essex, but, to mix matters, he keeps wrongly repeating that he was a Sir Robert and not Hubert. Powel, one of the oldest authorities, in the Welsh Chronicle gives an additional fact, that it was a Welshman and not one of the English who drew bow on the king and killed Hubert. The recent History of England by Knight pictures a very dramatic scene. The king's "faithful vassal Hubert", after the arrow has struck him and saved the king, "threw himself into Henry's arms, imploring him to remember his daughter".

Lord Lyttleton's account in his Life of Henry Second has aided most of the more modern recitals. "'Mortimer, though abandoned by his friends, would not lay down his arms. Henry, incensed at his obstinacy, led a great army against him, with which, having divided it into three bodies, he at once assaulted the three castles of Clebury, Wigmore, and Bridgenorth; and though it was expected that each of them would stand a long siege, they were all surrendered to him in a short time. Before that of Bridgenorth, which was defended by Mortimer, he commanded in person, and exposed himself to so much danger, that he would there have been slain, if a faithful vassal had not preferred his life to his own. For while he was busied in giving orders too near the wall, Hubert de St.Clare, constable, or governor, of Colchester Castle, who stood by his side, seeing an arrow aimed at him by one of Mortimer's archers, stepped before him, and received it in his own breast. The wound was mortal: he expired in the arms of his master, recommending his daughter, an only child, and an infant, to the care of that prince. It is hard to say which most deserves admiration, a subject who died to save his king, or a king whose personal virtues could render his safety so dear to a subject, whom he had not obliged by any extraordinary favours! The daughter of Hubert was educated by Henry, with all the affection that he owed to the memory of her father, and when she had attained to maturity, was honourably married to William de Longueville, a nobleman of great distinction, on condition of his taking the name of St.Clare, which the gratitude of Henry desired to perpetuate.'"

The oddest, and in some respects by no means the worst description, is that of John Speed in his huge History of Great Britain, published in London, 1611. His ambitious historic wings would willingly raise him to classical heights. Clio has not many such incidents, even among our brave English gesta, where valour is no rare quality. "'But Hugh de Mortimer, wanton with greatness, and the most arrogant man alive, stuffed his castles of Gloucester, Wigmor, and Bridgenorth with rebellious garrisons, which Henry notwithstanding reduced to subjection; though in the siege of the last named [he would have been slain] had not Hubert de St.Clere cast himself between death and the king, taking the arrow into his own bosom to preserve his sovereign's life. It bound Tiberius most of all to Sejanus, when a part of the banqueting cave in which they were, suddenly falling, Sejanus was found to have borne the ruins from the emperor, with the peril of his life; but Sejanus survived that adventure, which our Senclere did not, save only in the better renown thereof, which deserves to be immortal, being an act of piety worthy of a statue with Codrus, Curtius, Manlius, or whosoever else have willingly sacrificed themselves'".

The flavour of the heroic literary time of Elizabeth is to be felt through the long sentences of Speed, and it might be pity that his contemporary Shakespeare was not by his English dramas led to the embodiment of "our Senclere". He could put the true fire into such an incident, and he would not miss the fine effect of the Welsh background to the picture. "The most

221

arrogant man alive" could be as artistic a character as his Manlius Coriolanus, and even with fiercer and dramatically finer points in him. But on the earth there are "greaters than Shakespeare here". Life and its admirations are never exhausted till the Deucalion of the future stands without his Pyrrha, and the great world-play is in the last scene of its last act. The two ways of printing the surname in Elizabeth's time are remarkable, and, better than that, remarkably useful.

The knightly way of France has its counterpart in substantial English "Senclere"; and it is curious that taking away the final letter it is the spelling of the names of Richard and Britel, the former in The Domesday Book, "the big and the little Domesday", and the latter in the Exon Domesday. So steadily has this surname subsisted under the foam of various and interesting fashions. John Speed deserves a share of his hero's fame, not only for the sympathy with him that on opportunity would make himself go and do likewise, but because of this antiquarian variation of the name, which has its valuable suggestions for inquiries into the strange and often self-made suicidal names and surnames of Norman-English and even English periods.

What with the Danish soubriquet system; the pride of first name, and depreciation of the less noble surname innovation; patronymics by first names, those endless troublesome Fitzes; local surnaming, the chief element in present English names; and what with the usual obscurity of antiquity, it takes the wariest of stepping to find sure footing. By the strangest and certainly unforeseen accidents this name has curiously clear indications by which the lineage to which it is attached can be grappled with and held. Nothing liker to the doings in this matter of the eleventh and subsequent centuries is there than the mechanical, foolish, and destructive attempts of modern quacks (who cannot understand that difficulty is the very benefit of education), to destroy all knowledge of the early English literature by manufacturing a hidebound union of sounds and letters, because, forsooth, of ease of spelling and reading. Men outwit themselves by all dishonesties, be they those of laziness, pride, or whatever is not growing soundness in life and effort.

There is more yet about Sir Hubert Senclere, governor of Colchester. None of those accounts can possibly be of equal pleasure and value with that by Ralph Niger, the chronicler, who was contemporary with the event. The reference to those who like originals is, Radulphi Nigri Chronicon MS. Bibl: Cotton., under the division Vespas. D. x. 1 f 33, the year 1165. Raphe the Black was a monk, with the most skilful handicraft in black-letter writing, and his MS. is bound and gilt, with all the care it so well deserves, in the Cottonian collection of MSS. at the British Museum. The contents of the little but most careful work, are history from the beginning of the world to 1178; and the room he gives Hubert, considering his limited space, is out of proportion, short as it may appear, with the plan of his concise abstract of the leading events. Possibly a genuinely unselfish or supremely loyal act is worth a great deal of vulgar battles and intrigues. It is given faithfully as it exists. "'In this siege at Bridgenorth in the earldom of Hugo Mortimer, when the same king was sought by a certain arrow, a particular one of his peers, namely, Hubert Sinclair, constable of Colchester, put himself in his place with great judgment, and received death for his lord. Taking his only daughter into his own ward for him afterwards, her father dying in that place, and herself asking the king, he gave her in marriage to William Longville with her paternal heirship. He had by her a son, calling him also by his own name and surname.'"

The contemporary chronicle is probably the source whence some of these historians have drawn; and, if so, they cannot be complimented all round as to their knowledge of Latin. The romantic fever seems to have caught them, when they make William Longville be bound to Hubert's daughter, on the Jewish condition of raising an heir to him of the Sinclair and even Hubert name. There is no ground for this in the monk's MS. It says, what will be supported by charters existing still in the Harleian collection, that the young lady Sinclair bore William Longville a son, whom he called by his own name and surname, William Longville. Polwhele's tale is moonshine. The Normans were not of the mawkish order of human beings, and would neither wish others nor themselves to give up their individualities on sing-song principles. The value of the individual is perhaps the best moral of their vigorous and successful history.

Says Tindal, "'The Normans made themselves masters of Apulia, Calabria, Sicily, Normandy, and England in less than two hundred years;'" and when Rollo left his principality of the Orkneys, to prove strength of the individual head and hand, it is not likely his surroundings were very formidable except to seeing eyes. Charlemagne's tears at the sight of the long, low, dragonlike Norse boats show that he recognised the secret. Henry II, only half a Norman, had formulated the aphorism that the world has room for one great man at once, and there is deep meaning in his finding. No race aided the panoply of crusading chivalry more; but they never lost their heads, as the Celt, time out of mind, so easily does on romantic provocation.

Neither Hubert Sinclair nor his king could put such a condition on any Longville, and the lady's wishes, it may be guessed easily, were those of her sex in this respect, who have at least one subject on which they are the opposite of conservative. Her son was not named and surnamed after her heroic father, and the shortest proof lies in two charters of the Harleian collection in Bloomsbury. The one is "'Charter of Hubert Sinclair to the church of Holy Trinity of Norwich, about the church of Chalke, and land and an annual return in the same manor'". The other is, "'Charter of William Longville confirming the donation of Hubert Sinclair his grandfather as above; particularly various matters between the prior of Bermondsey and the prior of the church of Holy Trinity, Norwich, concerning the advowson of the church of Chalke.'". This is the William whom William Longvale, the husband of Hubert's daughter, called by his own name and surname; and the relationship of grandfather in the charter leaves nothing further to be desired as to the truth of the subject.

Here it is also seen that Hubert was not soldier et praeterea nihil. Besides his duties of constable or governor of Colchester Castle, and the management of the large patrimony left him by his father, Hamo de St.Clair, the sheriff of Essex and Hertford, he did not forget what was necessary to religious advance. It is rare that so much as the above has survived to memory of many a great man's numerous gifts; but there is another remnant of special interest, because referring to his own home county of Essex. In the reign of Henry II he gave a charter to one of England's most famed religious houses.

Mythology has embalmed the strangest tales of Osyth Priory, Chiche, Essex. Its abbess, who had her head cut off by the Danes, and walked with it in her hands for miles to the site of the future nunnery, is a jewel of the early popular reverent imagination. "'From the gift of Hubert Sinclair the tenpenny lands in Bromley '", is the gist of his grant; and it has, besides the religious interest, a genealogical one of a double character. Before his time somewhat, his relation William Sinclair of Corbeil was prior of the monastery of St.Osyth at Chiche, afterwards archbishop of Canterbury, and the first Englishman who was pope's legate, he who aided Stephen so effectually to the throne. He died in 1136, twenty years nearly before Hubert, but as a youth he was perhaps well known to the archbishop. Such a tie caused Hubert's gifts to flow in that direction. St.Osyth's is of interest afterwards by being the property of subsequent Sinclairs whose doings await notice.

It would leave a wrong impression of the hero of Bridgenorth to forget his position as a peer or baron of the land fulfilling well the civil and religious duties belonging to him as such, in the glory of doing one of the world's deeds which will not be let die while human nature has admiration for honour, loyalty, and devotion.

Chapter XXX
The Two Williams of Longvale

The first William was the husband of Hubert Sinclair's only daughter and heiress; the second, their son. It has been said by Polwhele that the husband of the heiress was a man of noble birth and in high favour with the king, which might go very well without saying, as the phrase sans dire puts likely things. The spelling of the name is rather variable in the records, but there can be very little doubt that he is one of the Giffard family which gave the two first Norman earls to Buckingham. The Walter Giffards were De Longuevilles in Normandy, the title there being earl or count of Longueville. It was Walter Giffard who commanded a division of the Norman army in the battle of Hastings, and he figures in the rhymed chronicle perhaps most in the scene where the Conqueror had taken his position for refreshment of food after the fight. Giffard was not there when it was decided to place "the tables" where Harold's last stand and death occurred, and on coming up he is amazed, and counsels care lest the Saxons be only half defeated yet. It is quite a dramatic interlude, but William would not move, and Giffard takes his place with the rest of the blood-spattered determined victors.

He fared well in the distribution of lands, getting no lordships; and he was one of the few in the council which aided William Fitz-Osborn and Odo to govern England. He was afterwards one of the commissioners who drew up The Domesday Book. In Rufus's reign he is remarkable for loyalty to that monarch at first, having fortified for his cause his castle in Normandy; but afterwards he sided more with Robert Curthose. He was a witness of the laws of Henry I, and died in 1103. He was buried in the abbey church of Longavilla, Normandy, of his own foundation. His brother, he who in 1128 first brought in the Cistertian monks, placing them in Waverley Abbey, Surrey, was William Giffard, bishop of Winchester and chancellor of England, whose aid to Eudo Sinclair, dapifer, at a critical time has been seen. The Monasticon in one place makes his sister, Rose Giffard, who was widow of Richard Fitz-Gilbert of Tunbridge, earl of Clare, Eudo's wife, but in another passage the right relationship is shown. She was the mother of his wife Rose Clare.

Bishop Giffard and Peter de Valence, Eudo's sister Albreda's son, helped to make the peace between Henry I and his dapifer. The Valences are the family who were constables of Hertford Castle, and who had for seat Orford Castle, Suffolk. As earls of Pembroke they took their best figure in history. William was the uncle of Edward I. The conqueror of Robert Bruce at Methven and elsewhere is a well-known figure, the Aylmer de Valence of the time of that Edward. Their relationships with Sinclairs are frequent. One of the marriages has monumental proof at Braybrook, Northamptonshire, as late as 1571.

Besides the bishop only another of these Giffards had the highest rank. To the first earl, a second, who was also Walter, succeeded, and he, who was a faithful supporter of Henry I in his many struggles, died without issue. He signed the charter of liberties by this king, as may be seen in Matthew Paris. The lands of his earldom of Buckingham came, through his aunt Rose Giffard's rights, to Richard, earl of Clare, and those of his earldom of Longueville in Normandy fell to William, the marshal of England and the "great earl of Pembroke" of the reigns of John and Henry III.

When the claims to the Scottish crown were being investigated by Edward I in 1291 at Norham, John Hastings, as descendant of the youngest of the three daughters whose rights were being founded on as best, demanded the partition of Scotland, on the ground that it was a fee of the English crown. In this case he would have a third, as if it had been an earldom or a knight's fee. "Fees are all partible", was his cry, and he was technically right. There is more insight got into the condition of England from this historic phrase than from volumes of investigation. The seemingly sudden extinction of families, the immense changefulness of possessions, the difficulties of tracing genealogies, the mixing of high Norman names in the most ordinary spheres, which are marked features of the centuries after the Conquest, have ample explanation in the words of John Hastings. The danger of exclusiveness, so open to poor human nature, its very strength throwing into weakness, had thus a powerful corrective.

It was much later that primogeniture came with its rather frosty fingers to preserve, but also to keep out energy from, select families. The division of possessions, by heiresses in particular, is the cause of lost lines to an immense extent. The barbaric equal division, on the elementary theory of fair play, had and has its evil consequences, however just, as the foundation of the primogeniture and male-succession system also has. In its rigour, the latter could only have been the work of pedants and mad genealogists. To have nobody worth chronicling about is the disconcerting result of this fossilising of best life. Via media, golden mean, common sense, or whatever phrase helps to keep us human, that is, not too divine, and never brutal, is the goal of all best culture, from peasant to king; and none of us can escape when we break the universal law.

The courses of lineage are subject to a thousand chances, suggestive enough of all the melancholies, in the midst of whatever honours and gallantry. For example, Hubert Sinclair of Norwich had descendants by the male line in Yorkshire and Lancashire who took some local or other accidental name, and grew into one of the greatest families of the district, Sir Henry Ellis says, as the Frechvilles. In the time of Charles II the last of them disappeared. Under the earlier system of succession to name and property, these surprises are endless. Disguised by new names England has now much blood in it of the old families, Sinclairs included.

Giffards there were to some number when the earl's lands were divided. In Gloucestershire there were the lords of Brimsfield, the liberal endowers of Gloucester Abbey. At the battle of Evesham in 1265, John Giffard was "the second man to the earl of Gloucester". Walter Giffard was archbishop of York in Edward I's reign. As early as 1071 one of the earl's family went to Scotland with William Sinclair among "the emigrants", and founded the Giffards there. Such Sinclair or Giffard might not try to heir anything here after favour for the Athelings. There was no want of male Giffard blood to succeed the earls of Buckingham, but the nearer female rights as then legal, kept them from succession, even to the titles.

That William de Longueville, the husband of Hubert Sinclair's daughter, was of this family, all the indications point; and that he took the Norman estate as his surname, is quite in accordance with facts. Polwhele is therefore right that he was of as noble blood as there was; and the close relationship of the Giffards or Longvales with Eudo Sinclair is good evidence that the king put the property of the last Sinclair lord of Colchester, by no means out of the family, in using his right of marriage over his favourite ward. In The Domesday Book there is a manor Longueville or Lanvalee in Kent, which was the right position for William's home to be, the chief scene of the family traditions. He may have been of a Norman family of this same lineage.

At Hubert Sinclair's death in 1165 at Bridgenorth, William Langvale was in his manhood; for he got after his marriage, not only his father-in-law's lands, but he was made constable of Colchester Castle. He held it under Henry Second, Richard I, and John. He is in record as paying 200 marks of the usual fine at change of monarch, to the latter. That he was also warden of the forest of Essex must not be forgotten. King John when he granted Magna Charta gave, or was forced to give, at the same time a charter of the liberties of the forests, which shows the importance of such office. The people's food, clothes, and fire depended on the wise provisions of the warden. In the chronicle of the abbey of St.Albans a few words which survive give a double inference, namely, as to the spread of his lands over England, and as to his religious liberality. William of Lanvale gave to it the villa or farm of Dissington in Northumberland, called "Ducentuna, in Northumbria", by the monks.

The first of the two William Langvales died in 1210 at a good old age. He was succeeded by his son "of the same name and surname" by the lady Sinclair. The position of the family is at once fixed by this that he is one of the barons (named by Matthew Paris) who wrested from John at Runnimede beside the Thames the charters which are the bulwarks of English liberty. "W. de Lanvalei" is the name as given there. He comes before Geffrey Mandeville, earl of Essex, in the list; and this reminds of the previous Geffrey, of Stephen's reign, who like this William Langvale was also a Sinclair by the mother. It is his charter of confirmation of the charter of Hubert de Sancto Claro, his grandfather, that is preserved in the British Museum among the Harleian charters, referring to the church of Holy Trinity, Norwich, and the monastery of Bermondsey, Southwark, already noticed.

He married a daughter of Alan Basset, a great surname. He is the twelfth of the sixteen nobles who appear at the head of Magna Charta as it is still to be seen. Thomas Basset is another of those, as the Latin has it, nobilium virorum. Bassets are the only family with this double honour. Gilbert and Philip were chief men in the Richard, John, and Henry III reigns. One of the Bassets was governor of Dover and warden of the Cinque Ports. The lady's grandfather appears in this, "'Richard Basset and Aubrey de Vere account for the fee-farm of Surrey, Cambridgeshire, and Huntingdonshire: In the treasury £414, 1s. by weight: Great Rolls, 5 Stephen, 4th roll'". This was in 1141. The Veres fell heirs to Eudo Sinclair's lordship of Colchester Castle, and the Bassets, as lords of Drayton, are long conspicuous in history. In Henry V's reign one of them, a Sir William Basset, was made governor of St.Cler Castle in France; the same fortress which was burnt by William Mandeville, earl of Essex, in Henry II's reign, of which king it was a favourite residence, who planted some trees there with his own hands.

An only daughter, Hawise, was the fruit of the marriage, and thus these Langvales came to their period. Her fortunes were also distinguished. In 17 John (1216) she was put under the wardship of Hubert de Burgh, who is one of England's greatest men. He married her to his son, John de Burgh, whose mother was the Princess Margaret of Scotland, sister of the king. Hawise had heired her grand-aunt, the daughter of Hamo Sinclair of Colchester and sister of Hubert Sinclair, in her properties of Stanway manor and Lexenden, Essex, given to her by Henry II; and her father had the bulk of the Sinclair properties already through his mother; so that she was an heiress to be desired, even in the large scheming of such a giant of distinction and honours as Hubert de Burgh. The earl of Kent, the seneschal of Poitou, governor of Dover Castle, ambassador repeatedly, chamberlain of the household, justice of England, and, on the death in 1220 of William, the marshal, the great earl of Pembroke, who was the only man to be compared with him of his time, governor in his room of the kingdom, Hubert de Burgh was a father-in-law such as few ladies secure. The lists of his lands and offices read like fable. His king, Henry III, not only when a boy but in his manhood was untiring in adding to this man's immense fortunes. Among the sixteen "noble men" of Magna Charta he stood eighth as, senesculus Pictaviae. The successful defence he made in 1216-17 of Dover Castle against Lewis, the dauphin of France, is famous.

Condemnation by him as chief justiciary, of Constantine, a London street-hero who had raised a dangerous insurrection in 1222, on his own fall from his position of first man next the king in 1232 to misery and persecution beyond all imagination, made 20,000 citizens swear to go and take him (a kind of monarchical Strafford, as they thought), from the altar of the church at Merton, Surrey, to revenge their republican's death by his. Only by policy were they prevented. There is no tale in English or hardly any other history so pathetically descriptive of human nature, both individual and collective, as his; and volumes could be filled to high and entertaining purpose in exhibiting his great but greatly chequered life. A brave man, he kept his courage up to the last. Not like Wolsey did he go down never to rise, but regained before his death probably as much of the world's goods and honours as he then thought sufficient.

His son, Sir John de Burgh, Hawise's husband, was knighted by Henry III in 1129, three years before his father was disgraced. He signalised himself, Matthew Paris says, in 1242 at the battle of Xantoignes in France. Matthew of Westminster and he, take note of the death of Richard de Burgh, "a baron of note", in this same year. Dugdale follows the history of these De Burghs, and from him it is worth noting that Lanvally was held for one knight and a half's service, the original but probably much cut up manor of the Langvales. Hawise de Lanvally had among other lands Kingstown, Hallingberrie, Waokre, and Lexenden. Henceforward there do not seem ties of Sinclairs to Colchester, its castle, abbey, and lands, though they figure for centuries in other parts of Essex.

Chapter XXXI
Commissioner of Domesday Book

To the modern reader a full account of the life of Adam Sinclair, the son of Hubert of Rye, would probably be more interesting and important than the biographies of dozens of feudal fighting warriors; and there remains most authentic knowledge of him and his doings. Even of his personal character considerable things can be gathered. Getting the clue to find him was nearly as difficult as making the eggs to stand proved to the Spanish dons deriding Columbus as discoverer, though the thing was fairly before the eyes.

Sir Henry Ellis in his Introduction to Domesday Book mentions Adam in the lists he gives of landholders, but the indexer of the Domesday Book printed by the government record commission never refers to him. The holders in capite are alone indexed, though it is notorious that many of the undertenants were far wealthier and more important. Examination of the wonderful volumes directly shows Adam at every turn, not only in the masterly arrangement of his subject with his three fellow "king's justiciaries", as the book itself calls its makers, but as a very large landholder.

Hasted in his History of Kent, has frequent notices, though from Domesday only, of this perhaps the greatest of all "the men of Kent". He was undertenant of an immense portion of the bishop of Bayeux, Odo's estates, the brother of the Conqueror, by far the richest landholder in England. Adammus filius Huberti has not one inch of soil by the in capite holding, and it may be safely said that this, with such a man, was by intention. That it was as practically useful to hold from the one brother as the other, no matter for the sovereignty, he must have decided. Alured, the chronicler of Beverley, wrote of Odo, "'Who was almost a second king of England'". Jealousy between the brothers kept Adam from all favours of grants from the king, is a possibility not at all likely. There may have been a pride with Odo which would not permit him to allow Adam to hold but from himself. Adam was treasurer, chancellor, in short, full dapifer to this richest sharer in the spoils of England; and he had the best of fields in which to glean effectually. In "Kent" his name occurs continually.

Pearson in his Middle Ages calculates that Odo's yearly income in England was about £3380, and that the king's other uterine brother, the duller Robert de Moretayne, the next wealthiest, had about; £1900 a year. These are immense sums of money, as the value of it then was. Odo accumulated in the sixteen years after the Conquest enough to buy the papacy, and he had already purchased a stately palace at Rome when in 1082 William seized him personally as earl of Kent, on his way to Italy to use all his power to become pope. His effects were soon after confiscated to the king's use, and as this was the very time of the compilation of The Domesday Book, it is not likely that Adam Sinclair suffered severely by the change. Had his lord become the king of all the world that the pope then was, his history would certainly have had great additional chapters in it. Odo's nephew, Rufus, re-established him in his estates, which had not lost anything by his absence for six years; but again he fell into trouble, and only got out of prison in Henry I's reign, when he went with Curthose to Jerusalem, and died at the siege of Antioch. The crown would be his nearest heir, but after the death of Henry, difficulties might occur to Adam's rule of the bishop and earl's estates.

William of Iypres got the earldom of Kent in Stephen's time, he who built the tower of the castle of Rye in Sussex, and it is probable he was of the Sinclair connection, by marriage if not otherwise. That he was by birth a Fleming nor aids nor hinders any question of lineage. Adam kept his "great possessions" in Kent and Northampton. The results of these changes could hardly but improve the fortune of so able a man. Hasted keeps repeating that Odo's property was confiscated to the crown by Rufus, but the change had no effect on an under-tenant, and there is documentary proof that Adam's lands remained to his lineage after his death.

Adam is one of the three chevaliers of Rye Castle in France who escorted William, then only duke of Normandy, when riding for his life from his enemies in Valence; and he followed his fortunes afterwards to Hastings with his three brothers in the usual way. Some time then he must have formed the friendship of Odo. The scholarship of both would draw them together. Most of the histories are quite silent as to the great and most practical love of learning of the bishop of Bayeux. Some of his worst troubles came from the fact that he was before and above his time, with all the cultivation there undoubtedly was among the Normans. It is as Odo's first man that Adam acted long after the Conquest, and this brought him continually into the presence of the sovereign, where his brother Eudo had first place.

In the *MS. codex in bibliotheca Cottoniana, Nero, D.S.*, from which Dugdale quotes the history of Hubert of Rye's sons into the Monasticon, there are additions of which he did not make use. Adam, like the abbot of the same name there, was "of Campes", and this opens a vista of information. The "two camps" are described by Hasted fully. They were near Kemsing, on the London side of Maidstone; and of all places in England this is one of the most interesting to those who have any interest in the lineage. Sinclairs for centuries have clung tenaciously to this particular Kent district. Adam's chief mansion was there, in front of the Hurst forest; and a more beautiful and fertile spot it would be impossible to find anywhere. This MS. says he was given "large possessions in Kent", and Campes was their centre. The name arose from three British and Roman encampments in the place. He was known as Adam of Campes as well as Adam the son of Hubert.

That he was of the first capacity the whole of The Domesday Book goes to prove, but there are also everywhere marks of self-possession and retiring sense of ability which have a most refreshing effect in seeing him among those, in their noisy clamant character at least, rather crude, brave mere warriors with the earth-hunger on them. He also had a hearty appreciation of the value of land, as is to be inferred from the great law-suit which Lanfranc, on his appointment to the archbishopric, instituted against Odo, for taking possession of properties belonging, he contended, to the see. Pinindean, where the court was held, on the west side of the Medway not far from where it reaches the Thames, became afterwards the possession of Adam and his lineage. Geoffrey, bishop of Coustance, sat as chief justiciary and viceroy on that great day, which had all that was best in Kent there. Richard Fitz-Gilbert, Hamo Vicecomes, the clerisy in its strength, were there; and no doubt Adam, as perhaps most interested, had a very anxious, and, as the case ended, a somewhat unsuccessful time. Lanfranc recovered pieces of lands attached to other properties; but it may safely be affirmed that the bishop of Bayeux, brother of the king, and Adam his relation and manager, took their own fully out of the whole affair.

Not many more remarkable events have there been in our civil history than this land reckoning at Pinindean. Adam had a most difficult task throughout, to keep Odo's business straight. His own fortunes probably rose and fell to some extent with Odo's very chequered life; but he did secure large lands despite all those storms of William the Conqueror seizing his own brother so that he should not become pope and be then his lord, of William Rufus conquering the bishop out of Pevensey and Rochester castles, and of many other such troubles into which fell often the able but perhaps fickle bishop of Bayeux, earl of Kent, and first governor or viceroy, with the earl of Hereford, of Norman England. It is easy to guess what opportunities and difficulties Adam had under such a lord.

That he was worthy of all trust, his appointment by William the Conqueror himself in 1080, as commissioner to reckon up his kingdom accurately for state purposes, is ample proof. It is probable that he was an expert in money business of the state. With the two Giffards (the earl of Buckingham and his brother the chancellor of England and bishop of Winchester), he kept continually conversant; and it is all but certain that he was, quietly as such men like to work, foot and hand in some of their most difficult duties. Walter was one of his fellow commissioners for The Domesday Book; the "'lieutenants of the king'", as they are called sometimes there, as well as "king's justiciars".

It is almost romantic how the names of these high benefactors of the nation have not been lost to memory and to fame. There is nothing in the record itself, to discover who its authors were. Heming's Chartulary, as it is called, preserved in the Cottonian library of MSS., Tib. A. xiii., is the register of St.Mary's, Worcester; and an extract from a claim of its monks for a cartula to certain lands in the Oswaldeslaves hundred, revealed this secret, to the infinite delight of the admirers of able deeds and able men. In proving their claims to the property, they go back to the time of William the Conqueror, and insert an extremely important passage of the very best kind of history. "'This testimony the whole county of Worcester confirmed by oath, at the instance and effort of the very pious and sagacious father the lord bishop Wulstand, in the time of William the Conqueror, before these same princes of the king, namely, Remigio, bishop of Lincoln; Earl Walter Giffard; Henry of Ferrers; and Adam, the brother of Eudo, king's dapifer, who to inquire about and describe the possessions and customs of the king, as well as of his chiefs, in this province, and in many others, were appointed by the king himself at that time in which he made the whole of England to be described'". The monks got their cartula, and if any proof were wanted, this would by its own antiquity and acceptance go far of itself to prove the authenticity of the account of the compilers of Domesday. There is not any question as to the value of the information among the most critical authorities.

The best, and surely an immortal, monument to Adam's fame, is the magnificent orderly record itself; and a reference to its pages, especially under "Terra Episcopi Baiocensis", in the various counties, might be amply sufficient to bring him fully before an inquirer's attention. His appearances solely in the smaller type of those not holding directly from the king have been explained. Practically, he was an in capite holder, though there was hardly any real social distinction between the highest and next highest forms of tenure. He is distinguished from nearly all the holders in The Domesday Book by the rather unique position of being properly of neither tenure, and for this variety from the monotony, the reader has to thank him, as for much other benefit.

What he held in Kent may be given as example for the other counties, and good example, because this was the chief scene of both his lord's and his own interests. In the lest of Sudtone, Achestane hundred, Adam the son of Hubert held from the bishop, Redlege; in Helmstrie hundred, South Cray and also Wickham; in Laroschefel hundred, Lelebourne; in Aihorde hundred, Sudtone, Certh, another Sudtone, Bogelei, Langvelei (the manor of which Hubert Sinclair's daughter's husband was afterwards lord), Otringdene, Esselve; in Rochester hundred, Pinpa; in Twiferde hundred he held some land without a name; in Medston hundred, Celca, Heham, Colinge, Bicklei; in Rovinden hundred some lands unnamed; in Faversham hundred, Ore, Stanefelle, and another Ore; in Ferleberge hundred, Fanne; and in Estrei hundred, Hamolde. To reckon up all the entries in the various counties over which Odo's lands, as was the method of land grants, spread, where Adam, the commissioner and his steward, had holdings, would be a miniature new Domesday. The object is gained that this son of the house of Rye is known to have succeeded, at least as well as his able brothers better known to general fame.

His brother Eudo Dapifer was his heir. It is not likely that Adam was married, or if so he must have had no children or all had died before himself. Like Hamo Dapifer he lived the individual life, and left his properties to his nearest relatives. There are several charters in the Textus Roffensis which amply prove this. Eudo died in 1119; and Adam (Eudo being younger, and living to a great age) it is probable died early in Henry Beauclerc's reign. Their gifts to one of the favourite churches with the lineage, St.Andrews, Rochester, aid, by the interposition of possession by a third between the brothers, the thought that Adam did not live long after the completion of The Domesday Book's pages. "'Eudo, dapifer of the king, gave to St.Andrews all those tenths which Adam his brother had formerly given to Anschetillus, archdeacon of Canterbury, and which the same Anschetillus afterwards granted to St.Andrews'". If anything were needed to add weight to the Cottonian account of the Rye family this would satisfy all criticism.

But there is still another charter in the famous Rochester set of rolls which shows the relations between Eudo and Adam well. Eudo gives tenths of various kinds of produce to St.Andrews from his lands of Buggeleia, Langley, Suthune, Leiburne, Readlega, Culinga and Merelea. These are some of the same places to which Adam's name is attached in

235

Domesday. Certainly the Fitz-Hamo or Corbeil Sinclairs had possession of some of his lands, and they may either have got them at his death or afterwards. From these charters there are incidental biographical lights on both Eudo and Adam.

One charter refers more perhaps to the former's ways of life. *"'Rodulph, the butler of Eudo, gave to the monks of St.Andrews a certain tenth of his, from Cooling, worth five shillings in the year, for the soul of his father and mother'"*. Eudo gave him this property of which he grants the tenths, Cowling being part of Eudo's heirship from his brother. The western and eastern sides of the Medway down to the Thames were the situation of these properties, which are easily distinguishable in their modern names as, for examples, Boxley, Ridley, Langley, Sutton, Leyburn, Cowling. The Celca which Adam had, is the Chalk which Hubert, the son of Hamo of Colchester, gave to the monks of tlie monastery of Bermondsey, and which his grandson, William of Langvale, confirmed to them.

In Edward I's time the monks, in answer to a Quo warranto, proved their right to it then, by the aid of Robert Sinclair, miles. How it came to Hamo de St.Clair of Colchester Castle, would be most interesting to discover. This will come up in discussing others of the name, who likewise possessed some of Adam's lands.

The Cobhams and the Brocs got parts of Sinclair lands. Whether they were of the lineage, it is more difIicult to see than that William of Eynesford, the sirs and lords Leyburne, and the several Sir Peters of Huntingfield were. One Eynesford created, inadvertently enough, the quarrel between Becket and King Henry II; the Cobhams, and the Brocs especially, seem to have had blood reasons for the part they took in it; Sir Peter of Huntingfield was one of Edward I's warriors in his early success at Carlaverock in Scotland: but they were all extinct in the male line before the fifteenth century. The Fitz-Bernards also cross the paths too frequently to have no closer than general ties.

The Aubenis were related through the daughter of Earl Simon Sinclair, and William Aubeny's name is the almost invariable accompaniment of Eudo's frequent signature to charters, and especially royal ones. William was the king's pincerna or butler, one of the very highest offices of the time.

With Adam, the commissioner of The Domesday Book, bachelor, learned, and extremely wealthy, the Sinclairs most under the rule of the Norman dynasty, of which they were part, must now be left for those of the days of the Plantagenets. Naturally they grew more of strangers, though gradually, to the royal court, when ties of kin got dim, and the reckoning only could be made by female connections. All that was highest in marriage, lands, or office they had in England for nearly a century after the Conquest, and the glow of their fame and their physical and intellectual powers kept them high for centuries afterwards, in a way rare to any one particular lineage. The weight of the life of the next to be considered goes into the era of the new dynasty of the Celtic Fulcs, though biographic facts shun too fixed lines.

Chapter XXXII
Hugo de St.Clare

History which deals with the most notorious of the archbishops of Canterbury, Thomas Becket, never overlooks Hugh Sinclair's position in the quarrel between the prelate and his king, Henry II. The family were as high at court, in his person, as when the dynasty of their own lineage was on the throne. They may have owed this chiefly to Matilda, the empress, though there is every sign that her son of the Anjou descent loved them dearly. How Hubert Sinclair saved his life has been told; and how Hugo stood by him in the worst struggle of his difficult and troubled reign, is equally worthy of remembrance.

The first preferment Thomas a Becket got in the church, after he left the bar, was from the abbey of St.Albans, to Bradfield, the property of the descendants of Richard Sinclair, the hero of Hastings; and Hugo de St.Clare knew of him through his relations more than others of Henry's court. Matthew of Westminster is authority for this. But Becket's prominence began on appointment to be archdeacon of Canterbury. After being made high chancellor his love of pomp appeared to the full. On becoming archbishop of Canterbury, his asceticism, even to want of clean linen and the consequences, grew equally notorious.

From 1163 till his so-called martyrdom in 1171, he tortured King Henry with an ingenuity which was ostensibly in the "cause of God", or, to use that phrase which was to the king as bitter as gall, "saving the honour of God", but which seems little if at all short of fiendish. Fifty years after his death, so productive of monastic miracle and popular pilgrimage, the clever heads of the university of Paris publicly debated whether then the soul of Becket was in heaven or hell. He was about the most malignant oflicial that ever stepped on English soil, and undoubtedly meant to bully spiritually from the sovereign downwards, if he had his way. The clergy committed murders, and not only were left unpunished, but against every right of humanity kept in their positions by the church, which claimed the full jurisdiction.

A glaring case of seduction and murder at last brought matters to a crisis, and Henry grew determined to have at least the punishment of felons completed, whether lay or clerical. The constitutions of Clarendon were articles of state and law to arrive at this point; and Becket, the archbishop, after severe struggle, made some movement of concession, but immediately afterwards retracted, as one who had been a Judas in the act to the "honour of God". He got absolution from the pope, and henceforth he nailed his colours to the mast. Disobedience and insolence to his king, devotion to the Roman hierarchy, were the rules of the rest of his disagreeable and miserable life.

The best and bulk of his own clergy despised the conceited stubbornness of the incorrigible ascetic, as being of like character at bottom with the buffoonery and license to correspondent excess of his lay days, and with the absurd display of his lord chancellor and ambassador period. The man was a parvenu and impudent mountebank, who, late in life, found a cause and a hot iron conscience. Such a canker becomes of necessity a grief to himself and every one with whom he has to do.

When he had to flee to France in the first year of the quarrel, 1163, the system of letters of excommunication by Pope Alexander's aid, who was only a schismaticised pope, began. Hugo de St.Clare was about the first to suffer from this kind of weapon. He was one of the lords of council. His special offence was that he took possession by the king's authority of lands and goods of the see of Canterbury. What could deserve more the clerical bitterest of all cursing and swearing than meddling, justly or not, with lucre ? Thomas "the saint", in his letter from Sens in France, ad suffraganeous suos, excommunicated John of Oxford, Richard of Ilchester, Jocelin of Baliol, Ranulph of Broc (Ranulph for cutting off his horse's tail during the quarrel in England), Thomas Fitz-Bernard, and Hugo de Sancto Claro. He gives particulars as to the crimes of the last two, *"'We have excommunicated also Hugh Sinclair and Thomas Fitz-Bernard, who have taken possession of the goods and properties of the same church of Canterbury without our permission.'"*.

Lord Lyttleton, in his *Life of Henry II*, gives the strangest details of the preparatio this designing or mad, or both, prelate gave himself before he felt fitted for this special effort. He had a whole night's watch before the sepulchre of some doubtful St.Dransius, whom popular opinion credited as favourer of victors in personal combats. Geoffrey Baynard did the same thing the night before the day on which he over-threw unfortunate Henry of Essex, the craven or mistaken standard-bearer of England. It is curious how well Becket gauged and engaged the people's affections on his side. Lest this might savour too much of the secular order of things, he took care to spend another night's politic devotion at the shrine of St.Gregory, whom he held to be the founder of the Anglican church. Thus supported, he went to Vizelay to do his self-imposed duty; and it was only by a pressing message from King Louis of France, saying that Henry II was extremely ill, that he was then prevented from including his king among the ministers he did excommunicate.

It was hardly to be wondered at that Henry once so bitterly cried out that his archbishop wished to ruin him both soul and body; and it is said that Becket knew him to be of so religious a tendency, despite all his gallantries, that he meant to drive him into a monastery as place of refuge from the world, of which he was often heard declaring his utter weariness. The penances he underwent after Becket was no longer his opponent are proof of the power the prelate thought thus to exercise over him.

Illness and King Louis saved him from the first stroke of St.Peter's or St.Thomas of Canterbury's vindictive sword; but Becket, says Lyttleton, "'pronounced several sentences of excommunication against his servants and ministers, particularly against John of Oxford, for the causes before mentioned; against Richard de Ivelchester, the archdeacon of Poictiers, for holding communion with the archbishop of Cologne, a favourer of the antipope; against Hugh de St.Clare and Thomas Fitz-Bernard, for having usurped the goods of the church of Canterbury (that is, for having obtained the sequestration of those he had forfeited by his flight); and, lastly, against the chief justiciary, Richard de Luci, and Jocelin de Baliol, as the favourers of the king's tyranny, and the contrivers of those heretical pravities, the constitutions of Clarendon'".

Again, in 1168, from Pontigny, he excommunicated Gilbert Folliot, bishop of London, who had gone wholly over to the side of his king; and, in a letter to the chapter of St.Paul's, Becket warns them to shun all the excommunicated. On the coming Ascension, he informs them, he is to have further heyday of new excommunications. Meantime, to keep their minds fresh on the subject, he sums his previous work, in addition to their bishop, thus: "'These are the names of the excommunicated: - Jocelin, bishop of Salisbury, Earl Hugo, Ralph of Broc, Thomas Fitz-Bernard, Robert of Broc, cleryman, Hugh Sinclair, Letard the clergyman of Northfleet, Nigel Sackville, Richard the brother of Hastings, who took possession of our church of Monocotone: Farewell'". Sackville he accused of holding a manor belonging to the archbishopric; but his views of law and right may be understood from the fact that the very beginning of his clerical arrogance was claiming Tunbridge Castle and its lands, the home and patrimony of the great family of Clares, as under-holding to the see of which Becket was holder.

Who were in capite holders if the Clares were not ? He excommunicated William of Eynesford, an in capite baron, against an express law; a thing never before done under any king, to whom the first lords were alone responsible. What made the matter worse was that it was on his own unjust presentation of a cleric to a church in prejudice of this baron's rights. To have claimed Tunbridge as a fief of his, seemed the top of insolence; but especially in a threatening letter to him, without the court etiquette of introduction, Henry himself soon felt the kind of man the saint that once was a devil could be with his crozier and sackcloth. The "great" Augustines, and others such, take all the fun they can out of both periods of life.

Other names, the best he could find, are in the lists of excommunicated, such as Alan de Neville and Richard de Poictiers. As early as 1165, Rapin says, he *"'excommunicated all that adhered to the constitutions of Clarendon, and particularly some lords of the council, who however despised his censures'"*. This is too general; but he mentions nine names, of which Hugh de St.Clare's is one. In the chroniclers there are plentiful details, and lists of the lords in council in particular who suffered. Matthew of Westminster, Fitz-Stephen, and Hoveden are useful references. Diceto and Matthew Paris are good, especially as to the names. In his letter to Pope Alexander, Becket, announcing what he had been doing, names Hugo and the rest; and with the consciously impudent intolerance which is only bred of clericalism in contest for the "honour of God", self included, adds that he had not excommunicated the king yet, but would not defer it long.

All the historians deal with this subject largely, and with these men. Goldsmith calls Hugo and his batch "the king's chief ministers". But he is not much of an authority on the subject. Another history says that they were Baliol, Lucy, and "four others of Henry's courtiers and prime favourites". Hugo is mentioned as one of these; and it is certain they were the six best men in England, next to its king. One of the latest compilers names Hugo de St.Clair and other three as the Norman favourites of Henry. In numbers such as four or six there is no great danger of that favouritism which has been so deadly in all annals.

The Thomas filius Bernardi who is specially mentioned as seizing, with Hugo de St.Clair, the goods and possessions of the see of Canterbury, must have had blood or affinity relationship to him. In the valuable gatherings of Benedict, abbot of Peterborough, the "burgh" from which Hubert took his local surname, there is a brother of this Thomas who plays a large part in the conquest of Ireland. He was sent beforehand by the king, with William Fitz-Adelm, his dapifer, to prepare for the arrival there of the sovereign, and he got Wexford and Waterford as his reward. Afterwards this Fitz-Adelm, then viceroy, has Wexford, and it appears Robert had left Ireland, for in 1176, when England was divided into six provinces for the better dispensing of justice, Robert Fitz-Bernard with Richard Giffard and another were the rulers of Kent, Surrey, Sussex, and several other counties. Hugh of Cressi, William Fitz-Raphe, and William Basset are names of others appointed which have genealogical pertinence. In the Great Rolls Robert Fitz-Bernard was farmer of the county of Kent.

It is supposable that in the seizure by Hugo Sinclair and Thomas Fitz-Bernard there may have been a revival of old claims, through their relation, Adam, the commissioner, as Odo's under-tenant, of large parts of whose lands they had already possession by heirship. The king's purpose, however, may wholly explain their doings. Hugo from the Great Rolls of Henry II was vicecomes of Kent as his uncle Hamo Dapifer was, and therefore by this office saw after the king's rights.

Not only did he get this title in heirship or by prescription from his uncle, but he was also king's butler or cup-bearer, the place that then retained most of the privileges of the original dapifer, seneschal, or mayor of the palace. In Henry III's reign, 1263, the appointment of Simon de Montfort, earl of Leicester, as high steward of England, and at the same time Sir Roger of Leybourne, of Hugo's lineage, as steward of the household, illustrates the history of the division of the original office. M. West., Wikes, and Tindal are authorities for these appointments, and Tindal says Sir Roger got made pincerna by the king, though accounted his greatest enemy, which is proof of hereditary claim. The Albinis, earls of Arundel, Salop, and Chester had been king's butlers. It was William Albini, pincerna or butler, who married Adeliza, the beautiful dowager queen of Henry I. The office seems to have left the Albinis, though they still claimed the privilege of being the pincerna of coronation days; and Hugo de St.Clare, by relationship to them, and as of near consanguinity to Eudo and Hamo, the dapifers, was the proper person to get the high office. The chronicler, Benedictus abbas Petroburgensis, says that one of the St.Liz was pincerna in Richard I's reign, who have been proved of the same lineage. Hugo Pincerna is to be found on the Carta Eudonis Dapiferi holding land of the extent of seven knights' fees.

Eudo's lands were then in the hands of the king, but this considerable portion of the estate shows that, despite the intricate female rights which affected properties wholly partible, Hugo's lineage to Eudo secured some possessions to him out of the great "feoda". Henry Fitz-Gerald, the king's chamberlain, managed it; and his brother, Dominus Gwarenne, a chief officer at court, well known to history, as the Fitz-Geralds became generally in this reign, holds portions, and also some other brothers, as from the king. Eudo's lands escheated to the crown, but not without considerable and prolonged honourable struggle. In the first four years of the reign, Hugo Pincerna as vicecomes Kanciae appears again and again receiving monies for the treasury; and there can be no doubt that he is the Hugo de St.Clare of the Becket struggle, and the lord of Aeslingham.

From the Textus Roffensis there could come accumulation of evidence about his connection as a dweller in the locality and as a relative to others of his surname. For example, to a confirmation of a charter, extracted from the Cottonian MSS., granted by Geffrey de Say to St.Andrews, Rochester, who could be more suitable and ready witnesses than "William, son of Henry of Cobham, Hugo Pincerna", and others? The title pincerna was at this period quite distinct from dapifer, having the conservative traditions as its pride, the dapifers becoming numerous and only divisional officers of state and law. The Bigods were never pincernas, and therefore do not confound with this Hugo de St.Clare, Hugo being a name frequent to that family, related only by affinity to the Sinclairs, through whose rights they got into their dapiferships. To these Fitz-Geralds, descended from Gerald, the steward of Arnulph Montgomery of the castle and honour of Pembroke, Geffrey Mandeville, grandson of Eudo Dapifer, had given a one-fee holding of Eudo's lands; but their property increased by geometric progression through their Irish doings of fame. What is of closer interest to discussion of Hugo Sinclair's life, Philip of Leybourne in Kent also held, like him, seven fees of Eudo's lands. The lords of Leybourne, who are frequently mentioned among the greater barons by Rapin, Tindal, and all the historians, were undoubtedly of Hugo's stock, and subsequent facts will help to make this clear.

Perhaps one of the most interesting entries among the gifts to St.Andrews, Rochester, is one which shows that Hugh Sinclair was not the kind of man to deserve excommunication from church or state or whatever else when human interests are to be dealt with wisely and well. "'Hugo, the royal butler, gave forty shillings to the Rochester alms, which he provided for from holdings in Southfleet and elsewhere, on the days of his birth, and he gives the charitable offering for the convent, and he has a smaller portion sent into the convent, and a distribution to the poor'". With the value of money then, and these gifts as yearly, the lord of Aeslingham might well have favours of chapel and house chaplains from the see at his further own charges. If the antiquity and brevity of such Latin records obscure the exact force of the words, there is no doubt about the general meaning of such an entry as the above. It is of such a man that Thomas Becket writes in 1169 to the pope or half-pope,

Alexander, as one of the "malefactors" deserving no mercy. In his epistle, the twentieth of the collections in the Bodleian and Cottonian libraries, so he designates them.

But let Lord Lyttleton's views of Becket be read in this respect. "'He also intreated him not to absolve the malefactors he (Becket) had excommunicated. These malefactors were several of the most eminent prelates and barons of England. Having waited the term prescribed to him by the pope, and being therefore reinstated in his former authority, he had at once excommunicated the bishops of London and Salisbury, the archdeacon of Canterbury, (whom in a letter to the pope he calls the arch-devil of Canterbury), Nigel de Sacville, and Thomas Fitz-Bernard, officers of the king's household, Hugh de St.Clare, Hugh, earl of Chester, Richard de Lucy, great-justiciary, and other chief men of the kingdom. All this was done between Palm-sunday and Whitsunday without any notice of it having been given to Alexander'". This was hardly clerical obedience either.

But enough of the famous historical quarrel. It will help to throw light on its nature if this "despoiler of churches" (could Thomas Becket's excommunicating letters be believed) is shown further in his genuine character as a reverent as well as capable man. The bishop of Rochester had another opinion of him and his family than had the archbishop. In the Textus Roffensis, edited by Dr. Thorpe, there is a double entry of a charter to the lord of Aeslingham, as it calls Hugo. Aeslingham manor is the Frindsbury district of to-day, and it is fruitful of information with regard to the Sinclairs generally. When they got possession of Aeslingham, it was not the fifth of the parish, but this name soon covered it all. The bishop grants a free chapel to Hugo within his manor of Aeslingham, as recompense for the many benefits of him and members of his family to St.Andrews, Rochester. This is the second John of its bishops. The servants of the manor were to be buried in the chapel, but though at a loss to the church, as the charter puts it, the family were to have burial in St.Andrews. For the monks' services of burial at the chapel, ten shillings annually were to be paid, with thirty sheaves of wheat, thirty of barley, and thirty of oats, from the harvest fields. Bishop John II further gives him the license to have his house chaplain at his own charges, as the previous bishops, whom he names, had granted. There is no doubt about the territorial position of the lord of Aeslingham if no further knowledge of him had been rescued from oblivion. Of this valuable charter the signatures are perhaps the very best part: Hugo de Sancto Claro himself, Philip Gruer de Sancto Claro, Robert de Clovilla, William Richard de Clovilla, another Hugo de Sancto Claro, Robert de Sancto Claro, Roger de Sancto Claro, and some others. Roger is mentioned as his brother.

The kindliness and respect to which this Latin charter testifies, are all the more genuine from the fact that Aeslingham manor was before this the best endowment the bishopric had. Offa, king of the Mercians, gave it to the bishop of Rochester in the eighth century, and Sigered, king of Kent, confirmed the grant, as also did Egbert. The charters with their exact dates are preserved in this Textus Roffensis. In The Domesday Book it is part of the lands of the bishopric, and if the exceptional threefold increase of revenue from it then, as compared with that in the time of Edward the Confessor, is indication, it could not but have been a most desirable possession. How it left the church will appear in discussing Hugo's lineage.

The point of importance now is that the favourite minister of Henry II, if he had no superstitious regard for the church and its officials, was everything but an irreligious personage. In the Report of the Historical MSS. Commission he appears in Normandy as witness, "Hugo de Sancto Claro", together with the chief men of Henry II's court, to the endowment of a religious house there by a Norman noble; and this is indication of full similar interest in such doings. He had too much traditional fame from his ancestors, as founders of abbeys and churches, to neglect his religious for state duties, however honourable. If he signed Stephen's charter in 1136 he must have lived to a good old age. In the list given by Richard Prior of Hagulstadt, one of the X Scriptores, or earliest authorities of English history, "Hugo de Sancto Claro" is the signature, and not "Hamo de Sancto Claro", as Lord Lyttleton's Cottonian MS. authority states. Perhaps the valuable fact is that one or other did sign then.

Chapter XXXIII
The Descent of the Baron of Aeslingham

Sir William Dugdale, England's facile princeps of laborious genealogists and antiquaries, found it the hardest part of his toil to fix the exact relationships of persons whom he met with in his endless but always useful researches. This has been felt strongly in these fields, even when there is no possible doubt about the lineage in itself. Records, having objects of their own, rarely show themselves as of direct use to historical purpose. By study and inference they give out their secrets. One crosses light back over another, and something unmistakably true is secured. To expect absolute accuracies of uncles, aunts, daughters, sons, grandsons, granddaughters, and further, without fail, is absurd with respect to contemporary families. If there is safe toiling within any particular stock at distant periods, it is all the most exacting ought to claim. A great delight comes when any of the established and authentic sources of national knowledge stand up as rocks to support weaker evidences, which could be rather grasped at than secured but for such help.

Hugh Sinclair's lineage is cleared up by an entry in the Rolls of 31 Henry I (1131), under the headings "Kent, Sussex, and Boseham". Boseham was the south-western part of Sussex. Hunter's edition of the passage from this state record runs, "'Hamo Dapifer owed when he died one hundred marks silver [as tax to the royal treasury] in regard to land and the marriage of the daughter of Robert of Cloville to his nephew Hugo'". This is the usual payment to the king when land changed hands and one's heir got married. That Hugo paid it himself, as heir to part of his uncle's property, goes without saying; and the entry in 1131 gives a safe inference as to the date of Hamo Dapifer's death.

His other nephew, Robert de Crevequer, his sister's son, pays; £156, 13s. 4d. of legacy duty on getting also a portion of Hamo's lands the same year, which confirms the probability of 1130 or 1131 being his last year. The Magna Britannia excels itself in praise of the "potent ancient and illustrious family of the Crevequers" who were "the lords of Kent by pre-eminence". It was this Robert with Hamo's lands who was its greatest English builder, making Chatham the caput baroniae, and founding the famous Leeds Castle and Leeds Priory of Kent. They were of affinity to Hamo by marriage of his sister, and not by blood, as Hasted risked guessing, this same rotulus proving the fact.

His nephew Hugo St.Claire was of his own strain, and the Clovilles by their frequent appearance together with the Sinclairs, as for example in the charter of the bishop of Rochester, seem to have been nearer kin than marriage would of itself account for. Cloville is certainly only a local name. The lineage gets numerous in Kent, the only place in England where this is very remarkable of it. Local naming grew to be useful, for distinction's sake. Patience would probably discover the baron Leybournes of Leybourne Castle, who ended in the heiress called from her riches the "Infanta of Kent", to be Sinclairs. Lords Gray of Codnor have been supposed the heirs of Adam the commissioner's lands of Cray. Their origin from the father of Arlotta, mother of the Conqueror, was discovered perhaps after their distinction in English history made them marquesses of Dorset and half the titles of the peerage. Boxley, once held by Eudo Dapifer, has its tenths confirmed to Rochester by the Leybournes, the gift of Eudo "their antecessor". The Brocs or Brookes and the Cobhams were locally named, and possessed much of Adam, Eudo, and Hamo's lands.

But let these stand for general specimens of inquiries which might profitably be made, and without limit. The Clovilles and the Sinclairs actually named in records are sufficient present quest. Besides the special juxtaposition of the Clovilles with Hugo as evidenced by his marriage and the signatures of the charter of the bishop, there is the suggestive fact that a William of Cloville and a Robert were proprietors of Okely, of which they, William by reason of his "devotion", gave the tenths besides other gifts to St.Andrews, Rochester, as the Textus shows. The tenths of Henherst in the parish of Cobham, a manor some time in the possession of one of the two Williams of Longvale, and of Goscelin, an ancestor of theirs, are given to St.Andrews, Rochester, by a William of Cloville, as well as by them, Goscelin's charter dating 1091. It is worth remembering that Edward the Confessor's internuntius to William, duke of Normandy, was the rich merchant Goscelin, whose marriage aided so much to the rise of the house of Rye, Hubert being the internuntius and sequester who volunteered the dangerous duty of getting the symbols of English sovereignty conveyed back to his lord. In 2 Edward I (1274) William de Sancto Claro possesses the Okely property. It may have come to him through the marriage connection of Hugo to Robert de Cloville's daughter. The period between is about a hundred years; and, with the valley of the Medway nearly in entire possession of

Sinclairs, there would not be want of male heirs if the Clovilles were originally of the lineage, as seems possible.

The Cloville connection proves Hugo to be of the Fitz-Hamo branch, by being the nephew of Hamo Dapifer. That he signed the national charter given by Stephen in 1136, is aid to the knowledge of him by the rotulus 31 Henry I, through his marriage then, 1131, to the daughter of Robert Cloville. At the time of the Becket quarrel, beginning 1163, he would be a man of age and experience upon whom the king could reckon securely. Hugo Sinclair's lineage as of the Corboil and ducal family of Normandy is certain. It was more difficult to discover his father than his uncle, Hamo Dapifer; but, solvitur inquirendo. There was a Peerage published in 1710, by Roper and Collins, London, which throws great light on the subject. The writer was fully acquainted with Dugdale's works, and with other records to which that Hercules had not access, adding valuable facts to the histories of various houses. Under "Granville, earl of Bath", has been found the clue to several of the knots which have been the most difficult to untie in the Sinclair lineage. These earls will have attention in their due place. Here enough of their story to show Hugo's descent must suffice.

Robert Fitz-Hamo, the "knight of Rye", when he went in 1090 to conquer Glamorgan and other parts of South Wales, had as the first two on the well-known list of his twelve famous knights, William of London and Richard de Granville. They were his own brothers. Richard's descendants proved this in the reign of Charles II, and got an earldom and the promise of higher rank, on the validity of the proof. There is no question amongst the genealogists about his descent. Richard had his local name from Granville in Normandy, near St.Lo, Thorigny (of which Fitz-Hamo was lord), Rye Castle, and the other neighbouring estates of his relations. He was at the battle of Hastings with his brothers, and got, says the Peerage, "'for his signal services, the castle and lordship of Biddiford with other lordships, lands, and possessions in Devon, Cornwall, Somerset, and Bucks., many whereof remain to his posterity to this day'".

The History of Cambria was translated from the much earlier Welsh in 1584. Miss Blanch Parry, a gentlewoman of the queen, had the copy of the original, and gave it to the translator. Stow and all the other antiquaries have got their best facts about Wales from this source, and it has a specially full description of Robert Fitz-Hamo's conquest, not forgetting to celebrate frequently the worthiness of the Norman, wonderful to say; even toward the Welsh also. It tells the measurement of his first acquisition of territory, with very particular reference to the places whence the twenty-two and twenty-seven miles are taken of length and breadth. Robert himself took eleven knights' fees of the thirty-six and a half which he ultimately secured, building Cardiff Castle as the chief of the eighteen castles with regal right within his rule. He "had his chancery, exchequer, and fair court-house" there. His Monday monthly court is described most interestingly. For his under-lords there was lodging provided by fixed statute in the outer ward of the castle. They came on Monday, the court was held on Tuesday, and on Wednesday they went away to hold the sub-courts of their own castles and lordships, after this monthly general enlightenment. There is the homely glimpse that Fitz-Hamo held, for the provision of his own house, a large grange in Boviarton.

But it is of his first knight, William de Londres, that inquiry is being made. Richard of Granville had the lordship and castle of Neth as his share of the new Welsh addition to his fortunes. It was made up of three knights' fees. But William had the castle and manor of Ogmor, which formed four knights' fees. Of the two brothers, it is certain he was the elder. If it is accepted universally that Richard was the brother of Fitz-Hamo, the relationship of William as another brother, is as firmly secured by the conditions of these Welsh possessions.

This William de Londres, of Ogmoor, and other lordships, was the father of Hamo of Colchester, and of Hugo, the lord of Aeslingham. Thomas Nicholas in his work, 1575, on the antiquities of Wales, says that he had a son Maurice, the builder with his father of Welsh abbeys, who became the lord of Castle Ogmor and the other Welsh properties, and that Maurice had a son William. He always takes care to note that the chief interests of the original William de Londres were in England and Normandy; but in describing the conquest of South Wales by the three brothers and the other knights, he puts this William farthest to the west, who from Ogmor pushed forward into Carmarthenshire. It is more than probable that he was the actual builder of that castle of St.Clare which still gives the name to the town near its ruins, and that his brother Robert Sinclair or Fitz-Hamo got the general credit of it as head of the expedition. The history of the Welsh branch of William's family might clear up the proper origin of Fitzmaurices, Fitzgeralds, and other Latinised "aps" who when they reached Pembroke pushed with Norman enterprise across the Irish Channel for fresh fields and pastures new. Such account sounds far more like the tenor of history than heraldic tales or sennachy heroics of Italian if not Trojan origin to the greatest ruling families of Ireland, who were Normans, and nothing more, and quite enough too for all rational purposes of distinction or heroism. Though it might be frightful heresy to Celtic minds, the flying shot may be risked, that even their Williamses may in their best branch have Norman ancestry, Oliver Cromwell, who was a Williams, taking origin from or near some of the South Wales castles always held by these gallant conquerors, William St.Clare, his brothers, and the rest.

It was William de Londres (William Sinclair of London) who founded with his niece, and not sister, Matilda Sinclair, countess of Gloucester, and wife of Henry I's son Robert, the abbey of Savigny in France, 1140. Their common charter, to which the seal of William de St.Clair is still attached, loses entirely its enigmatical, and gains the most sterlingly useful character. The theory that he was her brother, as the son of Fitz-Hamo by the Princess Nesta, his first wife, has to be given up; though it is yet useful from the help it gave to discovering the full truth of the matter. The scientific genealogists of the fifteenth and sixteenth centuries were right, in showing issue only from his second marriage, with Sybil Montgomery, the sister of Robert de Belesme. It was scantiness of evidence that compelled towards such explanation, which was not, after all, very wide of the mark.

Comparison of these findings with the accounts of Matilda and William Sinclair, already given, will easily correct and finish this part of the general inquiry. Hamo, who was sheriff and fee-farmer of Colchester, and holder of extensive lands in Bedfordshire, Norfolk, Suffolk, Essex, Huntingdon, and other counties, was the chief heir of this William of London, who is the signer of the charter by Stephen to Geffrey, earl of Essex; and Hamo's famous son Hubert, the hero of Bridgenorth, was his grandson. Hugo, the lord of Aeslingham, was a younger son of this William, brother to "the great Fitz-Hamo", as the Peerage says he was called from his distinction. It is easily understood why Hugo was high at court in Henry II's reign, with such near relationships to Robert, earl of Gloucester, the Empress Matilda's brother, and champion for her and this son of hers, Henry. How Hugo was nephew to Hamo, vicecomes of Kent and dapifer of England, the brother of this Fitz-Hamo, is quite cleared up. Conversely, as the Sinclair of English history in the Becket quarrel, he proves the Corboil or Hamo and Fitz-Hamo lineage to be that of Sinclair, which branched from the ducal house of Normandy, founded by Rollo, the greatest of the vikings or sea-kings.

Chapter XXXIV
Two Walters of Medway

In the reign of Henry I, Geffrey Talbot held great part of the valley of the Medway. In the reign of Henry II, beginning 1154, Walter de Meduana, the second of the name, was in possession of twenty fees of what was Talbot's land; and Hugo de St.Clare, the king's minister, had the portion of his properties nearer the Thames, of which Aeslingham was the head. Walter was Hugo's blood relation, and he heired Geffrey through connection with Eudo Dapifer.

It is through the same ties, but more distant ones, that Hugo got his share. Aeslingham or Frindsbury, Hasted says, was given by Gundulph, the architect bishop of Rochester, to Geffrey Talbot, except tithes, "after which this manor came into possession of the family of St.Clare". It would be interesting to know why this favourite and richest portion of the church's revenues went to Talbot. In the Textus Roffensis there are to be seen the charters of it given by Offa, king of the Mercians, in 789, and confirmations and additions by Sigered, king of Kent, and by Egbert, the first Saxon king of all England. In The Domesday Book the increase of its value from the time of Edward the Confessor is more than threefold, most property having decreased largely in value then. It is curious that the bishop of St.Andrews, Rochester, could part with it, even reserving the tithes. Hugo's estates were made up of this, and of what he heired of the lands of his uncle Hamo, the viscount of Kent and dapifer of England. With his wife, the daughter of Robert of Cloville, he got property also, in the same district.

To Aeslingham, and to its neighourhood on both sides of the Thames, where Hugo's descendants enjoyed their lives, it will be returned. Meantime, the question is who Walter of Medway was. We know of his grandfather, also a Walter of Medway, who came in with William the Conqueror. Already some notice has been taken of Walderne or Walter Sinclair, earl of St.Cler, and of his three sons, Richard, William, and Britel, with their sister Agnes. It seemed considerably mysterious that so prominent a noble of Normandy, and so nearly related to the Conqueror and his energetic family, fared slightly at his hands; but this discovery that the earl of St.Cler took the name of Walter de Meduana in England entirely qualifies matters, even though they are yet not the most favoured of their name. William's espousal of the cause of the Athelings does not seem to have damaged much any but himself, and he had the skill to find better things across the borders than probably might have been his in England. If so remarkable and, in Richard's case, so specially heroic a branch, had been entirely forgotten in the division of spoil among the comites, the garrulous chroniclers would have certainly all told more or less about it.

William the Conqueror's kingly generosity and manly justice are conspicuous in Walter's case as in many another's; but the Norman possessions of the earl may have hindered his presence here, enough to limit his advance to possessions of the first class. That he got land on the Medway shortly after the Conquest, is attested by a signature of his to a charter in 1075 as Walter de Meduana. It is preserved in the library of Magdalen College, Oxford, and the circumstances under which it was granted are full of suggestion. The granter was William Bruce of Brember, and William the Conqueror confirms the grant. St.Peter's Church, Sela, Sussex, was the object of his bounty, and the locality has some relation to matters. Odo Consul, Hugh [Montgomery], consul of Chester, Humphrey de Bohun, Heunes vicecomes, and Walter de Meduana, are the names most useful of those who witnessed the charter.

It was to William Bruce of Bramber, Sussex, or William de Braiosa, the founder of the great British family, that Agnes Sinclair, the daughter of Walter, earl of St.Cler, was married, many genealogists say. Some give his able son Philip Bruce as her husband. It is certain that one or other was, and here it is only of importance that the affinity tie existed between the Sinclairs and the Bruces in 1075. It is a commonplace that then, when witnessing charters was one of the great public duties conducted with special gravity, the nearest and weightiest members of families alone had the privilege of adhibiting signatures to such important writings. Walter, the elder, of Medway, was equally in place if his daughter was married to the granter or to the subtle and ultimately cross-taking religious son and heir Philip. In 1095, before going to the Holy Land, Philip confirmed the same charter; and, that Comes Simon and Thomas Talbot are witnesses, tells the tale of relationships. Again it is confirmed by his son William in Richard's reign, with Simon Sinclair, written Simon Comes, as a witness, having the interesting addition, "'Who then was dapifer'". Agnes Sinclair, daughter of Walter, was the bond between the Bruces and the various branches of Sinclairs.

But we have knowledge of this Walter and of his lineage from further unimpeachable record. In The Domesday Book he is an in capite holder under the title "Walter, the brother of the sewar". The sewar was the dapifer, and can only mean the great Hamo, father of Hamo, vicecomes of Kent, and of Robert Fitz-Hamo, "knight of Rye", the lord of Gloucester and Glamorgan. Walter of Medway, earl of St.Cler, could not have been the brother of Eudo, the dapifer or sewar. He must have been his uncle, and also the uncle of Hamo, vicecomes and dapifer. This would make Walter, the elder, a brother of the great Norman Hamo, the dapifer, and of Hubert of Rye, ambassador of Duke William to Edward the Confessor to get the legacy of the English crown.

Nothing is left unreconciled of what evidences appear in the whole subject, by this relationship of the Corboil Sinclairs; for they are all branched from the first earl of Corboil, son of the duke of Normandy. The fact that the Hamo who came from Normandy to fight with William at Hastings was first dapifer of the name, and his son Hamo, vicecomes, the second Hamo Dapifer, is proved by the showing, already made, that the latter died in 1130, and that the former's name occurs as witness to many charters in William I's reign. Even so late a charter as the great one by Bishop William de Karileph to Durham monastery, given at London 1082, could hardly have been signed by the younger Hamo, on any ordinary calculation of the length of lives.

The first Walter's lands in Bedfordshire, of the survey, are particularly noticeable, in that a Hugo is an underholder. Probably he was a younger son or nephew so provided for, and it certainly gives a hint that the name was not strange to the family. "Hugh" and "Roger" are frequently in the Aeslingham branch, and that these names came from the Montgomeries, earls of Arundel, Shrewsbury, and Chester, seems likely result of the marriage of Robert Fitz-Hamo to Sybil Montgomery, the daughter of Roger, and sister of Hugh, consul of Chester. Hugo Pincerna, an in capite holder of The Domesday Book; and occurring next in order to "Walter, the brother of the sewar", in Bedfordshire, is of the same stock; but this will have discussion when Hugo de St.Clare's descendants are treated.

Of Walter of Medway, the grandson of the earl of St.Cler, there are several glimpses. That from the Liber Niger Scaccarii of Henry II aids considerably our knowledge of him, and of his past and contemporary relations. His return or carta to the treasury of his properties has a Latin introduction to the king. "Carta Walteri de Meduana", is the heading of his return. Then comes the preamble.

"'To Henry, by the grace of God king of the English, his very dear lord, Walter of Medway health and faithful service: It has been known to you that in the year and day in which King Henry, your grandfather, was alive and died, Geffrey Talbot held twenty knights' fees in capite from him, which by your favour I now hold from you, namely '" ... Here follows the list of his underholders, of whom the most noticeable are named Willemus de Clovilla, holding three knights' fees; three milites, as they are entered in the Black Book, viz., Robertus de Sancto Clara, two, John Sinclair the same number, Ralph of Cloville half-a-fee; Hamo of Scottot, one fee; and so on till the twenty are accounted for. The carta ends with "Farewell".

The history of this Talbot feod or fief is instructive. Richard Talbot, Geffrey's father, a gentleman of Normandy, got 9 fees from Giffard, earl of Buckingham, who had 110 from the Conqueror. In 31 Henry I (1131), Geffrey acknowledges a debt to the treasury of 140 merks silver out of 200 due for being put in possession of his father's lands. In the Textus Roffensis he appears as the donor of Little Wrotham, Kent, in the time of Rufus, to St.Andrews, Rochester, the witnesses being, among others, Archbishop Anselm and Robert Fitz-Hamo. He took the side of Matilda against Stephen. His son was the William Talbot of Normandy who, Dugdale says, married Beatrice Mandeville, the sister of the great Geffrey Mandeville of chief fame in the struggle of Stephen and Matilda. This William Talbot was according to Tindal one of the ringleaders under Robert, earl of Gloucester, in championing Matilda, 1138, and it was he that seized Hereford Castle on her side. Beatrice was the daughter of Margaret Sinclair, daughter of Eudo Dapifer; and her brother Geffrey, earl of Essex, got her divorced from William Talbot, whom he disliked for some reason, and had her married for second husband to William de Say. The Talbot feoda in Kent got its enlargement from her, as heiress of Eudo Dapifer's lands after the death of her brother Geffrey, 1144; and it was through kinship to her mother that Walter Sinclair of Medway came to be the heir of part of it.

Beatrice, who lived to extreme age, and whose funeral at Walden Abbey was one of the grand events of the kind, heired, 2 Richard I (1191), her nephew, William Mandeville, earl of Essex, the last of his race; but though her son Geffrey de Say became lord of Berling, Kent, the caput baroniae of the Says, through her rights, this Say was not rich enough to contend against his sister's husband, Geffrey Fitz-Piers of Ludgershall Castle, Wiltshire, and William of Bocland. Beatrice Say was made countess of Essex, Fitz-Piers assuming the famous surname of Mandeville; and by his wealth and influence he secured much more than his just share of the lands in the right of the granddaughter of Eudo

Dapifer. Banks, in his Dormant and Extinct Baronage, says that when her nephew died, she, being aged, sent her son Geffrey de Say to have livery of her heirship, and that for 7000 marks he got the whole barony, but could not pay. After long contest, Fitz-Piers, and Bocland by right of his wife Maud, got the lion's portions by influence and money. Geffrey de Say, whom one genealogist makes earl of Essex by marriage to the sister of William Mandeville, died in 1214, and probably he thought he was wronged by his sisters and their husbands. The Says became the renowned barons of English history not long after.

But it is after the Talbots (of which lineage was the English hero of Normandy battles, and the existing family represented by the earls of Shrewsbury) that inquiry searches. Burke says that one of the early representatives became a monk, and that at some interval the family got possessions in the northern parts of England. At all events, the name lost the Kentish twenty knights' fees, and Walter of Medway possessed them in Henry II's reign. Beatrice Mandeville's first husband, William, seems to have lost them or given them to the lineage of his wife, whence they came, and in that most troublous of reigns, Stephen's. Matilda, besides giving all Eudo Dapifer's lands to her favourite, Geffrey Mandeville, earl of Essex, son of Margaret Sinclair, promised that afterwards he should have all Eudo's English lands also, and it is probable that Beatrice instead of him experienced the benefit of the promise when the empress and her son became triumphant. In a charter referred to by Sir William Dugdale, Geffrey actually got 20 knights' fees from her of Eudo's, and they must have been these.

If the first Walter of Medway was Eudo Dapifer's uncle, the second Walter of Medway would be second cousin to Eudo. The extinction soon in the chief lines of the Hubert of Rye family, gave these Walters and the Hugoes and Hamoes of the two brothers of Hubert of Rye next rights of heirship by blood. Out of the obscurity, though not impenetrable altogether, of antiquity, much more than this can hardly be expected.

From the chronicle of Abingdon monastery, Berks, much light is thrown on the related Bucklands; and Eudo Dapifer, Hamo Dapifer, Robert Fitz-Hamo, and others of the connection appear in it frequently and suggestively. Cornbury Park was a favourite place of the court in early reigns for signing charters and doing royal business, and Burke's interest in some arms of Sinclairs being found there in one of the herald visitations, might find its satisfaction from such source as this Chronica with its revelations. The difficulty of contemporaneous dapifers has already been completely solved by one of the charters; and a Walter, the son of Richard, as a witness to the same, may be a clue to the holder of the Medway fees between the Walters. Richard, son of Walter, earl of St.Cler, would be the father of this Walter, who is companion witness to Walter Giffard "the chancellor", which distinguishes the Giffards and Medways, related by marriage.

There was a Walter of Bocland of Stephen's reign; in the Textus Roffensis Geffrey Bocland is witness to a charter, and William gives a confirmation of lands from the Talbot feoda of which Walter of Medway was chief heir; but the Bucklands, who are at all events of close affinity to the lords of Colchester, of Eudo's lineage, may be left with the account of Hugo, who quieted, for Abbot Faritius of Abingdon, the violence of the men of Culham. Peace was made between them, "'in the presence of Hugo the viscount (an approved and wise man, who not only over Berkshire but also seven other shires was made viscount, so chosen and dear was the man to the king) and in the presence of many men present there from three shires'". To be so beloved of so able a monarch as Henry I, is an immortality of the permanent kind.

Carte, "the Englishman", in his admirable English history, says that Hugo got part of Robert Montgomery's lands, the notorious Robert de Belesme of Norman-English annals. A Hamo of Falaise also benefited by the ruin of that earl of Arundel, Salop, and Chester. The historian explains that they had not originally much property of their own. The close connection of Henry I, both by male lineage and contemporary marriage of his son Robert, to the Hamo, Fitz-Hamo, Eudo, and other Sinclairs, makes it more than probable that Hugh of Bocland was a young member of the same lineage. The threads are very close of their stories on both banks of the Thames, especially below London. But it must not be forgotten that Ordericus Vitalis says that on the ruin of many of the nobles, men of the merchant class, Geoffrey of Clinton, Hugh of Bocland, Ralph Basset, and the foreign Hamo got promotion, though this need not conflict irreconcileably, in Hugh's case, with what has seemed to be suggested by many circumstances. The Bucklands were heired by the Brooke or Broc lords Cobham.

In the various ties of blood and marriage of these earliest families of England, is to be found the secret of its greatness, as the kingdom with what Shakespeare calls "This happy race of men". That in the chief lines they often soon became extinct, does no more than tell the tale of departure of property from certain members; the lineages not being always extinct, but mixing, under change of names, which is the feature of centuries of English history, with new rising families for fresh courses of effort and distinction.

The Medways were not a lasting line, unless it be that the Joel de Meduana who pays large taxes from Devon and Cornwall, 31 Henry I (1131), and who was probably a son of Richard de Meduana, son of the first Walter of Medway, earl of St.Cler, Normandy, founded a family. But from what Jones in his History of Brecknock says, he perhaps did not; for he makes the "rich heiress" of Joel of Barnstaple and Totness, marry the William Bruce of Brember who appears so largely in Domesday Book. [Eva Marshall ?] This would well explain Walter of Medway's signing of the charter of the church of Seal, Sussex, the lady of Brember being his niece. In this light new relationships, besides Agnes Sinclair's, to the Bruces appear; and they give Joel of Meduana, who had estates in Cornwall and Devon as well as Kent, a recognisable and very substantial existence, though without male heirs, the Bruces getting his lands by the heiress.

In the Rotuli of 3 John (1202) Cecil, countess of Hereford, pays 50s. of scutage from the honour of Walter of Medway, and for a third scutage, or military tax, William Montchesney pays £ 14, 10 s. That these were of Walter's lineage is probable. The Montchesneys are a remarkable family after this time, and it is noticeable that in the records many Sinclairs hold of them, especially on both sides of the Thames, where Hugo St.Clare's descendants had their homes, in Kent and Essex. The head of the barony of Montchesney was at Swanscombe or Swain's Camp, where the Kentishmen surprised William the Conqueror and gained favours and freedom, bordering to Aeslingham and the other manors of Hugo; and if William Montchesney thus heired Walter of Medway, as the state record settles, it is easy to understand the general and even particular relationships of these Kentish lords. Chesney is one of the distinguished names of the county, and certainly was of local origin, though it may have had a double in Normandy, as was frequent. But even thus, these Medway heirs ended in the reign of Edward I, the daughter and sole heir of the last male Montchesney marrying Hugh de Vere, earl of Oxford, in the twenty-fifth year of that monarch (1296).

The William Montchesney who heired Walter de Meduana, married Joan, daughter of William Marshall, the great earl of Pembroke, whose mother was a Clare, and therefore the couple were of affinity. His son married one of the famous Valences, into which family Eudo Dapifer's sister, Albreda Sinclair, had been married. William increased the patrimony largely in Norfolk, Kent, Gloucester, and Northampton; and in Essex he got Ralph de Haie's lands of 14.5 fees, the Haies being descended from a nephew of Eudo Dapifer, on the authority of Le Prevost and Duncan. In 40 Henry III (1256), Montchesney was one of the principal barons with Simon de Montfort, earl of Leicester, probably his aunt Cecil's father-in-law if not husband, at the battle of Lewes. After the battle of Evesham his land was given to his brother-in-law, William Valence; but he got pardoned for rebellion, and under the government of the kingdom by Richard, duke of Cornwall, was restored to his possessions. For the short period of the Montchesneys, no English house did more brilliantly and successfully, getting the best honours, wealth, and marriages of their period. Stephen de "Munchensi" was governor of Acre after its conquest by Richard Coeur de Lion.

Dugdale's Baronage has good account of them, but he gives no help to the discovery of their lineage, beyond that the earliest of them were two Huberts, and that the first is in record as granter of lands. It might be more subtle than certain that they were Hubert of Rye and his son Hubert of Norwich Castle. One of them is a large in capite holder, in Essex, of Domesday survey, as "Hubert de Monte Canisio". There is at least recorded fact for this, that they were closely related with the barony of Hengham, Norfolk, which has already been shown to have been the home of the family of Hubert of Norwich for some generations. That Montchesneys heired Ralph de Haie's lands, is a fact which all but settles that they were a branch of the Rye family. The eldest brother of Eudo Dapifer, Ralph, castellan of Nottingham, and earl, did not found a family of long standing in the direct line, and this Ralph de Haie was one of that line, which suffered so extremely in Stephen's reign, as has appeared. It is known that Hubert's eldest son Ralph had the chief part of his father's lands in Normandy, and in the Liber Ruber Scaccarii - The Red Book of the Treasury, of Harry II's reign, Ralph of Hay held then 2.5 knights' fees, as from the honour of Plessy, the Sinclair-Mandevilles' baronry, and 1 fee and in another place 6.5 fees in the very region of most of the original stock, the Cotentin of Lower Normandy, especially the peninsular ending with the sea at Cherbourg opposite Portsmouth. There were Rye, Granville, St.Lo, Thorigny, Mandeville, Valence, and the rest of the names so familiar.

In the same Red Book under the heading, "'These are they who neither came nor sent nor said anything'", we have, with the best names in England, these two, Walter of Medway and Hugo de Sancto Claro, the latter specially mentioned as holding in Algia or Auge or Ou. Moulin speaks of this as "a submission list" to Philip Augustus, after his conquest of Normandy; but it is more probably one of the usual reckonings of some of Henry II's lieutenants or seneschals in France, like William Fitz-Raphe. Doctor Ducarel's Anglo-Norman Antiquities, has these and other interesting state records; though the doctor does not appear to know so much about them as he protests, to the depreciation of M. Moulin and others. The Chesneys or Monchesnis of Swanscombe,

Kent, their caput baroniae, seem to have picked up the pieces, in several counties, of that "house of Rye", about whom Freeman has wonderfully good words, for him to say; and it is not likely that a mistake would be made in claiming such brilliant but long since extinct Englishmen for the lineage. It is they who would have the honour in being proved of the line of Rollo, while at the same time they were worthy members of the Scandinavian, Franco-English, royal descent.

The story of the two Walters of Medway may be ended by noting that the Walter de Meduana contemporary with Hugo de St.Clare, was, like him, one of the great barons present, Lord Lyttleton being witness of this, at the framing of the necessary but as it proved extremely troublesome constitutions of Clarendon. There is no record extant that he also suffered by being "named", by the obstinate Thomas of Canterbury, to future reprobation, as the archbishop thought unwisely, of mankind; and to that eternal perdition which was the rod of correction, and, alas for the unselfishness of even clerical men, the rod of oppression in the puerile and senile epochs. It goes without saying that Walter was of the king's party, as all the intelligent and substantial Englishmen were, both clerical and lay. Was it not to take the excommunication off the bishops, the barons caring far less about the matter, that the final contest between Becket and the four nobles of the king's household was entered upon ? Any one reading Lyttleton's able and graphic account of the last days of the so-called martyr, must come to quite other than the usual conclusion about Reginald Fitz-Urse, William de Tracy, Richard Brito, and Hugh de Moreville as being, in any sense, murderers. Hours and days of expostulation and entreaty of every kind, and not for their own but his order, brought nothing but insult.

Had King Henry not been of a superstitious and loving nature, he would himself long before have ended the struggle in some such way as they did, if no other road opened out of the difficulty. Henry VIII knew short methods with far better and gentler clerics than this one. Did he not actually try and condemn, in a fictional court, this very so-called St.Thomas ? The vulgarity of the man came out in his clinging to a pillar, when, at last, they grew utterly hopeless of gaining anything from him, and the only poor chance of peace to his coinitry scorned to take him personally away to the king's presence in Normandy, to see what could be done in that case.

It is the unspeakable misfortune of those first men of the land that deserves most commiseration, whom oppression of a priest to themselves, their friends, their king, and their spiritual directors for years, would not have driven to violence but that this unknightly ill-bred man of the mob, began the rough play which could not but end as it did, with any men who at all respected their own manhood. It was in full keeping with the lowness of the man to call Fitz-Urse "pimp"; and that the immediate effect of such a vile insult, after days of honourable and reverent beseeching, was a sword across the head, could not but be. The unanimity with which the four completed the work is the apology for it.

He had outraged every instinct of royalty, nobility, and manhood; and it may safely be said if all that was noble, and most that was clerical, in the kingdom, had been there at that moment, having suffered as these men did, they would have had equally been in the great misfortune of killing, or helping to kill, a man who was stifling the souls of a whole people's select spirits. The consecrated place and person were the pities of the affair, but it was the archbishop who positively created the scene of blood. His previous sermons showed that he was courting martyrdom; in other words, searching after a full conclusion to his spleen of bitterly stubborn years. Lyttleton gives him credit for all that was good in him; but it would be quite a consistent view, to apply to him the nickname he himself invented for his archdeacon, and to call him, for the sake of brevity and truthful condensation, the archdevil of Canterbury.

Chapter XXXV
King's Chamberlain

In a century or more after the Conquest, the system of one man having manors in many counties, began to change, with the increase of families, with heirships by females, and for the general greater convenience of united property. There remain, however, to this day survivals of the Conqueror's peculiar but politic division of lands.

It has already been noticed that Richard "Sencler", the son of Walter, earl of St.Cler, and the first of Medway, appears in Domesday Book as the holder in capite of Wortham, in the hundred of Hartismere, and of house and lands at Norwich. Says the record, "'Of the burgesses who dwelt in Norwich, twenty-two are gone away and dwell in Beccles, a town of the abbot of St.Edmundsbury, and six in Humilgar hundred, and have forsaken the burgh, and King's Thorpe one, and on the land of Roger Bigot one, and on the land of William of Noies one, and on that of Richard de Sentcler one. Those who fled and those remaining, are altogether wasted or impoverished, partly through Earl Ralph's forfeitures, partly through fire, partly by the king's tribute, and partly by Waleran'".

Blomfield notes with a parenthesis a passage in The Domesday Book having reference to Norwich, "'And Richard de Sentebor (rather Sent-cler) has one house'". In the quelling of "the rising of Norwich", Richard, the king's chamberlain, was actively engaged, and received reward thus there of his loyalty. To fix his other lordships in England is not so easy as in these cases, where his name and surname occur in full. He was so well known, however, that the many entries under the name of Richard alone, now difficult to authenticate, are on all grounds of probability largely his. To found on this, nevertheless, would be for many reasons useless. It may be sufficient to assume that he took his father's place on the Medway, as well as occupied the Suffolk and Norfolk lands to which that record positively fixes him. The Textus Roffensis would make him to be Richard, the king's chamberlain, who had the property of Ros, from which he gave returns to the monks of Rochester. In Ingulph's Chronicle, who was a contemporary and favourite of the Conqueror, he is called "Richard of Rulos, the king's chamberlain", Rolph's being the Saxon name of Ros, which with "Chester" or castra added means Rolph's Castle. Ingulph praises the chamberlain highly, particularly about the kind way in which he got the historian's friend promoted to be abbot of the famous monastery of Glastonbury. This of itself shows Richard's influence with the king.

The barons of Ros were great men in the times of John and Henry III and subsequent reigns, and they were Richard's people. One of them married his blood relation, the heiress of the Todeneis, better known as the Albeneys, Aubenis, D'Aubignys, or D'Albinis of Belvoir Castle, Lincoln, and the same lineage with those of Arundel Castle, Sussex, descended from Rollo's uncle. The last of these barons Ros of Hamlake, Trierbut, and Belvoir died in 1508, and his sister heiring him, married Sir Robert Manners, the ancestor of the dukes of Rutland. Their son held also the barony of Vaux.

A complete reformation must be made as to the place in Kent called Ros. Dr. Thorpe, the editor of what he called the Textus Roffensis, is responsible most for the straying of the antiquaries on the subject. He mistook the old double "s" for the ancient "f". It is the Textus Rossensis his collection of charters and ancient papers ought to have been called. Bishop Tanner in his Bibliotheca Britannico-Hibernica of writers to the sixteenth century, quotes Dempster as to Henricus Sinclarus decanus Glascuensis et episcopus Rossensis, the ambassador for peace between England and Scotland in 1555. Rossensis here means Ross in Scotland, but the word is one and the same with that applied to the Rochester records.

Rochester, after a prevalent manner in England, means simply "the castle of Ros", the head of the lands given by the Conqueror to his relation, Walter, earl of St.Cler. The remarkable importance of Rochester and its castle in English history is hereby explained to satisfaction, being always in near relationships to the earlier sovereigns after the Conquest. Ros, or Rochester, as it afterwards came to be called from its castle gathering the town about it, was the first English chief home; and William when he became an emigrant and the cup-bearer or pincerna of Margaret Atheling, queen of Scotland, carried its name to his castle, on the linn of the Esk near Edinburgh, as was the Norman portable fashion. There is opening for insight as to the county of the name, in this view.

Walter of Medway, the earl of St.Cler in Normandy, and his sons and daughter, can be studied from no better central position than the English caput baroniae of Ros, with its monastery, its bridge of twenty-one arches, and its feudal castle; and the love of the lineage for centuries to the district and its institutions, civil and religious, has thus its eclaircissement. The outcome of the whole of this part of the inquiry might end in finding Walter himself to have been Wace's hero of the battle of Hastings, the "St.Cler who overthrew many of the Angles", and that he and his family (except William, who became pincerna to Margaret Atheling) got largely and choicely from their king, Rochester or Ros, as then called, being the English "Schloss Stamm" of this great and present branch. The Roll of Battle Abbey would aid such view, and also others of the lists of the Conqueror's companions of 1066, "the lord of St.Cler" being more applicable to Walter the father than to Richard his eldest son. But the latter has the credit with writers of being the gallant knight in conspicuous action on the famous October day. Between them, however, there need be no rivalry, the furthest descendants having equally in either case the honour of the deeds of their ancestor.

It is a popular delusion that families become extinct, even if whole lineage is taken into account. Many of the present most flourishing Englishmen might find their earliest home at Ros, could they wend their way back through the changes of surnames and the accidents of time. In Scotland, the earl of Caithness represents many there, who have preserved, like himself, the surname intact, the older system aiding against the English local naming method; and they are the genuine stock of Walderne, Richard, and the rest of these Saint-Lo, in Normandy, and Rochester, in Kent, heroes of Rollo's blood.

The Romans had a different title altogether for Rochester, and Bede, centuries before the Conquest, says it got its name from a Saxon lord called Rouph. The Normans would call it Rouph's; and this would satisfy the prevalent name among antiquaries, and that suggested as the at least equally true one drawn from the history of those barons of Ros who appear in the historic scenes and charters of the kingdom more than any others.

What aids the theory of Richard being chamberlain is that he had a son Joel who also owed returns to the monks for this Ros or Rosa. There is a Richard, the son of Walter, witness to one of the earliest charters from the Tunbridge Richard Fitz-Gilbert, and he must have been Joel's father, the son of Walter of Medway. Joel is authenticated by being mentioned in the Rotulus 31 Henry I (1131) under Devon and Cornwall, as Joel of Medway, who pays the large tax of £11, 17s. 6d, and still owes the treasury £25, 10s. 5d. Richard's brother Britel had his lands chiefly in the south-western counties, and this nephew of his was the founder of the Devon and Cornwall branch. Vincent in criticising too bitterly the account given by Yorke, the heraldist of the Veres, earls of Oxford, quotes Matilda the empress's charter of promise to Aubrey de Vere, the chancellor; and "Juhel de Meduana" is mentioned as one of the witnesses and pledges she gives for the fulfilment. This is of itself sufficient to mark him as one of the ruling chief Normans, and of a family of first wealth and rank. The castle and tower of Colchester was part of the gifts in this charter; and Joel Sinclair, as one of the relations male of Eudo Dapifer, by his adhesion to Matilda's proposals would be of special service. The castle subsequently returned to the Sinclairs, and then again the Veres got it; so that affinity is the likelier explanation than many political changes of the violent kind.

There is a Geffrey of Ros who gives the tenths of Ealdeam or Yaldham to Rochester monks. He is a descendant of Richard, and the founder of the Aldhams or Audhams, Robert de Aldham being his successor by the charter. Walter, the second of Medway, was the eldest son of the chamberlain, and this Geffrey was a younger brother whose son assumed the local name Aldham, from the remarkable manor which still keeps the name in the Yaldham-St.Clere of Kent, near Maidstone. Sir Thomas de Aldham was one of Richard Coeur de Lion's famous knights at the siege of Acre in 1189, and there is also a Sir Thomas de St.Clair among his warriors at the same success. They are probably one and the same. The proof of the lineage of the Aldhams is in this Rotulus in Curia Scaccarii: *"'The king takes homage from John, the son of John Sinclair, blood-relation and heir of Francis of Aldham, for all his lands and tenements which the same Francis held'"*. But this younger branch from Richard, the king's chamberlain, will demand much attention for themselves.

Richard must be followed to the north, where at the end of his life he lived most, in the centre of Norfolk especially. The Wrotham of Suffolk which he had from the Conquest, was by some of his descendants doubled in Wrotham of Kent, just as Norman names were brought across the Channel, causing doubles. William of Wrotham, who was appointed by Henry II the justiciary to decide proper weights, measures, and other necessities of honest dealing, was one of Richard's descendants in Kent. The family of Wrotham were of high rank and influence in the county, and they had lands also in Somersetshire. But the Kent relations are numerous, and, except two chief families cannot be reckoned clearly, with any amount of care, on the knowledge that has survived.

Of all his properties those near Norwich required, and had, most of Richard's presence. He secured part of the lands confiscated from the burghers for the rebellion of 1075, begun at the "marriage of Norwich". It is not likely, however, that his official and military duties left him much opportunity of living in any one district, till old age came. Then there is record of his gifting lands and tithes to the church at Grassenhale, Norfolk, for the good of his own and his wife's soul. The Norfolk lands were made to suffer fire and sword, but they had no doubt more than recovered their usual fruitfulness before the monks could accept of them as gifts, being nice in their appreciation of the world's goods even so early as that time.

Whether the eldest or a younger branch of his family, the Norfolk and Suffolk line seemingly grew independent in a generation or two from their Kent brethren. They become noticeable most near St.Edmondsbury, but they held lands also at the same time in Kent and other counties. Their presence was certainly most given to the north, and they may be dealt with as specially belonging to Norfolk and Suffolk, their other lands gradually becoming more and more subsidiary to where the chief hall was, the caput baroniae, or usual place of holding their courts as lords of manors. It was this that first corrected a little the extraordinary spreading of one man's lands through sometimes all the counties.

The earl of Moretaine, the Conqueror's uterine brother, had the enormous number of 793 lordships through the island, but gradually such lords built one or more head castles to dominate the best parts of their estates, and exchanges began to become frequent for the purpose of uniting properties, and saving toil of travel and expense of management. Sir Richard Pole says that the richest men took to buying properties near London and selling the distant ones. Richard Sinclair, the chamberlain, could not have seen much of this change, but his descendants in these counties grew to be permanent residents. Of this heroic son of Walter, earl of St.Cler, who "overturned many of the English", as the Romance of Rollo says, on the field of Hastings, nothing much further need be said. Position, wealth, and, in nge, the usual thoughtfulness of Norman chief men were his; and through his double line of Kent and East Anglian descendants, it will be seen that no branch of his name had more of the high qualities of the race. That he lived long has already appeared. It is probable that he died about the latter years of the reign of Henry I, later than his cousin-german, Eudo Dapifer, who died in 1119.

In his History of Norfolk Blomfield has various notices of him. From the Register of the monks of Castleacre, he has saved the knowledge that *"'Richard de Sancto or St.Cleer gave the said monks his right in the church in free alms for ever, for the health of his own and his wife's soul, his heirs' and ancestors' souls, with all the liberties thereto belonging'"*. He adds the list of witnesses to the document of gift.

Chapter XXXVI
Richard of East Anglia

The state records of Stephen's reign are scanty, and therefore it is lucky to find indirect evidence of men's existence and deeds from chronicles or other less authentic materials than the national archives.

Whether Anglian Richard was son or grandson of Richard, the son of Walter, earl of St.Cler and Medway, cannot be discovered absolutely, the guide of time allowing either possibility, He was the grandson, if the Robert, son of Richard, who was one of Stephen's dapifers in the first year of his reign, and who is a witness to a charter given then to the bishop of Bath, was the son of the chamberlain. The charter is among the codices of the college of Corpus Christi, Cambridge, and though insuflicient for proof of itself it might be a powerful link towards reaching certainty here. The Sinclairs at first were certainly in the highest favour with this king; whether by policy, or will on his and their part, are questions of subtle kind. "The charter of Stephen, the king, concerning the liberties granted to the church and the kingdom", is a peculiar, suggestive, and, luckily, an extant document. From the archives of Exeter it was copied, and the copy is in the Bodleian Library, Oxford. It begins, "'I, elected by consent of the clerisy and the people of England, and by the Lord William of Canterbury ... '".

This William was a Sancto Claro, and two others of the surname are among the extraordinarily select witnesses of this carta of 1136, namely, the son of Count Simon Sinclair, earl of Huntingdon and Northampton, and Hamo de Sto.Claro, by this express and full name. William of Aubeni is there, a relation by blood and marriage; Robert, earl of Gloucester, Matilda Sinclair's husband, the son of Henry Beauclerc, is there; and, indeed, nearly all who were noblest in England. Gilbert de Laci is the last on the list.

In the general confirmation by Henry II of all the previous charters of the Tewkesbury monastery of St.Mary, founded by Robert Fitz-Hamo Sinclair, the signatures to one of those Henry I gave, would make "Brience, the son of the count", who is one of the witnesses of Stephen's national charter, also a Sinclair. But this is a mistake on the part of both Sir Robert Atkins and Rudder, the careful historian-antiquaries of Gloucestershire. They print the signature, "Brience, son of Earl Hamo, steward of the household". Hamo Sinclair had no children, all the authorities agree, and "Brience, son of the count" is of another relationship than this to him. Both were related closely to the Montgomeries. The difficulty is at once solved by putting a comma after "Earl", thus making it the signature of two persons. In this same charter Hamo and Robert Fitz-Hamo appear, mentioned as brothers. The question who Brience was, is at once settled, however, by the list which Richard Prior of Ingulstad, one of the X Scriptores, has given, where he appears as the son of the earl-constable, which office Hamo had not.

But return must be made to Richard, whom it is safe enough to assume as grandson of the first Richard of his branch, the son of Walderne, earl of St.Cler and of Medway. Something about his character and general position is attainable from a history by Matthew Paris of a quarrel between one of the abbots of St.Albans and William de Albini, pincerna, the earl of Arundel, whose fierceness was notorious and almost fabulous because of the story of slaying a lion by his own personal vigour. It was Abbot Robert who claimed the right of lodging in the cella or priorate of Wymundham, Norfolk, as being subordinate to the monastery of St.Albans. The prior and the earl of Arundel joined issue, in ways strangely characteristic of the period. That Abbot Robert bearded the terrible earl in this matter, was always afterwards his highest tribute so far as courage is concerned.

But there was more at work than the arrogance of an earl in Stephen's time of fortified castles. The prior of Wymundham had run scant of money, and had taken the liberty of making away with some of the valuables of the priorate. He was of the supple order of cleric, and contrived when the abbot of St.Albans, his superior, heard of the larceny, to make it appear that the proceedings were by order of the lord of the manor, the earl of Arundel. This he cunningly thought would of itself prevent all attempt at inquiry.

Abbot Robert recognised how matters really stood, having had much experience of monkery, and duty was clear to him. He set out with a company of clerics from Hertfordshire to see for himself. Before reaching Wymundham he was met by some of the prior's agents, who said that the cella was in possession of the earl's men, and that by the earl's command the abbot should have no lodging there. Abbot Robert could not sleep outside. He and his thirty or forty of a company must have something done for them. Hospitality was the monastic privilege and duty, and how much more to their own head, the abbot. Meantime, something alarming had occurred, probably by the instigation of the prior, at his wits' end. The abbot's cook, who had gone on in front to prepare food, was attacked and driven back on the main body, with the loss of his baggage of pots and kettles; and it was only by the highest flutter of monkish garments that the earl's minions, or the prior's, could be frightened from their savoury prey. At this point the prior in person appears on the scene. With him came Henry of Gorham and Richard de Sancto Claro. The abbot must be resisted if he should attempt entrance.

It became serious, even to fears of martyrdom; and though Robert did not shrink an inch, he was willing to make some compromise. His company might go to Norwich to find shelter, but he himself would sleep at all hazards in that cella of his own. The prior, Henry of Gorham, and Richard Sinclair had better go and tell the earl what was done, and that he was prepared to meet him next day at Norwich for any explanation on either side. Immediately on this treaty Abbot Robert went forward, pressed through angry soldiers, without active opposition, and did sleep in his own cella.

The ambassadors arranged the meeting rightly, and the abbot and the earl had their tug of war. "'What business have you on my lands with your company ? Your right is to lodge yourself there for a night and pass on; the priorate is my affair'". So the earl, but he was not match in logic for the abbot. "'As head of St.Alban's monastery, I and my company, large or small, can visit or stay when and as long as I choose, without any reference to the lord of the manor'". But if he gained his point he did not go much farther. His sagacity told him that with an earl so violent, and a prior so shifty, too close inquisition were not desirable. He departed, and found the credit of bearding Arundel worth his considerable journey.

Richard Sinclair as peacemaker, implies that he was well known to the earl, as well as one of the magnates of the district himself. He had a castle or manor there, though Wortham, which his antecessor Richard, the chamberlain, possessed in 1080, was the chief demesne. His successors showed still more inclination to reside in Suffolk, and the story of those of the great centre of St.Edmundsbuiy will exhibit this. He appears in the Great Roll of the Pipe, 1189-1190, at the beginning of the reign of Coeur de Lion: "'Norfolch' Sudfolch' De Plac Cvrie: 1 Richard I. Gerard de Wachesha redt comp de XX.s.p recogn res Ric. de S Claro de tra de M'lingef: In thro x.s: Et deb x.s.'". This is one of the usual transactions in the king's court about the receiving of taxes from lands. Richard Sinclair pays a tax from another estate of his, Marlingford in East Anglia. Gerard of Wachesham is the sheriff, and if Wachesham is the same as Wercham, it will be seen that Richard later had his chief land, which implies affinity for such heirship. But nothing can be added to the subject, and Wachesham and Wercham may not after all be the same places.

This Richard, residing near Wymundham, in Norfolk, at the time of the monastic adventure, is the same also with the Richard de Sancto Claro who appears in one of the charters of the Rolls of 7 John (1206). It is a confirmation to the abbess of St.Edward of Shaftesbury. "'And the tenths from the demesne of Richard Sinclair of Wercham, which he himself gave with his daughter: And in the same "town" 30 acres from his demesne'". There is little doubt that this, though the spelling is somewhat different, means the in capite domain of Wrotham, and also the Wachesham of 1189-1190. Between this district and St.Edmondsbury there was a Werham, and it is likely that the names had one origin, and the places one proprietor, if modern Werham had any particular estate existence then at all.

It may be thought curious that Richard did not send this daughter for whom he thus provided, as a nun to some convent nearer his home demesnes. It may, however, be remembered that the Sinclairs had great traditions in connection with the nunnery of Shaftesbury. Hawisa Sinclair, one of the daughters of Robert Fitz-Hamo, had been its abbess from the reign of Henry I, as her sister Cecilia, on Dugdale's authority and Glover's, was abbess of Wilton in Wiltshire. Some say Cecilia was that of Winchester. It was woman's highest ambition of those periods to be abbess. Lillechurch nunnery, Kent, had King Stephen's daughter for abbess, and hardly any such position in England was not filled by relations of royalty. The career Richard opened for his young daughter was one of the most privileged, and only wealth and birth could get on this path to feminine eminence.

Henry I when he provided that Matilda Sinclair should inherit the greatest part of her father's lands, to grace and enrich her husband, the king's son, whom he created earl of Gloucester, made ample amends to Hawise and Cecilia by giving them these high and coveted positions, of which the wealth was as great as the other advantages. Whether this young daughter followed the steps and reached the eminence of her relations, has yet to be discovered. That this is a charter of confirmation, may throw back the original gift by Richard considerably beyond 7 John (1206) and so go to the proof that the Richard of Wymundham was the donor.

Chapter XXXVII
Gereberd, Viscount of Norfolk and Suffolk

The brother of the young lady sent to Shaftesbury convent for her education (and profession, it may be) was a man of much business in political and particularly in financial affairs. Gilbert, Gerebald, Gerebert, or Gereberd Sinclair is one of the most frequent names in the state papers of his time. The variations in his first name do not cause any doubt, for the title follows them, "viscount of Norfolk and Suffolk". This, with the dates, which cannot be more authenticated than by state entries, makes assurance doubly sure.

It was he who founded the fine English home of Bradfield St.Clare; a name which his property near St.Edmondsbury still retains, to keep him and his lineage in remembrance. The park around his manor was one of the most remarkable of those greatest lovers of the forest and its sport, the Norman rulers of England. It was a few miles from the monastery of St.Edmondsbury, part of it being an underholding from the abbot. The district is remarkable among other greater things as being the ancestral home of the notorious Francis, Lord Bacon, the shrewdest and most overrated philosopher of Christendom. The natural and political advantages of Bradfield St.Clare, as in the neighbourhood of the best city, socially and clerically, of East Anglia, induced Gereberd to make it the caput baroniae of all his estates wherever else held; and his good judgment is supported by indications down to this day.

English history has largely transacted itself near Bradfield. St.Edmondsbury and its abbey were very celebrated in the reigns of Richard Coeur de Lion, John, and Henry III, under all of whom Gereberd was in state service. In 1182 Abbot Samson got his election, he whom Past and Present has so vividly preserved as a specimen of that olden time; and it is of interest to know that Gereberd held parts of Bradfield as from him. It might not, however, be too much to say that better specimens of heroism than Abbot Samson, disentombed from Jocelin of Brakelond's chronicle, could have been got from the period. Lachrymose and spiteful, his stubbornness for good, as he saw it, was of the puritanic, essentially vulgar, rather than the manly and chivalrous sort. Monk's cowl and frock of the twelfth, or clothes of the nineteenth century, cover very similar pieces of human nature.

St.Edmondsbury Abbey was especially honoured in King Richard's time. To it he offered in religious duty after his return from Palestine, by way of the Austrian prison from which he was ransomed by English gold, the rich standard of Cyprus, taken from its tyrant king, Isaac, whose beautiful daughter had so much of the Lion-Heart's favour.

Sir Francis Palgrave in his Ancient Calendars and Inventories, has given various extracts referring to Gereberd from the sixth year of Richard, 1195, to the accession of John in 1199. The earliest is about the advowson of the church of Bradfield on the home manor, Thomas a Becket's first living. Robert, the son of Simon, makes a claim, and succeeds, about part of the returns of the church, Gereberd not appearing to contend against it. The passage is from the Rotuli Curiae Regis or Rolls of the Justiciar's Court, under "Suffolk" - *"'Rob fil Sim. ... Girebt de Sco Claro ... de Bradefeld ... Walt de Hope ... '". Besides the light it throws on the law business of the time, this extract is of the special use that it notes the indifference of spelling his name Gilbert or Gereberd. Another is: "'Suff ... Gereb d Sen[c]ler ... Rob d Cokef. ... Petr fil Elie. ... R d Cokef ... Ric fil Ric ... '"*. It is difficult to discover who all these are, except Gerebert himself. The family of Cokefield, however, are in frequent relationships with these St.Edmondsbury Sinclairs, the descendants of Richard, son of Walter, earl of St.Cler, and also with his descendants who took the name of their place of Aldham. There is a charter in the Monasticon of a Nesta de Cokefield, the wife of Matthew of Leyham, to the church of St.Mary and St.Anthony, Kerseya, which has witnesses of undoubted kin, as William de Huntingfield, who represented as much land in Suffolk as in Kent, Roger of Aldham, Hugo de Aldham, and William de Aldham. Palgrave's suggestion of a 'c' in Senler is more kind than useful, the original spelling aiding other searches, especially in the midland counties.

Richard, the son of Richard, might have been Gereberd's father. Certainly at this period Gereberd was very young, and not in the full throng of business in which he is engaged afterwards. From a later record he was attorney to this Adam of Hilleg, who here appears to be sheriff. It might be an undue supposition that he was thus fitting himself for the same office, which he held subsequently both in Suffolk and Norfolk. The Jews were extremely busy in those reigns, and Gerebert has many dealings with them. Evidence cannot settle whether he succeeded in his younger period as he did later. Rather does it point to the opposite. In 1196 whether for enterprise or necessity he sold the lands of Marlingford, Norfolk; the same place which is referred to in the Great Roll of the Pipe of 1189-90 as being in possession of Richard de Sancto Claro. There is account of him selling other lands of the same county in 1208.

But there is warning not to run to the conclusion that he was in "the hands of the Jews", as the phrase is now (1887), by the fact that in John's reign he is also a buyer of properties. He bought Berwicks-and-Scotenays, in Essex, from Alberic de Wic; and, with additions, this became one of the remarkable places held by him and his descendants. There is a description of it by Morant in his county history. It is known in charters as Topesfield and Topefeud, and Morant gives the suggestive further information, that Camoys Hall, which was one of several manors included in it, had been a residence and property of Hamo Sinclair, the dapifer. It is in the Hingford hundred, and was held as from the honour of Bolonia or Boulogne, Eustace, the earl, bridging the Channel at an earlier period with his possessions, France and England being curiously united then, and in other also than the Normandy relationship. Alberic was probably one of the Veres, and the connection with the Sinclairs through Eudo Dapifer's family would also aid such a bargain.

Richard's ruinous reign as to money, both by his own crusading madness and that of his most gallant subjects, explains great revolutions in family matters, and his successors John and Henry were not the men to heal the wounds of the body social. Gerebert, however, seems to have prospered, and many things indicate that he well knew how. The value of being a wide underholder, especially to the church, which then had half the income of England from the soil in its possession, is shown by a notice of holding lands, not only from such as Samson, the abbot of St.Edmondsbury, but from the prioresses. With several others of social standing he pays rent to the prioress of Algarsthorp for possessions, no doubt the most profitable of all in this kind, men being then much better arithmeticians than women.

In the Rotuli Litterarum Clausarum in turri Londoniensi anno 2 Henry III, 1217, in a summons by a Say to a Ferrers about the manor of Bercot, "Lincoln" being the heading, the case having about one hundred and fifty witnesses, "'Gilebt de Sco Claro Vic de Norf & Suff,'" appears. This settles his position at the beginning of Henry III's troubled reign, as viscount of Norfolk and Suffolk, or king's substitute for the rule of these counties. In the same year there is one of these secret letters from Henry to the sheriff of Essex to put Alan de Creping in possession of lands which Alan had lost by rebellion against John, in which appears James de Seincler - "'Eod m scribitur Vic Essex p Jam de Seincler'". At this period

Gereberd is old enough to have a son at manhood, James; and, in the year after, he gives lands in Stone and Bishopstone, Buckinghamshire, to a Hugo de Seincler, who is another son.

On the carta of St.Edmondsbury in the Niger Liber Scaccarii of Henry II. Gibert de Sancto Claro holds one miles or knight's fee, as from the abbey. Henry died in 1188, thirty years before, and the return of the charters of the holdings of the church and barons might have been considerably earlier. That Richard Sinclair was dead in 1189-90, and that his heirs paid the taxes on Marlingeford, is proved by this reference to Gilbert as holding from St.Edmondsbury in Henry II's time. Another name in 2 Henry III (1218) is of close lineage to Gerebert: "'Eodem m scribitur Vic Suff p Rob de Seinclow'".

The public affairs of Gerebert have much light thrown on them by Cole's Documents. This is a volume of extracts from the tax accounts of Henry III during the third and fourth years of his reign. Here Gerebert is sheriff of Norfolk. But the next entry with regard to Suffolk (in which the famous Jew, Isaac of Norwich, appears) shows him in another character, as the attorney of Adam of Hillega, who seems to have then been viscount or sheriff of that county. Three years previously Gerebert has been shown as viscount of both Norfolk and Suffolk. "'Gereberd for Adam, the sheriff, claims the taxes from Isaac of Norwich, due by Hugh, the son of Richard, the Jew being his agent and money-lender'". Another entry puts Gereberd himself in exactly the same position as Isaac. "'Here the taxes are taken at Westminster from a Norfolk man, Gereberd being his agent, and it is of value to notice that William of Hengham was the king's agent'". He was one of the descendants of Hubert Sinclair, the governor of Norwich Castle and earl of Norfolk, of the Rye family. They became best known as the barons of Hengham, Stephen's reign putting them out of the very highest rank, which they held in previous reigns.

In Warwickshire Gereberd next has transactions for himself and for the king with a world of Jews, and it is probable that he was then sheriff of the county, that office alone explanatory of this entry. The ghost of the learned Gereberd would have to be invoked for perfect explanation of all this legal money business. Joseph, Manasseh, Leon or Levi, Bendico or Benjamin, Jacob and his brother, lent £41 to the king. Rudder in 1766 said that the Norman silver pound, which meant weight, was equal to £3, 2s., and it could buy what perhaps £10 then could not. Compared with the present value of money, this £41 lent by the Jews would be equal at least to half-a-thousand, and, if limitation of circulation is considered, to far more. It was, therefore, quite worthy of the "lord king" and his sheriff's best attention, the teeth of the Jews having got to their usual length again after Richard and John's dentistry. It is possible, however, that England owes a good deal of its greatness to the freedom of circulation which usury encouraged. If these were gold pounds (and one such was worth £48 in 1711, according to Sir Robert Atkins), the £42 then would be worth several thousands now. The subject is too subtle for satisfaction.

The gist of Gereberd's settlement with Joseph and Co., is that the king pays them back £22 of the loan of £41 which he had for four years, and the rest is to come with interest by instalments during the three remaining years, and further that if Gereberd pay some of it Joseph will give him reckoning for it, and, chiefly, Gereberd wishes that if he have any of the payments to make he may make them to the king, the Jews and Henry to deal with each other. He gets the grant, but the transaction is too distant in the far time to be at all sure of its special meaning.

The general effect of it is easily discernible, namely, that kings and king's viscounts had difficulties then of keeping the wolf quiet as much as private and public men have now, if not more. There are paragraphs and paragraphs of this and other such Jewish and business transactions in shaky Latin, but already more than enough has been written of what is nearly obsolete to much useful general purpose. Here Gereberd denies his liability to pay 62 merks to some Jews of Oxford and elsewhere, on the very good ground that they have forged the bill against him. The cyrograph was a parchment to which the wax seal was attached as to charters, and these Jews seem to have known the theory and practice of palimpscst, and also of detaching qucucs or wax hangers from the original parchment to put them to new ones. Cheque forging is a much more difficult process for sharpers now. To take off the previous writing, as the monks for economy often did, and write anew, was as good for the swindlers as for them.

Tindal's elaborate essay rather than note on The Exchequer of the Jews in England, is as valuable as it is exceedingly interesting on the subject of cyrographs, money business, and indeed of the whole Jewish economy in this country, the civil, religious, and political bonds and privileges included. It is to be found in vol. I, book viii, p. 346, at the end of Henry III's reign, in Rapin's History of England, which Tindal annotated most usefully, and continued from the beginning of the reign of William and Mary in 1689, when the able Frenchman left it.

But a work on the subject could be written, from the information in such records as these about Gereberd Sinclair in Cole's Documents, that would give great pleasure to a limited class of students of history and life.

That Gereberd succeeded through all his transactions is to be inferred from his generosity to others, as well strangers as relations. In the hundred of Piriton, Oxfordshire, he gives a portion of his lands there to a widow, to the termination of her life, free from all rent and from all services whatever; and in 1227 Hugh Sinclair, to whom he gave the properties in Buckinghamshire in 1218, gets large additions from him in the same district, though he did not live much longer to enjoy them. In Palgrave's Ancient Calendars and Inventories, from 6 Richard I to John, this Hugo is one of a court in an Essex settling about the heirship, probably his own, to a Sibilla of that county, before he got his lands in Buckinghamshire. John de Sancto Claro succeeded Hugh as heir in 1237.

In a record of 36 Henry III (1252) is an entry by which it appears that Gereberd and his successor John were both dead at this date, and their properties awaiting possession by the new heir. They must have died within a year of each other; for in the Calendar of Inquisitions after Death of 36 Henry III (1252), number 22 deals with Gerebert as quondam proprietor of Topesfield, of the honour of Bolonia, in Essex; and number 48 of 36 Henry III (1251) John de Sancto "Clauro" for the same place. In 37 Henry III (1253), John is again mentioned as formerly of "Bradfeud maner, Suffolc", which was the Suffolk pronunciation of Bradfield St.Clare.

Chapter XXXVIII
Two Johns

There is further information about John who succeeded Gerebert and died so soon after. In the Patent Rolls of the Tower of London, year 40 Henry III (1256), there is mention of him as "lately dead", in connection with 50 acres of land and one messuagium which he held for the third part of a knight's fee, the arable land being always a small portion of estates then. This also occurs, "'The same held two knights' fees in Bradfield and Wethersfield from the abbot of Saint Edmondsbury, in which Alesia was formerly, the countess Warenne, sister of the king'". Henry III had three sisters, and one brother Richard, the duke of Cornwall and king of the Romans. Rapin and Tindal give no account of the third of these ladies, who was Alesia the countess Warenne here noticed; but Rapin mentions Joanna and Eleanor, the former being queen of Alexander II of Scotland, the latter wife, first of William Marshall, earl of Pembroke, and then of the Simon de Montfort, earl of Leicester, who cost all that trouble of battles of Lewes and Evesham to Henry and his son Edward, the greatest of the Plantagenets.

It would be interesting to know how John Sinclair succeeded this sister Alesia, in holding Bradfield and Wethersfield from the abbey, to the extent of two knights' fees. Gerebred certainly had the former, to one knight fee's extent, from the abbot, besides his own held in capite. The explanation is that Bradfield was of several fees in extent. There was a Monks-Bradfield besides that which had the name St.Clare. Of Wethersfield, however, this is the first mention, and John got it directly after the countess. The honour of Bolonia was then in the crown, and he was one of the underholders; though this could only be an occasion rather than the reason why he should be next after the king's sister. But he may have got these two fees through ties to the count, Warenne. In the Testa de Nevill, the book of the fees in the court of the treasury, he appears under "Norfolk" as holding half-a-fee of Elvedon from the feoda of the count.

John had possession of the Bucks, and Oxford properties for twenty-five years before his father Gerebert's death, and for a short time of less than a year he had possession of most of his lands, except what Robert Sinclair had got of Gereberd's to the north. John was the principal heir to the various lands of Gereberd, and died in 1252; the family branching into two, in the persons of John, his successor, and of Robert. This second John, had Bradfield St.Clare as the head of his barony, and of him considerable account has survived. He "kept court" at Bradfield from 41 Henry III (1257), which means that he held the baronial court which settled local cases. Mr. Gomme says that the baron court was much the same as the hundred court. Between them they did most of the civil and criminal business of the counties, and John had the best of traditions to be equal to his position.

On his father's death a mandate was sent with regard to the Essex lands. De terris capiendis, is the heading of the record. "'The king commanded the abbot of Pershore [Gloucester] that without delay he must take into the hand of the king the manor of Topefield, which was that of John Sinclair, who held in capite from the king of the honour of Boulogne, and that he keep that safely till the king has given further order: With the king witness, at Woodstock, 16th Aug'". It was in 1252. The inquisition after death being held shortly thereafter, this is the result in Essex, where Topefield was the head property: "'John, the son of John Sinclair, is his nearest heir, and is of the age of nineteen'". It was in the following year that by an exactly similar legal process he was declared heir of the Suffolk lands. There are no records for other estates that may have fallen to him, and if twenty-one was majority, then his lands, so far as these two counties were concerned, remained some time longer in the king's hands. What he hold as undertenant is not of course to be discovered in state papers, the superior answering to the treasury for the whole feoda or fief.

His father and his father's predecessor, Gereberd, are known by various incidental notices to have been wide underholders to the earl of Warren, Peter of Kennet, the abbot of Edmondsbury, and others. In the Open Rolls of the Tower there are transactions about the Essex and Suffolk lands in 40 Henry III (1256) and it would appear that John did not get actual possession till that year. This is supported by the fact that he did not begin to keep his manorial court, at his beautiful seat of Bradfield St.Clare, till the year 1257. In 1250, Henry III had taken the cross, to go against the Saracens as soon as he could get ready. In 1252, Rapin says, the voyage to the Holy Land was still being contemplated, and "'as money was the most necessary preparation, he took occasion from this voyage to extort great sums from the Jews, nor were his

Christian subjects less spared'". Henry's needs in this way being chronic, it is likely John Sinclair had to wait in nonage for the regal profit longer than was necessary. Kings had learned to apply to the nobles the system, so fruitful with the clergy, of deferring occupancy.

That John had some bitter grievance to put right, is implied by his taking sides, as one of the barons, with Simon Montfort, the earl of Leicester, against the king. His patriotism, however, may be sufficient explanation of this. The appointment of the twenty-four barons, and afterwards the founding of England's greatest institution, the house of commons, in 1264, had his active co-operation. It was the year after he began to hold his manorial court at Bradfield St.Clare that, in 1258, when he was twenty-five, the provisions of Oxford were drawn up, and twelve commissioners chosen by the king and twelve by the barons, to regulate the disorder of the troubled reign. He was at Oxford on that day with a goodly following, as most of the military feudal tenants of the kingdom were, to compel progress. Simon de Montfort, earl of Leicester, was made president of the council. They had the appointment of the sheriffs through all the kingdom, with general powers almost unlimited.

But Henry and his son Prince Edward (afterwards Edward I) could not endure the thraldom, as they thought it; and, in 1263, the civil war began. Prince Edward's violence in coming with his army from Wales suddenly, and forcibly taking possession of £10,000 from the treasury of the Templars, London, began the system of reprisals in similar way through the kingdom; and perhaps Stephen's reign was not worse socially than Henry's at this period. The Londoners naturally took the side of the barons after the prince's doings; and they even threw dust at the queen as she tried to pass up the river from the tower palace, as well as words of insult, to express their feelings. It was Edward's special hatred to the Londoners for this, that lost Henry the battle of Lewes in 1264; he pursued them too far, and the royalists were meanwhile defeated by the earl of Leicester. Percy, Bohun, Basset, Baliol, Bruce, and Comyn were made prisoners by the barons. John Sinclair was on the victorious side that 14th day of May in Sussex. The first house of commons parliament was summoned some months after, the greatest step in English civil freedom. But the escape of Prince Edward from surveillance renewed the war, and the battle of Evesham on the 4th August 1265, in which Simon Montfort, the earl of Leicester, was killed, put the political game entirely into the royal hands. The estates of the confederated barons were confiscated, and London lost her gates, magistrates, and 20,000 merks, as punishment of her love of liberty.

Simon, the earl's eldest son, left Kenilworth Castle, his home, in despair of pardon, and fortified himself in the isle of Axholme,

Lincolnshire, where many of the confederates joined him. Prince Edward compelled them to surrender, in December, their lives and limbs to be spared, and their estates to be given back or not as himself and his uncle, the king of the Romans, might decide. Montfort got a pension of 500 merks, but he soon after turned pirate in the English Channel, the Cinque Ports conniving at his doings. Meantime the malcontents had possession of Kenilworth Castle, and besides a new batch of barons in Axholme Isle, there were risings in the north and in Hampshire. But the chief centre of the barons was where Hereward made his last stand, in the isle of Ely among the fens.

While blockading Kenilworth, Henry called a parliament, and articles of terms were drawn up and offered for the acceptance of the rebels. Their pardon was to be general, but before having possession of their estates some were to pay five years' value, others three, others one. John Sinclair was among these barons of Ely, with several of his lineage. The terms were rejected, and soon after they, and he as one of them, made an expedition to Norwich, returning to the isle with £20,000 sterling and all the necessaries they could take with them. Tindal says they did as much for Cambridge, "'in their return to Ely, carrying away not only several Jews, but also the richest of the townsmen, whom they kept prisoners till they would ransom themselves at exorbitant rates'". The Annals of Waverley Abbey, Wikes, and Rishanger support him in this. After more than a six months' siege Kenilworth was lost, and about the 25th of July the founders of the house of commons surrendered their last refuge, the semel et iterum famous isle of Ely. Says Rapin, "'The only conditions granted them was the saving their life and limbs'".

By the suffering of its benefactors humanity seems alone to be well served. There are signs, however, that these patriotic rebels did not submit tamely to be kept out of their properties, and some of them undoubtedly contrived to secure portions if not all from the greedy hands of weak Henry. John Sinclair of Bradfield St.Clare was of this number. In the state rolls of 51 Henry III (1257) there is a graphic account of his particular sins. A commission, or king's sham parliament, was sitting at Ipswich, in Suffolk; and a presentation was made there by Richard de Bosco, or "Richard of the wood", against John Sinclair and various others. They may have been claiming their own estates, and this accusation could be used as potent argument against recovery; or, the king and the prince, now at their leisure, may have been revenging their troubles of five chequered years of alternate imprisonments and successes. Those named might be greater adventurers than the others, being, as local men, best acquainted with the resources of the district around Ely; and so had to suffer more than the loss of their estates. The whole roll, however, in which these troubles are being settled, does not show special vindictiveness. A William Sinclair of the Thames district lost and recovered again his estates there, though with difficulty, because of espousing the side of the barons. But of him again. There is record that John was fortunate.

The presentation before the court by Richard de Bosco was, that John de Sencler, Robert de Mundeville, milites, Edmund de Seincler, Peter de Sender, parson of Wethersfield, summetar John de Sencler, and others, sent by Robert Euel or Howel (the head of the malcontents in the isle of Ely), had come with horses and arms to his house in Walberwickam, and had taken all they could lay their hands on. There is a particular account of the cups, dresses, gold-rings, weapons of war, and other valuables which they found, and the value of each article is given in the presentation, throwing quaintest light on the social as well as political condition of that troubled time. But John de Sencler and his equestrian armed company did not stop at this point, in their enthusiasm for popular liberty as against royal prerogative. This royalistic Richard de Bosco must have incurred the special hatred of the earl of Leicester and his barons. Probably, however, his personal stubbornness or disinclination to be quietly fleeced, is suflicient explanation of the treatment he got. No doubt the love of ransom money, which was one of the belles passions of these and much later times, Agincourt included, aided the general necessity of frightening Richard de Bosco thoroughly. He says they took and stripped him, carried him into the wood of Bukenhelle, possibly his own wood, so hoisting him as it were with his own petard, and there kept him bound a day and a night. The length of detention was evidently his own doing, the time being required for him to make up his mind as to what he would do. Only after the aid of striking him on the neck with a kind of sword (and he was lucky that it was only a kind of such speedy weapon) and sundry additional whippings, did he make a finem or settlement by paying a ransom of 65 marks. This sum would be value for perhaps £500 now, and though such doings were the fashion, Richard de Bosco had some reason to grumble. Whether these Sinclairs, of grave social and official standing, and more than the half of England and whole of London, which they thus represented in the struggle for rights, are to be blamed or praised, may be left to ingenuity. Might and right coalesce as laws weaken and tyrannies strengthen.

It is of importance to note that the surname is spelt in this roll exactly as Richard, the son of Walter, earl of St.Cler, has his spelt in The Domesday Book, with the exception of Edmund de "Seincler". To other things, this is corroborative of their descent from him. Edmund is a side branch of the same family, who, for distinction, made the difference of spelling; and to them the attention is next to be directed. Then only thirty-four years of age, none of his name-fellows were John's sons, though the parson of Wethersfield church, which being on one of his estates was an advowson of his, was his brother, who went into the clerisy, and ought perhaps to have kept his natural war instincts within the pale of that body. John, "the summetar", was of an older generation, or a cousin; but these are not alternatives of surety or importance. As to John Sinclair, the lord of Bradfield St.Clare manor, he did not make the phrase permanently applicable to himself by his patriotism which the followers of Simon de Montfort, earl of Leicester, were known by after the royal victories, "the disinherited". He recovered his position though he did give rough handling to Richard de Bois, once bailiff of Norwich, and who had a name of considerable standing, in his own person and in those of landholding descendants. Morant says John occurs in 52 Henry III (1268) next year after this presentation, as a lord, the width of his possessions compelling him to the full duties of a baron of the kingdom.

The Rotuli Hundredorum was drawn up by a commission subscribed under the great seal, 11 Oct of the 2nd year of Edward I (1273), and was the result of forty-seven articles of inquiry as to the state of the demesne lands of the crown, the manors in the crown's hands or their alienations, the tenants in capite and their skill of evading tax by subinfeudation and other schemes, alienations to the church under pretences of frankalmoigne or free gift, wardships, marriages, escheats, fee-farm, services, tolls, murage, customs, unlawful exportation of wool, and other of the curious social institutions of the thirteenth century. There were ten local men appointed for the St.Edmundsbury district to find the true state of matters there, and John de Sco Claro appears as one of the four of best rank, milites, among the ten. They made inquisition concerning the liberties of St.Edmundsbury on oath. This shows that he had not suffered much, if at all, by the previous period of rebellion. It is acknowledged that Edward appreciated the motives of the barons by himself summoning parliaments and paying them the highest respect. If there were nothing further than this of explanation of John's continued prosperity it might be enough.

In Laing's Scottish Seals there is notice of a Sir William at the date of 1292, and the fact that his seal was in the chapter house, Westminster, might suggest that he was one of these Englishmen. His shield is a cross engrailed in a centre of rounded tracery, and in each of three compartments a boar's head couped. The inscription is "S Willelmi De Sco Claro militis" - "Sir William Sinclair". Edward III's connection with Scotland at the period may be explanation of a Scottish knight's seal getting placed among state relics, though it is open to discuss the locality implied by the boars' heads. But this William only in passing. It may be added, however, that he may have been the "Sir William de Santcler" in Robert Crawfurd's History of the Royal Stuarts, who was one of the representatives of King Edward Baliol's claims in 1294 before Edward I at Norham against the earlier Robert Bruce.

A John de St.Cleer pays his feudal respect to the abbot of St.Edmundsbury as late as 30 Edward I (1302) for some possessions connected with the manor of Bradfield St.Clare; and it is as probable that it was the hero of the island of Ely who was thus living so long and happily ever after, as that it was a successor of the same name. It is true that the homage to the abbot suggests a new reign at the manor or the abbey. Either way serves the genealogical narration, for history there is not, of these years, as far as is discovered. Most men of the period had substantial dealings with the church in preparation for the close of life, and John Sinclair of Bradfield, baron, was no exception to the rule. He was too old to join Edward I in the wars against Wallace and Edward's own relation and English vassal Bruce, who headed the Scottish or, better word, Norman independence which was secured in 1314 by the battle of Bannockburn.

Chapter XXXIX
Vicecomes and Escheator

Guido or Guy de St.Cleer was the son or grandson of the baron of Bradfield of the raiding adventures. His mother was a Neville of the famous earl of Warwick "king-maker" family, and to the maternal side he owed his first name. The earliest notice of him is in 1335 as, with his wife Marjory, holding Wyrun Hall, Norfolk, which would be connected with her marriage dowry, this being a new name in the properties of the lords of Bradfield. In 22 Edward III (1349) he was made king's viscount or sheriff of the united counties of Cambridge and Huntingdon, in both of which he had properties. At this time sheriffs had their appointments only for a year, with rare exceptions, as can be seen by the extant and easily accessible lists; but Guy's ability or influence, or both, gained him this coveted position again and again. He held it in the 23rd year also, and had it renewed in the 24th and 25th of Edward III's reign. It was the period of the glorious but expensive battles of Cressy and Poictiers in France when Guido had so much management of the king's affairs in the counties where his lands lay, and it is safe inference to draw that he was personally popular with both his lord and the people, when the official connection was so often kept up. His wealth also would have its good effect in such times of pressure. At the interval of a year he had the consulship of the two counties for the fifth time, 1354. The year after he was out of this particular harness, but in 29 Edward III (1356) he was made escheator for the king in the counties of Norfolk and Suffolk.

Escheats were one of the principal sources of the king's revenue, and they included not only the lands properly so called, but also those which after the Conquest became vested in the crown by devolution, seizure, forfeiture, or other contingency. The records are full of references to such honours, baronies, or fiefs as that of Bolonia, "quae est in manu regis" - which is in the hand of the king; and this family itself, is remarkable as holding from such escheats some of its fees. Those baronies were often farmed to the favoured nobles at a yearly payment. But besides the great fiefs, the lands of the lesser barons and gentry, as well as the produce of hereditary offices and serjeanties, fell frequently to the crown. Usually the escheats merged into the royal demesnes, claims getting gradually quite dead. In Henry II's reign was instituted a public office of escheatry, managed by custodes or keepers. These afterwards got the name of escheators, and one of these Guido was. Small escheats the sheriffs took care of, the justices itinerant putting them in their charge. But perhaps the most lucrative part of the escheator's duties was taking possession for the king of the temporalities or estates of the church on occurrence of vacancy from office by death or otherwise. Of these the bishops could not get possession, and cannot yet, without writs. Rufus and Anselm, king and archbishop, figured in the game of profit and loss early, and the crown never lost this useful and necessary hold on the rich demesnes of the church, at one period worth more than the half of England.

Next year, 1357, Guy was sheriff of the united counties of Norfolk and Suffolk. Among the charters still preserved in the British Museum, there is an order by him as vicecomes of Norfolk of that year. It is a parchment carta of ten lines' length, in Latin, seven inches or so by four, and in good preservation, except that the queue and seal are gone. With four other similarly ancient Sinclair charters, its interest is of considerable public and very particular genealogical importance. The five are in absolutely safe keeping henceforward. One is from John de Seintcler of Penshurst, the poet Sydney's place afterwards; and, written in old French, his seal with the shield of blazing sun is attached to it. But this will probably recur, and Guido's course requires further following. Of Norfolk and Suffolk, as previously of Cambridge and Huntingdon, he was exceptionally made viscount again and again. In 1358 he had reappointment. The last of his sheriffships traced is that of 1359.

But he was often escheator at other periods. In the Rotulorum Originalium in Curia Scaccarii Abbreviatio temporibus Henry III, Edward I, and II there are to be found no fewer than seven king's mandates to him in this office. One of them under the heading Canc or Kent is addressed to Guido de Seintcler, escheator of the king in the county of Cambridge; another under Cant or Cambridge is addressed to him as escheator of the county; the third is to Guido de Seyntcler, escheator of the king in the county of Suffolk, under the heading Suff; in a fourth belonging to Suffolk he is "esc.r.", in the county of Huntingdon; under Huntingdon he appears as its king's escheator; Canc or Kent has him as escheator in the counties of Cambridge and Huntingdon; and lastly there is a mandate to him under Cantab as escheator of the king in the county of Cambridge.

The names and business which are in these mandates are of special value. In Suffolk he was to put Robert Corbet, chevalier, son and heir of Sir John Corbet, in possession of the manor of Asyngton, held by Sir John in capite as from the honour of Hatfield-Peverell, then in the king's hands. On doing certain service in the court of the honour or barony, and paying a reasonable relief, Sir Robert was to get full possession. It would be valuable to know if Guido was aware of the unity of lineage of these Corbets or Corbeils with himself.

In Cambridge he was to take possession for the king of Barnton and Iskelyngton, and also of the "house of St.Michael" in the town, of which house the master was dead. The manor of Bramton with its pertinents had to be seized in Suffolk. In Huntingdon, Richard, the brother of John, the son of John Farndon of Newbury, after a reasonable tax, was to get a house and 86 acres of land, with 15 of meadow, and various returns. In Kent, Guy was to give Thomas de Wanton his mother's lands, and also those of another lady relation. Walter Hamelyn, then dead, who had been himself escheator of the king in the county of Cambridge, had a son John, to whom Guido Sinclair, the ruling escheator, must give lands, houses, mill, meadow at Badburgham, as the heir to his father, who was holder from the crown by services.

One of these mandates may serve as specimen for the others: "'Kent: It was commanded to Guido Sinclair, escheator of the king, that having accepted security from Thomas Oky, who married Matilda who was the sister of Andrew Stenene, dead, concerning his reasonable tax, he make full possession as heirs to the same Thomas and Matilda of one homestead, sixty acres of arable land, two of meadow, and twelve pence of returns from the assize with the pertinents, which was held from the king in capite by the service of the sixth part of one knight's fee'".

In Blomfield's History of Norfolk there are useful notes of Guy, especially in connection with Grimston, which he possessed, a manor that afterwards was called Morley's, because of its coming into the possession of the lords Morley. It was part of the old barony of Hengham, which the Hubert Sinclair family held from the reign of William I. Kimberley of the present peer, of Wodehouse lineage, is another of its parts, once held by the Gournays of the Vexin. Grimston or Morley's manor, near Hengham, the caput baroniae, is a few miles south of Kimberley Castle. Says Blomfield: "'The family of the St Cleers or de Sancto Claro were also ancient lords of this manor'". He thinks that "'good part of this manor was alienated by some of the family, who had a noble seat and park at Bradfield abovementioned'". Whether Guy was the seller cannot be fixed. It is more probable that it was John, or perhaps

Gereberd, as in his younger days he seemed dealing with the Jews overmuch. At the time in which Guido lived it was not possible to recover matters by raiding in the Jewish quarters, the kings themselves being precluded from the extraction of Israelitish teeth in default of the required liberality. It is certain that he had great opportunities of enriching himself, whether he took sufficient advantage or not of his position and influence.

His son Pain, or Paganus, de St.Clair, must have died without male issue. In 49 Edward III (1376) he preleases to Edward de St.John and Joan his wife and her heirs all his right in the manor of Grimston. She may have been his sister or daughter, as she was certainly his heiress. The St.Johns are said to have been a Kent family descended from the rich Hugh de Port of Domesday Book. The lands of this branch of Sinclairs could therefore fall into hands far less worthy; but it is melancholy, nevertheless, to see the end of so much vigour as exhibited itself in these northern and eastern home counties. Of Pain Sinclair little is known, and he must be left with the remark that his mother was of the Beauchamp family, from whom he got a first name unusual to his paternal lineage. A Joan was the heiress of the Bradfields.

The chief estates, indeed, ultimately reverted to Sir Philip St.Cleere, known most as Sir Philip of Bristow, in Surrey. Blomfield says he was lord of Bradfield and Wethersfield in the reign of Henry IV; but in the inquisition after death 9 Henry IV (1408) he is returned as having Wethersfield manor in the county of Suffolk, without mention of Bradfield. Wethersfield must have grown into the head manor by which the others, if any, took their designation. He also is one of the descendants of Richard Sinclair, the king's chamberlain and son of Walter, earl of St.Clair and of Medway; but his relationship to Pain was very distant, and it is difficult to believe that he inherited as heir-general, though this would seem to be the fact. Sir Philip's history, however, will occur again in following his own powerful branch of the lineage; and it is enough here to know that the Suffolk lands were not yet lost to the name, Sir Philip having descendants to possess these and many other estates. The following refers to one of them: Henry V, from whom Sir John Sinclair had Wethersfield by direct holding, gets the custody of the manor after his death.

Chapter XL
Cousins

"Cousins" must be used in its general sense. It is impossible to reckon exact degrees, though there is ample security of nearness between various others mentioned and the Bradfields. Contemporary with Gilbert or Gereberd, Robert Sinclair appears as signing a mandate for the viscount of Lincoln from the king, 2 Henry III (1217). Gereberd was viscount of Norfolk and Suffolk at that very time. Fulc Baynard, one of the Baynards of Baynard's Castle, beside the Thames, London, was to be possessed of land in Lincolnshire, and in the Rotuli of secret letters in the tower of London this is, "'In the same manner it is written to the viscount of Suffolk for Robert Sinclair'". It would be only a guess to say that Robert was own brother to the viscount Gereberd, and it is enough perhaps that they were thus friends in all senses. As the pious gravestone puts it, "In their death they were not divided".

One of the open rolls of the tower, 36 Henry III (1251), the year of Gereberd's death also, gives account of Robert and his son Robert. "'Concerning homage taken: The king took homage of Robert Sinclair, the son and heir of the late Robert Sinclair, for all the lands and tenements which the aforesaid Robert, his father, held from the king in capite in the day on which he died, and he restores to him those lands and tenements. And it was ordered to Master William Clifford, escheator for this side of the Trent, that having accepted security from the aforesaid Robert about his reasonable tax to be rendered to the king at the treasury of the king, he make him heir, without delay, with full possession, to the same Robert with regard to all his lands and aforesaid tenements, and in respect to which the aforesaid Robert, his father, was possessed in his own demesne as of a fief in the day on which he died, and what by reason of the death of that Robert was taken into the king's hand: with the king witness, at Saint Edmundsbury, 14th Feb, 1252'". The two records taken together, show that these Roberts held much of their lands in Lincolnshire, the "escheator for this side of the Trent" being the rather general title of the officer north of the home counties;

and the king's business being done at St.Edmundsbury, gives the inference, otherwise substantiated, that they held in Suffolk also.

That Robert junior had Edmund for successor, and that he was the Edmund de Seincler who was one of John Sinclair the baron's followers when from the isle of Ely they raided against those who hated parliaments, is rendered likely by a charter among the "additional charters" in the British Museum. The carrying away of Robert de Bois for ransom was in 1266, and in 1294 Edm. de Sco Claro and others are witnesses to a gift of lands to a gentleman and his wife in Codeham of Croffield, in the county of Suffolk, by Hamo Wygge of Croffield, whose green seal is still attached. William Leneday of Codeham also gives a charter of lands similarly, to which an Edmund de Sco Claro is witness with others, in 13 Edward III (1339). To one by Robert Sacc of Codingham he also at the same time subscribed. John Loneday of Croffield gives lands in Croffield to three several holders; and to this charter, with a broken seal of black wax yet preserved, Edm. Seynclowe and others are witnesses, 25 Edward III, 1351. Edmund was seemingly the continuous name for the heads of this family. John de Hochara, parson of the church of Eston Gosebek, granted a charter of lands to Gilbert Debenham and others to which Edm. Synclowe is one of the witnesses, 34 Edward III (1360). But not much more can be got out of such details than substantial proof of the existence of these cousins to the Bradfield Sinclairs.

Those in Buckinghamshire are somewhat better known. Stone or Stanes in the hundred of Stanes in this county was their seat. It has been noticed that Gereberd gave it to a Hugo who had also Essex properties. Hugo dying in 1227 the seat reverted to Gereberd's heir presumptive, John, who died in 1252. A younger son again got it at a later period. He appears as Robert de Seyncler of Stone at an inquiry in which he took part about the rights of the dean and chapter of Be. Marie, Lincoln, to certain houses and tenements in the town of Aylesbury, Bucks. In the Hundred Roll of 2 Edward I (1274) William de Sco Claro, a proprietor of large substance, appears as of Stanes, Bucks., having tenentes and hominies and the other grades of clients common to a feudal lord. He held Suthcote by serjeanty, which most honourable tenure implied personal service at court to his king. He had lands also for which he paid certain sums directly to the king's treasury, the usual method of doing when one possessed part of a barony escheated to the crown and farmed.

At this same time there were Stephen Sinclair in the hundred of Balberg, Suffolk; Gerard Sinclair of the hundred of Piriton, in Oxfordshire; and a Geffrey in Upthorp, Huntingdon. Thirty years later a John held Calendon in Bedfordshire.

In Leicestershire, 41 Edward III (1368), John "Seincoler", as the record spells it, had Lobenham, and his son John in 46 Edward III (1373) is put in possession of this same manor. Another John still, with his wife Alicia, held it in 3 Richard II (1379) Adam St.Clere, who was born out of wedlock, had, 11 Henry IV (1410), Warton, Stippershall, and divers messuages and lands as from the castle of Tamworth. These properties were in Warwickshire, but there is no certainty that he was of the Bradfield Sinclairs, because at this period the more southern members had got possessions by purchase or heirship in the central counties.

A Peter held Chaddesden, 11 Edward III (1337), and in 36 Edward III (1362) a Margaret Sinclair died possessed of Boyleston manor as of the honour of Tuttebury Castle in Derbyshire; but they are more probably of the Ralph of Rye family, whose chief possessions lay there.

Maria, the wife of Sir Roger Bellers, formerly the bride of John Sinclair, possessed, by the Inquisitions after Death, 10 Richard II (1387) Fromlond hundred, Grymston, Estwell, Goutby, some dues from the Leicester burghers, Scalford, and Thirsington, all in Leicestershire, and also Cryche in Derbyshire. Part of this she got with her first husband. Cryche, in particular, was always a Sinclair possession from the time of Ralph Fitz-Hubert, the brother of Eudo Dapifer, the Frescheville Sinclairs succeeding the Fitz-Ralph ones. The unity of the whole Rye lineage with Sinclairs is proved by this Maria, the widow of John Sinclair, holding Cryche, Derbyshire, in 1387. Grymston seems a reminiscence of the Norfolk manor, Grimston, where the baron, John Sinclair, of the Simon de Montfort, earl of Leicester, parliamentary party, is noted as having kept his first court in the 41st of Henry III (1257). Who the latest John is, has not been discovered, though it is likely he was of the more southern families also.

In 19 Richard II (1395) Rowland Sentclire had land from the fief of William de la Zouch, miles, of Haryngworth, in Northamptonshire.

Industry might add many more such names, rescued from periods often dark exceedingly, but it may be enough to notice one other remarkable family whose story is of similar broken, but fuller, kind. In the Roll of the Hundreds, 2 Edward I (1274) Philip de Sco Claro appears frequently as a prominent proprietor in Cambridgeshire. In the eighth year of this king, he is one of a jury sworn upon the articles of commission of the king's justiciary, Lord William Muschet, miles, and his colleagues at Cambridge. William de la Haye, miles, Warenne of Barenton, Ralph le Heyr, and four others are Philip's fellows. This Haye was of his own male lineage, as Duncan shows.

Roger of Thornton and Philip de Sco Claro appear again and again together in near relationship. Robert of the Island holds land of them in Westwyk and Hogytone, which they had from their wives, who were sisters. The ladies held as from the castle of Richmond, and certain dues had to be paid into the court of the earl of Brittany as the superior. Malketone, Cambridgeshire, was the place in which these properties were situate. There is account also of the villeins of Philip connected with some of his manors. Haslingfield manor had freeholders under him, and Cotes had his villenagii. In Cotes, Lord William Vesci held the third part of one military fee from Philip and Roger, as of the barony of Ledeth. In Wynepol also Philip Sinclair had various tenants.

There is a Robert de Sco Claro in this roll record who was of the family. He appears in the hundred of Bosemere, Suffolk, as doing certain things at the town of Cretyng which require challenge from the commission. The following up of the inquiry called the Hundred Roll was a long process, and the records are called Quo Warranto, because many had to prove their rights, or tell by what warrant they held lands, or did certain things the commissioners were not satisfied with. It was not till 27 Edward I (1298), that the king had business in this connection with the Cambridge Sinclairs. Nicolas de Sco Claro had succeeded Philip, and the affinity relationship to the Thorntons seems closer than before. Roger had been followed by Barthus Thornton, and he too had gone over to the majority, his daughter Alianor still under age being his heiress. She was in the wardship of Nicolas Sinclair. Her estates claimed exemptions and rights which the king challenged, and she was summoned to show warrant before the justiciaries. She came to the court, by her attorney, and also Nicolas. Nicolas seemed to be reaping benefits from the state of things, and was in no hurry to settle matters. Alianor through her attorney pleaded that she was under age. Nicolas followed up by maintaining that he could not answer without her, and for that time decision was deferred. Like the Thorntons, this family also must have ended in an heiress, and their lands may have gone to the building up of some newer English name. But they are further traceable in the Bodleian library, Oxford, where among the Rawlinson MSS. are notices of their genealogy. They are called in them the "family of Malton".

Chapter XLI
The Adams Sinclairs

Near Kemsing on the railway line from London to Maidstone, the county town of Kent, the ancient seat of the Aldham family still preserves the name of St.Clere, and with the addition of Upper and Lower Sinclair, as the Kentishmen now distinguish. Yaldham is also a synonym. A more beautiful situation for a home is not in England. A large modern mansion is there now (1887), which by its condition, and some of its surroundings, raises thoughts of better days. The magnificent beeches, whose height seems endless, can hardly be reminiscence of the ancient owners; but they are certainly reminders of the splendid traditions of the place. High on a gently sloping hill, it has a view over an English Eden of several miles, the most fertile, soft, and luxurious basin that can be imagined. Where Adam, the commissioner of The Domesday Book, had his home, is a short distance to the east; and every way the gaze turns memories are roused of Sinclair lineage. Igtham, Seal, Knockholt, the archiepiscopal palace of Otford, a favourite home of Henry VIII, are in sight.

Of events the most classical in the kingdom's history, this has been the scene. Near where the mansion was built, the caput baroniae of estates in many counties, there still exists some very ancient remnants of building. Low square doors, pent roofs, walls built alternately with lime and heavy oaken beams, make the thought come that these portions must have known the presence of some of the family. The soil and sky are, at all events, as pure and sweet as when they looked with the varied emotions of their periods, and of their particular natures, over these fields, so full of growth and beauty. "Tis the place and all around it". In the neighbourhood of London there was no more favourite spot for royal and noble leisure than that mid district of the historical county. Instead of the peaceful English mansion which now rests on the hill slope, the Aldham-St.Cleres had the strong feudal castle usual to the chiefs of wide lands, and the clang of arms was the hourly familiar sound for centuries above the rich vale beneath.

It has been already shown that Aldham was the local name taken from this home, and that the lineage was Sinclair. The way the double name of

Aldham-St.Clere came was that a St.Clere of the same family married the ultimate heiress of those who had taken the name of Aldham, and thus their local surname got preserved. The Aldhams were Richard the son of Earl Walderne's male descendants, and the John St.Clair who married Joan de Aldenham, Aldham, or Audham, about 1300, was of the stock of the same Richard, and the proprietor then of the neighbouring Igtham. He did not, however, possess the caput baroniae of Aldham-St.Clere. Through the right of the mother, this Joan, it was his son John St.Clere of Igtham who heired Francis de Aldham, his cousin, and founded the new family of the old strain. One of the rolls of the treasury has been referred to, showing that he was not only his cousin by affinity but that they were consanguineous besides, this being the word used to show unity of blood male, John was aged twenty six when he came into possession of the properties of the Aldhams.

In 1312 the earl of Warwick, the leader of the barons, had beheaded Piers Gaveston, the favourite of Edward II; two years after, the English army was destroyed near Stirling; and from 1315 a dreadful famine of three years had paralysed the country. The king was in continual trouble with his barons, of whom the earl of Lancaster was then head. The barons, jealous of Edward taking up with favourites, had got the office of king's chamberlain for Hugh Despenser or Spencer, the young son of one of themselves, of whom they thought they were sure. But he and his father, Hugh the elder, became worse scourges of their own friends than Piers Gaveston himself; and in 1320 a new baronial war violently ended this rule of unexpected favourites by clearing the kingdom of them both. The tide, however, completely turned in favour of the king next year, and recalling the Spencers, he overpowered the barons and, says Rapin:"'never, since the Norman Conquest, had the scaffolds been drenched with so much blood as upon this occasion'". The nobility blamed the Spencers inexorably for the severity. The earl of Lancaster was beheaded, John Giffard was put to death at Gloucester, and among many others, Francis de Aldenham, whom Tindal puts among the lords, also lost his life thus, at Windsor, the last of the earlier Aldham Sinclairs. The Hugh favourites had their surname from an office at court of the nature of public almoner; and the elder being a Norman himself, and by marriage to Eleanor Clare, a sister of the last earl of Gloucester of the Clare line, who was killed at Bannockburn, securing the earldom, the disappointment of the barons with him and his son Hugh was of the keenest. Francis de Audham, the neighbour of Tunbridge Castle, and the relation by many affinities of its lords, had hard lines measured to him. Many knights were hung in chains, but Francis had the higher privilege of getting beheaded in the court of Windsor Palace. He may have been in royal office, and had to suffer, for example and terror, on the spot. He was a young man, and died without issue, John de St.Clair of Igtham succeeding him as above.

Before following John's course, and that of his descendants, the ancestors of this Francis Sinclair of Audenham have to be considered. Their connection with Northamptonshire, helps towards the purpose more than that with their own peculiar county of Kent. His father was Baldwin of Aldham, in Kent, and of Wodepreston, in Northampton. His sister was John Sinclair's mother. The father of Baldwin and Joan was Thomas de Audham of Kent, and not of Northampton till by his marriage with the widow of his kinsman, Robert de la Haye of Sussex, Isabel Montacute or Montagu, he got, uxoris jure, Wodepreston, and some properties in the west. She was daughter of Sir William Montacute, or, as Nicholas says, of the 4th Baron Montacute, who died 1249, both being of the great western family who were earls of Salisbury, princes of Man, and played first parts in political events generally. Thomas de Audham died in 1276, his son Baldwin being then only fifteen. Margery Montague, Isabel's sister, was married to William, one of the lords of Echinham, "the knightly family" of Sussex; and it is worthy of note that in the ancient church of Echinham, the Sinclair arms of the later Aldham family is quartered with theirs, than which there could not be any better proof of, at least affinity.

Sir Thomas Aldham, knight, followed Richard I to Palestine, and was at the siege of Acre in 1191. The Robert of Aldham previous to Sir Thomas, is in one of the charters of Rochester; and the family go back, through the lords of Ros, in Kent, to Richard, the king's chamberlain, son of Walter, earl of St.Cler and of Medway. But there is a gap between the two Thomases, which Peter de Aldham fills up perhaps, who appears as a witness at Winchester, then a great scene of national business, in a charter of land to their favourite St.Andrews of Rochester, dated 1245.

The connection of the Aldhams with Geffrey of Ros is shown thus from the Textus Roffensis. Geffrey of Ros, and afterwards Robert Aldham, gave the tenth part of Aldham, namely, Stownfield, containing 22 acres, Brodefield containing 42 acres, Piryefield containing 20 acres, Donnfield containing 40 acres, and Freythe containing 18 acres: total 180 acres. This has various interest. These acres show what was actually in cultivation around Aldham, and compared with the usual patches laboured then gives the impression of wealth and energy. "Peerie" is the Norse word for "little", and has philological value.

Robert of Burnaville held Ros, and is one of the Aldham line, though it is impossible to find an exact date for him.

William of Ros held it in 1163; for Carte in his History of England says that Thomas a Becket claimed two of his manors as belonging to the see of Canterbury, at the very beginning of the great quarrel. William held six and a half knight's fees as of the king, in capite; but Becket claimed the manors of Hethe and Saltwoode as his.

Hugo de St.Clair and his kin were very closely interested.

William of Eynesford, who is often referred to by ordinary historians as chief occasion of the dispute, was one of them, as well as William of Ros. Ralph of this family was in 1199 prior of Rochester, and showed the usual love of, and capacity for, architectural work, being a prominent builder of the churches of his time. Hamon de Hethe, bishop of Rochester, would also seem to be of the same house.

The Aldhams appear very often in Northampton, and less frequently in Somerset. The Monasticon has three of them, Roger, Hugo, and William, signing a charter by Nesta of Cokefield, Northampton, to the church of St.Mary and St.Anthony, Kerseya; and, in 30 Edward I (1301), Osbert Aldham is a juror in a great cause at St.Edmundsbury, Suffolk, as to the seneschalship of the abbey. Cokefield has suggestive relations to Gerebered Sinclair and his family, which might reward search; but that Robert of Cokefield in 1222 gave his right over it to John de Montacute, grandfather of the lady who married Thomas Audham, accounts for the Aldham prevalence there. That they held part of the property of the Montacutes in Somersetshire, the manor of Chiselberg in particular, explains their appearances in histories and records of that county, the original home of the Montagus, their name being local to that district, the "sharp hill", from the situation of their home castle. The connection with this county will appear through the history of their heirs, the Sinclairs of Aldham, who added to their Somerset properties, having relations there continuously from the Norman Conquest. They kept the Sancto Claro name religiously untouched by the prevalent pride of locality appellation.

Much can still be collected of the earlier Aldham Sinclairs; but as it would be of the same substantial rather than remarkable character, enough is stated. That they were of the baronial order expresses a great deal in those periods, when all that was being done which was notable, was the work of the barons, to whom kings were but the foils. Franciscus Aldeham, the last of the branch, he who was executed as one of the rebel barons, is mentioned in one of the Harleian MSS. as the antecessor of John and Philip St.Clere, and as holding fifteen military fees from the honour of Morteine alone, which is ample evidence of his baronial position. Mortayne or Morteine was escheat and practically demesne of the crown since its early forfeiture by William the Conqueror's nephew, and to hold from it was equal to in capite tenure. He held much besides of other baronies, Aquila for one, Aldham being probably of ancient in capite possession, and not as of any barony, itself the caput baroniae of the family. The Aldham coat of arms was, Azure, a pile, or.

Chapter XLII
Three Johns in Succession

The first was John de St.Clere of Igtham, Kent. Igtham, or, as it has been explained, the "eight villages", is not far from Sevenoaks, and is in the immediate neighbourhood of St.Clere, which had the name of Aldham in his time. The properties of Igtham and Aldham bordered each other, and the evidence goes to show that the Igthams were a younger branch of the Aldhams, and both families the descendants of Richard, the king's chamberlain, son of Walter, earl of St.Cler, and in Kent known as Walter of Medway.

Nothing grows more certain, as the facts are further discovered, than that the Sinclairs got numerous in this favourite county of theirs; and, despite the difficulty of assuming local names, the lineage in the more influential cases cannot be hidden. It is better to err on the side of restraint, for the likelihoods lead to their identification with many territorial families of Kent; but this, to be thoroughly satisfactory, would require time and accuracy of research beyond all ordinary or perhaps useful purpose.

There are state records enough of those periods to make such a special inquiry distinctly satisfactory to the scientific sense. It would, however, have to be a labour of love and leisure. History, especially English history, is only to be known thoroughly by investigation of the progress, rise, and fall of families; and in this way reward might be reaped from a devotion of years to even one such county as this, where the Sinclairs, if not as thick as the leaves of Vallombrosa, undoubtedly composed a large part of the ruling men, under their lineage or local names, from the Norman Conquest downwards.

Madox and Tindal say that the Great Rolls of most of the years of Henry II, Richard I, and John are in being; but, if so, a good many of them are not yet printed. With such valuable burdens of history and antiquity as they carry, it is a national scandal if one line of them will be left in the obscurity of MS. Twenty thousand common contemporary bills of parliament are of less urgency than a bill which could save for posterity such knowledge of national history as any one year of these rolls, "great" in many senses, contains. For what is already available, the historian and antiquary, as teachers of the piety of loving country, and as illustrators of notable action by examples, are grateful beyond all expression; but if there is more to be done, it is a disgrace which cannot be too soon wiped off our body politic, so proud of its modern cleanliness of civilisation. No madness of antiquarianism prompts the warning; it is the knowledge that a nation's most precious thing is its past history, this being the chief factor, if well considered, of its best condition.

John Sinclair of Igtham married Joan Audham, his neighbour and kinswoman, in the desirable, but not romantic, way which is still familiar to England. It does not appear that he got any dowry or heirship with her; but, through her right, their son largely increased the patrimony. The first John, who was survived by his wife Joan Audham, died in 1327, the year which began the reign of Edward III. He was in manhood in Edward I's reign, and it is probable he may have had his share in the French, Welsh, and Scottish wars of that time.

Of the battles in the last, none might have so much personal interest to him as the three-in-one contest of 24 February, 1302, fought near his kinsman's "castle of Ros or Ross", as Rapin has it, the Roslin Castle of Scottish history, "lin" being descriptive only of its situation over a linn or fall of the Esk. Sir William Sinclair, or, as English records would have written, Sir William de Ros, was one of the leaders who beat thrice on that day the three English armies of Edward's guardian of the kingdom of Scotland, John de Segrave. These considerations of naming would almost give the colour of fact to Stow's statement, that the Sinclair who founded the Scottish families went with William the Lion from England, on his return thence by ransom. What is more likely, and it agrees in most respects with authentic ancient documents and histories of date near the Conquest, is that William Sinclair who went to Scotland with Malcolm's English wife, Queen Margaret Atheling, in 1069, had possession for two or three years of Ros, in Kent, and carried the love of it with him. William de Ros he would be known as, according to Norman fashion, and he would have no choice here but to use his local name. When he became an "emigrant", his brother Richard would get the lands he left; and from him descended the Ros and Aldham names now being followed, with clearer evidence than there is for the earlier time.

John may have witnessed Wallace's execution at London on an August day of 1305. If the same race lighting on each side as leaders could make a civil war, that struggle throughout was so. The populaces of both countries were only assisting at the bitter settling of a Norman family quarrel; the Plantagenets, the Bruces, Cleres and St.Clairs, Comyns, Baliols, et hoc genus omne, being in the scientific sense of this abused phrase of the "closest blood" and of innumerable affinities to each other. It has always been easy for ambitious intellect to dupe popular instinct, as to national and other fallacious independences. The moral training of wars has hidden fountains, as the Nile once had.

What side John de St.Clair took in the struggles for and against the favourites, in the first place, Piers Gaveston, and in the second, the two more formidable Spencers, during Edward II's reign, can only be guessed at, through the execution of his wife's nephew, the baron, Francis Audham. Double kinsmanship, so to put it, and being his nearest heir, would keep John's sympathies warm with him and the other barons, against the tyrannical men of their own order, the two Hugh Despensers. These had then the earldom of Gloucester, so long associated directly and indirectly with his lineage since Robert Fitz-Hamo's time, the elder getting it through marriage with a Clare; but it is difficult to decide how this would, or if it would, affect inclinations. That strong personal interest in the chief problems of the period held him, is enough to have shown for further purpose. The triumph of Queen Isabella and her favourite, Roger Mortimer, earl of March, by the execution of the two Spencers and the deposition of Edward II, her husband, took place in John de St.Clair's last year; and he may have lived in 1327 long enough to know of the crowning of the boy of fifteen who proved so great a king, Edward III, and of the tragic death of the deposed monarch in Berkeley Castle.

It is of more genealogical interest to find from the archives of the "city" of London that he had a contemporary there, Thomas "Sencler", as the name is spelt; but more than the general connection of blood cannot be asserted. In Riley's Memorials of London and London Life in the thirteenth, fourteenth, and fifteenth Centuries there is a "Petition of the Hostelers and Haymongers" to the mayor, sheriffs, and aldermen against the freedom of trade taken by foreigners who paid no taxes, municipal or national, and yet landed hay, to undersell and ruin Englishmen. This was in 1 Edward III (1327). It was agreed that the foreigners should be allowed to sell only in shiploads, not in bottles, and a commission was appointed, two to act on water and four on land, to see that this protection should be afforded. Thomas Sinclair was one of those who watched the land proceedings, which would require most attention. One of the sheriffs of that year was Roger Chantecler, which is probably another form of spelling the name. In 1315 Sir John de Pulteney or Pounteney was mayor, and it will be seen that he had close connections with Sinclairs, who were as busy in London's commerce as in England's ruling and landed interests.

John Sinclair of Igtham died in the year when Thomas Sinclair appears thus in the records of the "city". This John of Igtham was succeeded by his son, also John of Igtham, till by his heirship to his cousin, the baron, Francis de Aldham, he became John of Aldham, or, as it then began to be called, Aldham-St.Clere. It was the same year, according to Baker, in which he heired both his father and this cousin of his, 1327, and he is certainly registered as twenty-six years of age when heir to Francis. His birth took place in 1301, when Edward I was in the midst of his great wars, if this is correct. But Tindal and his authorities give 1322 as the date of Francis de Aldham's execution, and though not at all a very unusual thing, John Sinclair, his cousin, could hardly have had to wait five years for possession, unless he too may have been rebellious, and did not get his rights till the barons were triumphant over the deposed king. One record, however, mentions him as in actual possession in 1326, which was before his father's death, of Brambletye, in Sussex, as heir of Francis de Audham, who had been holding it of the crown by knight's service as of the honour of Aquila, one of the great baronies then in the hands of the king. The Norman family from Aquila had been dispossessed; and Francis of Audham's position as baron, is further illustrated by the fact that he held of this honour, as well as the fifteen knights' fees of the honour of Mortayne, besides his own demesnes.

John of Igtham had land in Sussex, but the bulk of his son's property in that county came from his cousin Audham, and he got possession of the whole Audham barony soon after 1322, in his father's lifetime. He was born earlier, therefore, than 1301, and about 1296 is the date. Their original local name of Igtham stays with several subsequent to these two Johns, and at the same time they get mentioned as of Aldham and Aldham-St.Clere, the lineage names luckily appearing in all the instances. Henceforth Sussex has much to do with them. In the subsidy of 7 Edward III, (1333-4), this John, heir of Francis Audham, pays double of any other in that county. He and his wife Alicia were in 1339 challenged by Quo Warranto in Northamptonshire for the privilege of free warren they took in connection with their estate there of Wodepreston, and by proving that John Sinclair, his father, rightly possessed the same, it was confirmed also to them. As this was an Audham property, and was in the actual possession of his father, John Sinclair of Igtham, here is further proof that Tindal and his authorities are right as to the earlier date of the death of Francis Audham. His aunt's husband had immediate possession, and this may explain fully the few years between, before the cousin, his aunt's son, came into these lands. But the question is one of piquancy more than of importance; the facts become the same so far as the change of large property from the one branch to the other of the lineage is concerned.

The Calendars of Inquisition after Death begin to be of the greatest use about this time, throwing much light on the men and women having properties in land. This John Sinclair died in 1335, on either of the above reckonings a comparatively young man; and the list of his properties will help to illustrate his own, his father, and his cousin Francis of Audham's positions to useful extent. The record, translated from the Latin in which it is, reads: "'John, the son of John Sinclair (de Sco Claro), Chiselberg manor with the fief pertaining to it, West Chinnock manor, Penne, the fief Chilterne, Dumere, and Michell Weston, Norton manor, near Taunton, all in Somersetshire; Wodepreston in Northamptonshire; Beustede manor with additions, Hampshire; Aldham manor, Lullingstone, Kemsing manor, in Kent; Jevington manor with its members, namely, Brambeltye manor with additions. Heighten manor, and Lampham manor, and as from the castle of Pevensey, Willingdon hundred, part of Rype, two-thirds of Torring manor, two-thirds of Excete manor, Lavertye, and in the manor of East Grinstead the lands and tenements of Newborne, all in Sussex; Preston-Parva manor in the county of Northampton'".

In the Rolls of the Court of the Treasury there is an entry of a John de Seintcler, senior, making a money settlement with John de Chigehull about the manor of Wolveston, Derby; but he and the junior John are presumably descendants of Ralph of Nottingham and Derby, the eldest son of Hubert, the ambassador to Edward the Confessor. It must not be forgotten that one writer says that "Wolveston manor with its pertinents" was in Hampshire, at Southampton; and he mentions John of Kent as being in possession of it by heirship 2 Edward III (1329), which seems the true account. He probably gave it away before his death to his Hampshire relations, since it does not appear in his list of properties then. Of John of the Calendars of Inquisition there are two entries from these rolls of the treasury which are their own evidence. Under "Wall", which included some of the western counties now within England's borders, this notice of the heirship of the Audham part of the above lands comes: "'The king took homage of John, the son of John Sinclair, blood-relation and heir of Francis of Aldham, for all the lands and tenements which the same Francis held'". This is of as much enlightenment about lineage as property, but it has to be remembered that it refers only to all the lands inherited in the parts then called Wales. Some of the lands in England proper went to other heirs, as well as to John Sinclair.

The following from the same rolls would go to show so: "'And it was declared that the said John Sinclair recognised that the said Francis of Aldham held the manor of Wodepreston from the king by the service of middle fee of one knight, the manor of Chiselberg with its pertinents by the service of one military fee as from the honour of Moretayne, and the manor of Brambeltye as from the honour of Aquila by the service of middle fee of one soldier'". John Sinclair may have heired more than these manors from Francis, for they are but a portion of his many fees. He must have divided his baronial possessions to others besides John, and there is the further probability that the crown on his execution for treason seized and kept a large share. It is thus that gifts to John's son are noticeable, as will appear hereafter.

Lavertye manor is known to have been in the hands of the Montacutes in the thirteenth century, who became earls of Salisbury for aid to the valorous seizing by Edward III in 1330 of Roger Mortimer, earl of March. Roger was the favourite of his mother Isabella, queen of Edward II. Her son with his party got entrance into Nottingham Castle by a subterraneous passage still called Mortimer's Hole. Isabel Montacute married Francis Aldham's grandfather and brought Lavertye to the Aldhams. John Sinclair was in possession of it at death, and yet it is not mentioned in this roll; so that the account is only incidental to three of the many manors he held from all sources.

The last John was not the least important of the trio. A quotation from the twenty volumes upwards of Sussex Antiquities may introduce him. 'St Clere - Proof of the age of John, son and heir of John de Seintcler, deceased, taken at Chichester on Monday after the Annunciation, 25 Edward III (1351). The deponents say that he was born at West Whittering, and baptized in the church of St.Peter there on Palm Sunday, 27 March, 2 Edward III, (1328). John de Polyngfold, Alice, widow of Sir Nicolas Gentyl, knt., and William de St.George were his sponsors. Robert de Bromer recollects the day, because a dispute which had for a long time existed between him and John de Seintcler, the father, was on that day settled in the church and enrolled in the missal. Born thus at the beginning of Edward III's reign, he lived through its eventful fifty years, and died 12 Richard II (1389) aged 61.

The following notes, chiefly from the Archaelogica Cantiana, throw some further light on the Aldhams and Sinclairs: - Margery de Peckham [nee Aldham] had a sister and coheir named Isolda in 1347. This sister was the wife of John St.Clere, and paid aid for land in Igtham when the Black Prince was knighted. The land is described as a moiety of a knight's fee, which Christina de Kirkeby and the heirs of Nicolas de Cryel held in Igtham from the archbishop. It is recognised by Ciriac Petit as being the manor of Igtham or The Mote. The inquisition after death of William Inge states that he and his wife, Isolda Inge, acquired from Nicolas de Cryel the moiety of Igtham manor. These facts suggest very strongly that Isolda Aldham, Isolda Inge, and Isolda St.Clere meant the same person, who may have married John St.Clere after the death of William Inge, who was chief justice of the king's bench in 1316, and had been married first to Margaret Grasenel, and second to Isolda Aldham. The Cryels or Kyryels were settled in Hadlow, near Yaldham of Wrotham, and about 1680 Thomas Cryel married Mary, one of the distinguished Kent and Lincolnshire family of Dalison, whose seat in the southern county has been Hamptons, Tunbridge, three miles from The Mote, Igtham.

The assizes of Sussex county were held at Horsham, now known as Shelley's birthplace, sometimes at Chichester, and oftenest at East Grinstead, where Sir John resided most. On the manor of Lavertye, East Grinstead, Cooper says he had his park; and his public connections with Sussex would make it appear that it was as much his home as Aldham-St.Clere, in Kent. In 50 Edward III (1377) he became sheriff of Sussex and Surrey. He and his family were in very particular relations to the spirited and generous queen of Edward III, Philippa, she who took David, king of Scots, prisoner at the victory of Neville's Cross, near Durham, and who in the same year, 1347, obtained the pardon of the six doomed burghers at Calais from her husband.

Under Sussex, Edward III, of the Rolls of the Treasury this comes: "'The king confirmed the grant which Philippa, the queen of England, the very dear consort of the king, made to John Sinclair, chevalier, of her manor of Maresfield, which is from the honour of Aquila, together with the king's park in the same place, the town of Grinstead, and the keepership of her forest of Ashesdoune, and her other properties in the county of Sussex, to be held to the end of her life, returning thence annually thirty pounds to his lady, the queen, for the military fees. These properties, extending widely between East Grinstead and Lewes, remained for his descendants, being expressly mentioned as belonging to his grandson in 1408; and the probabilities are all but certainties, that the queen pledged them for money received in that very expensive reign'".

Nor is this the only transaction which indicates the mutual helpfulness of ruler and ruled in this connection. After forty-two years of happy marriage Queen Philippa died in 1369, and in the Issue Rolls of the following year, the lord high treasurer of England, the bishop of Exeter, whose crook had perhaps as well been guiding the sheep as raking money tables, pays to Richard, earl of Arundel, in Sussex, £1377, 14s. 6d. by order of the king for relief of Philippa's soul. Of this, at that period, large sum £100 was due to the earl himself, and to Mary St.Clere "20 marks altogether". Mary was the daughter of Sir John Sinclair of Grinstead, and this is not all that is known of her. Like her father, she had been a favoured friend of Philippa, and the scene of gift is Essex:

"'The king confirmed the grant which Philippa, the queen of England, the very dear consort of the king, made to her maid-of-honour, Mary Sinclair, of all the lands and tenements which were those of William de Teye, in the town of Havering-at-Bowre, in the county of Essex, which fell lately into the hands of the king as escheat, and called Markdiche, which are to be held to the termination of her life'".

The prevalent French has a noticeable effect on the Latin, and it is further noteworthy, that the words of the grants to the lady and her father are suggestively similar. In Rymer's Foedera a letter from Pope Eugenius in 1147 shows that Teia was part of the lands of Hubert Sinclair, the king's chamberlain, one of the Norwich family; for he gave land from it to the church of Algate intra muros, London. Mary therefore had lineage claims to succeed William of Teye, though it is impossible to trace them now. Royal free gifts were very rare indeed in English history, apart from relationships, and above all in the times of the expensive French wars.

But Sir John's affairs were not only in the home counties. From Somerset an example has survived: "'The king has committed to John Sinclair the custody of one messuage, one garden, sixty acres of land, and seven acres of meadow, with the pertinents, in Estham, in the county of Somerset, which belonged to Letitia, who was the wife of William Sinclair of Kingswood, dead, for the heir of Nicolas Seymour, dead, who is within age, to hold them up to his legitimate age, rendering from them to the king forty shillings per year and doing service'". The nearest relation had the right to this kind of custody, all other things equal; and these Sinclairs of Kingswood, Somersetshire, are a younger branch of Sir John's line.

Before William it was Thomas Sinclair of Kingswood, and in the right of his wife, Juliana Pipard, he had lands also in Gloucestershire, as appears from the following charter in Latin of the "additional charters" preserved in the British Museum: "'Thomas Sinclair of Kingswood and Juliana his wife get possession from Walter, the son of Thomas Pipard of Salisbury, of their lands in the town [district] of Durham, in the county of Gloucester, the dowry of the said Juliana, who was formerly the wife of the said Thomas Pipard'". The date of this writing is 39 Edward III, 1365, and a portion of red seal remains. There is another connected survival, namely, the letters to his attorneys by this Walter to see to the settlmg of the claim.

Having wealth of money and lands, Sir John seems also an adept in the state and county business of his time; and he made valuable additions to what patrimony he received. Another of his daughters, Margaret, married Sir William Walleys of Glynd, long since an extinct Sussex family, and heired by the lords Morley. Mrs. Gladstone of Hawarden

Castle is a Glynd, and may be a financial offshoot from the landed Walleyses of Glynd. It would be a more curious thing, if the Scot of Scots should, on close investigation, turn out to be a most energetic but unfortunate Norman of this Sussex ilk, the heroes beyond the Tweed being almost invariably Anglo-Norman. The suggestion, however, is dangerous enough to raise a new war of independences.

Why Mary Sinclair heired the Teyes might be a question of interest, if her heirship were anything else than the gift of crown property. Henry Teye was executed at London in 1321, at the same time and for the same reason as Francis Aldham, when Edward II and the Despensers got the advantage of the barons; but the estates did not then come into the king's hands, for William de Teye was the antecessor of Mary. There is a Sir Robert Tey or Teyes in English history later than Mary as one of the commissioners for the commons in the parliament of Shrewsbury, 1398, a king's favourite; but the property of Havering Bower which she got from Queen Philippa, is again in the crown during and after the time of Richard II. It was in 1397 a seat of this king. Here he came, on a pretended hunting excursion, to entrap his uncle the duke of Gloucester in the basest possible way. Froissart tells the tale of how he left his seat of Havering Bower, near Rumford, in Essex, and came on a quasi visit at five o'clock of a summer's afternoon to the castle of Plessy, his uncle's dwelling, as it once had been Margaret Sinclair's (the countess of Essex, William Mandeville's lady), as it was her son's (Geffrey Mandeville), and that of several constables of England. After supper the duke was to go with him to London for a supposed council, but on coming towards the end of Epping Forest, King Richard galloped in front, leaving him to be seized by an ambush under the earl-marshal, Thomas Mowbray. But this is public history. Mary's care put Havering Bower into good enough shape for a royal seat. She was the immediate previous possessor. Her court experience may have kept royal acquaintance fresh as to her Essex home, so that unlike her father she did not transmit to her own friends. In 1437 Joan of Navarre, Henry IV's queen, died there. Sir John Sinclair was married to Mary, the widow of Sir Roger Bellers. There is a notice of Sir John and his wife Mary holding jointly in 1386 inter alia Brambletye and Lavertye, her death taking place in 1390, the year after her husband's. Their son was Philip, who may be called Sir Philip St.Clere, the elder, of Igtham, to distinguish him from his own second son, Sir Philip of Burstow, in Surrey, and from the son of his eldest son Thomas, Philip, the second of Igtham.

Chapter XLIII
Sir Philip, Thomas, and Philip

There are three eldest sons, father, son, and grandson, in direct succession to Sir John Sinclair. His heir Sir Philip, whom Burke's Peerage describes as "'Sir Philip St.Clere, knt., M.P. for Sussex in 1377'", married Joan de Audley; and it was by her right that Farthingo and Stean in Northamptonshire came to one of his successors. Her father was Sir James de Audley of Wold, son of Hugh de Audley, earl of Gloucester, one of the six earls created by Edward III in 1337, on the occasion of making his son Richard duke of Cornwall, the first use in England of the ordinary ducal title. James had perhaps still higher rank than his father, by being one of the twenty-six knights in the list headed by Edward III and his son Edward, prince of Wales, who are known as the founders of the order of the garter. One of these Audleys, covered with wounds, was publicly acknowledged by the Black Prince after the battle of Cressy, as being the most valiant that day, of all his heroic Englishmen. The Stanleys, of whom the earls of Derby are the chief representatives, changed their original name of Audley to what it is. The historical fame of the Audleys and Stanleys belongs to the same male stock. The king's cousin, the beautiful countess of Salisbury, was the occasion of the famous institution of which the motto is Honi soit qui mal y pense, and which has always preserved twenty-six as the number of its select knights. William Montacute, the earl of Salisbury, was one of the founders, whose family contributed estates to these Sinclairs, as has been seen.

Sir James, the knight of the garter, had connection to Farthingo and Steen through his mother, who was Margaret Bereford, daughter of Sir William Bereford of these properties, and of Langley, Warwickshire. The Berefords played their part in the reigns of Edward III and Richard II. On the young king Edward seizing the government from his mother Isabella, and from her favourite, Roger Mortimer, earl of March, Sir Simon Bereford as one of her party was executed in 1330, and in 1388 Sir Baldwin was banished as a favourite of the latter monarch. The fortunes of all the set hang around that dramatic entrance by underground passage of Edward III, with Montacute, three Bohuns, and others, into his mother's apartment in Nottingham Castle, and seizure of Mortimer, despite the queen's "Bel Fitz, Bel Fitz, ayez pitie du gentile Mortimer". The amazing thing is that the "gentle" gallant had then four sons and seven daughters. Their father's position seemed only to have made the daughters the more popular, their marriages being the best possible in the kingdom, such as those with Beauchamp, earl of Warwick, Hastings, earl of Pembroke, and others similar.

But it is his daughter Joan, or as some say Margaret, Mortimer, that has present interest, having married James, lord Audley. It was their daughter, named also Joan, who was wife of Sir Philip St.Clere of Igtham and Grinstead; and in her person she centred some of the courtliest traditions and most royal relationships of the period. The earldom of Gloucester seems never far from St.Clairs, from Robert, the "knight of Rye", downwards through Mandevilles, Clares, Audleys, and, it might be found, the Despensers besides; so strongly tenacious have Norman natures been of the rights and delights of consanguinity. The three heiresses of the Clares married, the eldest, Eleanor, to Hugh Despenser, the son; Margaret, first to the notorious favourite Piers Gaveston, and second to Lord Audley, the father of James; and Elizabeth to William de Burgh, earl of Ulster, and other two succeeding husbands, as the History of Cambria tells fully. But this sea of best genealogies of the time is to be shunned now with care.

Sir Philip and his lady, Joan de Audley, had Thomas Sinclair as eldest son. He was one of the heroes of Agincourt, who "fought with us upon St.Crispin's day", to take the words of King Harry V, as dramatised. In the roll of the Sussex men who were there, "Thomas Sencler" appears as one of the five armigeri who, with the earl of Arundel and Surrey, and lords Cobham and Camoys, were the officers of this contingent, consisting mostly of archers. The earl led them to Dover, but he fell ill, and lords Cobham and Camoys were their leaders on the battle-field. Both of these appear to have been of the same lineage as the heir of Igtham. But this will find its evidence in connection with the descendants of Hugo St.Clare of Aeslingham.

After the siege and taking of Harfleur, King Henry was returning with his sick troops to England, by way of Calais. Met by many times their number of French, who barred the passage northwards, he secured against all hope and likelihood perhaps the greatest, at all events, the most joyful, victory in English record. The strangest tales are told of the consequences of the flux which afflicted his army even before it left England. At Agincourt it made them exhibit the berserker fury to an unparalleled degree of heroism.

Thomas was one of those who outlived that day, and came home to Kent and Sussex. It would seem, however, that he succumbed soon after, whether from illness or wounds. His death certainly took place in 1416, and the battle being on 25th October 1415, the likelihood is that his decease was the effect of that trying campaign and victory.

His wife was Margaret Philpott, daughter of Sir John Philpott, lord mayor of London. As an alderman, he got knighted at the same time as Sir William Walworth, who was then lord mayor, because of his aid in arresting and slaying the rebel Wat Tyler at Smithfield. Sir William had £100 a year of pension given for his courageous deed, and Sir John Philpott and two other aldermen £40 a year each for ever for their services to the young king, Richard, at the crisis of England's most dangerous rebellion. Tindal speaks of Philpott as the "famous", and Walsingham gives support to this enthusiasm of his.

When Edward III died, his grandson and successor Richard II was only eleven, and a regency was appointed of his three uncles and others. His eldest uncle was the duke of Lancaster, called king of Castile, and he was quite as proud as a Spaniard. The parliament would not trust the regents with money. Says Rapin, after showing that the parliament granted a subsidy for war, "'but it was clogged with this condition, that the money should be lodged in the hands of Philpott and Walworth, two eminent aldermen of London, who were ordered to take care it should be expended only in repulsing the French and Castilians in league against England'". Cotton's Abridgement gives details: two fifteenths and two tenths out of cities and burghs, the fifteenths of all lands, and tenths of all goods, to be levied before Candlemas, and deposited in the hands of William Walworth and John Philpott, merchants of London. Lancaster stopped defence of the sea-coasts till he got the money.

Meanwhile piracies were going on, and John Philpott gained high honour from occasion. Mercer, a Scotch pirate, had taken merchantmen out of the harbour at Scarborough, and was proceeding to further brilliancies, when Philpott fitted out some ships at his own expense, and putting, a thousand soldiers on board, went in quest of the pirate, found him, defeated him, and brought him prisoner to London in 1378, to the admiration of the people generally, and to the dangerous jealousy of the regency. Several of Rapin's paragraphs are devoted to the fame of Thomas Sinclair's energetic father in-law. "The king of Kent" was not the first of his kind whom honest Philpott looked out of countenance, and out of rebellious life. A lady of the distinguished Sandford family was his own wife, and he himself appears as a miles.

The Tyler rising was in 1381, and three years after Sir John Philpott died. This daughter then could not but be young, her marriage to Thomas Sinclair, the heir of Sir Philip, taking place necessarily however before 1395. She married a second time. One of the monumental tablets of the church of Greyfriars, which was situated where Christ's Hospital now is, Newgate Street, had the following inscription, preserved from the barbarous destruction which overtook that place of sepulture for the great: "'Margaret, daughter of the baron John Philpott, lord mayor, and knight beforesaid, and wife of Thomas Sinclair, armsbearing, and afterwards of John Nelond, arms-bearing: she died 18th Sept 1438'". On the same tablet when perfect, there was account of her father, as this survival shows.

Bridges in his History of Northamptonshire gives further knowledge. Describing Wold, Orlingbury hundred, in that county, he says Thomas Seyntcler died 4 Henry V (1416), which is the year after Agincourt, possessing jointly with Margaret his wife a manor in Wold, which he left to Philip his son and heir. Thomas heired it from his mother's family, the Audleys; but it is possible that Sir John Philpott may have had land there also, and that some of the Wold properties were Margaret's dowry. In 20 Edward III (1347) the Audleys had them. Thomas de Audley had heired his brother William, and himself dying left an only daughter Elizabeth under age. A suggestive record of 10 Richard II (1386) says that her guardians were, Wm. Montague, earl of Salisbury, and John de Ros.

The result of Sinclair's city connection is sufficiently indicated by a charter in the British Museum, which shows him to have had a grant of Southwark in 1415; and this at once helps to explain the wealth of Sir John Philpott and the parallel prosperity of Thomas Sinclair of Igtham's brother, Sir Philip of Burstow. As this was thirty-five years after the lord mayor's death, it must have come to Margaret Sinclair or Philpott by lapse of heirships, the Philpotts having much London house property.

Of Philip Sinclair, the eldest son of Thomas and of Margaret Philpott, less is known than of any of the line. He was twenty-one when his father's properties came to him, 4 Henry V (1417); and he, with paternal traditions of victorious war so recent, must have followed King Henry in his triumphal conquest of the kingdom of France. Much may yet be discovered of his doings, if so; but, for the present, it is certain that he died without issue, the too general fate of the soldier of that brilliant period. His mother, Margaret Philpott, with her second husband, got Wold manor in 5 Henry VI (1427) which was in Philip's possession. She gets it, however, not from her son, or on her son's death, but from his cousin-german. The latter heired it by lineage, and it would seem on his cousin Philip's death, giving it over to Margaret Philpott and her husband John Nelond, armiger.

The duke of Bedford, regent of France after the death of his brother Henry V, was a personal friend of the Sinclairs of Aldham; so much so that he bought part of their property near Aldham St.Clere, where he resided usually when in England. It might point inquiry, to say that Philip Sinclair spent his life chiefly with him in Paris; which would account for how little appears of him, wealthy and splendidly connected as he was, in the survivals of this country. If he died in 1427, as has been supposed, the dream of English continental supremacy had not been to him dashed for ever by the hysterical furies of the Maid, so appalling to his brave fellow-countrymen. Of the French wars of those two able brothers, Henry V and the duke of Bedford, much has yet to be gleaned.

It is of genealogical interest that the "lord of St.Cler" was one of the Norman-French earls who fell at Agincourt, but the doings of another Sinclair in France are too characteristic to be passed. The contemporary chronicle of the religieux of St.Denis, 1380-1422, tells in vigorous monkish Latin of the personal strength and high gallantry of "Messire Bruneau de Saint Clair", and of how he figured in the struggle for the regency between the dukes of Orleans and Burgundy, the brother and uncle of the sun-struck Charles VI. In 1414 this king warred against the duke of Burgundy; and so serious was the war expected to be that he went first to St.Denis monastery, to take with all ceremonies the oriflamme, the standard raised when France was in danger, to lead his army. To "Messire de Bruneau de Saint Clair" and to the "Sire d'Aumont" it was given for last defence, as the bravest men of all the French. It was made of silk of a gold and flame colour, with three flying points, and eighteen divisions. The flag was of no great size, if pictures may be trusted; but it thrilled the patriotism of the country to its highest when displayed. After Joan of Arc drove the English from their conquest, the white coronet has been the banner of the country. The earls of Vexin had hereditary claim to carry the oriflamme; and, as St.Cler is in the Normandy Vexin, Bruneau must have had this to aid him to his office. By the "Sire de Bacqueville" on similar occasion he was again selected for his known gallantry and physical strength. One of his military duties was at command of the king to go, with a marshal, Bouciault, and the count de St.Pol, against bands of brigands qui infestaient le pays chartrain. They were, in those troublous times, of all ages from fifteen upwards, but short work did these three make of them. When the Armagnac party were devastating as they pleased, he drilled the inhabitants so thoroughly that they swept them back entirely out of that part of the country. In that time of faction, when coups-de-etat were as common as in days of civilisation, Parisian modern, Bruneau Sinclair was made provost of Paris, as of the Burgundian party. When a change came he was re-established in his functions of grand maitre de l'hotel du roi, the office so well known in French history as mayor of the palace.

But though France and England were one country in the days of Henry V and of his brother, enough has been here said of Bruneau. That he should be dapifer or seneschal then, points to the hereditary faculty of high ride in his lineage. It might be a pity, however, to pass one rather isolated fact of the wars of Henry V, which has double genealogical interest, namely, that in 1417 the castle of St.Cler on the Epte, whence the name came, was put under the governorship of Sir William Basset. The Bassets had been of close affinity to the Sinclairs in England, and King Henry and Sir William knew this, and acted and benefited accordingly.

Whether Philip St.Clair of Igtham figured under the English rulers of France, is more probable than provable, till further evidence is found. He is the last of these three eldest sons in succession.

Chapter XLIV
Sir Philip of Burston and his Sons

There were three Philips altogether, and he of Burstow was the second son of Sir Philip of Igtham, and the uncle of the Philip who died without issue. He was the brother therefore of Thomas Sinclair of Igtham, the warrior of Agincourt. Baker, in his History of Northamptonshire, is authority for Sir Philip of Burstow being the younger of the two brothers; but how then is it that Sir Philip dies in 1408 possessed of nearly all the paternal estates (see the Calendar of Inquisitions after Death), and his brother Thomas dies in 1416, having Igtham and Little Preston chiefly ? Could there be gavelkind or parage of such sort as to make the younger brother's portion the larger of the two ? Or did the elder elect the soldier's life of adventure for new possessions, and leave the other the provision of money and the mastery of the bulk of the lands ? Fees were partible; and the first Philip of all, their father, may have favoured his namesake. Certainly the weight of influence and property follows with the younger; for it is better to accept the recognised account, since it does not affect anything which was the first-born, Thomas's line dying out in his son Philip, and much if not all of their properties going to Sir Philip of Burstow's sons.

However he came to possess so much of his father's lands, he had faculty, and did not rest content with what he had. In 44 Edward III (1371) he made a great marriage, which increased his already large estate. But the right version perhaps is that he made this marriage first as a younger son, and that then his power brought him the paternal and fraternal kindnesses, on his proved capability of clever deeds. What aids this is that he took his usual title from Burstow and Godstone, in Surrey, which he had by his wife. She was Margaret de Louvaine or Lorraine, and the widow of Sir Richard Chamberlain of Sherburne, Oxfordshire, and of Cotes. The only sister of an only brother, Sir Nicolas de Louvaine, she heired him, and brought his properties to her husbands, with the latter of whom they remained, for his family.

The father of Sir Nicolas and Margaret, was also Sir Nicolas, and he had married the widow of Sir John de Pulteney of Offspring, Kent, held by "a yearly rose", getting Offspring and other estates with her. Sir John de Pulteney was lord mayor of London, and gained also high political fame. Penshurst, in Kent, he got the privilege of embattling for his residence as a baron of the kingdom. It was he who by wit, or by being the cause of it in others, made roses, red and white, peaceful and bloody, current in English mouths. Quite a galaxy of London plain but warm-hearted humour gathers around his name and surroundings. The Poultry of Cheapside is a change of Pulteney's name, just as Buckingham or the Duke's Foot Lane there became Ducksfoot Lane, and Green Lattice Lane, Green Lettuce. Shakespeare, in King Henry VIII has the authenticating lines, "The duke, being at the Rose, within the parish of St.Laurence, Poulteney ..."

The lord mayor gave his name to the whole district thus, and "The Rose" had as often the title of "Pulteney's Inn". "Cold Harbour", in Thames Street, however, was oftener "Pulteney's Inn", another of the mansions of this great draper. He gave Cold Harbour to Humfrey de Bohun, earl of Hereford and Essex, for a rose at midsummer to him and his heirs. In 1533 it became "Shrewsbury House" for Francis Talbot, the fifth earl, but reached ultimately the very reverse side of high fortune. Sir John had property in many parts of London, even as far east as Stepney; but it was from where the Mansion House stands, and towards the river, he held most largely. "The Rose", says Thornbury, in his Old and New London, "was a spacious mansion, originally built by Sir John Pulteney, knight, five times lord mayor of London in the reign of Edward III". He adds that the Hollands, De la Poles, Staffords, Courtenays, and Ratcliffes all enjoyed it subsequently.

These Louvaines were a branch of the dukes of Lorraine, of whom Tasso's Godfrey of Boulogne (for on Stow's authority it is the same family) is the most renowned among many such; and they had large baronies in England such as Eye in Suffolk, and the honour of Bononia, so long in the king's hands. The beautiful Adeliza, or Alice Louvaine, second queen of Harry I, and afterwards countess of an Albeni earl of Arundel, was of this family. But the remarkable Percy earls of Northumberland, were really Louvaines, Joscelin, Queen Adeliza's brother, having married the heiress of the Normandy Percies on condition of changing his name. The descendant of Charlemagne, he is another proof of the monopoly of great deeds in world history by great breeds.

The renowned "Hotspur" of Chevy Chase, or the battle of Otterburne, in which James, earl of Douglas, was slain, dying in the arms of Sir John Sinclair, was one of them. Though he and his brother, Sir Ralph Percy (Louvaine), were taken prisoners, they had good right to be brave. He fell performing prodigies of valour at the battle of Shrewsbury in 1403.

Shakespeare has immortalised him, had he never been one of the heroes of Chevy Chase. In the Genealogia Europae of Henninges, published 1598, both the sons of a Sinclarus, are with James Douglas at Otterburne in 1388, Johannes and Gualtherus. John Sinclair is made father of William, comes Orcadensis. This earl of Orkney appears as father of John, bishop of Brechin. Though this is short, and difficult to fit with some pedigrees, it is of considerable value in the reference to Otterburne, where the Louvaines and St.Clares so strangely cross. Sir John, father of the earl of Orkney, was next in command to Douglas, and had the honour of the Louvaines as his prisoners. The present duke of Hamilton owes much of his position to heiring these Sinclairs and Douglases, who were intermarried frequently. Sanquhar or St.Clair, the caput baroniae of Nithsdale, was held by the Hamiltons at one time. Shakespeare, in Henry V, says that the Louvaines were "sole heirs male of the true line and stock of Charles the Great". The foreigners discovered the greatness of lord mayors of London long ago, and brave ones lived even before Sir Richard Whittington of the fifteenth century.

That Sir Philip of Burstow had city sympathies as well as affinities and real heirship, the following charter of 20 Richard II (1396) shows: "'Philip Sinclair, chevalier, and others, for the church of All Saints at Fenn in Roperia, London, two messuages in the parish of All Saints called "The Coldeherburgh", for enlarging the church, and making a cemetery'". Here is the history of "Fenchurch" Street in short compass; and the Cold Harbour of Sir John Pulteney had, before 1397, come by the right of his wife to Sir Philip Sinclair. He must have had high public spirit, or interest in other London properties, to have gifted these messuages of fame and value. Making an intramural cemetery then, was the most advanced sanitary city improvement. Over these favoured citizens' dust, so provided with a shapely resting-place, the office, the street, and the cab have long since taken permanent position, Bunhill Fields being modern compared with the graveyard of the Fen Church in the rope-making waste of ancient London. It is noteworthy as a survival that there is a Cold Harbour near St.Clere, Kemsing, Kent.

Blomfield, in his History of Norfolk, says that this Sir Philip was lord of Wethersfield and Bradfield, in Suffolk, in Henry IV's time, but on his death he possessed only the former. How he got either of them, by what degree of consanguinity to the Sinclairs of Bradfield, or if by purchase, or if from the crown on the death of Pain St.Clair as escheat, is open for inquiry. It is difficult to believe that lineage by exact steps could be reckoned, though both houses were descendants of Richard of 1066; three hundred years upwards being very estranging except with the most fortunate of families.

In 1405 Sir Philip was sheriff of Sussex. Among the Harleian charters this is to be found about his wife and himself, dated 7 Henry IV (1406): "'Acquittance of Elizabeth Mortayne to Philip Sinclair and his wife Margaret, for 10 marks of annual pension, and 20 marks from the manor of Tyllesworth'". But what will throw most light on their histories are the lists of their possessions, from the Calendar of Inquisitions after Death. Sir Philip's was taken 9 Henry IV (1408) and his wife Margaret de Louvaine died the next year, for hers is taken 10 Henry IV (1409).

Philip Saintclere: Cheseberg manor, Somerset; Swaffham Prior manor, Cambridgeshire; Wethersfield manor, Suffolk; Barton St.John manor, Staunton St.John manor, a certain manor in Chalgrave, as from the honour of Wallingford, Oxfordshire; Lagham manor, as from the manor of Tandridge, Merden manor, Heggecourt manor, Burstow manor, Leweland manor, tenement in the manor of Lagham beforesaid called Stroudland, Hegecote manor, parcel called Shavenore as from the manor of Shiffield, and other parcels of the aforesaid manor of Hegecote called Lyllye, Wimbledon manor and service, Surrey; Laverty or Lanerty manor, Torringe manor, Brembletye manor, Hegton manor, Jevington manor, tenement in Meresfield called Newnham, as from the honour of Leicester, Nuttborne manor, Chudham manor, Excete manor, Ashdoune forest, service of the honour of Aquila, Sussex; Ashby Magna manor, as from the honour of Peverell, Leicestershire; West Aldham manor, as from the castle of Eynesford, Kemsing, half of 180 acres of land from the manor of Wodeland, Wodeland, 80 acres of land as from the manor of Otford in gavelkind, the returns of Lullington Castle, Yemesfield manor, as from the castle of Tunbridge, Penshurt manor and Otford manor, tenement then called South Park, Falkham manor, Eshore Park, tenement in Penshurst called Lathehames, Sutton-at-Hone manor, Chiddington tenement called Mercheshopes, Remesleghes manor, Penshurst tenement called Hameden, Chidingston manor, Bytberwe tenement called Hereland, Leghe manor, Leghe tenement called Bernestesgrof, and the park called North Park, Faukham manor, Kent.

Margaret, the wife of Philip Seinclere: Zeneford manor as from Tunbridge Castle, Penshurst manor as from the manor of Otford, South Park, 80 acres of land named as from the manor of Faukham, Eshore Park, tenement called Netherham as from the manor of Sutton-at-Hone, Chidingston tenement called Marcheshope as from the manor of Romesley, Chydington manor land, Hoveland in Betterberwe, land as from the manor of Leghe, Leghe land, called Blackheath, Bernetsgrove, North Park, and 100 acres of adjacent land, Kent. These formed her portion after the death of her husband, the bulk of the property being put under guardianship for their sons, John and Thomas, the elder of whom was only twelve at the decease of his father. In the charters of the Museum there is one by Sir Philip providing for Margaret de Louvaine, if she should become his widow. With many other things of note in these lists, it is remarkable that he held the Staunton St.John, in Oxfordshire, which was the home of Lord Bolingbroke of Queen Anne's time, the famous author and politician, Pope's friend.

On the whole, the marriage of Margaret de Louvaine to Sir Philip was more a stroke of fortune for her than for him, as comparison of the list of even his great-grandfather's properties shows. His able grandfather, Sir John Sinclair, sheriff of Sussex and Surrey, the manager of Queen Philippa's property and its ultimate possessor, seems to have had his hand over the affairs of the De Louvaines. That thus Sir Philip, his grandson, had introduction substantial to his consort, whether also romantic, may or may not be. Among the Harleian charters one of historic as well as private interest remains, written in the language still used at that period for legal transactions, the French introduced by the Normans. Its date is 44 Edward III (1371) and given under Sir John's seal at Penshurst - "mon seal a Penshurst". This was nineteen years after the death of the lord mayor Sir John Pulteney, baron of Penshurst and Ospring, whose widow married Sir Nicolas de Louvaine, father of Sir Nicolas and Margaret, the wife of Sir Philip of Burstow. The writing runs: "'John Sinclair: surrendered to Sir Nicholas de Louvayne all the estates which I had of his lease in all the manors, fees, and advowsons'". They are both called armigeri in the document; which is a parchment 2.5 inches by 11, folded double and three, of 6.5 lines of well-written but dim old French, the seal being yet attached, and hardly imperfect, since "EINTCLER" remains, and nearly the whole of the shield, with "the sun in its glory" blazoning its entire field.

Sir Philip married Margaret de Louvaine that same year, says Philpott in Villare Cantianum, and this surrender of leases on the part of his grandfather to his bride's brother, may have been to put them in possession of some or all of the estates, by way of her dowry. The Surrey properties of Burstow and the rest, were the chief aggrandisement to the family in the transaction; and if Sir John Sinclair had no claims against the Louvaine properties, the lands she brought her husband were princely enough. It is suggestive of Sir John Sinclair's ability and wealth, that he was in possession so early as 1371 of Penshurst, though it may have been only by lease. Sir Philip had it fully on the death of his brother-in-law Sir Nicholas, to whom his wife was heiress.

In considering Sir Philip of Burstow's properties, it need not be forgotten that his elder brother, Thomas of Igtham and Parva Preston, who lived eight years after him, must be supposed to have got the lion's share of their father and grandfather's properties; the grandfather living, as the above shows, long after the marriage of Margaret de Louvaine, and having then power over his affairs. Rev. Thomas Cox in Magna Britannia says that Ospring came to Sir Philip St.Clere of Aldham through his wife, Margaret Louvaine, and continued with his posterity till the reign of Edward the Fourth; but it does not appear in the inquisitions. It certainly was in possession of some of the family, and the suggestion occurs that it may have been exchanged by Sir Philip of Burstow, for some of the large proportion of the patrimony he holds, with his elder brother, Thomas of Igtham, whose estates lay in more convenient proximity to the somewhat eastern Ospring, long a royal demesne. Cox's finding could be true that it remained in the family till Edward IV, if Thomas of Igtham's son Philip, who died without issue about that time, heired it. Sir Philip of Burstow's sons were dead twenty-seven years before Edward IV held the throne (1461). There are not evidences enough to discuss further.

The two sons of Sir Philip of Burstow have to be treated, John the elder, and Thomas the younger. In 1409 they were orphans, the elder thirteen; and Sir John Pelham, the earl of Chichester, got the wardship of the boys from King Henry IV. The Inquisitiones ad Quod Damnum of 7 Henry V (1419) are proof of this: "'The jurors say that Henry, lately king of England, father of our lord the king now, by his open letters, committed to John Pelham, miles, the custody of all the manors, demesnes, lands, etc, which were those of Sir Philip Sinclair, dead, who held in capite from the said Henry'". It is under "Sussex" and as if to make assurance doubly sure, the record commission has entered it twice. The occasion of this inquisition is the death of John Sinclair the heir, at the age of twenty-three, in 1419.

The earl had got the marriage of John arranged to his satisfaction. In Collin's Peerage his daughter Joan Pelham is married to Sir John Seynclere, and Collins gives his evidence, namely, a letter in his time extant from the earl in the reign of Henry V to this young Sir John. He himself died 12 Feb, 1428, leaving this and another daughter and a son to succeed him. Sir John Pelham was one of the ambassadors for the marriage of Henry V to the Princess Katherine of France, of whom Shakespeare makes so much, and he had various similar political experience. His daughter fell heir to some of her husband Sir John's lands, but the chief portion went to the younger brother, Thomas Sinclair. They had a sister Margaret Sinclair, who married one of the lord mayor connection, Thomas de Pulteney, armiger, but much more is not known of her yet. A charter is preserved in the British Museum of thirteen lines of writing, given by a Thomas Saintcler, who must have been their uncle of Agincourt fame, and in it there is mention of a John, this last Sir John, and a Juliana Sinclair, probably another sister whose history has also to be discovered.

In 1422, the first year of the reign of Henry VI, Thomas Sinclair is the sole male survivor of his line. That his cousin-german, Philip of Igtham, died a young man, seems proved by Thomas being, in the escheats of the year 1422, written as of Igtham and Parva Preston, which could not be with his cousin alive. The year before, by prior settlement of Sir Baldwin Bereford, one of the favourites of Richard II, through the marriage of the grandfather of Thomas, Sir Philip, to Joan Audley, daughter of one of the ladies Bereford, Farthingo and Stean in Northamptonshire first came into actual possession of the family. His brother Sir John Sinclair died in 1419, so that he had his lands earlier than either the Igtham or the Northamptonshire estates. He was born in 1401, and in 1422 he was possessed of most if not all of the lands of his family, the single representative of their antiquity, ability, and wealth. Among the Probat aetatis records of Sussex he appears in 2 Henry VI (1423) as "'Thomas Sinclair, brother and heir of John, the son of Philip Sinclair, Chevalier'"; so that his relationship is quite clear.

Then he got his properties, it is said that some of them were not in sufficient order to please him, and that he sold distant ones that he might put those nearer London in good shape; but of this the list of his possessions at death does not show much sign. That he was energetic, perhaps to too great degree, there is indication. Says a Sussex antiquary, "'The fishery of Cuckmere Haven was vested in the St.Clercs, lords of Firle and owners of Excete'" (Inquistion After Death, 1 Henry VI (1422), No. 30. Later the mayor of Rye had his battles over this fishery, but Thomas Sinclair had fierce legal business about rights there interfered with, and to his heirs the legacy of strife went down.

That he had the contemporary love of battle the following, if it refers to him, would go to show. It is taken from the Issue Rolls of 15 July, 4 Henry VI (1426). "'To John Vincent. In money paid to him for so much money expended, by command of the treasury of England, for expenses of twelve jurors of the county of Middlesex dining at Westminster, and there attending and waiting to give a verdict upon a certain inquisition taken, the lord the king and Thomas Seyncler, esquire, upon a certain security of the peace broken by said Thomas Seyncler; which verdict, so delivered by said jury before the treasurer and barons of the exchequer, the same Thomas was convicted for the lord the king in 100 marks. By direction of the treasury, etc - 13s. 4d.'"

It may be a libel to refer this to Thomas of Aldham St.Clere, but the date, circumstances, the esquire, which had then its meaning, and the large fine, for some quarrel such as could arise about the Cuckmere fishing, point in his direction. Besides, the time near Agincourt, and when Talbot was making his name so terrible in France, gave honour to men for vigour of this kind, while not forgetting to make them pay into king's treasuries for the amusement. It is probable also that, like his uncle Thomas, he was a soldier in the French wars; and if so, he knew the change of fortune the maid of Orleans, Joan of Arc, began in his twenty-eighth year. With his family's knowledge of the duke of Bedford, the regent, he could hardly have not been in those gallant struggles which followed so indecisively from her capture till the last years of the duke. Meanwhile he is not known as distinguishing himself there, though it is extremely probable that he died in France the early death of most soldiers. As lord of the manor of Stene he presented Simon Smyth to the incumbency 18th Feb 1427. He died on the 6th of May, 13 Henry VI (1435) age of thirty-four.

He had married Margaret Hoo, the daughter of Lord Hoo and Hastings, and left issue, three young daughters, he and they the last of this wealthy and distinguished branch of English Sinclairs. The history of these coheiresses and of their mother, will throw much light on the short life of Thomas; so that there is no fear of him being left, without justice done to his position as one of the landed magnates of his time.

Chapter XLV
Mother and Daughters

One of the writers of the Sussex Archaeological Collections has taken great trouble in tracing the lineage of Margaret Hoo, the wife of Thomas Sinclair; and he is justly proud of his success, as compared with the efforts of other genealogists in this particular inquiry. He has drawn up a table of pedigree, besides writing his careful paper; and to them for full knowledge it would be instructive to go. Sir William Hoo of Hastings had served three sovereigns in ambassadorial, diplomatic, and other distinguished ways during forty years. He died Lord Hoo and Hastings, 22nd November 1410, aged 75. His first wife was Alice de St.Omer, daughter and coheiress of Thomas de St.Omer, her mother being Petronella, coheiress of Nicolas, Lord de Malmaynes, of the baronial Kent family who came with the Conqueror, and who were heired chiefly by the Crevequeres, barons of Chatham and Leeds Castle. Sir William Hoo and Alice de St.Omer had Thomas, who succeeded his father, and in more ways than one.

When after fifteen years of war from the appearance of Joan of Arc both French and English grew exhausted, and a peace was desired in 1444, Sir Thomas Hoo, Robert, lord Ros, and others, went as ambassadors of England with De la Pole, earl of Suffolk, to Tours, according to Rymer's Foedera, and got a two years' truce, at the same time getting a queen, Margaret of Anjou, for Henry VI. In the roll of the knights of the garter, Sir Thomas Hoo, lord Hoo and Hastings, is entered as elected in 1445, and these services are the explanation of his K.C. In 1460 William, lord Hastings, had K.G. Sir Thomas had two brothers, John and William, and one sister, Margaret, who married the wealthy Thomas St.Clere, from which marriage the family of Gage is descended. The antiquary adds, "'The descendants of the daughter Margaret were ultimately the heirs of Thomas Hoo who died in 1486'". This was the last of the line.

Margaret's brother William was also a distinguished man, holding a command as Sir William Hoo in the Sussex contingent at the battle of Agincourt. He was knight to Lord Camoys, having both respectively, as money then went, 2s. and 4s. a day. Brady's Appendix has a table of pay from the prince at 20s. a day to the Welshman at 2d. But this was earlier, 20 Edward III, though little or no change occurred. The French war, for a year and one hundred and thirty-one days, had cost altogether only £127,101, 2s. 9d. Sir William and Thomas Sinclair of Grinstead, the uncle of Margaret's husband, were fellow-officers under Henry V on the memorable day.

It was the inquisition in Bedfordshire, where the Hoo from which the name came was, at the death of the last male, Thomas Hoo, in 1486, that gave the clue to the antiquary as to Margaret, the wife of Thomas Sinclair, the last of his branch. Sir Wilham Boleyn, aged 36, entered on his cousin Thomas Hoo's manors of Offley, Cokern-Hoo, and Hoo in Luton, under the feoffment of 10 Dec 1473; and the Bedfordshire jury found that he had for coheirs,

1. his cousin, aged 50 upwards, Elizabeth Lewknor, born Sinclair, the daughter of Margaret Sinclair, born Hoo, sister of Sir Thomas Hoo, knt., the father of this Thomas Hoo that died without issue.
2. William Gage, aged 40, the son of Alianor Sinclair, the next daughter of Margaret, wife of Thomas Sinclair.
3. Miles Harcourt, aged 18, the grandson of Edith Sinclair, youngest daughter of Margaret Hoo and the same Thomas Sinclair.

This Sir William Boleyn, first cousin to these three Sinclair ladies, their mothers being two sisters, was grandfather of Ann Boleyn, queen of England, Henry VIII's fortunate and unfortunate consort. His mother was Ann Hoo as theirs was Margaret Hoo. Tindal says "'Ann was the eldest daughter and coheir of Thomas, lord Hoo and Hastings'", and that she married Sir Geoffrey Boleyn who was "'lord mayor of London in 1458'". A Kent guide-book takes care to state that he was a tradesman. He is yet another connection for these Sinclairs with the city of London's mayoralty, but it is also the courtly connection, which unions became more and more common as feudalism grew milder by decay.

The English nobility is now made up much more of commercial than feudal blood, and the road to this was paved considerably by the Kent and Sussex nobles in particular. Sir William Boleyn himself was married to Margaret, daughter and coheir of Thomas Butler, earl of Wiltshire and Ormond: and it was through her that her son Sir Thomas Boleyn, the great ambassador of Henry VIII's reign, after being Viscount Rochford, got the title of earl of Wiltshire and Ormond, the father of the marchioness of Pembroke who became the queen, Ann Boleyn. Her mother was Elizabeth Howard, sister of the duke of Norfolk, and

Camden says her daughter Ann was born in 1507. Rapin declares that "'Ann Boleyn was of a good though not a noble family'", by which he must mean that Geoffrey the lord mayor was one of the people. After him, all that was noblest in England seems to have connected with the Boleyns. Ann Boleyn's daughter, Queen Elizabeth, the Gloriana of England's poetic age, could easily trace kin with these ladies, the daughters of Thomas Sinclair by Margaret Hoo; and the favour at court of their descendants is explainable thus, in good degree. But this is enough of anticipation, before returning to the history of the coheiresses after 1435, when their father died.

Elizabeth the eldest was then twelve, Edith the second eleven, and Alianor the youngest nine; their mother, Margaret Hoo, about thirty, able to give them every motherly care and devotion. Whether educated at home or by the religieuses of the famous four nunneries of England, whose abbesses were baronesses, might be discovered; but the public records find them quite equipped with, all the charms of womanhood, natural and acquired, the chief figures at what must have been a triple marriage in 1446, their ages twenty-three, twenty-two, and twenty. The division of their lands to the respective husbands took place on the eighth of July of the same year. To their father had come all the estates which gave names to the family, Igtham, Parvapreston, Farthingo, Stean, Aston-Clinton, Burstow, Aldham-St.Clere, East Grinstead, and the rest; and out of them provision had to be made for the young widow, and also for his sister Margaret, married to Thomas Pulteney, armiger, of the Ospring and Penshurst baronial family founded by Sir John de Pulteney, lord mayor of London. But enough remained after these and perhaps other similar claims were satisfied, to make the coheiresses the best prizes for loving husbands of the period.

- Elizabeth married William Lovel, a scion of the Lord Lovel and Lord Zouche families, and he got with her the manors of Brambletye, Lavertye, Excete, Nobbout-Seynt-Clere, all in Sussex; the manor of West Aldham in Kent; Wethersfield in Suffolk; the manor and advowson of Clopton in Cambridgeshire; the manors of Wodepreston and Hey ford, Northamptonshire; the rents, during the life of William Sydney, from Merden manor and Lageham manor, in Surrey, with similar rents coming from Devenish and part of Nobbout-Seynt-Clare in Sussex.
- Edith married Sir Richard Harcourt, of the earl of Oxford family of this name, and he had as her dowry the manor and advowson of Jevington, the manor of Lampliam, the manor of Brighthelmstone, now the watering-place of Brighton, the manor of Portesdale and that of Newnham, all in Sussex; Lageham

manor in Surrey; Ashby Magna and Willoughby manors, Leicestershire; and Chaldegrave, Oxfordshire.
- Alianor became the wife of Sir John Gage, to whom fell the manor of Heyghton, the manor of Hothye, and the advowson and manor of Torryng, in Sussex; the manors of Burstow, Heggecourt, and Merden, in Surrey; Wodeland in Kent; Aston-Clinton manor and Chenery, in Buckingham; and Wolde in Northamptonshire.

If comparison be made with the inquisition lists of the family properties in 1335, and again in 1408, both already given, it will be seen that the coheiresses did not by any means divide all among their husbands, princely though their dowers were. The Somersetshire estates must have remained with their mother, or gone to their aunt Margaret, as well as Igtham and various other manors which Thomas Sinclair is known to have possessed besides those mentioned. Lyghe manor in Kent he sold, or had to sell perhaps, from friendly or other cause, to the brother of Henry V, John, duke of Bedford, regent of England till the warlike Henry died, and afterwards that of France till his death at Rouen in 1435, the year in which Thomas Sinclair died. Bickmersh in Warwickshire had come to him from Sir Baldwin de Bereford; Covelingley, Caterham, Home, Wolksted, Tanrugge, and Godstone, where Diana's fountain gives back youth to London maidens, were his, in Surrey; in Kent he had Eythorne Court, and Hasted in his history gives the tale of a South Court which John de St.Clare held, 20 Edward III (1346), as one knight's fee from the castle of Eynesford (whose ruins were then large and remarkable), and which came to Thomas. This is indication to be added to what has been said before of the relation between the lords of Eynesford and these Sinclairs of Aldham.

Aldham St.Clere itself was at one period held from the castle of Eynesford, probably as being by a younger branch of the family which Thomas Becket's interference made the occasion of all that trouble to himself, and to his king, the greater martyr of the two. Hasted also gives account of Woodland, which came from "the lords of Kent", as by pre-eminence he calls them, the Crevequeres, to John, son to John St.Clere, in 9 Edward III (1336). Stone, too, in Buckinghamshire, called "Sentler's Stone" or "Sencler's Stone", which was shown to have been for many generations in possession of a branch of the Bradfield St.Clare lords in Suffolk, seems to have fallen by heir-general to this family. But there were difficulties about it, and opposition to some of their claims. Sir Philip of Burstow urged his right of presentation to St.Mary's Church there in 1407, but it was not admitted. Probably Wethersfield, Suffolk, came to him by the same connection. They had in Hartwell of this county, West

Orchardson or Seyntclares. Four miles from Newmarket they held in 1408 a St.Cleres in Cambridgeshire, and in Norfolk, Huntingfield. But antiquity, though singularly favourable to them, does not give up every point; and perhaps enough has been said for all purposes, their tale being quite safe in many records, books, and manuscripts of their country. That they had large share of Kent and Sussex in particular, is easily remarked.

Elizabeth Sinclair, the eldest daughter, married a second time. Richard Lewknor was her choice, and they built the Brambletye House which is so well celebrated by Horace Smith's novel of society, and whose ruins are now one of the favourite studies of artists. There are older and later portions of buildings about which there is antiquarian dispute, but there is no doubt that Lewknor and his lady were the founders of the mansion. The Lewknors were one of the best Sussex families, bearing knightly title and holding sheriffships and commissionerships to parliament frequently. Under various kings history shows that they held legal, court, and state offices. Sir John Lewknor was killed at the battle of Tewkesbury, 1471. Such heirships as Elizabeth's to Lord Hoo and Hastings must have aided considerably to their aggrandizement. On her death she was succeeded herself by a daughter of Lord Say, who was Sir Thomas Grey's widow, and one of the ladies of the queens of Edward IV and Henry VII. The historical associations connected not only with this but with many others of their manor-houses are endless. Within sight of Aldham-St.Clare the road of the pilgrims to St.Thomas' shrine at Canterbury went, and these coheiresses may well have had Chaucer's gay ambassadorial company at the beautiful home there, when he was gathering ideas as to the twenty-nine types of society then and ever. They could have seen the Jack Cade gatherings to revenge the loss of Normandy by putting the house of York, in other words the Mortimers, on the throne, from their castle-tower; and many a tear for slaughtered friends must the wars of the roses have cost them.

Edith Sinclair was not a long liver. Her husband Sir Richard Harcourt married a second and a third time, dying himself in 1487. His heir, however, was Edith's son, Sir Christopher. She had a daughter Anne who married Henry Fiennes, lord Say and Seal, a Kent neighbour, son of the learned high treasurer, James Fynes, lord Say and Seal, barbarously beheaded by Jack Cade in his rebellion of 1450. Lord Clinton and Say is the later title. There is a well near Kemsing which is called St.Edith's Well, and it is probable that the character of this one of the coheiresses is immortalized in the name. The history of the Harcourts, afterwards earls of Oxford, and in the heart of the good things, needs no illustration.

The youngest lady, Alianor or Eleanor Sinclair, was married to Sir John Gage, and went with him to found a home in England one of the most ancient and honoured by distinguished dwellers, Firle Place in Sussex. Sir John was a Yorkist, and figured like most of his descendants as a warrior. General Gage of the American independence war a century ago, is a more recent historical example. Their son William Gage died 1496, and was buried in the Greyfriars Church, London, having married Agneta, daughter of Thomas Bolney, armiger, M.P. for Sussex in 1459. Sir John Gage, the son of William, was knight of the garter, and elected in 1541 lord chamberlain to Queen Mary, the general who quashed the rebellion of Sir Thomas Wyatt; his wife, Philippa, daughter of Sir Richard Guildford, an equally distinguished man of the time.

Collins says that the first Sir John bought lands in Cirencester, Mursater, Sidington, and Brimsfield, Gloucestershire, "'and made a further addition to his estate by his marriage with Eleanor, daughter and heir of Thomas St.Clere, esquire, lord of the manor of Aston-Clinton in county Bucks, and Offspring in Kent'". In Henry VIII's reign Leland the antiquary speaks of Master Gage, "controller of the kinges howse", a descendant of the Gages, and says, "'One told me that much of the lande that Mr. Gage hath are landes of the S.Clares in Kente'". Leland gives further information about other counties where he inherited thus, and use of it will be made in due place. "'One told me that Mastar Gage hath miche of S.Clares lands in Kent'", is another version Hearne gives of his deciphered MSS. called the Collectanea, parts of which are lost and other parts difficult to master.

This Sir John Gage, K.G., was constable of the tower, and in the dissolution of the monasteries reported on Battle Abbey. The Sussex Archaeological Collections sings his praises greatly as not only knight of the garter and constable of the tower, but chancellor of the duchy of Lancaster, privy councillor to Mary, soldier and statesman previously to Henry VIII, his death taking place 1557, at the age of 77. The ancient MS. by his 3d son Robert, quoted in Burke's Peerage, is still more remarkable by its list of offices and honours. The Segraves or Sulgraves of Northamptonshire, prominent as governor of Scotland in Edward I's reign, and as chief justiciaries and other such officers of other reigns, seem to have been consanguineous with these Gages, originally of Gloucestershire. A Harleian MS., however, makes the first Sir John have a father John and a grandfather of the same name lords of Cirencester.

But these Gages, well known lately in all the English wars with France and America, have relations to other branches of the Sinclair lineage in the reigns of Henry VIII and his successors. The Peerages of Burke and Foster give plentiful details of their honours, lineage, and marriages. Two quarters of the shield of Viscount Gage have the arms of the St.Clere family, "Azure, the sun in splendour, or"; and the marriage which gained them has good genealogical treatment by the professionals. The historical MSS. commission of 1863 reported on the charters then in Lord Gage's possession; and of one in "box 5", it is said: "'24 Henry VI - To a deed of this date is the seal of William Lovell, Esq., of Rotherfeldgrey; the arms are barry, nebuly, quartering St.Clair (a sun in splendour)'". This is evidence of the connection of the Lord Lovell with the Lord Gage family through these Sinclair ladies. The court rolls of Heighton St.Clair in the times of Edward III, Henry IV, Edward IV, Henry VII, Henry VIII, and Elizabeth are still among the Gage documents, as well as bailiffs' accounts for Shovelstrode in East Grinstead in the time of Elizabeth, and for Heighton St.Clair in the reigns of Henry IV and Edward III.

As early as the eleventh century Earl Simon Sinclair is a witness to some of the family charters.

By the death of Thomas, the father of the coheiresses, those wide and numerous lands were lost to the Sinclair name irremediably, and the chief satisfaction is that so much wealth went to building up names for other English houses worthy of all the fortune which energy and gallantry deserve.

Chapter XLVI
William, Son of Hugo Pincerna

It is now returned to the other branch of the same lineage, whose chief estates at first were in Kent, and particularly in the lower part of the valley of the Medway, till it enters the Thames at Sheerness. In the person of Hugo de St.Clair the stock was left, the lord of Aeslingham in the reign of Henry II whom Thomas Becket singled out as one of his chief enemies, and whom, as one of the king's ministers, he had excommunicated. Hugo was shown to have been nephew to Hamo St.Clare, the dapifer; and Ralph of Ingulstadt in the X Scriptores, or X Chroniclers, gives his name in full as one of those who signed Stephen's charter to the kingdom in 1136. How he was related to Walter of Medway, father of Richard, king's chamberlain, of whom Thomas of Grinstead who died in 1435 was last landed descendant in Kent and Sussex, has also been indicated. Hugo was of the Hamoes, earls of Corboil, lords of Thorigny, lords of Granville, lords of Gloucester and Glamorgan, in direct succession. Walter of Medway, earl of St.Clere, was brother to Hamo, the father of Hamo Dapifer, viscount of Kent, and of Robert Fitz-Hamo, "knight of Rye", lord of Thorigny, Gloucester, and Glamorgan. It is thus that Hugo de St.Clare or Hugo Pincerna stood connected with those whose doings have just been described.

How Hugo Pincerna got, with many other estates, seven knights' fees of Eudo Sinclair the dapifer's lands, is explainable by similar relationship, which has already had treatment. The purpose was to follow from that twelfth century the successors of his branch, as far as knowledge could be got of them by considerable but by no means exhaustive search, the wealth of English record being not yet available enough. For example, this is an accidental entry rescued from the Great Roll of 1182 which will at once show how well such inquiries as the present might be completed if the whole series of the Great Rolls were under full literary command: "'Odo de Dammartin accounts for 500 marks for having the custody of the son and land of Hugo, king's butler or cupbearer; In the treasury 200 marks and he owes 300 marks; Great Roll, 28th Henry II'". To have the care of the son and land of Hugo Sinclair, Odo must have been, by marriage, of near affinity. William de Dammartin signed the charter of the earldom of Essex with William de St.Clere, given by Stephen to the second Geffrey de Mandeville; but a much more suggestive fact is that Manasseur de Dammartin held three knights' fees from Walter Sinclair of Medway's twenty, heired from Geffrey Talbot. This appears on the carta of Walter sent to Henry II, of whom Hugo was a favourite minister. Manasseur's son Odo was as neighbour not less than by affinity a fit and proper person to have the wardship of Hugo Sinclair's son, and the management of the lands till he came of age. His, for that period, heavy payment, is sufficient index of the wealth of Hugo Pincerna, the lord of Aeslingham. The scantiness of such happy accident of information leaves much untold. What this son's name was who is thus taken care of would be interesting and valuable.

In the notification upon the dedication of the chapel of Aeslingham in the Textus Roffensis there are Hugo, Philip, and Robert Sinclair, besides Hugo himself and his brother Roger of the name; and if any of these were his son it would be Robert, because Hugh and Philip were monks of Rochester. Probably a minor, which he must have been, could not sign documents, and in that case information is still lacking as to the name of his son and successor. We know that a Robert de Sancto Claro held then two knights' fees from Walter of Medway, and he is in all likelihood the signer, the Clovilles also, similar holders, adding their names. There is a Roger Pincerna in the Textus Roffensls who might be the brother mentioned, but nothing definite can be made of this, though his gift to Rochester of property in Plumstead has some aid of locality.

It is possible that this Roger was of an earlier period altogether, for Morant's History of Essex seems to give the right clue as to Hugo St.Clare's sons under his account of Danbury. The manors of St.Cleres and Heyrons there, were, he says, originally one, and a William Pincerna and Ralph de Heyron, who were brothers, possessed them towards the end of the twelfth century. In Essex Hugo and his successors gained considerable footing, especially opposite their Kent estates on the south side of the Thames. Palgrave's Rotuli Curiae Regis has account of a William at Greenwich engaged on cases of disputed lands. Four milites were usually summoned to elect twelve arbiters for decision. William de Broc is one of the disputants in a case, and William de St.Clare, William of Cloville, and Henry of Coddeham, since known better as Cobham, are some of those who act. William and Simon of Plesingehow require similar decision, and William de St.Clare and Roger of Cheny or Chesney are members of the deciding court, held at Greenwich also.

There is a third case in which William de St.Clare does the same duties at Greenwich. He pays his Essex taxes at Stratford, these rolls having reference to the years 1194 till 1199 in Richard I's reign. From Essex and Hartfordshire he pays in the Rotulus Cancellarii his share for those counties of the ransom for this monarch, 1196, "'Of the second shield-money for Richard: William Sinclair pays 30s.'". "'Of third scutage William Sinclair pays 30s. scutage: of his lands and military taxes William Sinclair owes 3 marks from the same'". These scraps are indication of similar doings at other times and in other counties which detailed inquiry could amplify for special purpose. His position is pretty well known by his immediate succession to his father Hugo, though his brothers may have curtailed the patrimony.

A Thomas St.Clare went to the East with King Richard, and died there. He has, however, been claimed for the Aldham St.Clere family on good grounds. Ralph has been referred to as dividing with him the property at Danbury, Essex, where there are monuments still of crusaders of their branch. Morant's general account of the name there has rather more reference to the Kent and Sussex than to the Kent and Essex branch, though it applies to both as to lineage. Says he, "'The family of St.Clere was of great antiquity in this kingdom: the lord of St.Cler being one of those officers that attended William the Conqueror into England'". He then gives such authorities as the Chronicle of Bromton, and the various other well-known sources of proof of this. It is Hugo de St.Clare he thinks signed the charter of Stephen, though his Essex leanings might be supposed to make him agree with Lord Lyttleton and his authority of the Cottonian MSS., that it was Hamo de St.Clair, the well-known castellan of Colchester Castle, and fee-farmer of that city. But he may only have met with Richard Prior of Hagulstad's Chronicle.

About this William the difficulty is that in King John's time he seems to have lost all his honours, according to the Liber Ruber. He had a park at Danbury, but it is certain that Aeslingham was his usual home. Besides Ralph who got Hesdon, part of St.Clere manor in Danbury, there were two other brothers at least. John, as Palgrave's Rolls from the King's Court show, held a fee from William Munchensi in Kent, as he from the see of Canterbury, and there was considerable dispute about its tenure in this court in Richard's reign. But Dunleia in the county was also his, as the Rotuli Chartarum, 9 and 10 John (1208-9) proves. There is among these rolls a charter of confirmation to Henry of Cobham "'from the gift and grant of John Sinclair, the whole tenement of John to him at Dunleia'".

About the time of Magna Charta, 1215, John would seem to have come into the position and honours of his elder brother William. It is he who follows John Marescall, the husband of Eleanor Sinclair, as "John, the son of Hugo", one of the sixteen nobles who advised King John to give the great charter of England's liberties, and whose names are on immortal record at the head of the venerable document. There was no Hugo in England of first magnitude except Hugo de St.Clare to whom John could be son then, the Hugh Bigods always being mentioned as such. Around him the fifteen names are of the sounds most familiar to his lineage, male and female, the Albineys, the Marshalls, the Bassets, Warrene, Fitzgerald, Hugh of Newton or Neville, and Hubert de Burgh. It were almost impossible that some one of the lineage could be out of such a closely-related gathering, for whatever purpose, and the advice Johannis filii Hugonis was altogether in place and keeping with the position of his kin.

But to return to his gift of Dunleia to a Cobham. The Coddehams or Cobhams of the early period are of close relationships with the Sinclairs, whether of like lineage or not; and this would seem further evidence to much already indicated. Sylvester Sinclair appears as the brother of John in signing a document of the Textus Roffensis, but of his lands or doings nothing more has been found. Large dividing must have occurred at this period, the name Sancto Claro being numerous in the records of the district near the Thames, especially on the south side. A Robert signs one of Henry of Cobham's charters to Rochester Church, but the date is not to be fixed, nor can he be said to be another brother of William Pincerna the son of Hugo de St.Clair of Aeslingham. In Dugdale's Monasticon William Pincerna gives Elham to the monks of Rochester, and with regard to the same property King Henry I gave a charter earlier through "'Hamo Dapifer and his faithful barons of Chent'".

The early history of Danbury and East Tilbury is obscure, but some streaks of light cross over them. This William Pincerna held the former and possibly the latter. Morant in his History of Easex says that the Kameseck or Kewseck family held East Tilbury, and that they also held Camseys and Great Sandford, in Essex. But in describing the manor of St.Cleres, East Tilbury, he says that it was "'so named from its ancientest owners on record'".

Camseys or Kamseys from which the Kamesks had their name, clearly a local one, was the Camoys Hall which Hamo Dapifer had for one of his residences; and as Hugo de St.Clare was his nephew, he must have heired this also. It was part of the Topefeld which the Bradfield St.Clare family held later. One of Hugo's younger sons is probably the first Edmund of the several who appear in this Camoys line, from whom Lord Camoys who held a command over the Sussex draft at Agincourt must have descended. East Tilbury went certainly for nearly a century out of the possession of William Pincerna and his direct successors, and it was not till Henry III's reign it came back to them, from their friends the Camoys or Kemescks, who appear in a Quo Warranto of Edward I on this very matter.

Danbury and East Tilbury are extremely interesting localities. Danbury is the highest hill in Essex, and was used as the watchtower for London against the Danes, Spanish, and other enemies from the sea. The Danes, from holding it at one of their successful invasions, gave it its name of the "fort of the Danes". The ruins of this fort are still discernible, and in its centre was afterwards built the church with its three figures of crusading St.Clares so dear to the antiquaries. The mansion of the family was a quarter of mile from this church.

Tilbury is remarkable for Queen Elizabeth's haranguing of her soldiers in expectation of the descent from the Spanish Armada. This scene on the north side of the Thames gradually and finally became the remarkable home of William's descendants, holding, as they did, in Essex greater possessions than in Kent, after some generations. But this will develop gradually as the successors appear.

Chapter XLVII
Governors of Rochester Castle

The successor of William Pincerna, the royal cupbearer, or of John, the baron of Magna Charta, was William; and he is known by the part he took in the wars of the barons, led by Simon de Montfort, earl of Leicester, against Henry III and his son Prince Edward, afterwards King Edward I. That he was a baron himself is proved by his signature to a charter of lands given to a Cobham in 30 Henry III (1246) written Dominus William de Sencler. Of this his history is further confirmation, if any more were necessary.

Immediately before the battle of Lewes, the royal army had come from the north (and from Oxford, the scholars of which suffered at its hands for sympathy with the barons, upholders of "the provisions") to the castle of Rochester to relieve it. It was besieged by Simon de Montfort, and defended by William de St.Clare, the governor, till the approach of Henry and his son the prince compelled the insurgent lords to raise the siege. William Sinclair died the same year, in possession of this office of castellan; and it is not improbable that he was either killed in the battle of Lewes, fought on the fourteenth May 1264, or in defence of the important stronghold of Rochester, which had already seen so much fight since the Norman Conquest. Not the least interesting part of its story is told in connection with the architectural bishop of Rochester in the time of Henry I. The king would not confirm Hedenham manor, Bucks, to the church of Rochester except by gift of a sum from the bishop of £100. The bishop would not agree, and Robert Fitz-Hamo Sinclair, then the first Englishman next to the sovereign at his court, compromised with the disputants by getting the bishop to build the additional part called from his name "Gundulph's tower", which he did for about £70, and got therefore confirmation of the manor, with other favours.

William de St.Clare had much tradition to make him be valorous captain of so renowned a castle, and so near his family's home, as Rochester. For situation on a mastering site in the varied and comparatively deep valley of the Medway, there like a regular basin around it, and for its impressive Norman architecture in white Caen stone, it is one of the finest and most picturesque relics in the country. It is now in the hands of the corporation of Rochester, which bought it recently for £8000 from the earl of Jersey, who stipulated that it should be kept as a ruin, and that the corporation would preserve its surrounding gardens in the same condition as when it was on lease to them at a yearly rental of £240. It has had a long eventful history, and as much as the tower of London the English people ought to watch so precious a monument of their Norman period.

If its governor of the middle of the thirteenth century, William Sinclair, had been its builder it would have noted antiquarian and national value, but it was grey and grand with age as now when he was its lord. The rebels coveted its strength in vain in 1264. In the official guide the following is to be found: "'Henry III entrusted William St.Clare with the custody of this castle, whose ancient seat was at Woodlands, in Kingsdown parish, in this county'". That in 1228 it was held by Hubert de Burgh might have come from the marriage of his son to the daughter of William Langvalee, her mother being the daughter of Sir Hubert Sinclair, constable of Colchester Castle, who saved Henry II's life by expending his own during the siege of Bridgenorth. But there may have been political rather than property reasons for the justiciary of England to be constable of Rochester Castle.

Of Simon de Montfort's attack upon it just before the battle of Lewes in 1264, it has been told that the earl of Leicester made a furious assault upon the castle, but the brave governor and his associates defended every inch of ground with so much ardour and resolution that, although Leicester made himself master of some outworks by burning the bridge and its wooden tower, he was unable to succeed after a siege of seven days with his whole army. The tenure of its lands in this and other counties was perfect castle guard, and every tenant who did not pay his rent on old St.Andrew's Day was liable to have it doubled for the return of every tide of the Medway. It was probably on these terms William Sinclair dealt with his castle vassals. His death at the critical period had its effect, but success went to his side of the struggle by the battle of Evesham in 1265.

The strange thing is that his son, also William, is as vigorous on the parliament's side, and suffers accordingly on the turn of the wheel. Of him there is a good deal known. It was he and not his father who was the William de Sancto Claro indicted at Chelmsford in 1255 for having knight's fees and not being knighted. The Liber Ruber speaks of him as having no honours, and it was the advantage in those periods of English history to keep out of such prominence as long as one could, taxes being less, and the demands upon a man being generally the milder. That he was a person of strong individuality several things besides this indicate. His indictment may have helped to estrange him from the cause of Henry III, of whom his father was so strenuous a supporter. As a knight he followed Simon Montfort to the battles of Lewes and Evesham; and having possession of his patrimony at the latter fight, he lost all, as is shown by this transaction from the Curia Sccacarii of 51 Henry III (1267) two years after the battle of Evesham: "'William Sinclair: The extent of his lands which by reason of transgressions charged against him the king had given to Baldwin of Hackney'".

But the Great Rolls of Henry III gives further information about William's peculiar fortunes at that critical period. The sheriffs took possession of his lands in East Tilbury soon after "'soon after the battle of Evesham, at the instance of the earl of Gloucester, and the said William Sinclair made a settlement with the said count, and kept his land'". Roger Clare made possession easy for him, and reasons are not difficult to find beyond the natural ties of blood between them. They were both on the side of the barons at Lewes, and the king or his son must have showed suspicion of the favour experienced, for afterwards the roll says, "'My lord the king gave that land to Baudwin D'akeney'". To this reference has been made already. But the roll ends by showing that the same William de St.Clare redeemed that land from Baldwin of Hackney and retained it. If all is well that ends well it was not without great energy that he escaped being finally one of "the disinherited", as the barons who lost their properties at that time were called. Between the time he was possessed by the earl of Gloucester and dispossessed again by the king, he had drawn returns, but this did not prevent the successful invasion of royalist Baldwin from the neighbouring quarter of Hackney coming east upon him at Tilbury.

The difficulties of his relation, baron John Sinclair of Bradfield, at the same time, 51 Henry I (1150), one of the isle of Ely marauders, well got over, must have aided William in Essex and Kent. In the Patent Rolls in the Tower of London of 1267 this is found: "'The king has restored to William de St.Clare all his inheritance'"; which is a kind of quod erat demonstrandum to this passage of biography. Morant says that in Essex he held, 51 Henry III (1266), St.Cleres, East Tilbury, and Coringham, and also that he had a park at Danbury. It was this year he died, and the Calendar of Inquisitions after Death gives the list of his inheritance under the heads of Estilberry, Danigbury, and the lands and liberties of the castle of Rochester. It is, however, doubtful whether he was able to be at that time, in the circumstances in which he had been placed, de facto governor, as he was it de jure. His early death so soon after his possessions were regained, must have made in any case his governorship and residence there of the shortest. The actual holding of the lands of the castle at his death, answers all doubts as to his position; like his father, governor of the most historic stronghold in the most characteristic spot in England.

Further, the William who succeeded these two Williams would get his father's inheritance; though there was nothing in history to bring him forward in the military character. It is in civil capacity he wrought most, as now discernible. In 1279, twelve years after he succeeded to his patrimony, he was sheriff of the counties of Essex and Hertford; and before this his name is noticed in connection with disputed lands, and especially as to a half-fee about which he was arbiter on the part of his relation William Mountchesney or Monte Canisio, the same people probably as the lords Chesney so familiar to early Kent. In the Quo Warranto of 2 Edward I, 1274, he himself holds two half knight's fees from this William Mountchesney in the hundred of Shamele, Kent. *"'Also William Sinclair holds half a fee in Merston from William Montchesney by underholding, and the same William of the king, in chief, and it is worth ten pounds a year: And that William Sinclair holds half a fee in Higham from William Montchesney by underholding, and the same holds from the king in capite, and it is worth per annum 100 s.'"*.

His transactions about lands are of curiously incomprehensible character. Through Cicely Sinclair, the wife of Ralph of Osyth, a sister or some near relation, he got in 1266 Chichridell and other manors near St.Osyth, Essex, and also some property of hers at East Tilbury. The East Tilbury portion, Morant found in some ancient record, consisted of 140 acres of arable land, 8 of meadow, a marsh for feeding 200 sheep, 50s. 2d. rent assize, and a windmill. This portion of East Tilbury was held from Humphrey de Bohun, earl of Hereford and Essex. But East Tilbury contained several knights' fees, and all is explainable if these Sinclairs from Hugo or Hamo Dapifer's time had one portion, and added subsequently to this as opportunities came.

In 1285 an Edmund of Kemesck or Camoys certainly held the greater part of East Tilbury, and Kemescks of Camoys Hall also fell heirs by relationship to Hugo's uncle, Hamo Dapifer. They may have been Crevequers by the sister of Hamo already noticed. In the records of a Quo Warranto court at Colchester, 13 Edward I (1285), particulars are given. "'Edmund of Kemesck or Camoys was summoned to answer to his lord the king, by what warrant it seemed good to him to claim as heir the frank-pledge and returns of corn milled in Estillberry, without the assent and wish of his lord the king: And Edmund appeared: And says that a certain William Sinclair held the said manor to the end of his life, by the grant of Edmund himself: He says also that Edmund himself and all his predecessors, from a time of which no memory remains, held the said liberties in the said manor: And he showed no special warrant from his lord the king: And William of Chiselham, who summed up for the king, said that the liberties of it depended on the crown, and they were allowed to no heir without the special warrant of the king'". The justice, William of Chiselham, sent him to the king's court for final decision; but of this there appears nothing. No doubt when John Warren, earl of Surrey, opened Edward I's eyes as to the tyranny of these proceedings, by openly drawing his sword in court and declaring that by that he held like his ancestors his lands, and when the judicious king stopped the inquisitions, Edward de Camoys got all his liberties without challenge. John Warren gave the further valuable warning, that the Conqueror himself had his lands as only a comes among their ancestors as comites, and Quo Warranto business was put out of court for that reign.

It would seem that William Sinclair had neither this nor the other parts of East Tilbury returned, by the post-mortem calendar of his lands. He died 11 Edward I (1283) possessed of Danehoberry Park alone in Essex, Chichridell and its related manors at St.Osyth had gone out of his hands also, and the presumption is that his Kent lands and Rochester Castle privileges went over to others, probably his relations. Besides Higham, Merston, and Green manor, he had Great Okeley manor and Little Okeley, as no doubt much more in the western angle the Medway makes with the Thames, the stem-land of a little world of his lineage. Misfortune, extravagance, or, being without children, generosity to his relations, suggest themselves as to his strange doings.

In Norfolk particularly all kinds of discoveries are on the verge of his actions, yet without satisfaction quite solid as to him and his people. Between this county and Kent there is a continual state of business for the Pincernas or Butlers, as they began to be called, of which lineage he was; and he may have made the fortune of the famous earls of Ormond and Ossory, while giving away his own. These Butlers are said to be descended from a butler of one of the earls of Leicester by some of the modern Peerages, and Theobald, king's butler at the coronation of Henry II, is mentioned as one of them. It is not likely. Never was it so difficult as then to get good place without birth of the highest kind; and, besides that the Pincernas or Botelers were mostly a Kent race, it is all but certain that this line of Hugo St.Clair, king's butler or pincerna, the descendants of the Hamoes and Fitz-Hamo of the ducal house of Normandy, is one with the Butlers of West Wickham,Kent, earls of

341

Wiltshire, and with those distinguished men of Ireland. Theobald, archbishop of Canterbury, was possibly one of them, first names being much weightier than now that surnames are general.

In 1270 this William Sinclair of Danbury Park married one of the two coheiresses of Nicolas Pincerna or Nicolas the Butler or Nicolas le Boteler, and got the half with her of Walcote Hall, North Burlingham, Wilton, Swalfield, Burgh Hall, Butlers or Herewards, and Upton. North Walsham, Blomfield says in his History of Norfolk, he got, as himself heir to the half of Sir Richard Butlers land there. His marriage, as was so much the Norman way in their desire to hold and increase their lands, was therefore a lineage one. In Burgh Hall there was Nicolas Pincerna or Le Botiler, he says, before the last Nicolas who died in 1250 lord of this and other manors.

In 1242 William Sinclair, governor of Rochester Castle, the father of this William, had possession of half of Burgh Hall, and sold it to William of Heveningham, Suffolk. The rights of it were afterwards gained by Guy de Botetourt, whose descendant was made a baron, 9 Edward III (1336), on the aggrandisement it gave. The husband of the other coheiress, Adam of Brancaster, followed the sheriff in all his transactions about these properties, Guy getting much from him also. The older Nicolas Boteler or Pincerna had a part of Swafield, which the sheriff's father sold to William of Heveningham as early as 1232, having heired it from Nicolas. But a clean sweep of the coheiresses' lands was made in 51 Henry III (1267), three years after they were married. The son William of the William of Heveningham who had already bought much at an earlier period, purchased and got every inch both husbands acquired by their wives, why or how it is impossible to see. North Walsham, of which the half fell to William de St.Clere from Sir Richard Butler, William conveyed by line to William the younger of Heveningham in 1273, "'to be held of him and his heirs by the service of a sparrow-hawk'". They also had Suffolk lands by the coheiresses, which went similarly.

William Sinclair and Felicia Butler his wife had no heirs as far as can be traced, and this may account for favours to William of Heveningham, who was a magnate of the eastern counties. The puzzle is made still more perplexing by Felicia Butler his widow advancing a claim in 1285 over the Suffolk and Norfolk estates of her father thus disposed of. The claim was for something she called her "dower", which she contended had not gone with the rest at transfer. That the husband and wife had reduced themselves to poverty is an impossible supposition, and yet this claim of something shadowy by the widow two years after his death in 1283, points to that. Danbury Park went to his male heir, a brother or nephew, as well as the Kent and other chief manors. In the Inquisitions ad Quod Damnum of 11 Edward I Williemus de Sancto Claro appears; and as late as 18 Edward I, 1290, seven years after his death, in these same records, Inquisitiones ad Quod Damnum there is suggestive notice of him.

Before dealing with this, however, something may be said of the William of Giselham who was the king's justice over the Tilbury affair. Edward I had been three years beyond sea before returning to England in 1289, and he found, or pretended to find, great evils in the dispensation of justice, from the chief justiciary Weyland downwards. What makes his punishment of so many able men suspicious, is the immense fines he put upon them all. A clerk of the court, Stretton, was fined no less than 32,000 marks besides jewels and silver plate. Such a vein of cash as this the royal heart and need could hardly be expected to spare, the Jews no longer being oppressible. Indeed they were banished next year for the very reason of impecuniosity, or possibly to secure by confiscation, as the king did, their immovable goods in England.

Sir Ralph of Hengham, chief justice of the higher bench, a descendant of Hubert Sinclair, castellan of Norwich, was fined 7000 marks, on similar accusation to that for which Lord Bacon suffered. The Chronicle of Dunstable MSS. and Wikes give eleven others who lost their offices of the very first rank. Such a swoop has never fallen before or since on the highest personages of the administration of law, and it is far more likely that political chicanery or violence was at the bottom of it than corruption among so many knightly and distinguished men. Sir William of Giselham, who had made his fortune with Edward by being an enthusiastic Quo Warranto inquisitor, got, four years after the Tilbury decision, a seat as judge on the king's bench. He was of a Kent family, and it is of genealogical interest to find his father, John of Chiselham, in a Cottonian MS. as a witness to the confirmation of a charter to Rochester see by Geffrey de Say, son of Geffrey de Say and Alicia de Chemuney, side by side with such signatirres as William, son of Henry of Cobham, and Hugo Pincerna. Henry Bray, judge and escheator for the Jews' treasury department of the nation, suffered a fine of 1000 marks at a time when the imposition of tallages and all other manners of collection shows the crown at its wit's end for money.

Edward had the skill to use parliaments for his purposes. He was just opening the drama of political scheming which the state of the Scottish monarchical succession offered him.

But to return to the lord of Danehoberry Park. He is twice mentioned in the Inquisitions ad Quod Damnum of 18 Edward I (1290) "'John, the son of Simon, executor of the will of William Sinclair in favour of the chapel of Danbury'"; and again, "'William Sinclair gave land for making a chantry'". Such glimpses are at Danbury helpful to give outline of the kind of man he was; and in his generosity to the cause of the religion of his time, he seems to have had the hereditary spirit of his people well developed.

The chapel of Danbury is one of the most historically interesting ruins in the kingdom, and it enhances its claims on consideration that this sheriff of Essex and Hertford, so incomprehensible, and still so comprehensible, in his doings and character, had a hand in part of its foundation and in its permanent support. It was his family chapel, and he fully realised his duties in regard to it. But there are no grounds for believing that his patrimony in largest part, and his acquirement of estate with his wife, coheiress of Nicolas Pincerna, left him, by fanatical enthusiasm for dying to endow college, cat, or chapel. The shapeliness of the Norman nature, which never forgot either secular or religious duty, had in him also a sufficient representative. The crusading ecstasies were over before his time, else this might be explanatory of his transactions. It was his forefathers who took the cross, three of whom already had their monuments in Danbury Chapel, to inspire him with the pietas which is next to the divinest thing in man.

Chapter XLVIII
Robert, Nicolas, and John

Morant says that in 1301 Robert de S.Claro or St.Clere possessed the manor of St.Cleres in East Tilberry, which was of the extent of one knight's fee, held under Bohun, earl of Hereford. To him also came the manor of St.Cleres, Danbury; but it is impossible to fix what relation he was to William its former possessor, called the lord of Danbury Park, the sheriff, whether son, nephew, or further. There was no want of heirs to any of the name at that time and place, and this implies nearness. His executor, Simon, the son of John, was probably of his lineage in the Northampton connection. His son's wife leaves money to Robert de Sancto Claro.

Hasted in his History of Kent mentions that Robert held Merston in that county in the reign of Edward I, and that it was one knight's fee held from Warin de Montchenzie. It is he who is a witness with Hugo de Windsor, vicecomes Kanciae, Henricus de Gren, and others to a charter by Henry of Cobham to Rochester see.

But there is earlier, and entirely trustworthy, knowledge of Robert Sinclair in the Placita de Quo Warranto of 21 Edward I (1292), com "Kanc". This is eight years before the notice of him as at East Tilbury. Near Rochester on the north side of the Medway, Hoo is, and of it the abbot of Reading monastery had part or whole, which the king's justice de quo warranto, challenged as belonging to the king. Robert of Higham and Robert de Sancto Claro, milites, and neighbouring proprietors, were of the jury to settle the question.

But this is only one of a series of such transactions for Robert. These two are part of a jury about Peeche being the property of Lesnes Abbey. The prior of Canterbury had to answer as to his rights over Estrie, which is one of the furthest to the north-east of the holdings in Kent of Adamus, filius Huberti, in the record of Domesday Book, near Sandwich and Deal. The abbot of St.Catherine's, Canterbury, was challenged to show his right to the advowson of the church of Selling. If this is Cellinge or

Cowling, the church of which had Adam Pincerna for its first patron, Robert ought to know its history well, being in his own special angle of Kent, and at one time, if not then, on his or his family's lands. He is one of the jury sworn, and supports the abbot's right to it; and he must have, from his influence and knowledge, largely aided the abbot to prove his right, which he did, and was established in it. Something closer to his family history still, appears when he is one of a jury who support the right of Henry de Grey to the manor of Eylesford with its pertinents.

Unlike many of that period, Henry has a charter to meet such challenging, which was given to his grandfather Richard; but he is none the worse of the aid he gets from Robert de St.Clair, who knows both sides of the Medway as only traditional memories of the noblest kind can inspire. As "Sir Robert de Seynt Cler" he is once again engaged in these Quo Warranto troubles in connection with the manor of East Chalk, Kent, which had and has many associations with the name he bore. This is the Celca which Adam Sinclair, commissioner of The Domesday Book, holds in that record, as he holds likewise the above Colinge, Bicklei, and the Hegham still in Sinclair possession, all of Maidstone hundred.

Hubert Sinclair, the hero of Bridgenorth Castle, gave part of it to the monks of the famous monastery of Bermondsey, Southwark, London, as an extant Harleian charter shows. His daughter's son, William of Langvale or Longueville, confirmed his gift. The husband of his daughter Hawyse, Sir John de Burgh, son of Hubert de Burgh (Shakespeare's "gentle Hubert", who could not kill Prince Arthur at the tower, and whose honours and glories would burden a Spaniard to bear) and of Margaret the king of Scotland's daughter, gave the rest of the manor of Chalk to the monks of Bermondseye. Here Edward I by his judges is challenging the prior of St.Saviour's, Bermondsey (a church since noted by being the marriage-scene of James I of Scotland and his love of the King's Quhair) to show right to the manor and its pertinents.

With Sir Robert's aid on such a question only one conclusion could be arrived at, namely, that the prior's right was inviolable; but it serves to show the eagerness with which this hated search after flaws of title to lands was pursued, that so remarkable a property as this did not escape querying. Sir Robert had three milites as his companions in getting to their conclusion by jury in the prior's favour.

After two hundred and seven years, this Sinclair still possesses some of the commissioner's property as described in The Domesday Book; and his brother Nicolas took his local name from Oare in the Faversham hundred, of which Adam entered himself as possessed, holding it from

Odo, the bishop of Bayeux. There is hardly a place in the whole sweep of Kent, except perhaps the extreme north-east, which at some time has not had associations with the name as holding land; but the Medway to wide extent on both sides was always the favourite district.

Both Sir Robert and Nicolas appear together in another of the transactions in the Placita de Quo Warranto. Ralph, the son of Bernard, one of the Fitz-Bernards so distinguished in the Irish Conquest and by state offices, gave a charter to Radulph Pincerna, and Ralph is challenged to show his title to Kingsdene, Otterdene, another of Adam Sinclair's holdings in The Domesday Book. The charter was of Henry II's time, when the Fitz-Bernards were at their height; and this possessor surely is fully entitled to what he has. The result was that Ralph had more right than the king to Kingsdene, Otterdene.

Both Robert de Seincler and Nicolas Sinclair of Ore appeared in favour of their relation, Ralph Pincerna. He is of the eldest line, and heirs Hugo Pincerna's office, though less is known of him than of them. Offices grew obsolete, and he became founder of some of the Kentish Butlers in all probability, and in this name-dress they are no more to be followed with certainty. They might be the Butlers of West Wickham, once held by Adam, the commissioner, which property rich Sir Samuel Lennard held after, progenitor of an earl of Sussex, and related to the lords Dacre. They seem the Butler earls of Wiltshire.

The latest notice there is of Robert Sinclair has to do with Essex. The abbot of St.Ann's, Colchester, has to get "the concurrence of the whole convent", before some transaction about land can be completed. This was 3 Edward II (1310); and like his time, he would then be making provision for his soul in the prospect of death. There was a St.Cleres manor near Colchester which was in his possession.

Of Nicolas some further reliable items have survived. His name Nicolas was frequent among the Pincernas or Botelers, which is some aid to reflection; and the remarkable Fitz-Nicholases of several reigns, dapifers and other similar state officers, look in the same direction for origin. Hasted says that Great Okely and Little Okely were held by William Sinclair in 1279 from Montchesney and the bishop of Rochester, and that soon after these estates were possessed by different branches of this family. Great Okely he says descended to Nicolas Sinclair, and after some time Little Okely also became his.

In 20 Edward III (1347) Little Okely was possessed by John Sinclair, who paid aid for making the Black Prince a knight in that year. Rev.

Thomas Cox, the antiquary, in Magna Britannia, says that this John held them united, and that he also held Merston manor, and a quarter of knight's fee in the same district as from Swanscombe Castle of the Montchesnies. They had other properties, like Oare, in Kent; but John came also into possession of the Essex properties, being holder of them in 1334.

Great Okely was some time in the possession of Walter Neale of London, a relation of the wife of Nicholas. It finally left the Sinclair name with John's life, but on what ground is obscure. In Berry's MS. Genealogies of Kent he was married to Elizabeth Colepepper, daughter of Sir Anthony Colepepper of Bedgeberry. Her mother was Constantia Chamberlain, daughter of Sir Robert Chamberlain, Sussex. It was to Sir Richard Chamberlain that Margaret Louvaine, the wife of Sir Philip Sinclair of Burstow, was previously married; but that was not the first tie of afiinity between the families. Were it not too easy an inference, the stronger tie of consanguinity might be suggested, in connection with Richard Sinclair, of Hastings fame, the king's chamberlain.

It will throw light back over much that has been hinted of this kind, if a passage be given from the General History of the Kings and Queens of England by Francis Stanford, Lancaster herald, with additions by Samuel Stebbing, Somerset herald, and published in 1707, when such subjects were closely searched after. The authority of two specialists besides, cannot but be weighty. "'In The Domesday Book in the exchequer, surnames (so termed by the French because they were superadded to the Christian name) are first found, and were brought from France to England by the Normans who not long before took them: many of which were noted with de such a place of their habitation, as, Alberic de Vere, Walter de Vernon, Gislebert de Venables; or with filius, as Gulielmus filius Osberni, Richard Fitz-Gilbert, and Robert Fitz-Hamo (the father of this Mabel who being Frenchified looked upon it as a high disgrace to take a husband without his two names); several also taking surnames from their offices, as Eudo Dapifer, Gulielmus Camerarius, Herveus Legatus, Radulphus Venator. There may not be much more than impression in this, and it certainly cannot be pressed in respect to those sirs Chamberlain of Oxford and Sussex."

Sandford's reference in parenthesis to the daughter of Fitz-Hamo, Mabel or Matilda Sinclair, is in relation to his quotation of the rhymes of the chronicling Robert of Gloucester, who puts them into the mouth of the lady when sought in marriage by Robert, the son of King Henry Beauclerc, his suing being ultimately successful: '

> "'Sir, sheo said, well ich wote your hert upon me is,
> More for myne heritage, than for my self, I wis;
> And such heritage as ich have, hit were to me grete shame,
> To take a Lord but he liadde any surname:
> Sir Robert le Fitz-Hayme my Faders name was ... '"

and so on goes the lively monk for pages, making all happy at the end like a good-natured modern novelist. There cannot be a doubt that many of our noblest surnames took their origin from offices, though perhaps Sandford could have missed Dapifer as a good illustrative example.

The Colepeppers were a remarkable family of Kent and Essex. In 1321 Thomas Colepepper was governor of the castle of Leeds, in Kent, when Edward II deceitfully attacked it in his quarrel with the barons. Having taken it he hanged the governor and his officers. This misfortune made the fortunes of a family who appear frequently in subsequent history. Berry says John St.Cleere, married to Elizabeth Colepepper, died without issue. The families are again knit in friendly bonds, as will show by degrees.

There is a John Sinclair of Hardaness, Kent, who had close relations to Hethe and various localities near; but it would be difficult to identify him. He is mentioned frequently in the Report of the Historical MSS. Commission, especially in connection with the endowment of a chapel of St.Clare on Hardness property. This is the Upper and Lower Hardres of the present, quite close to Canterbury.

There was a William Sinclair also holding property in Essex, but nothing genealogical can be made of him, only one scanty note surviving of his life. It is extant in the Bodleian Library, Oxford, among the codices manuscripti of Roger Dodsworth, vol. XXX. "'Charter between William Sinclair and John Sutton, knight, concerning the advowson of the church of Tendring, made at Colchester'". Its date is 2 Edward III (1329) and if William was a clergyman he need not further be referred to, the lineage then being able to supply a number of such, though now so few. The above description of the charter, however, would imply proprietorship, and the district is recorded as some time afterwards in the hands of the Tilbury people.

Chapter XLIX
Coroner of Kent

In his Political Vocabulary, Maunders says that the coroner and sheriff took the place of the older ruling earl of counties, and that the coroner had to be a knight. Green, in his History of the English People, gives Hubert Walter, bishop of Salisbury, the credit of creating the office in the reign of Richard First. The bishop, as premier, took the pleas of the crown from the sheriff, and gave them to the coroner, "a new officer". The title itself implies attention to the king's interests as chief object, and it was later that duties of inquest came to be considered principal. There was a law, Maunders adds, that the coroner must be possessed of high influence and large lands in the county for which he acted. John de St.Clair fulfilled these conditions, and more; for he is a baron or dominus in the Hundred Rolls. His antecessor, and some successors, may be grouped around him as central figure. He held office under Henry III, who died in 1272, and also under his son, Edward I.

Thomas Sinclair of Aeslingham manor was his antecessor, the Frindsbury of later times. That it was a ruling centre of Kent there can be no better proof than that Pinindene was in it, where the great law-suit de terris was held, Lanfranc, the archbishop of Canterbury, against Odo, William the Conqueror's brother, bishop of Bayeux. Whether as being eldest or younger son, gavelkind not unknown in his time, Thomas got possession of the chief seat of Hugo St.Clare, his ancestor, cannot be decided. In the Textus Roffensis there is a charter of the prior and convent of Rochester, to which Thomas de St.Clair is a witness. Nicolas of Ore, the brother of Sir Robert Sinclair of Estilberry and Merston, the latter estate bordering on Aeslingham, also signed this document; and the facts must have been that they were three brothers, and had received their portions, "fees being all partible", as they are found locally named. To the chapel for which Hugo got the notification and grants of privilege from the bishop of Rochester, Hugo left a charter, which is confirmed by Thomas in 1289. The church of Frindsbury or Aeslingham must have been this same chapel, and it gave returns to the see of 100 marks yearly, which is considerable evidence of the importance of it and its surroundings. He granted Nelefield, Kent, to it. Hasted says that John, the second bishop of Rochester, dedicated St.Peter's Church, Aeslingham, as part of other favours, to Hugo St.Clare, who paid liberally in return.

Of John, the coroner, his successor at Aeslingham, more is known. Next to putting down nationalities, the greatest of the Plantagenets was remarkable for his desire to put down the lawyers. From the Hundred Roll and Quo Warranto inquisitions, instituted at the beginning of his able reign, to the commission of trail-baton, or "draw the staff on them", in 1305, cudgelling all those who held legal offices on slight or no occasion, was his favourite relaxation from the bloodier, equally unjust, cudgellings of war of this "hammer of Scots", and of Cambrians besides. His extreme respect for the purity of law could be interpreted on commercial principles, perhaps; but there always was, and will be, jackal's provision for such lions of scrupulosity as this King Edward.

John Sinclair the coroner's busy public life could not possibly escape the envy of some detractors, and in the Quo Warrardo rolls he is found arraigned on the most trivial injustices, or supposed acceptances of too much for the performance of his duties as coroner.

- In the half hundred of Bernefield, county of Kent, the jury, jurati, say that John de Saint Cler took from the half-hundred of Bernefield eighteen pence for making an inquisition de infortunio, and retained the money.
- In the hundred of Brenchesle, county of Kent, the jurati say that when Richard Horsman was slain, John de Saint Claro took four shillings from the hundred for burying him and for the inquest; and also that the same John took from the hundred half a mark for John of Mettlefield for the same duties.
- In the hundred of Chatham, then in the list of Aylesford, county Kent, the jurati say that John de Seint Cler, who was coronator in the time of King Henry, took four shillings from the men of Gren more than they wished, for purifying the church of Gren from two criminals, who had fled to the altar there, for the murder of Adam of Stretton, and John of Aldinge, clergyman.
- In the hundred of Eyhorne, county Kent, the jurafi or sworn men also say that Lord John Sinclair, coroner ("dns Joh de Seint Cler, coronator", in the record), took from the burgh of Stokebir, in the exercise of his office, three shillings for burying William, the son of John of Bykenore, slain; and for a certain dead man slain in Frethenestede, five shillings; and for the death of Roger of Edelonde in Holingeburn, four shillings; in the same manner also

for John Kemblelof, his chaplain, for the same duties, two shillings; and for the death of Stephen, filius Pollard, in Selve, etc.
- In the hundred of Ho or Hoo, in the list then of Aylesford, county Kent, the jurati say that John de Sancto Claro, coroner in the list of Aylesford, took from the burgh for performing his duty for Henry Prude four shillings; and the same John took from the burgh four shillings in respect to Robert le Hok for the same; and from the town of Stoke, for the same, two shillings for the same duty; and again from the town of Stoke, for the same, two shillings.
- In the hundred of Twyford, county Kent, the jurors also say that (in rather hieroglyphical Latin) the meaning seems to be, that the coroner, Lord John Sinclair, would not perform his duties till he was first paid, and that in his time he had drawn for them, from this hundred of Twyford, the exorbitant sum of twenty shillings.

Without remembering that land was at 3d. an acre then in Kent, and that 6d. a head was a tax in full of all demands of the king's treasury for a year, enough to raise a rebellion like Wat Tyler's, the consideration of these charges of the coroner cannot be well understood. But with that in mind, these complaints of the populace are on their very face absurd, and the coroner was triumphant over this small attack upon his public integrity. In Brady's Appendix he appears as Magister Johannes de Sancto Claro in 25 Edward I (1297); and Edward was not the man to have him promoted into his intimate court business if he were not of the very best metal. He signs Letters of Protection of the Clergy, with the king, at Langley.

That he underwent a challenge of Quo Warranto in the young enthusiasm of the new king was a fate common to him with John Warren, earl of Surrey, and many another of the most dignified and historic men in the kingdom; and, for all Edward's energy, they had the impudent radicalism of the thing sent to its own place long before the end of the reign. The criticism to which Edward subjected his best legal officers and in capite holders would have turned any less able and less popular monarch infallibly off the throne, and, as it was, he left a legacy of discontent that took centuries to quiet. It was under number ten of the articles of inquiry put into the hands of his commissioners of the great seal, 11 Oct, 2 Edward I (1273), that the king challenged the coroner of Kent, Dominus Johannes de Sancto Claro, viz., "'Exactions and oppressions of sheriffs, escheators, coroners, and other ministerial officers under pretence of law'". Let a commission be armed now, or any time, with such a weapon, and summon popular juries, and what is to be expected ? Sheriff Aristides or Coroner Camillus would be hunted into exile.

The illustration of thirteenth century life given by the coroner's appearance in these Hundred Rolls is sui generis, and does him not a particle of discredit, but, to judicious interpretation, honour as an earnest and exact man, having no love of oppression, but of order, and of the means required to keep it at its due tension. He married the fourth daughter of Baron Camville of Clifton, Nicolaia Camville or Campvill. The Harleian MS. 807 by Robert Glover, Somerset herald, of the sixteenth century, calls her father Dominus William de Campvill, and he had properties in Kent as well as in the west. Gerard de Camville was viscount or sheriff of Lincolnshire in 1194, of which office as well as the castle of Lincoln he was dispossessed that year; and Richard de Camvilla was one of the barons who signed the constitutions of Clarendon, as may be seen readily in Stubbs' Select Charters. William was the last baron, the male issue having failed; and the barony being in abeyance among the co-heiresses, Nicolaia had ultimately heired the title for her husband, if he had not already had baronial rank. Hamon de Crevequer, "lord of Kent", got the wardship in Henry III of the heir of Thomas de Kanvill of the same family. The Crevequers, by their mother, the sister of Hamo Dapifer, heired their uncle, so that this was connection by John on some of the old lines of relationship. Dominus Johannes de Sancto Claro is one of the signatures to the returns from the bishop of Rochester's feu at Dartford.

His nearest successor is difficult to discover, but the next to that was Thomas Sinclair, who is noticed as holding the Essex properties in 1384. But there is earlier account of him. Chiche and other manors about twelve miles from Colchester, which had been in possession of the name and had fallen into other hands, again returned to it in the person of Thomas. Among the Harleian Charters there is one bearing description, "'Charter of John Cavendish and Leo de Bradham to Thomas Sinclair of the manor of Frothewick with pertinents in Chicheridel, St.Osyth, Crustwich, Chiche, Comitis, and Chichesrethwick: with two seals: 37 Edward III (1363)'". This is 1364, and for a time these eastern properties had been out of the lineage, and not improbably so going by William's arrangements, the sheriff of Hereford and Essex, if not earlier.

How this Cavendish held it may be illustrated by the fact that the Cavendishes were a Suffolk family near Bradfield St.Clare, and heired it by marriage. They became afterwards the brilliant duke of Devonshire Cavendishes of naval and other state fame. This is not their only connection, that has survived, with the lineage. In Henry VIII's reign one of the successors of this Thomas of Frothewick, Tilbury and Aeslingham, married Margaret Cavendish, and affinities were the explanation of property thus changing. In the full history of the Cavendishes, if such at all exist, this ought to be found.

About 1384 the Kent properties must have finally parted from the Essex Sinclairs in favour of a younger branch of the family. Of the latter only glimpses at intervals appear, but the Tilbury and Danbury men long increased in position and distinction. Some account of the younger descendants of Lord John Sinclair, the coroner, may be given before returning to his direct line. The Easter Issue Rolls of 30th June, 28 Henry VI, 1450, have this historic entry: "'To Alexander Eden, sheriff of Kent, and to divers others of the same county: In money paid to them, viz., by the hands of Gervase Clifton, £100, and by the hands of John Seyncler, £166, 13s. 4d., in part payment of 1000 marks which the lord the king commanded to be paid to the same Alexander and others, as well for taking John Cade, an Irishman, calling himself John Mortimer, a great rebel, enemy, and traitor to the king, as also for conducting the person of the said John Cade to the council of the said lord the king, after proclamation thereof made in the city of London, to be had of his gift for their pains in the matter aforesaid: By writ of privy seal among the mandates of this term, £266, 13s. 4d.'".

Shakespeare, and the historians more than he, could correct themselves from this best of authority. The drama Second Part of King Henry VI is more dramatic than historical, and Jack Cade's slaughter by a giant Alexander Eden at Hothfield or elsewhere in Kent or Sussex, is popular legend seemingly for the miserable facts, as they were, of the cold hand of law condemning, hanging, and quartering him whose father was a Mortimer, mother a Plantagenet, and wife descended of the Lacies. Lord Say, because he could speak French and Latin, "and corrupted the youth of the realm by erecting a grammar school", lost his head by command of this John Mend-All, the kind of sovereign who deserves to die high. Such pleading as Say, according to the drama, made, was pearls before the very king of the swine. It was by his mother that this Say was of the chivalrous family so closely knit with the early Sinclairs, he being the first of the Fynes.

"'Kent, in the Commentaries Caesar writ,
Is termed the civilest place of all this isle:
Sweet is the country, because full of riches;
The people liberal, valiant, active, wealthy:
Which makes me hope you are not void of pity.'"

But this is not the only appearance of John Sinclair in the records of that alarming rebellion and its sequels. In the acts of the privy council there is a letter from King Henry VI himself, dated 8th June, 1456, to "John Saintcleir, squier" and other knights and esquires of Kent, calling upon them to meet at Maidstone, and see that the king's justice be done in reckonings with rebels. This is twenty-one years after the Kent and Sussex Aldham-St.Clairs had failed in the male line in the person of the wealthy Thomas Sinclair, father of the three coheiresses, who must have seen much of the Cade rising, recruited from their own wide estates to large extent. With this John in official activity and himself a squire, if there were no more of their lineage in the county of landed rank, the name was not friendless in the consanguinity sense.

In the report, or rather the digest, of the recently created historical MSS. commission, whose wise purpose is to save as much out of private records as possible, there is quite another aspect than that of loyalty in respect to another John Sencler, lord of Faversham, Kent. He is an armiger in the pardon he gets from Henry VI at the special instance, or rather by the absolute power, of the queen, for taking part with this same "John Mortimer" in the rebellion. The list of pardoned begins with this lord of Faversham, then one called "gentleman", then a dozen to a score of Faversham glovers, brewers, fellmongers, butchers, wool staplers, suggestive of the combination of trades attributed to Shakespeare's father and himself a century later at Stratford-on-Avon. The leadership of John of itself implies his influential position, and it is not without valuable suggestion, as to the reality of good grounds for the popular discontent, when such a name is found in the ranks of the Kentish rising. Jack Cade was perhaps more and less than a Captain Mend-All of the Wat Tyler order.

England had been disgraced by the loss of Normandy, and our French-blooded queen, Margaret, with an imbecile husband, Henry VI, and favourites of detestable and treasonable characters, had outraged not only the popular but the baronial feeling. Only thus can the Kentish enthusiasm for an Irish gallowglass, expressed by thousands of followers, be explained. He was the sham Mortimer to the real one in the background. The duke of York had rights, by a female Plantagenet, towards the crown; and it is not extraordinary that, as his ancestor Hugh Mortimer gallantly fought side by side with St.Cler in the battle of Hastings, Wace witness, this John Sinclair was of his party. The duke's sons, Edward and Richard Mortimer, the Edward IV and Richard III of England, had for first stepping-stone towards their elevation, Cade's movement.

Five years after, all the kingdom was white or red rose, in fiercest civil warfare. Says Rapin:"'Though Cade's enterprise had miscarried, the duke of York had reaped the benefit he proposed. The great number of people that embarked in it, discovered how much the nation was displeased with the queen and the ministry, and that the memory of the rights of the house of March was not entirely abolished'". The house of

March, so called because of its Welsh border standing, being Mortimers, and only noblemen, had no lineage claim whatever, but affinities unfortunately played great part in English regal politics. Adventurer and cruelty are perforce connected, and the Mortimers of historic pages prove so, though there have been far vaguer pretensions than theirs to highest place. The Nevilles, heirs of the Montacutes and Beauchamps, and of royalty affinities also, the earl of Salisbury and the earl of Warwick, king-maker, their great representatives, had their influence most in Kent, and they were favourers of the Mortimers with effect, at the beginning of the struggle. That Jack Cade was inspired by chief men of the county is very certain, and the division of lineages to parties then is no single experience of the van-district of England's vigour.

The date of John Sinclair's pardon is four days before the capture of Jack Cade, about which another John Sinclair was much engaged, as already shown. The report itself by the royal commission is well worthy of examination for the light it throws on the history of the period. Such an inscription as the following would imply that Kentishmen of the name, in lower ranks, then prevailed: "'Here lies Roger Sentcler, formerly serving the abbot and convent of Lesnes, who died on the first day of the month of January, 1425. Whose soul ... '". This is preserved in Weever's Funeral Monuments, as well as in the Vet. MSS. in bib. Cot., from which he took it. Lesnes Abbey was founded by Sir Eichard Lucie, chief justice of England, the fellow-excommunicate of Hugo St.Clare, pincerna; and he himself became its abbot, Roger must have had dignified service under the later abbot of his time before they would give him funeral immortality in the sacred building. Many individuals could yet be discovered of such kind. In Henry VII's reign the Issue Rolls of the Privy Purse tells of a court doctor, Rauffe Sentcler, and gives the interesting information that the royal medical fee was then, at the palace of Sheen, the sum of £1.

Hasted in his History of Kent, under "Woodland", has most difficult account of no fewer than four of the surname holding it, the last of whom was Thomas, who held it 12 Edward IV (1473) "whose descendants passed it away at the end of Henry VII's reign". His information cannot refer to the Aldham St.Cleres, though the names are similar, and must mean these Medway and Thames people. In 9 Edward III (1336) John, son to John St.Clere, enjoyed Woodland, he says, and the former John of these two was Duminus John, the coroner, as far as can be made out. What adds strength to this is that Hasted says that Hamon Crevequer of the "great family", held it before the St.Cleres, and that the second John was succeeded by a Thomas, who could quite well be the Thomas of Frothewick and Tilbury already noted. Thomas died 4 Henry IV (1403).

The wife of a Philip Sinclair, Margaret, also is recorded as its holder 1 Henry VI (1423). Thomas of 1473 referred to by Hasted, separates them entirely from the Aldham St.Cleres of Kent and Sussex, because the last Thomas of them died in 1435, the end of male descent to his branch. It is one of the Aeslinghams who is meant by an entry in the Calendar of Inquisitions after Death, and seemingly he of 1473 - "'Thomas Sinclair, armsbearing, 15 Edward IV (1476): He held no lands nor tenements in the county of Essex:'" which record of 1476 was written in transactions about his will. This appears to give the history of the separation of the Aeslinghams into the family at Tilbury and Frothewick, Essex, and into this Kent family whose remains are as interesting as they are difficult to reduce to clear coherence.

The coroner's successors must be closed, on the knowledge yet attained, with the history of some Anthony Sinclairs of curious character. In the national record office, Fetter Lane, details are to be got of a Sir Anthony of Kent as late as the time of Charles II. In 1666, the year of the great fire, he, poor as Job, petitioned the king for some consideration on the extraordinary grounds, which do not seem questioned by the ungrateful or impecunious gay monarch, that he had lost £2500 a year, which was an immense income at that time, and £5000 in goods, by raising troops for the royal service in Kent; that he had three brothers who were slain in the king's battles; that he himself had been severely wounded; and, lastly, that arrears were due from the exchequer both to his father and grandfather. Such men as these did not deserve to have their representative beggared, and then for ever neglected. He is certainly the last landed Kentish Sinclair, but his descendants may now be numerous men of the people, if right inquiry were made, "in the civilest place of all this isle". Such a tale as this would make the hackneyed catch once again respectable. Sic transit gloria mundi.

What aids to corroborate it effectually and finally, is an entry in the Pell Records. It is a payment by the privy seal, 31st Dec 1606, to John Williams, London goldsmith, for "part of a gold chain" which James I gave to Sir Anthony "Sencleer", as it is spelt in the record. This was soon after the gunpowder plot, when the popular enthusiasm for the king's safety opened for him the purse of the house of commons, and he was unusually liberal of presents accordingly. The union of Scotland with England was also on the carpet, and gifts were more than somewhat free. The spirit of the time is shown by the Spanish ambassador giving a chain to one who brought him the news that the report was false that James had been killed by a poisoned knife. At this period also, the king of Denmark, the brother-in-law of James, came to visit his sister the queen, and for him fabulous feasts, masquerades, and generosities were provided. The Danish ambassador was Sir Andrew Sinclere, knt., of Scandinavian birth, and he was a special favourite of the English court on that occasion. The Pell Records have, "'By order dated last of April 1614: To George Herriott, jeweller to the queen, the sum of £320, for one diamond bought of him, and by his majesty bestowed upon his trusty and well-beloved servant, Sir Andrew Sinclere, knight, without account, imprest, or other charge to be set upon him for the same or any part thereof'". This is the Edinburgh Heriot of whom Sir Walter Scott has made so much. Sir Lewes Lewknor has various attentions to pay of the hospitable kind, by virtue of his court office, to Sir Andrew, the Lewknors of Sussex being already familiar names. But he who got the piece of a chain is the Sinclair or Sencleer of present interest. His Danish kinsman no doubt enjoyed his English hospitality and friendliness. Sir Anthony Sencleer of this reign was the father or grand-father of the Sir Anthony Sinclair of Charles II's time, and that the exchequer owed the elder Anthony money is somewhat suggested by such gift-giving. James was curiously easy in getting into money ditficulties, and amusingly cunning in staving off results from day to day, if his describers are to be believed.

With the later Sir Anthony this branch must be left entirely. He seems to have been quenched out of the noblest chivalry of England, by the chronic generosity and loyalty of his line to the wretched Stuarts or "stewards", who never really rose above the official temper of the distinguished Scottish office from which they took their names, for all their unfortunate and at last tragic coquetting with autocracy. The genuine monarchical spirit of the Norman dynasty they never could, by reason of the fate and stamp of nature, arrive at by any of their miserable assertions. If a Sir Anthony, of stranger's blood even, had had such a bill of deeds to back him as this one had for Charles II, and came with it to a duke of Normandy of the descent of Rogenwald the Rich, the father of Rollo the Rich, and progenitor of the truest men of Europe, the Sinclairs among them, or to a William I or II, or a Henry Beauclerc, he would have not been sent empty-handed away, but kept as a comes worthy of their best lands and titles. Gold chains and similar miseries were the measures of the Stuarts for such supporters. In some books Sir Anthony is a St.Leger.

But let swift return be made to the Essex Sinclairs, who are the last of the Aeslinghams to be described, the descendants of Hugo St.Clare of Becket fame or notoriety. Mention must be made of a Robert de St.Clair who had properties near Dover, and especially the manor of Hastingleigh, in the neighbourhood of Ashford. Of him next to nothing, however, is known. There is record of his marriage to a Joan in 1331, and also that he had four sons, Robert, William, Richard, and Thomas.

Jeake's Charters, page 49, shows that a Guy St.Clere held the then perhaps most coveted position in the kingdom, constable of Dover Castle, and warden of the Cinque Points. He held them separately and together; and if he was one of these Hastingleighs, they also are not without distinction down to this day. These offices were objects of ambition to even king's sons, Henry VII's second boy, Henry, afterwards Henry VIII, being appointed to them in 1493.

Chapter L
The Essex Men

The John Sinclair who is recorded as possessing Tilbury and other Essex estates in 1334, married the daughter of Sir Anthony Culpepper, died without issue, and the family of his relation Dominus John, the coroner, succeeded him. Thomas has been referred to as holding Frothewick and other manors near St.Osyth in 1364, and Tilbury with its pertinents in 1384. His descendants remain in possession. In the rolls of parliament A.D. 1391, there is a complaint by the abbot of St.Osyth against John Rokell. John Sinclair had sold a wood to several persons who at the instigation of Rokell refused to pay their duties to the abbot. The latter gained the cause.

The Sinclairs had never lost footing in this county from the Conquest, or at all events from the time William Rufus granted the lordship of Colchester to Eudo St, Clare, his dapifer, the builder of Colchester Castle, and the founder of its abbey of St.John the Baptist. The De Veres, earls of Oxford, by marriage secured the lordship of Colchester, but the lineage did not forget to secure some of the estates of Eudo, their kinsman. Though of the Hamo Dapifer family, they were near enough to share some of Eudo's fees as well as heir parts of Robert Fitz-Hamo's, and much of his brother's, Hamo, the dapifer and viscount of Kent. But compared with these magnates the Essex men of the fourteenth century had small portions. They grew into distinction none the less. They are mentioned in 1406, 1446, and in 1454 as of standing.

At the prolonged and imposing funeral ceremonies of King Edward IV in 1483, first at Westminster Abbey and then at Windsor, Sir Thomas St.Claire took a leading position. In a little work printed from the MSS. of the lord lyon of Scotland, Sir James Balfour, in the Advocates' Library, Edinburgh, there is a remarkable account of this event in English history. Divers knights and esquires of the household bore the body, accompanied by the nobles of the kingdom, to the services held at Westminster. "The large and broad cloth of gold on a rich canopy of cloth imperial, fringed with gold and blue silk," which formed the pall, was borne by four knights, of whom Sir Thomas St.Clair was the first. When the procession arrived at Windsor, Sir Thomas is mentioned first of the "eight knights without the hearse".

More of his history has not been found, but that he held high rank and office in the royal presence is clear enough. The hereditary ability shines fully out from the history of Sir John Sinclair in the reign of Henry VIII, 1509 till 1547. His father John had added the manor of Coldhall, Great Bromley, in the Tendring hundred, to the patrimonial estates. He died, Morant says, on the 26th August 1493. Henry VII's troubled reign he lived in, dying about the time Perkin Warbeck presented himself as one of the princes in the tower, reputed murdered by Richard III their uncle. Willoughby, lord Brooke, was steward of the household to Henry VII, and Thomas Butler, earl of Ormond, a chief figure, both of whom could reckon kin with John Sinclair. The lords Lovell and Zouche, hunted to sanctuary at Colchester as being the favourites of Kichard, and illustrious rebels of the reign, were related to the Kent and Sussex family by the marriage of one of Thomas Sinclair's co-heiresses. The Guildfords and other such names of the time were familiar by close ties.

When the young successor of this John of Essex appeared at Henry VIII's court he was no stranger, and took due place accordingly. His father resided till his death at Hedingham Castle, and the chief possessions were its pertinents, with Chichridill, St.Cleres, Frodewick, Fenhouse, Danbury, and Cold-Hall. Portions he held from his relations, by frequent affinities, the De Veres, earls of Oxford, and the lords Darcy; but he was also an in capite holder. There is record of him in 1512 as "'John Seyntclere of St.Osith's, alias Chicheridill, sheriff of Essex and Hertford'". In 1513 it is noted that he had by king's appointment the same sheriffship, and that he demitted it on 23d Jan 1515. There are survivals of some of the accounts of his office, such as sums he paid to the king as duke of Lancaster, to Henry, earl of Essex, to the infirm men of St.Albans, to the prior of the Carthusian house of the salutation of St.Mary near London, which have at least an antiquarian interest. He was a commissioner of the peace for Essex.

In Brewer's Letters and Papers of the Reign of Henry VIII he appears knight of the body in the royal household as early as 1516. In 1523 and 1524 he is a subsidy commissioner in Essex, the officers of the household being then those responsible that the king should have money. He has fresh grants of commission of the peace in Essex for the years 1525, 1526, and 1530. It would seem, too, that he acquired about these years some land in Kent, for he has returns from Newington in this county. As a relic of him there actually exists one of his writings among the Harleian charters of the British Museum. It is entitled: "'Indenture between Sir John Seyntcler, knt., and George Harper and Thomas Colepepper, son and heir to Sir Alexander Colepepper, declaring a bond for 200 marks to be void: Cum sig., 34 Henry VIII (1543)'". Its seal is not the least interesting part of the document, and it is of value further as showing that ties still existed to the Colepeppers.

Sir John Sinclair's most remarkable work was the share he took in the suppression of the monasteries and nunneries in this reign. In 1535 Henry VIII ordered a general visitation of the monasteries, and appointed Thomas Cromwell, the famous earl of Essex, visitor-general. Cromwell appointed commissioners, and armed them with eighty-six articles of inquiry, the visitation beginning in the October of that year. In 1536, the lesser monasteries, to the number of 376, were suppressed by act of parliament, adding; £32,000 yearly to the income of the crown; £100,000 being the value of plate and goods seized. In 1537 there was a visitation of the larger monasteries, disclosing mysteries demanding further reformation. The report of it was published next year. The complete suppression took place in 1539. Camden says that the monasteries numbered altogether 643, the colleges 90, the chantries and fee chapels 2374, and the hospitals 110. There were twenty-eight mitred abbots, peers of parliament, of whom three had superior positions to the rest. Abbot John Beche, one of the latter, was hanged at Colchester in 1539 for obduracy in not subscribing to the king's supremacy over the English church. He was the abbot of St.John Baptist there, founded by Eudo Sinclair more than four hundred years previously. Times and necessities change.

Sir John Sinclair of his lineage was now one of the most active in practically levelling such foundations, and had Eudo lived in the latter period he would probably be of the same mind. In a communication from Sir John Sinclair to the lord privy seal occurs this passage: "'Yesterday I was with the abbot of Colchester, who asked me how the abbot of St.Oswith did as touching his house; for the bruit was the king would have it. To the which I answered, that he did like an honest man, for he said, I am the king's subject, and I and my house and all is the king's; wherefore if it be the king's pleasure, I, as a true subject, shall obey without a grudge. To the which the abbot answered, The king shall never have my house but against my will and against my heart; for I know by my learning, he cannot take it by right and law. Wherefore, in my conscience, I cannot be content; nor shall he ever have it with my heart and will. To which I said. Beware of such learning; for if ye hold such learning as ye learned in Oxenford when ye were young ye will be hanged; and ye are worthy. But I will advise you to conform yourself as a good subject, or else you shall hinder your brethren and also yourself'".

In Dugdale's Monasticon Sir John appears in the history of the monasteries. Himself and two other knights, with about twenty armigeri, and Thomas Cromwell, earl of Essex, visitor-general, were the commission which inquired into the nunnery of Polesworth, in records which have survived; and he no doubt took a large share in that greatest religious revolution of English history. Cromwell, the blacksmith's son of Putney, could be trusted as to his choice of sufficient adjutants in so perilous a reform, which was the real cause of the loss of his head ultimately. See Froude's history.

From being knight of the household Sir John Sinclair became master; but he could not have held the office long, for Sir John Gage was controller of the household in 1544, the descendant of his relative Alianor Sinclair of the Aldham family. Gage went that year to the French war under the duke of Norfolk, and is mentioned as controller. In 1554 he was Queen Mary's lord chamberlain, and was engaged quelling the London rebellion of Sir Thomas Wyatt, one of whose adherents, Sir George Harper, seems to have been he of the Harleian indenture. Sir John Sinclair of Danbury died 25 November 1546, a year before the death of his vigorous sovereign, the first secular head of the English church.

His son John succeeded him, and in 1554, the year after the accession of Mary, Morant says that he passed St.Clere's Hall to Thomas, lord Danbury, by fine. Other parts of his property went also, a Gason being another successor. As far as can be discovered he was the last of this branch. If there were more of them they must have lived the dignified but often very quiet life of lords of the manors. The history of the manors is, however, silent about them after Mary's reign, and John, son of Sir John, must have died without male issue.

These Essex men have left relics both of their existence and antiquity which take high place among archaeological remains. The chapel at Danbury Place, which has been mentioned, makes one of the curious chapters with all antiquaries. Gough's Monumental Tablets gives the fullest account of its three crusading figures, St.Clares of the Essex branch, with the usual crossed legs and lions at the feet. By drawing comparisons between the figures and their niches, as also from the character of the building, they give their date as early as Richard Coeur de Lion. One knight was carved in the attitude of prayer, with his hands palm to palm, his sword sheathed, and his lion looking towards him; the second, drawing his sword, the face of his lion turned away from him; and the third, returning his sword into its scabbard, the lion looking half. An imaginative writer has evolved a world of symbolic meaning from these attitudes. The first hero means, home a returned crusader; the second, one who died in the holy wars; and the last, death on his way home to England. It would be delightful if faith could agree fully with symbolism generally; and in the instances of these three Sinclairs, encouragement might come to verify by long research such romantic possibilities of chivalrous biography as these sculptural attitudes might indicate. It is more to be depended on, that they were distinguished warriors of the gallant periods of English knighthood, when fighting the Paynim or the Saracen was far less an affair of bitterness than of high poetical sentiment.

But after looking on that picture of antique devotion to the cross and the sword, look on this of modern sacrilege. On 16th October 1779, some men of the temper that would botanise on their mothers' graves, went by forwardness or stupid magisterial permission into the north aisle of this church at Danbury, and commenced, for antiquarian curiosity of the unpardonable kind, to dig beneath the figures of these knightly crusaders.

They found their leaden sealed coffins; opened them violently; pulled off the shrouds, with dismembering effects; and, worst of all, invited the vulgar mob for a livelong day to examine the remains of these great men of other times. There were fabulous curiosities as to the liquid by which knights, templar and others, were perfectly preserved for centuries. Here was an opportunity not to be missed by the "gropers among dead men's bones", in the spiritual as well as material sense of that phrase. But a veil must be drawn over the test which their enthusiasm applied towards analysis of the preservative fluid in those leaden coffins.

Gough tells the story, to which there is nothing parallel, not even the experiments of nineteenth century scientists. To disturb the ashes of the dead is always next to being a cursed employment, in whatever interest it may de done. The genial symbol-reader might not be singular in wishing that the figures had fully drawn their swords on that occasion, and used them with crusading energy and efficiency. One hundred and eight years ago, this the last sight of the Essex branch was seen, and such a last ! But so strangely are human things related that such sacrilege may go more to keep their names immortal than even the noblest deeds could.

The hill of Danbury, Essex, by the Thames, beneath London, is a land-mark and a watch-tower to this lineage, as it had been for ages to the world's greatest city; and its chapel will always stand fixed to memory as something notable that has been. Gough's engravings of its three crusaders pay tribute to their handsome forms and faces.

Chapter LI
Wolsey's Appreciator-General and Others

The story of none of the lineage might be more instructive than that of a John Sinclair of Henry VIII's reign, if it could be well revived from the considerable evidence which still exists. It is impossible to state with security whether he was one of the Essex branch. He may have been one of the younger members of some of the landed families who were out of property, though he himself is in possession of lands. But there is no necessity for speculation, and it is best that he should have independent treatment.

John "Sencler", as Wolsey wrote his name, was his vice-chamberlain and appreciator-general; and when about 1527 the suite of the cardinal-legate contained such men as William Stanley, earl of Derby, Cuthbert Tonstall, bishop of London, Sir Thomas More, chancellor of the duchy of Lancaster, author of Utopia, and thirty to forty similar names, with 500 horse, as Cavendish writes, to be vice-chamberlain was a post of honour and much business. Tindal has culled from Hall, Stow, and Herbert that when the cardinal went to France to confer with King Francis for Henry the Eighth, he had those named. Lord Sandes, king's chamberlain, Sir Henry Guilford, and others like, with 1200 horse.

Of John Sinclair's doings there are glimpses as early as 1524. On May 28th, John Seint-Clere, esquire, appreciator-general to the most reverend father in God, Thomas, lord legate-cardinal, archbishop of York, and bishop of Durham, takes an inventory of the late Thomas Howard, first duke of Norfolk's goods, "'plate, Jewells, and quick catell remaining in the castle of Framyngham and thereabout in the county of Suffolk'". On 12th July 1526 there is a letter which seems of the nature of sequence to this valuation, from the reigning duke of Norfolk, son of the first, better known as the earl of Surrey, victor at Flodden Field. Says he: "'My sister will deliver the goods, and the coming of Master Synclere shall be nothing displeasant to her.'". He writes from Henyngham. At this time the cardinal was intent on gathering money,

> "' For mine own ends: indeed to gain the popedom,
> And fee my friends in Rome.'"

The duke of Norfolk was his supporter when, the year before, his raising of money from the people without consent of parliament stirred an insurrection in London. To save himself he got the ringleaders pardoned, barely escaping King Henry's anger at this earlier period of his fortunes. The duke was probably his debtor in some way. But in passing from this suggestive record, the duke's title of "master" to John Sinclair indicates his position as one learned in the law, the word having then a technical force, though not confined always to erudition in law. The foundation of his secular colleges was the stalking-horse by which the cardinal compelled money into his purse. It was he who began the suppression of the monasteries, to get revenues ostensibly for the new institutions. In 1524 Pope Clement VII gave him a bull to suppress St.Frideswid's priory in Oxford, on the site of which to build his college of Christ Church, and another on 11th September to suppress as many monasteries as would make 4000 ducats annually for his colleges. The practical part of these doings was in the hands of John Sinclair, thus a forerunner to his kinsman Sir John, who was so busy a few years after similarly on the greater scale.

It is curious to remember that one of the Simon Sinclairs, earls of Huntingdon, Northampton, and Lincoln, was a generous donor to this same priory, which was in the diocese of Lincoln.

But the institution of Wolsey's heart was the university or college of Ipswich, his birthplace in Suffolk. Its dean, William Capon, writes in 1528 to the cardinal, advising him as to additional improvements, and giving many details of the merrymaking of the season, quite conscious of his lord's sympathy with the subject. He tells of nine "bukks" sent to help the popular mirth, "oon from Mr. Sentclere, your grace's servaunt"; and they were "'spent on our said Lady's day in your grace's college, and in the town of Gipeswiche'". Not long after this the proud cardinal came into the compass of a praemunire, and "fell like Lucifer, never to hope again".

Great events occurred the next few years, and John Sinclair took active part in them. He was one of those to whom the papal bull, connected with the divorce of Katharine of Arragon, Henry VIII's first queen, was first read in solemn assembly, 31st May 1529; and he had his responsible share in the arrangement by which the bishops of Lincoln and Bath, after oath taken, were appointed to summon the king and queen to appear on June 18, between 9 and 10 o'clock A.M., in the parliament chamber, Blackfriars, London. Cardinal Wolsey's opposition to Anne Bullen caused his overthrow. Ralph Sadler, who played diplomatic and warlike parts then, discerned as early as 1st Nov 1529, that "divers of my lord's servants, Mr. Sayntclere, etc., are sworn the king's servants".

This "master's" traditions were his king in preference to the clergy. But John was friendly with Wolsey after his fall, and they have business together about ships on the Thames, Mr. Sayntclere then living 12 miles from Oxford, the date of communication being April 1530, and the cardinal dying 30th November of the same year.

The heraldic visitators of Oxford of 1574 found the Sinclair arms in Stafford manor-house, Cornbury Park, now a seat of the duke of Beaufort; and Burke could make nothing of the puzzle it was to him when he found it among the Harleian MSS., where the visitation is. It is worth while suggesting that this John was holder of Cornbury Park, which in Henry I's time was a royal seat, and appears in connection with Hamo and Eudo, the dapifers, and other lineage names, as signatures and otherwise, of which the Chronicle of Abingdon monastery gives details. In the list of the gentry of Oxfordshire, drawn up by Henry VI's commissioners in 1433, a Johannis Chantclere occurs. There must have been a permanent Oxford family, of whom John, the vice-chamberlain of the cardinal was, the fellow-servitor of Thomas Cromwell before both became king's servants. As early as the fifth year of this reign, 1514, there is notice of a John Seinteler, armigerus, of Kebworth, who bore arms, "The sun in its glory, or"; but it is not possible to discover whether he is one with the appreciator-general. Several families of the line used this blazon.

From the Conquest one branch of St.Cleeres held under the Mohuns of Oxfordshire, better known as earls of Somerset. The same Oxford visitation of 1574 testifies to this, and it is probable that the Oxfordshire family's origin may thus be traced: "'William de Mohun or Moyne came into England with the Conqueror, and was the most noble of all his host, having divers noblemen under him, as St.John, St.Cleere, and others'". Another record says he had forty-five nobles in his troop. "William de Moyon", Auguste le Provost and Duncan found, "'was lord of Moyon, three leagues to the south of Saint Lo. The remains of the castle belonging to this family, one of the most distinguished in England under the Norman dynasty, may still be seen'". He fought at Hastings; and his locality of Saint Lo, the home land of Sinclairs, together with his following, would seem to prove him of the ducal lineage. It is only so that such underholding and trooping can be understood.

In July 1524 the vice-chamberlain got a lease of the manor of Lammershe in Essex, which belonged to the countess of Richmond a little before. Wolsey, who was abbot of St.Albans among his many other dignities, gave, 1st June 1528, John Sender the office of keeper of the woods of Brumeham and a dozen places besides belonging to the monastery. For this he had a salary. He had previously, in 1525, been granted the keepership of Tyteinanger, Hertfordshire, with so much a day. These are but specimens of many similar benefits. Of their public relations, "the inventory of all I have, it is the king's", of Shakespeare's celebration, shows John Sinclair's ordinary work and duties. The means are extant on which something like a biography of him might be made, but more industry in his favour perhaps is not here required.

That there were distinguished kinsmen of his then in England, not necessarily holders of land, may be inferred from a note of "Capitaine John Seinctclier". King Francis of France had equipped 150 greater ships, 60 smaller ones, 25 from the Levant, and 10 Genoese, to make a descent upon England in 1545. It was all but as formidable an invasion as that of the Spanish Armada in 1585, and the more to be dreaded that at first there were only 60 ships to oppose to them, though afterwards increased to 100. The French made landings on the Isle of Wight and three places in Sussex, and had some severe skirmishing with the English fleet, but nothing was done. The greatest effort of France at sea ended in a siege of Boulogne of the fiasco character, and a peace was patched up. The English fleet when it had orders to sail on 10th August 1545 to find the enemy, was made up of three divisions of 25 ships each. The van ward division was commanded by Sir Thomas Clere, admiral, the second ship of which was Captain Sinclair's, one of the largest. Its name was "The Jhesus of Lubick", its burden 600 tons, and carrying 300 men.

Out of the landholding ranks it is only incidentally that any lineage in England can be seen. Even the clergy cannot from the records they have left be traced much further than as isolated individuals. The Sinclairs of England grew scarce, but they have not become extinct even in the lineage name. Could the local names be followed with some scientific accuracy, it would be discovered that noble and good branches of the same blood are now flourishing. But certainties must be given that may leave such inferences.

In 1627 Thomas Sinclair was vicar of Broke, near St.Edmundsbury, Suffolk, in the very district some descendants of the Bradfields might be expected.

Dr. Thomas Tanner, bishop of St.Asaph, author of Notitia Monastica and other antiquarian works, writes a letter to Peter le Neve, Esq., Norroy king-at-arms, dated Mar 30, 1704, in which a suggestive final paragraph occurs, the more as being written from Norwich, where he then resided. "'The gentleman that brings this, Mr. St.Clair, travelled with Mr. Windham, and has since lived in his family; is a well-wisher to English antiquities, and has taken great pains among the old writings at Felbrigge, of which he will be able to give you a good account. He is now going again beyond sea with Mr. Gray. By letting him have a sight of The Domesday Book, or any other old things you have in your custody, you will very much oblige a person of his curiosity; and also, sir, your humble servant, Thomas Tanner.'"

A note says that the part of the survey wanted was county of Norfolk, of which Peter le Neve had a fac-simile copy from the original. This Mr. St.Clair is of the Norfolk stock, and seems to have been a learned tutor. His antiquarian temper has had recent example in his kinsman, the genealogist, Alexander Sinclair, H.E.I.C.S., who died in 1877, the second son of Sir John of Ulbster. On all that relates to the Scottish line he is an authority, as the kind favour by his nephew, the earl of Glasgow, of his MSS. for examination, enables to be distinctly stated on real knowledge of his work.

Broomhall manor, Norfolk, was held by Robert St.Cleer in 1721, and he combined the proprietor and clergyman, as a kind of link to plainer lives which some of the name must have lived there.

Another Rev. Robert appears in a bond, preserved in the Bodleian Library, Oxford, among the Rawlinson MSS., in which on appointment to the rectory of Bulphan, Essex, 8 June 1722, he promises to indemnify John Robinson, bishop of London, against all actions. He was, however, the son of William Sinclair, commissary of Caithness, his mother being one of the Inneses of Sandside.

There is a monumental tablet to "'the good Mrs. St.Clair, who died in 1727, the year terrible for fevers'". She was the wife of Patrick Sinclair, rector of Norfolk livings from 1700 till 1750, to one of which Horace Walpole presented him.

In the Miscellanea Genealogica et Heraldica there is a monumental inscription taken from Wilford, Nottinghamshire: "'Near this place are deposited the remains of George Sinclair, M.A., late rector of this parish, who died 12th June 1775) aged 46 years'". The arms are those of the earldom of Caithness, impaling a chevron between three roses, gules, and on a chief as many mullets of the first. It is suggested that this is for the Stevenson Sinclairs, descendants of the baronets of Longformacus. In the parish register his burial is noted as having taken place on 23 June 1775. It is probable that he was not of English but Scottish birth.

There was a Robert Sinclair, recorder of York, who married in 1811 Elizabeth Sothern, daughter of Sothern of Darrington Hall, Yorkshire. He was Irish, if so modern a date is of interest at all.

Other professions might add quotas to such collection as this, but the reading would possibly be less lively than what is desirable.

Thornbury in New and Old London tells of a parliamentary commission inquiring into the evils of farming the Fleet prison even to murder of the prisoners by the officials, and he mentions "the case of Captain David Sinclair, an old officer of courage and honour", as a very bad one against the lessee Bambridge for wringing guineas out of those in his power. "'Bambridge, who disliked his prisoner, had boasted to one of his turnkeys that he would have Sinclair's blood. Selecting the king's birthday, when he thought the captain would be warm with wine, he rushed into Sinclair's room with his escort, armed with musket and bayonet, struck him with his cane, and ordered the men to stab him with their bayonets if he resisted being dragged down to the strong-room. In that damp dark dungeon Sinclair was confined, till he lost the use of his limbs and also his memory; and when near dying he was taken into a better room, where he was left four days without food'". This was in 1726.

In one of the rolls of the treasury of Henry III, Edward I, and Edward II, the king gave John Bray, hostianum of the king's treasury, the custody of the heir of John Sinclair, lately keeper of the king's palace, Westminster, and of the gaol of the river of Fleet, on payment of £10 yearly. These offices were then in capite and hereditary. Only men of high quality were given such power over their fellows, and comparisons and coincidences are curious and instructive at interval of four or five centuries.

But Dr. Johnson's Life of Savage has equally melodramatic incident connected with a Mr. James Sinclair. The blackguard verse-writer, Richard Savage, who claimed to be the unacknowledged son of an earl, Rivers, and of the countess of Macclesfield, was roystering in Robinson's coffee house, Charing Cross, and, wounding a servant-girl who tried to stop the quarrel raised by his insulting some gentlemen there, he ran Mr. Sinclair through the body, "when he was not in a posture of defence", his point held towards the ground, as the evidence bore. Savage was taken to Newgate, and tried at the Old Bailey for murder, but had the king's pardon, through the pleading of the countess of Hertford, Lord Tyrconnel, and Mrs. Oldfield, the actress. It is said the countess of Macclesfield "did all she could to bring Savage to the gallows". Dr. Johnson, like Lord Tyrconnel and others, noble and simple, was credulous that she was his mother, as he said; and there are many fanciful tales of his birth and upbringing, hidden in the humblest of London scenes; but a drunkard's imagination is apt to be a troublesome one, like his weapon. The tragedy took place in 1727. To be murdered thus in doubtful company by "the bastard", as he loved to call himself (the greatest monster intellectually, morally, and physically of his time without compare, whether of shoemaker Holborn blood or of the vilest of countesses and earls, whose adulterous shamelessness was sui generis) seems not an enviable fate. The incarnation of ungrateful clever tavern rascaldom, rhymed on this as on all other subjects; and the devil may himself mend, since there are in the lines marks of remorse that he cut off a young man whom he figures as probably doing great things for his country but that he had met with him.

To prevent, howewer, too sudden wandering down to modern times, a short return may be made to Henry VIII's reign, when his business with Scotland brought him into close personal relations with one of the kin, who was as much English as he well could have been, whether native or not. Henry's sister Margaret was queen there, and after the death of her husband in 1513, James IV, at the battle of Flodden, a French and an English party began to develop. Alexander, duke of Albany, a Frenchman by birth and speech, had been declared regent, but did not come from France till 1515. He was the head of the French party, while the English faction rallied around Queen Margaret, aided by her brother Henry VIII's protection and active interference. Alexander was the son of the first duke of Albany, second son of James II, who had first married Lady Catherine Sinclair, daughter of William, prince of the Orkneys and earl of Caithness, but was divorced from her because of nearness of blood, as the church decided, making their son the bishop of Moray illegitimate. The French Alexander was the son of another wife.

Queen Margaret's parallel character to that of her brother, in the matter of marriages and affairs of the heart, complicates the politics inextricably. In 1516 Henry tried to have the regent removed, because it was dangerous that the heir presumptive to the crown should have the guardianship of Queen Margaret's young son, the king. She had married the earl of Angus, and their daughter Margaret was born at Harbottle Castle, Northumberland. Her husband left her then, and her domestic troubles never ceased afterwards. In 1522 Henry again wrote to the parliament to expel the duke of Albany, on the pretence that he wished to marry the queen, his sister; but this also came to nothing, though he sent

Lord Dacres to the borders with some troops. Margaret even joined with the regent. Henry, however, sent the earl of Surrey across the borders to get the regency for her.

The duke of Albany Henry tried to seize on his passage from France, but he passed through, and landed with 3200 French soldiers, the French interests being his. Indeed much of the coquetting rather than war on the border was to aid the wars going on in France. The English party made Albany's attempt to meet Surrey futile. Next year the regent was away again, and the queen and her favourite, Hamilton, earl of Arran, stirred up the king, now fourteen, to assume the reins of government, they being the real rulers. Douglas, earl of Angus, her husband, with other nobles, upset this arrangement; and he became regent in the king of England's interest, holding the young king's person, which was the prize of ambition. In 1526 an attempt to seize the boy failed. Queen Margaret had married next to Henry Stuart, and induced the king, her son, so that she might rule again, to escape to Stirling. The Douglases had to retire to England, 1528, Henry VIII agreeing to a truce of five years.

During all this scheming a Patrick Sinclair figured conspicuously. In the State Papers of Henry VIII the references to him are quite voluminous. There are many letters written to, by, and about him in the collection. Queen Margaret commends herself heartily to him in one, and signs her strange literature, "Yours ye know", Surrey writes Wolsey from the borders, 'Sinclair says that Albany must invade England or send the Frenchmen (6000 upwards) home, for Scotland cannot support them.

As she writes to her brother, "'Patrick Sinclair was her trusty and true servant, and ever hath been to the king my husband'". At no time was he more of a friend to her than when she was writing to Henry VIII, her "dearest brother", "'to preserve your sister's son, who is nearest to you next to your own children'".

In 1526 he was ambassador to the king of England, and many letters testify to his kind reception. One by Cardinal Wolsey is especially remarkable, recommending Patrick Sinclair as "right trusty" to Henry, then at Winchester, and reciting long and faithful services to his sister's party. Bishop Clerk's letter thence telling of the king's imperturable silence as to what passed privately between himself and Patrick, is a study as to secular wisdom baulking the clerical curiosity of the cardinal-legate's scouts. Master Magnus, the English ambassador at the northern court, writes to Wolsey that Patrick is one of the six nobles then wholly devoted as "right good Englishmen". He is never tired of praising him as "an honest gentleman", "our good friend and special lover", and as "very forward" in the cause. "'Patrick Sinclair and Mr. John Chisholm are nightly with us'", writes the ambassador. Queen Margaret Tudor's letter to her brother Henry VIII in Patrick's favour, is one of the high historic documents, part of which runs, "'Wherefore I beseech your grace kindly to be his good prince for my sake, and that you shall give commandment to the earl of Surrey and the lord Dacres, that he may be received and well treated in your said realm, if he has need: And this you will do at my request'".

But Patrick's throne of favour with the lady was not always so steady as this, though he was true to her when the duke of Albany's hard hand gave her, as she writes, "not £1000 Scots" yearly, and when her "cupboard must be pledged". There are worse clues of Ariadne than the money supply for getting through the labyrinths of monarchical politics. His temporary eclipse is explained by letters between Cardinal Wolsey and the duke of Norfolk, who was earl of Surrey at Flodden. Margaret had complained to the cardinal that Norfolk slighted her in not answering one of her letters; and to the priest's inquiries the soldier writes that Patrick Sinclair and Henry Stuart, who was becoming the favourite, had fallen at variance, and he could not write letters then by Patrick as bearer because Patrick "cannot please her now". Henry Stuart, he informs the cardinal, is made lieutenant to Lord Maxwell of some two hundred men of special dignity, and "'he doth put in and out at his pleasure, which Patrick Synclere did before'". He says for final, "'To please Henry Stuart she quarrelled with Patrick Synclere for not bringing a letter from me'".

By and by Sinclair regained his position, but the Maxwell connection kept up the variance with native bitterness. Margaret's letter-writing was almost as strong a passion with her as Henry's theological books were to him. From 28 Dec 1515 when Lord Dacre received her in great state at his castle of Morpeth, with the lord chamberlain, Archibald Douglas, Will Carmichael, Dan Carr, and, as she writes in a letter of 1520, her "man of law, Pet Synglar", throughout the entassement of interests she is continually busy. In 1523 she writes to Surrey that she wishes to "steal out of Scotland", because Albany keeps back her income, and will compel her to sign papers detrimental to her son.

Her marriage to King James IV had brought considerable correspondence between the two parts of the island. Lord Dacre writes Henry, 20th July 1512, from Carlisle, of a huge ship the gallant monarch had built, of which Lord Sinclair was the captain; and few things from these valuable State Papers are more amusing than another letter of 13 April 1513 on the same subject to Henry from his ambassador. Dr. Nicolas West, telling of an interview with James. "'He talked of his great ship, said that she shot 16 pits of great ordnance on each side, that he had two more ordnance in her than the French kingdom ever had to the siege of any town: which methought to be a great crack'". West speaks of one piece of ordnance three yards long, carried from Edinburgh Castle, which "'shoots a stone bigger than a great penny loaf'". The ambassador went to see Queen Margaret Tudor at Linlithgow Palace, and was "fetched by Sir John Sinclair on Sunday".

When she died in 1541 of palsy at Meffen she left no will, but wished the king her son, James V, to be told to be good to the earl of Angus, and to her daughter Margaret Douglas. The attendants were to ask him if this daughter could get all her goods. She had no more money than £2500 Scots, equivalent then to £625 sterling. The king came on the day of her death too late to speak with her, and soon went away, leaving orders that Oliver Sinclair and another member also of his privy chamber should lock up all her goods for his use.

This Oliver seems to have heired Patrick's position and traditions. The jealousy and feud, especially of Lord Maxwell, had their satisfaction next year in the person of this the so-called favourite, who has received so much ignorant abuse. Solway Moss ought to be the scandal of the Maxwells and others who, quarrelling with their king, preferred to be prisoners than to do his just commands. It was not that they refused to war under Oliver. He was of better blood than any in that kingdom, the lords of Roslin, Nithsdale, Newburgh, etc, princes of Orkney and also in Scandinavia. They never questioned his dignity.

He was Oliver Sinclair of Pitcarnis and Whytekirk, a younger son of Sir Oliver of Roslin, and the nephew of the lord Sinclair and earl of Caithness. His grandfather had been lord chancellor of Scotland, prince of Orkney and Shetland, doing homage to the king of Norway, earl of Caithness, lord of Roslin, Pentland, Herbertshire, Nithsdale, etc.; and he himself held the tack of Orkney and Shetland when, for state reasons, they were given to the crown by his family. Because he loved the king, and his nobles hated him, a handful of English cavalry were allowed to disgrace both the sovereign and his first minister.

The death of James V was largely caused by shame at the event, and sorrow for the disobedience of his nobles. Lord Maxwell's yearly income was only £166, 13s. 4d., from the returns Henry VIII got taken of the estates of his prisoners; and he was one of the richest. It could not be much of indignity to serve under Oliver with a pocket of that weight. But the historians are wrong, and Froude as much as the others; it was no matter at all of ignorance of war, inequality of condition, or of plebeian versus patrician. The patricianism was all the other way, as King James knew; and probably he was taught so by his English mother, Patrick's eulogist. James Sinclair and Alexander Sinclair were also prisoners requiring to be ransomed, by that vile day's work of betraying them and their brother. Wolsey, Cromwell, More, Surrey, the Despensers, Buckingham, and even a Gaveston, are ignoble only after they are politically dead. Every little dog can bark complacently and courageously on the bodies of dead lions.

Oliver's daughter's husband, Hamilton of Bothwellhaugh, fought out part of justice from a Linlithgow window for him in the destiny sense. The "favourite" awaits vindication, and he shall yet get it, being as honourable and as brave a man as was in the kingdom. Of his military sufficiency his governorship of Tantallon Castle is proof positive. Sir Ralph Sadler, the English governor of it at one period, had the most careful respect for his warring skill, as his letters to England show still. But more perhaps than enough of this semi-English discursus.

That Henry VIII knew the family well, as of his own people as well as beyond the Tweed, one of his last public acts is testimony, if such could be required when Sir John Sinclair was one of the great men in his household as in his state and clerical affairs, and when John Sinclair was the vice-chamberlain of the cardinal-legate, and fellow king's-servant afterwards with his vicar-general, Thomas Cromwell. In 1546, the year before his death, the king, having his council with him at Guildford, Surrey, writes to the council at London: "'His Majesty prayeth you also to write to the warden of the Westmarches, that he signify to Olyver St.Cleare (who offereth to come in to redeem his pledge), that whensoever he come to Carlisle, his pledge shall be truly and safely delivered to return at liberty to Skotland'".

Chapter LII
The South-West

Robert Fitz-Hamo, lord of Thorigny and Estremeville, and the earl of Corboil, in Normandy, lord marcher of Wales generally and of the lordship of Glamorgan in particular, was lord of Tewkesbury in Gloucester also. He was the earliest Sinclair in this county, but enough has already been said of him as the "knight of Rye" of the first two Norman kings' reigns. Carte the historian usually calls him Robert de Thorigny.

The History of Cambria, translated in 1584 from Blanch Parry's Welsh MS., a gentlewoman of the queen, is full of his story; and certainly not the least interesting part of it is the account of the rise of the famous Cecils, through this Robert Sinclair's favour to the first of them, Robert Cecil, who came to Wales with him for the conquest so celebrated. The writer of the history says he gathered the details faithfully from records in custody of the right honourable Sir William Cecil, knight of the garter, the lord Burghley, and lord high treasurer of England, the well-known minister of Queen Elizabeth. These Cecils were the earls of Salisbury, of whom the conservative marquis is now the representative.

But Robert Fitz-Hamo was succeeded by no son, his daughter Maud, married to Robert, the son of Henry I, Beauclerc, getting his lands in the west; and her son accumulates under his earldom of Gloucester no fewer than 230 knights' fees. That some of Fitz-Hamo's own lineage found their homes in these border lands the frequent record of their name of Sancto Claro amply testifies. They may have been the descendants of his brother, William of London, to whom he gave the castle of Ogmor and the four knights' fees in South Wales in 1091. The whole region on both sides of the Severn, "Sabrina fair, virgin, daughter of Locrine", half way up to its source, was well under the sway of the Sancto Claro gens; though they held most on the Welsh side, as far as Pembroke. The king's son Robert, and John Lackland afterwards, swallowed up much of it for want of male heirs, or rather by skill of marriages.

Fitz-Hamo's other brother Richard, however, is certainly the ancestor of some of the name in these counties. He got as his share of the Welsh conquest the castle of Neth and three knights' fees, the properties of both him and his brother William being large and frequent in various parts of England besides. Richard took his local name of Granville from a side estate of Thorigny in Normandy, to which he was made heir, and it had variations such as Greenfield, Grandeville, Greenvil, according to the fashions of time or place. Much has not been discovered of members of his family as actually possessing estates in Gloucester, their chief situation being in Devon and Cornwall, as will appear.

There is a Thomas Sinclair, among the "additional charters", British Museum, of Kyngeswoode, near Bristol, the scene of Wesley's first foundation of methodism in 1739. He claims lands in the town of Durham, Gloucester, 39 Edward III (1346).

In the Placita de Quo Warranto of Edward I, Johannis de Sancto Claro in "'Com. Glouc. Cir. Langetr'" is one of those swearing in favour of John Maltravers as to his right, against the king's challenge, to Wodecester. John Sinclair was himself a Gloucestershire holder, and, as it would seem, of Staverton, and of a St.Clare which is long out of local memory.

Staverton, of 287 acres, with a rental of 1575, between Cheltenham and Gloucester, was held in the Returns of Owners of Land, 1873, by Capt. Louis St.Clair, but he may or may not be of the ancient house of Richard.

The Exon The Domesday Book has already been quoted to show that Britel Sinclair, the brother of Richard and of William, all three the sons of Walter, earl of St.Cler, held property in Somersetshire shortly after the Conquest: "'And from the half hide which Britel Sinclair held the king has no tax'". This was in the Bolestane hundred. Reference has also been made to a signature of his to the charter of the foundation and endowment of the priorate of Montacute, Somerset, and to two of his fellow-witnesses, Robert Bruce and Jordan de Barneville. Bruce was probably his nephew or brother-in-law, from the marriage of his sister Agnes Sinclair to Bruce of Bramber, Sussex, and of Brecknock, Wales. The Barnevilles were not only closely connected with Britel, but with the Aeslingham Sinclairs of Kent and Essex, who were directly Hamoes, Robert and others of Barneville appearing in the Rochester register and the Monasticon. They held land in Kent as well as in Somerset.

Britel Sinclair does not occur, with his surname, in any of the ancient records except the Exon The Domesday Book; but the Exchequer Domesday, after the fashion of the time, gives a Britel, without other indication, an immense number of holdings in the south-western counties, especially under his blood-relation, William, earl of Moreton, half-brother to the Conqueror. There can be little doubt that this is he, and that he knew the value of Adam Sinclair's system of underholding, in preference to the incapiie, particularly from those of the royal lineage. That Ralph Sinclair, the castellan of Norwich, Adam's brother, was the steward of the earl of Morton, goes to show the same. It would hardly be safe, however, to assume as proved that this is the only Britel of the large magnitudes; but it is extremely near a proof, compared with the proofs usually possible of such antiquity.

The question arises, Was he the ancestor of the Somersetshire family who are so frequent in the documents of all the reigns down to the sixteenth century, or were they of the "Hamo" Sinclairs ? Was Richard of Granville, the son of Hamo of Normandy, their ancestor, as he was that of the Devon family and of the Cornwall ? The brother of Eichard, king's chamberlain, ancestor of the Bradfields and Aldhams of England, and brother also of William, dapifer to Queen Margaret Atheling of Scotland, ancestor of the Roslins, the princes of Orkney, dukes of Oldenburgh, and a whole series of other noble branches, Britel is more difficult to fix as an ancestor. Indeed, what evidence there is from Somerset seems to point that he died without issue, though this cannot for a moment be asserted.

Describing the parish of St.Clare, Cornwall, the Complete Parochial History of Cornwall has a passage that, if founded on good authority, might help to settle the question: "'From this parish was denominated an ancient family of gentlemen surnamed De St.Cleare, from, whence are descended the St.Clears of Tudwill in Devon, who, suitable to their name, gave for their arms, in a field azure, the sun in its glory, shining, or, transparent; of which tribe was that Robertus de Sancto Claro qui tenet decem libratas terrae in hundredo de Mertock in comit. Somerset'". With apparent mistake, such as that the parish gave the men their name instead of the men the parish, some of this seems as well-grounded as it will be found illustrative.

If Robert of Martock was of the Cornwall family, then the Somerset people were the descendants of Richard Sinclair of Granville, brother of Robert Fitz-Hamo, Hamo Dapifer, and William Sinclair. Britel's successors in Somersetshire, if he had any, are forever in the hades of antiquity, it must be feared, should corroboration of this quotation come. One thing is at least gained, namely, that the unity of the lineage of the "knight of Rye" with Sinclairs is fully settled by this account of matters in itself, if there had been no other evidence. In the face of the Parochial

History it is hardly possible to credit Britel with the chief Somersetshire house, and one of the Hamoes seems the only other ancestor for it.

The author of The Norman People, however, finds that Britel was the ancestor of a Dorsetshire family, and this clears up many if not all difficulties. It is not perhaps fair to suspect his research, because he makes William, the dapifer of the English Margaret, queen of Scotland, one of Britel's Dorsetshire descendants, though he is certainly as wrong in this as the industrious Stow was in making William the Lion on his ransom take the Sinclairs to Scotland.

The Bolestane estate in Somerset was only one of many in several counties, as was the Norman system of tenure then, and Britel may have had no more connection than such particular one with Somerset.

There is, in the most absolute state records, various reference to a Dorset high family; and this author, being an enthusiast for Norman things generally, is more than likely to be right, and to have had facts for his statement that Britel founded it.

In the Magnum Rotulum Sccacarii of 31 Henry I (1131) under "Nova Placentia 7 Nov Conventiones" this occurs: 'Dorseta: In pdon bi R Willo de sco Claro vj s 7 viij d,' and in another entry 'xix s.'. These sums as taxes represented considerable property in this county alone.

As far as times and places are concerned he could quite well have been the son of Britel, and it is he probably whom the author of The Norman People sent wrongly to Scotland. It is true there is not much subsequent trace of him, or of any descendants of his, unless those in the neighbouring county of Hampshire were his branch.

Winchester had great attraction in the earlier periods. The Chronica of John of Oxford mentions a William de St.Cleer engaged in important money business with the bishop of Winchester, 19 Edward I (1291).

A William de St.Clare appears prominently in papers about Edward I's Welsh, Scottish, and French wars; and in a charter of lands in the Monasticon to the abbey of Tichfield, Southampton, by Edward II, Dominus William de Sancto Claro is a witness, Stanewoode being part of the grant. This Lord William had a Geffrey de Sancto Claro of Southampton, Hampshire, as one of his antecessors, who is noted as holding some land from the counts of the island, the Brians of the Isle of Wight, in 7 Henry III (1222). It is he who is mentioned in the Rotuli Litterarum Clausarum, in Turri Londoniensi as holding land in the counties ruled by the viscount or sheriff of Winchester and Dorsetshire, "'The seventeenth year of King John (1216): It was commanded the sheriff of Winchester and Dorset, that he give to Philip Brito or Britel, the land which belonged to John de Boneville or Bameville, and to Geffrey de Sinclair, held in his bailliwicks or provinces of jurisdiction, to be held as long as the lord the king shall please: at Reading, 7th April'". If the Britoes could be identified with the descendants of Britel, no more distinguished race is there in English history; but such a possibility would open endless worlds of inquiry. The carta of Walter Brito for Henry II gave him as holding 15 knights' fees in Somerset as from the earl of Mortaine, from which Britel held most of his lands in the Conqueror's time. John of Boneville would seem to be one of the Barnevilles so much connected with Britel Sinclair and the Sinclairs near Rochester on both sides of the Thames. Another curious thing which might connect this Geffrey Sinclair with the Hamo Sinclairs of Stapleton, Somerset, if indeed these were not, after all, Britel's people, is the fact that in 9 Henry IV (1408) Sir William Boneville held a part of the lands of the Somerset family, as the half of the manor of Stapleton and Sayes Place in Martock. He is the descendant of the John of Boneville of the record.

But this will have further light upon it in the account of the family, for whom it is difficult to settle origin decisively as from Richard, the brother of Robert Fitz-Hamo, or Britel, the third son of Walter of Medway, earl of St.Cler in Normandy.

On the whole, it is safe to leave Lord William Sinclair of Dorsetshire as the representative of the line of Britel.

The Somersets may be reckoned, on preponderating grounds, the descendants of Richard Sinclair of Granville, the founder not only of this branch but of the Devonshire and Cornwall Sinclairs,

The Aldham Sinclairs of Kent and Sussex held largely also in this county of Somerset. In 4 Edward III (1331) John, the son of John, was possessed of Chiselbergh manor. In 17 Edward III (1344) his wife Alicia died seized of it. It seems to have come with Alicia, for it was by the death of John Daubernoun it went to the Aldhams, and as Alicia was a widow she may have had it through her first husband.

Much has already been said of this manor in describing the Aldham-St.Cleres.

In 9 Edward III (1337) this John died, and the Inquisitions after Death find him possessed in Somersetshire of not only Chiselbergh manor with the feoda appertaining, but of West Chinnock manor, Tenne, and, in one feoda, Chilterne, Dunmere, and Michell Weston, with Norton of Taunton manor. The greater portion of these came to him by his father John's marriage to Joan Aldham, who brought him much of the Aldham properties, and, through her mother, of the Montacute or Montagu estates. The Montacutes, the earls of Salisbury, were a Somersetshire family, and it was at their castle of Montacute, Somerset, Britel Sinclair signed its lord's charter to the priory of Montacute near the castle, and such signatures were usually a fair presumption of affinities.

The Aldham Sinclairs held large footing in the county till they became extinct in the male line, 1434, their three co-heiresses dividing these among the other properties to their husbands.

In 10 Richard II (1387), John Sinclair, chevalier, and his wife Maria had Norton, Wele, Pennard, Chiltern, Chiselbergh, with the advowson. West Chinnock manor was given to her as part of his widow's provision, 11 Richard II (1388). Sir Philip Saintclere has it in 9 Henry IV (1408).

But the Somersetshire estates were regular part continuously of the Aldham-Sinclairs' estates, and enough has been written of them under their other lands. They, in any case, were later holders in the county than the original descendants of the Hamo family, and their origin and history belong in greater degree to the districts near London.

One further general line of inquiry may be suggested. In the List of the Norman Barons who fought at Hastings this is, "'William de Moyon, with several manors, received Dunster Castle, in Somersetshire, which became the principal abode of his successors. His grandson, also called William, was created earl of Dorset, by the empress, Matilda, on account of the services he rendered her in the war against King Stephen. The barons Mohun, of Okehampton, were descended from him, and this branch was not extinguished before the commencement of the eighteenth century'". Among the Harleian MSS. the Oxford visitation of 1574 has a description of the first William, who came from Moyon, near St.Lo, which became his local surname: "'William de Mohun or Moyne came into England with the Conqueror, and was the most noble of all his host, having clivers noblemen under him as St.John, St.Cleere, and others.... He was earl of Somerset'". It is a question where this St.Cleere settled; and it is also discussible whether William, "the most noble of all his host", was not of the same male Rollo descent as this nobleman who, with forty-four others of rank, followed him to England. The Mohuns, Yorke says (and Vincent cannot contradict him, he confesses), were earls of Somerset and Dorset together.

Chapter LIII
The Somerset Family

A quotation from Colinson's History of Somerset, printed in 1791, gives some knowledge. "'A little to the northwest of Ash is Stapleton, which for a number of successions belonged to the family of St.Clare or De Sancto Claro. In 6 Henry III (1221) Robert de St.Clare held of the king in chief ten pounds a year of land in Stapleton, by the service of finding an armed servant with a horse in the king's army for forty days at his own cost. He was succeeded by his son Robert, who, 7 Henry III (1222), paid ten marks for his relief of the land which he held here of the king by serjeanty. This Robert died 2 Edward II (1308), being then certified to hold the manor of Stapleton of the crown in capite, by the service of holding a towel before the queen at the feasts of Easter, Whitsuntide, and Christmas, and likewise at the king's coronation. Robert de St.Clare, his grandson, succeeded to the manor of Stapleton, of which he died seized 10 Edward III (1337), leaving issue another Robert, his son and heir. Which last-mentioned Robert held only a moiety of this manor, of which he died seized 33 Edward III (1359), and was succeeded by Richard, his son and heir. The other moiety was held 42 Edward III (1368) by Ralph Seyncler (as the name was sometimes written), who died without issue, as also did the above-mentioned Richard and Margaret his wife, upon which the manor reverted to Robert de St.Clare, a cousin of the above-mentioned lords, who died 46 Edward III (1372), and Sibill his wife had an assignment of the third of this manor for her dower, remainder to Sir William Bonville, knt., and his heirs, 9 Henry IV (1409). Sir William Bonville held a moiety of the manor of Stapleton, and a messuage and one carucate of land in Martock, called Sayes-Place (after the family of Say), from the earl of Somerset. At this time there was a chapel in Stapleton, which seems to have been built by one of the St.Clares. It was subservient to the church of Martock, but has long since been destroyed, and nothing further appears memorable of it or the place'".

Colinson's conclusion is rather too absolute, but he deserves all commendation for what he has preserved. In the will of Sir Wm. Bonville, who was generally described as of Shute, Devonshire, which he made on 13th August 1407, in the time of Edward III, he gave, among an extensive list of benefits to friends, priests, etc., £20 to his daughter Dame Catherine Cobham, £20 to his daughter Elizabeth Carewe, and to Raulyn Sayncler, to purchase a corrody for his life, £20. Whether Raulyn was of the Somerset or Devon Sinclairs there is not anything to show.

There are considerable records existing which are safe to keep the memory of this family to indefinite periods, and Stapleton was only one of their several manors.

A calendar of old documents has, under the heading of "Dorset and Somerset", Richard I, 1195-6, "'Ralph de Seincler owes forty marks for having recognisance of 5.5 knights' fees, of which his father was possessed in the day when he took the garb of religion, by the pledges of Herbert Fitz-Herbert and Henry de Alneto'".

Among what are called new promises by Hubert, archbishop of Canterbury, is the pipe roll extract, dated 7 Richard I (1196), "'William de Seincler accounts for twenty marks for having plenary seizin of his land of Stapleton, and he has delivered them into the treasury, and is quit'".

An early notice is "'In the third year of John, A.D. 1202: rolls of aids or offerings: Somerset: Walter of Esselegham gives to his lord the king 60 marks silver as the peace-offering because he arraigned Ralph Sinclair, and because he remanded him, and that he did not use, as regards the rest, except what Walter had of his right of office'". It could well be that this sheriff Walter was a son of Hugo Sinclair, pincerna, of Aeslingham; and that Ralph got free in the rebellious year of some of the barons, on 60 marks, is possibly owing to his relationship to the sheriff.

This is confessedly difficult to infer about, but it is quite possible that Ralph had reason to be among the rebels at the beginning of John's reign. His treatment of the queen, Isabella of Gloucester, by divorcing her after he had secured by her most of the lands of her grandmother Matilda or Mabel Sinclair, daughter of Robert Fitz-Hamo, was one private cause that the Somerset family should have no love for him, and there was enough public cause besides. But they do not seem to have been ruined by Ralph's course, whatever it was in the full light of his time.

There must have been two or three antecessors of his before Richard of Granville or Britel, the ancestor, could be reached; and here is the only difficulty of tracing, to unusual fulness. The successors are plain.

At the beginning of Henry III's reign the baron Robert held Stapleton as the caput baroniae to his other manors.

On 18th October 1264, in this monarch's reign, there is a Somersetshire inquisition made in virtue of a writ dated Canterbury 3d October, on Saturday, St.Luke's, by command of W. de Wenlige, the king's escheator citra Trent, before Robert de Sancto Claro, escheator of the county of Somerset, regarding the age of Hugh Lovel for proof of heirship to the barony of Kari Lovel, worth £150. Lady Eva Lovel being dowered in tierce.

The escheator's son was one of the king's courtiers, and held various lands by serjeanty the tenure sought after as the most honourable, because testifying to a family's personal services or relationship to the crown.

Richard de Sancto Claro died in this same year possessed of Mertock, Stapleton, and other lands. In the Rotuli in Curia Scaccarii of Henry III, Edward I, and Edward II, he appears with his wife, under Somersetshire: "'Somerset: Richard Sinclair and Margaret his wife give ten pounds for license to acquire two parts to the two, of the divisions of the manor of Stapleton, with its followings'".

Of Robert, his son, The Hundred Rolls have notices, and it is to be remembered that this valuable survival has not its fame by showing the best side of men, being Edward I's challenging of the rights all round of landholders in England. In the hundred of Martock, Somersetshire, the jurati have their statement thus: "' Dicunt et quod Robs de Sender Rict de Bolougne etc peipuunt et retinuit avia de astraura set nesciunt quo waro'".

In the Hundred Forinsec de Sumton: com Soms, concerning subtractions made, or supposed to be made, from the crown's possessions, he occurs again: "'And Robert Sinclair has taken possession of a part of the hundred for twelve years past, which part his predecessors were accustomed to pay for, and this section was possessed in the time of Thomas de Perham, fee-farmer of the manor and hundred of Somerton'".

This is evidently bordering land which from paying some rent went by purchase, heirship, gift, or other accident into possession of the lords of the manor, and the king would know, or his commissioners, that no parchments or particular grants could be shown for the possession; and hence the crown's opportunity, so widely and often unjustly exercised by Edward I.

Another Robert Sinclair had a deal of trouble of this kind. In the Quo Warranto records, which are an account of the following up of the knowledge gained by The Hundred Rolls, as to whom attack should be made upon, he appears several times, and especially about some disputed parts of his manor of Somerton. He was summoned to answer as to his rights in a court in Somersetshire; but the most valuable account of him is his being summoned by William of Chiselham, the king's commissioner, to Exeter, to state his rights to parts of the properties which he held. The piece at Somerton in particular had to be fought for. Says the record, "'Robert Sinclair came and said that Richard le Bure, his grandfather, had it with certain tenements, as gift from Ralph de Huse or Hussey'". These le Bures were his lineage, who had taken this name first in Normandy and then in Essex; and the curious corroborative thing is that branches of them were on the Thames in close local and other connection with the Sinclairs there, showing the universal knowledge Sinclairs had of each other then all over England. The Bures afterwards, too, became dukes of Dorset, which is another fact binding the south-western counties, in themselves, and also to Kent and Essex.

Sir Francis Palgrave's Rotuli Curiae Regis throws considerable light on these antique but piquant relationships. In 1199-1200, for example, Hugo de Bures and Hugo de St.Clare are arbiters about lands in Tilbury, Essex, belonging to Sibilla, aunt of John of Wirre field in that county. Jordan de Bures was a donor to St.John's Abbey, Colchester, of which Eudo St.Clare was founder, and the Jordans were a Somerset family as early as the Jordan who signed the Montacute priory charter with Britel Sinclair. The Huses or Husseys are also of similar connections in old records with the Bures, Topesfield, Essex, having two of its manors in their possession, Gerebert St.Clair's family being its regularly accepted proprietors.

The Brocs, of Canterbury fame, early lords of Cobham, had Ilcestre, Somerset, as one, perhaps their original, seat, situate exactly between Somerton and Martock, belonging to these Somerset Sinclairs.

"Simon", the pet name of the earls of Huntingdon, Northampton, Lincoln, and, had they pushed their rights, of Northumberland, Cumberland, and Westmoreland, was a favourite also with the Bures.

But this Robert Sinclair who appeared at Exeter, must have been the son of the Robert of The Hundred Rolls, 1274, and he died in 1309.

The Richard Sinclair mentioned was one with Richard le Bure.

The name Robert, from Robert Fitz-Hamo's fame, became popular even above their ancestor Richard's. It is Robert, a grandson, that dies in 1337, the successor of the Robert who died in 1309. He was possessed of Stapleton manor, Andredseye, Saltmore, Bergham, and indefinite moor and pasture lands.

In passing, it might be inquired if Walter de Stapleton, bishop of Exeter and high-treasurer of England in the reign of Richard II, was one of the lineage.

When Queen Isabella and Mortimer got the Spencers upset and hanged, and the king dethroned, Walter, whom Richard had left guardian of London for him, was beheaded in 1326 by the populace.

Tindal says: "'He was a great benefactor to Oxford, founded and endowed Exeter college, and built Hart hall. The reason of the mob's fury against him was that, being the treasurer of the kingdom, he had persuaded the king's council to cause the itinerant justices to sit in London, who finding that the citizens had offended in many things, deprived them of their liberties, fined some, and inflicted corporal punishment on others'". He gives Walsingham as his authority.

Rapin says of him as a churchman, "'Walter Stapleton, bishop of Exeter, was eminent for his learning and capacity in the administration of the public affairs; and particularly for loyalty to Edward II, his sovereign, for which he lost his life'". Tindal notes that, "'With him maybe joined Walter of Merton, bishop of Rochester, and founder of Merton college in Oxford in 1267'". But this were opening too wide a field, the Stapletons being of themselves a great English family, whatever their further consanguinity.

Before leaving Edward I's searches for anything which had no charters, mention must be made of an Everard Sinclair who in the hundred of Stane, county Somerset, was challenged as to some payments and possession of tenements said to be subtracted from the hundred and added to his lands in Allberry. He was a side member.

Robert died possessed of Stapleton, Somerton, etc, and also of Budelege manor. This is another of the same to Buddleigh in Devonshire, which binds these Stapletons to Richard Sinclair of Granville more closely. In 18 Edward III (1345), Elizabeth Seincler had at her death Stapleton and its pertinents. In 1352, a Robert holds these manors, who died in 1360, leaving two sons, Richard and Ralph, between whom there was a division of the lands. Richard married a Margaret, but died without issue, as also died Ralph in 1369, the properties being left to their cousin Robert, showing that there were several branches in the county.

In the Rolls of the Court of the Treasury is account of Richard put in possession of his parts of Stapleton: "'Somersetshire: It was commanded to John of Bekington, escheator of the king in the county of Somerset, that having received security from Richard, the son and heir of Robert Sinclair, dead, of a reasonable sum, he may make full possession to Richard of two parts of the manor of Stapleton near Martock, which he holds of the king in capite by the service of half one knight's fee'".

The same escheator, who had also Dorset county under his jurisdiction, has business of settling estates heired through an "Edithe Seintelere".

The manors of Athelardeston, Hywyssh, Chanflour, with returns and advowsons, were of her right in Somersetshire, and Podyngton and West Chikerill, with the pertinents, in Dorsetshire.

There is a dateless entry in these rolls referring to a Robert which is worth transcribing: "'The king, for five marks which Thomas Warrene paid, granted to Robert Sinclair that he may give two parts of the manor of Stapleton with the pertinents, etc., to Thomas the aforesaid, to be held for his whole life as fee-farm'". This may mean the much earlier Robert who had connections with a Thomas who farmed Somerton manor as already referred to.

Of the present, the cousin Robert, there is a charter preserved in the British Museum, dated 29 Edward III (1356), having devices on a shield on the still attached seal. He is Robertus Saincler de Somerton et de Stapleton, and his parchment conveys a gift of lands to the famous abbey of Glastonbury in his own county of Somersetshire. The chief men of the kingdom were the granters of such, and this would be some evidence of the position of these lords of manors if there were not any more facts. He died in 1372, and his wife Sibilla Sentcler next year. His manors were Stapleton, Botecle, Coker, Somerton, etc., mentioned 1352.

In the escheator's Account and Inquisitions from 6 Edward III (1333) to 1 Richard II (1377) in the national record office, Fetter Lane, London, where worlds of information are lying dead, or as good as dead, in stores of ancient MS., Sibilla Sentcler, Co. Somerset, was the subject of an inquisition after death. Her properties were put in list by the escheator, William de Cheyne. She had the third part of Stapleton, Milton, Fauconberge, part of Lymington manor, Todenham manor, Somerton manor, Compton manor, Dowden, etc.

After this the family became even more numerous in the county, and the consequent divisions of fees impoverished the branch gradually, till they passed, chiefly under local names, which were the fashion, among the body of the great English nation, which owes much to the decline of its nobility into the stream of energetic everyday life.

But there were good branches who long held lands.

Sir John Sinclair of the Aldham Sinclairs, Kent, had the custody of Estham for the heir of the wife of William Sinclair of Kyngswoode in Edward III's time, and the beginning of that of Richard II, Laetitia, dying in 1377. Besides Estham she had part of the manor of Castlecary, with the advowson of the chapel on it.

In 20 Richard II (1397), William Seyntclere held Ashebrutell manor, and at the same time Robert held Andredseye manor.

There is a mention of a William Seint Cler in the Rolls of the Treasury, Henry III, Edward I and II, and also of a Nicholas, his brother, as of Somerset. They had a cause at Westminster about land, and Ivo of Ashelond was their fellow defendant.

John of Legyh and Isabella, the wife of Nicholas de Helmunden, recovered some lands from the three in Croukhern. They are not dated closely enough to be fixed in pedigree, and indeed they may be an indirect branch of the main Somerset Sinclairs.

There is much yet to be gathered of these westerns of the Hamo or perhaps, though less likely, of the Britel blood; but for the present their tale must end with Nicolas Seyntcler, miles, who had Alicia as wife, the Calendars of Inquisitions after Death of 19 Edward IV (1480) state. This is forty-six years after the extinction in the male line of the Aldham Sinclairs of Kent, Sussex, and also of Chiselbergh and other manors in Somerset.

Sir Nicolas Sinclair, in all probability, left heirs to his three properties of Pokeston, Cammelerton, and Churchill. He would, however, by the manors he held, seem to have been of yet another side branch from that in which the Roberts were so numerous.

It is difficult to do sufficient justice to these holders by serjeanty and men of distinction, on the materials yet made available, of which there is good further abundance lying undisturbed, in Fetter Lane and elsewhere, awaiting shape.

Chapter LIV
The Devenshire House

In the reign of Henry VIII, John Leland the itinerant and antiquary wrote. The Itinerary was begun and finished in 1542, but his Collectanea lay in MS. till his death. Both have valuable notes of the branches of the St.Clare family in Devonshire and Cornwall.

Said he, "'There is yet in Devonshire one of the Sainct Cleres, a man of meately fair Landes that descendith of a Younger Brother of the Principal House of S.Clere of Devonshire'".

He tells something also of this "principal house": "'Mr. Gage Controller of the Kinges House hath the substance of the lands of the Sainct Clere that was the chiefest of that name yn Devonshire be the Heire Generale'".

Another of his notes attaches suggestively with this: "'One told me that much of the Lande that Mr. Gage hath is landes of the S.Clares in Kente'". This Sir John Gage, controller of the household, knight of the garter, was the grandson of Eleanor Sinclair, the third daughter of the Thomas Sinclair of Kent, Sussex, and half a dozen counties more, who died without male to heir him in 1435.

If Leland's hearsays are right, and certainly he had the best of contemporary information, this Devonshire family was a branch of the Aldham St.Clares, descendants of Richard, the son of Walter of Medway, earl of St.Cler, and they might have been treated under that special lineage.

But though it may be true, as Leland says, that they were the "principal house", they may serve to introduce another, and a greater English house of their kin, whose first holdings were in their county. As these were the "principal house" of Devonshire, so the other was of Cornwall, though the latter did not confine itself at all to one county, as the chief Devonshire family appears to have done.

The latter's lands centred around Exeter, looking towards the English Channel, while those of the Cornwall family were on the other side of the county to the north, looking over St.George's Channel and the estuary of the Severn to Wales, where they had large properties. But the name Leland gives those on the Exeter side, of the "principal house", need not be disputed, in favour of the more famous and probably wealthier kinsfolk, their importance belonging in greater degree to Cornwall.

It was the regular way for a family to have its church founded near its seat, and the ecdesia de Sancto Claro is mentioned in 29 Henry III (1245) as giving more than double the returns of seven others in the county. There were "debts to the king", and in that year the bishop of Exeter was ordered to distrain on these churches, the debtor being John Wak, a cleric.

This was the home church of the elder main line.

In the Inquisitiones ad Quod Damnum, No.128, Anno 14 Edward II (1321) appears, "'Seintcleer: William Sinclair: Baunton bailliwick and hundred, a portion of the manor of Baunton, Devonshire'".

These inquisitions were as to losses to the king, and he here seems to make a claim to a part of Baunton manor, the seat of the "principal house".

It is the younger brother's descendants who have survived to memory most. Sir William Pole, who died in 1635, leaves account of them in his Collections, under the heading "Todwell", a well-known place a few miles from Exeter. Says he, "'Todwell or Tudwell in this parish, was possessed by inhabitants of that name. The first of which, that I find, was Jordan de Todwilla, whom lineally succeeded John, Jordan, Raph, Raph, and William Todewill, the last whose daughter Jone married unto John St.Clere, of which name of St.Clere seven succeeded each other, and the last being a man well qualified, but that by prodigality have consumed his estate, whereof being ashamed, did (a malo ad pejus) counterfeit lunacy, and in that humour pulled down his house, and sold timber and stones, affirming that none of his posterity could prosper as long as that house, where so much sin had been committed, stood, and it was credibly reported that a dead man, booted and spurred, was found in one of his fish ponds, and also the bones of divers children. It is now built by Arscot, a young brother of Arscot, of Annery, who married the said Gabriel St.Clere's daughter, and is now the dwelling house of their son'".

Sir William gives other particulars of the younger branch.

"'A manor called Buddeleigh, after the dissolution, was sold unto St.Clere of Tudwell, and by Gabriel St.Clere sold unto Thomas Ford of Bagster, esquire'".

This St.Clere of Tudwell, probably bought it from his kinsfolk, the Somerset house, who were in possession of it. If it could be proved that it was heired from them, the younger branch may have themselves been descendants of Kichard Sinclair of Granvill, Cornwall, and Wales, though it is safer to follow Leland, these proprietors of Toodvill and Buddeley being not very early possessors of them in any case.

Of another property Pole says, "'William Hidon had issue Eliza or Isabel, wife of Richard Seint Clare of Todewill, and Clisthidon continued in the name of St.Clare unto Gabriel, who sold the same unto Edward Parker, esquire, his brother-in-law'".

Again, "'John Carew, of Bickleigh, married Gilbert St.Clare's daughter, and died without issue'".

Of Kynawersy, of "the Knights" Hidon, which was a property made up of seven farms, he says it "by the heir came unto Seintcler".

It belongs to the Lord Iddesleigh (Northcote) family in later centuries.

Those Sinclairs had a third part of Torrington Parva. Egidia, one of the three daughters and coheiresses of William Carews, became the wife of William St.Clere, and brought this to him.

The Rev. Richard Polwhele, in his History of Devonshire, published in 1797, goes over Sir William Pole's ground.

Says he, "'The manor of Polsloe, to which Budleigh is subservient, was sold after the dissolution to St.Clere of Tidwell. By Gilbert St.Clere it was sold to Thomas Ford of Bagster .... Tidwell, in this parish, is called in a deed of the thirteenth century Toddewille, in another Thodewille. But its etymon is generally referred to a well on this estate, which ebbs and flows like the tide. Tidwell had lords so named. The first I find was Jordanus de Tidwella. Joan, the daughter of the last of that line, was the wife of John de St.Clere, of which name (St.Clere) seven came successively in that pleasant place. Gabriel St.Clere, after he had wasted his estate by excessive hospitality, began to take his house to pieces, and sell the timber, stone, and glass; affirming that neither he nor his posterity could prosper as long as one stone stood upon another of a house where so many sins had been committed'".

Polwhele then goes on to tell the tale of Hubert Sinclair of Bridgenorth fame, who died to save Henry II's life, "we are told a descendant of this family".

This has already been discussed, Hubert proving to be one of the Hamo family who were constables of Colchester Castle, as far as can be discovered, and not one of the Aldhams, though they are all one kin.

He continues, "'Tidwell was rebuilt by Arscot, a younger brother of Arscot of Annery, who married Gabriel St.Clere's daughter; in Sir William Pole's time it was the residence of their son. About sixty years ago the Arscots sold Tidwell to counsellor Walrond, who on his purchasing the estate built a new house, leaving the old mansion as a residence for a tenant'".

These Sinclairs had also Nether Ex by heirship from the lords Carew of those parts.

On the western side of the parish in which they had Toodville, was Hayes Farm, the birthplace of Sir Walter Raleigh. Many other brave men by sea and land were their familiar friends in the district of "Little London", as Exeter was called, from its importance and spirit. It was the house of that farm, of which his father had the remnant of an eighty years' lease, that Raleigh's still existing letter of 26 July 1584, shows him to have wished to purchase, so that he might enjoy again his early experiences. He was unsuccessful in the attempt, great courtier of Elizabeth though he then was.

The Devon visitation of 1562, Harleian MS., 889, gives various items of information.

The Fords were bound by many affinities, and in the end made but too practical use of them.

Joan Ford was the wife and widow of Gabriel Saintclere, esquire; George Ford married Joan Sinclair, the daughter of Gilbert Sinclair of Budleigh, in Devon; and a Joan Ford married John Sinclair, son and heir of Gilbert.

There was a Mark Sinclair who married a lady of the name Bois in this county.

But the Hulls of Lackbeare are equally intertwined. John Hull, armiger, four generations before this visitation of 1562, had for second wife Johanna, daughter of Richard St.Cleere of Ashperton or Ashburton, armiger, a property which afterwards gave title to one of the Fords.

Hervey, the Clarence king-at-arms, in 1567 drew the shield of William Hull of Larkebeare with seven quarterings, of which the Talbot arms and the St.Cleere arms, per pale or and az the sun in his beams counterchanged, made two.

John Holbeame of Holbeame, of another distinguished Devonshire landed family, had in the generation previous married Maria, daughter of Gilbert St.Cleere of Budleigh.

There is one scrap in the printed Harleian Miscellany, which, for all the parenthetic additions of some editor, does not give much satisfaction: "'Gilbert St.Cleere of Toodwell, in county Devon, married Joan daughter of John Strawbridge of Collyton, and had Agnes wife of John, Ann and heire of Thomas Carew of Bykeley, county Devon [son of Edmund lord Carew Joane wife of George Ford [of Islington aet 17. 30 Henry VIII] George, William, Thomas, and Philippa St.Cleer the daughter'".

At Wilton, of the great nunnery, in Wiltshire, in a church there, a ten-inch monumental pictorial brass exists to John Coffer and to his wife Philippa St.Cleer, this daughter. John is in the kneeling attitude. The date is 1585. Above the female effigy is the shield of her husband, an armiger or squire, and one quarter has the St.Cleer arms: Per pale or and azure a sun counterchanged. A professional heraldist might on this evidence fix the house of Devonshire as a branch of the Kent and Susses great family, their arms being all but the same. There is no reason why they should not be fully so accepted, if it be remembered that they were not the only family of the lineage in that county.

This John is also called Consure for surname with some coats of arms, and is supposed to have been born out of England. He was dapifer or steward to the earl of Pembroke, then great master of the household to Queen Elizabeth, and his surname Coffer, like so many, grew from his office.

Names were at that time nearly as fluently poetical as they were with the Greeks in their legendary mythological period.

He had been steward or dapifer then for 38 years, dying in 1587 at the age of 77.

While he held this office royalty twice visited the earl at Wilton.

It is also said, somewhat contrarily to prevailing literary tradition, that it was then and there Sir Philip Sydney wrote the Arcadia for the countess of Pembroke, his immortal sister, who "herself could sing Clorinda lays".

Here too, on Sir Philip's introduction, Edmundus Spencer Londoniensis Anglicorum Poetarum nostri seculi facile princeps, became a friend to Pembroke. Spenser dedicated his poem, The Ruins of Time, celebrating his heart's ideal, his "Phillisides", slain 1586 in peerless prime, to the mourning sister, "'the right noble and beautifull ladie, the ladie Marie, countess of Pembroke'".

If Philippa Sinclair was one of the Kent family, she would be close enough friends with the Sydneys, who were tenants, "keepers of sheep", a Howard once said, previously on her peoples estates there. Some of Spenser's lines actually seem cunning hidden compliment to the steward of the earl, who no doubt was very kind to him as a stranger. "'Coffers made of heben wood that in them did most precious treasure hide'", is one of the poet's visions, which Philippa Sinclair's husband may have been substance for.

At such a home the mind of England was in its highest flowering.

To have transformed Consure, for his entertainment of the angel visitor,

"'Into that starre
In which all heavenly treasures locked are'",

suggests the rather wild but fruitful wantonness of Elizabethan art. However good an earl's dapifer, and friend to one of the worthiest, this destiny seems too elevated.

There is a notice of the younger branch in The Proceedings of Chancery in the Reign of Elizabeth, and it seems to be their last appearance in records.

S.s. 19. No. 61 reads, "'Elizabeth Saintclere, wife of Gabriel Saintclere, plaintiff: Thomas Ford and Robert Mylls, defendants: object of suit - premises: For relief of the plaintiff and her children, charging the defendant Thomas Ford with keeping away her husband from her and family, and by fraudulent means procuring a conveyance of the capital messuage, barton, and demesne of Tudwell, on which the plaintiff had a settlement as jointure, and also his manor of Budleigh, and lands in Budleigh and Ashburton, and by fraudulent practices and promise of payment to plaintiff of a rent-charge of £10, procured her to levy a fine with her husband of all his estates, to the utter ruin of the plaintiff and her family, the defendant not allowing her access to her husband: county Devon'". Who the members of her family were, male and female, it would be interesting to know, but they seem to have made nothing out of this Ford of sharp practice, and henceforward had to be of the people, to gain some livelihood instead of the plentiful one thus lost to them by the frantic follies of the "well-qualified" Gabriel, whose conscience grew too tender for his people's good, and too fitted for the schemes of designers.

But total ruin cannot have come suddenly to such wealthy landholders, and there is ground to believe that they survived Ford's skill.

In the Proceedings in Chancery: Elizabeth, No. 10 is another entry of interest: "'Hugh Pomerye, Esq., plaintiff; Gawen St.Clere, Sampson Letheby, Barbara his wife, John Keyner, and Thomas Jones, defendants; object of suit to quit plaintiff's possession; premises, the manor of Engesdon, otherwise called the manor of Over Engesdon, in the parish of Ilsington, and divers lands in Ilsington the inheritance of plaintiff: Devon co'". Gawen St.Clere is thus holding some of the patrimonial estates, and the names with him are his managers or tenants.

The parish of Ilsington is at Ashburton, a town a dozen miles or more south-west of Exeter, while most of the rest of the estates, as Budleigh, Clisthidon, Tidwell, were on the other, the eastern, side of the Ex river. Gawen St.Clere was a proprietor later than Gabriel, but more with regard to him or his descendants has not been found. He lost in this case, as may be inferred from Prince's assurance that the family of Pomeroy is one of great antiquity, and that "the particular branch from which the noble house of Haberton springs was settled at Engesden, Co. Devon, temp James I" Viscount Haberton of the Irish peerage, therefore, is the present representative of Gawen St, Cleres opponent in the time of Queen Elizabeth.

A Peter Sentle devised a messuage and land in Morton-Hampsted some time previous to this from his fee to Nicolas Loskey, but it may be doubted whether he is of the Devon houses at all, though the locality argues in his favour.

This distinguished branch has some of its members in the church, of whom one may serve for more.

In the Valor Ecclesiasticus of Henry VII, the estimates of the revenues of the church, under Decanat de Plymtr: Infra archdiaconat 9 dioc. Exon in pdco com Devon, comes Clysthydon, of which George Sinclair was rector. There is a detailed account of the sources of its income from returns, offerings, lamb's wool, the total being £20 and 5d. money, which represents more than that of a rectory in general now.

That the Devonshire house is the same with the Aldham-Sinclairs, one other monumental record would seem to prove, especially by similarity of arms. In Braybrook, Rothwell hundred, Northampton, there is a mural monument with the arms, a sun in its glory, and having two side inscriptions, "'The woman reverencing her lord shall be praised'", and "'Gracefulness is fleeting and beauty is hollow'". The chief inscription runs, "'To Mary, risen from the Devonshire family of the ancient and honoured nobility of the Sinclairs, his very faithful and good wife dead by too bitter fate at Braybrook, Thomas Valence her surviving husband has placed this therefore with the highest love and eternal devotion: She died in the hope of the resurrection on the fourth day of September in the year of human salvation 1571. Tears will remain her monument '". These are the Sancto Claro and Valoniis families in the dearest nearest relations in the sixteenth century, as they so often were from the Conquest, and long before it in Normandy. The Valences, constables of Hertford Castle, most famous as earls of Pembroke, married to royalty; and, influencing in the first degree England's interests as generals and statesmen, they are one of the chief stocks of its brilliant history. The Sinclairs were even of more ancient and honoured nobility than they, for if the Valences had royalty ties by marriage the others had it by lineage of blood.

One other house, the last to be described, will go further to corroborate this, which has been shown perhaps too abundantly.

Chapter LV
The Sinclairs of Cornwall

The parish of St.Cleer is very well known by the strange stones so interesting to antiquaries and all others called "The Hurtlers and Wringdon Cheese".

It took its name from the family which were its proprietors.

At the time when The Domesday Book was written, the place was still called Treloen (from which the Trelawney, beloved of 40,000 Cornishmen), Niveton, or Trethac; but in 1288 till 1291, when Pope Nicolas had sent a commission over England for his taxatio ecclesiastica, or annates to the full value without escape, the family had its church of St.Clair in full order, which meant that its mansion there was equally perfected, giving the name to the whole district. The annate or yearly tax to Rome was 10 marks for the church.

It had all the peculiarities of construction by a Norman family.

The massiveness of its doorway of Norman architecture was celebrated, and this part of the building remained for ages to attest the wealth and civilisation of the men of the period.

St.Cleer is pre-eminently a mining parish, and this most ancient of all British industries made the proprietors of it then of similar weight to those who now have minerals in their estates.

The Ferrers earls of Derby had their names from being iron-masters, and were for this the first barons of Normandy.

There is, or was, a chapel also of fine building in St.Clear, and the carefully built well a little north of the church, attached to it, was one of the wonders. The well and chapel were connected with a great ancient nunnery here also. The baptistery of St.Cleer and the wayside cross are remnants of a state of things once very imposing and brilliant in that end of the island.

Some think that the "Schloss Stamm" of all the south-western families was situated thus in Cornwall, and one writer expressly says that the Somerset family of Stapleton, Somerton, and other manors, and the

Devon houses, the principal and side, were all branches of the original Cornwall lords of the parish of St.Cleer, Cornwall.

A suggestive fact is that the heralds have bracketed Cornwall and Essex Sinclairs as having the same arms, Azure a sun in its glory or; on a canton gu. a lion pass, ar., which is somewhat different from the Kent family.

This Essex family must have been from Hamo de St.Clair of Colchester Castle, fee-farmer of Colchester, the signer of Stephen's charter in 1146; and thus the heroic Hubert, his son, could be considered of the Cornwall branch as well as the Essex. But the Essex men who succeeded to Eudo's extinct male line were seen to be of the Hamoes, and this paves the way to what appears the origin of the branch, namely, that they were the descendants of Richard Sinclair of Granville in Normandy, of Biddiford in Devon, of Neth in Wales, and of various other estates in England and France, the brother of Robert of Thorigny, the "knight of Rye".

They are certainly of the same lineage thus, directly or indirectly, and it may not be of great difference whether the Sinclairs of St.Cleer, Cornwall, be accepted as his descendants, or of some member of the second Essex family, of the nearest consanguinity to Richard. Richard de Granville was his local name, and the history of his successors is by no means lost. Other descendants of the Cornwall house are difficult to find.

Had we the remarks of Leland on the Cornwall branch, which were originally in the MS. of his Collectanea, there might be full knowledge; but the indexes to such information remain, while the text is gone, like the tantalising abstracts of the lost chapters of Livy's history.

An entry in The Great Rolls of the Pipe, 4 Henry II, 1158, Nova Placentia 7 Nov Conventiones, shows a Hugo Sinclair, it may be, the king's butler, doing business with Cornwall: "'The same sheriff accounted for 20 marks silver for Roger, the fisher of Moneth, Cornwall, paid to Hugo Sinclair for king's tax'".

A Peerage, published in 1710 at London, throws light in the quaintest style on these affairs. Under the heading "Granville, earl of Bath", the author's account comes.

Says he, "'This ancient and noble family takes its descent from Rollo, the first duke of Normandy, which Rollo had two sons, William his eldest, surnamed Long Espee, who succeeded to his dukedom, and Robert his second son, who was the first earl of Corboile; Richard, fifth earl of Corboile; Hamon surnamed Dentatus, sixth earl of Corboile.

The said Hamon Dentatus had two sons, the eldest called after his own name Robert Fitz-Hamon; the second, as it is still the custom of those countries, after the name of one of his lordships, Richard de Granville, which surname of Granville, or by corruption Grenville alias Greynville, Graynfield, and Grana-villa has remained to his posterity ever since.

The said brothers, Robert Fitz-Hamon and Richard de Granville, accompanied William the Conqueror in his expedition into England, and were present with him at the great battle of Hastings in Sussex, where King Harold was slain, and for their signal services the Conqueror bestowed on them very large gifts and honours, particularly to Richard de Granville the castle and lordship of Biddiford, with other lordships lands and possessions in Devon, Cornwall, Somerset, and Buckingham, many whereof remain to his posterity to this day."

After the death of William the Conqueror, the said Robert Fitz-Hamon choosing twelve knights for his companions, of which his brother Richard de Granville was one, entered Wales with an army, and defeating the Welsh slew Rhese their prince; made an entire conquest of Glamorgan, and made the rest of Wales pay tribute to the king of England. Wherefore King William Rufus, in consideration of these and other great services of the said Fitz-Hamo, and being likewise his near kinsman, created him a free prince in all his conquered lands in Wales, holding the same in vassalage of the king as his chief lord: which the said Fitz-Hamon divided between himself and his twelve knights, his companions.

King William Rufus dying, the said Fitz-Hamon, who by his great exploits had now gained himself the name of The Great Fitz-Hamon, was sent by King Henry I as general of his army against France, when he received a wound by the push of a pike upon his temples whereof he died. The style of the said Robert Fitz-Hamon ran in this manner, Sir Robert Fitz-Hamon, by the grace of God, prince of Glamorgan, earl of Corboile, baron of Thorigny and Granville, lord of Gloucester, Bristol, Tewkesbury and Cardiff, conqueror of Wales, near kinsman to the king, and general of his highness' army in France.

Robert Fitz-Hamon thus dying, and leaving issue, one only daughter, Richard de Granville his brother, as the nest heir male, inherited by the Norman laws all the estate and honours of his family in Normandy, and thereby became earl of Corboile, baron of Thorigny and Granville. At his town of Keith in Glamorganshire he founded an abbey for religious monks, and endowed the same with all those lands he held in Wales.

In his old age, according to the devotion of those times, he took upon him the sign of the cross, and setting forward to Jerusalem died in his journey; leaving issue his son Richard de Granville, earl of Corboile, etc., who married Adelyne, widow to Hugh Montford, and elder brother to Robert de Bellemont or Beaumont, earl of Mollent in France and the first earl of Leicester in England after the Conquest, by Elizabeth, daughter of Hugh, the great earl of Vermandois, son of Henry, king of France;

mixing thereby with the blood of the house of Normandy the blood-royal of France; from whose loins are directly and lineally descended this family, and the ancient family of the Granvilles seated in Devon and Cornwall.

No subjects ever surpassed them in valour and nobleness of birth, nor in loyalty and fidelity to the crown, which they have most eminently shown in all ages since the Conquest; amongst whom must be always remembered that famous Sir Richard who in the reign of Queen Elizabeth, being then vice-admiral of England, with a single ship encountered the whole armada of Spain, and with 100 men fought against 10,000, of which memorable action Sir Walter Raleigh has written the relation in a particular treatise; and Sir Bevill, who so generously lavished his blood and substance in defence of his king and country in the civil wars, dying like his great ancestor Fitz-Hamon fighting with his pike in his hand at the battle of Lansdowne.

He left issue by Anne his wife, eldest daughter and coheir to Sir John St.Leger, knight, John, his son and heir, who by an immediate succession from father to son beginning at the year of our Lord 876 from Robert the son of Rollo, being upwards of 800 years, was the thirtieth earl of Corboile, baron of Thorigny and Granville. He was created by King Charles II, anno 1661, the 20th April, earl of Bath, viscount Lansdowne, baron of Biddiford and Kilhampton, groom of the stole, first gentleman of the bedchamber to his majesty, lord warden of the stannaries, lord lieutenant of the counties of Cornwall and Devon, governor of Plymouth, etc., and one of the lords of his majesty's most honourable privy council.

This addition of honours he got by his signal services and sufferings in the civil wars, having upon the death of his father Sir Bevil taken upon him the command of his regiment, being then but sixteen years of age, and being present in several battles and sieges, particularly in the fight at Newberry, where he was left among the dead.

But he was happily preserved for an action of the greatest glory and importance to his country; being the first and chief instrument of that famous negotiation with his kinsman, General Monk, by which the royal family was re-enthroned without conditions.

In memory of which, besides the aforesaid additional honours, his majesty King Charles II did pass a warrant under the privy seal, whereby he obliged himself, and recommended it to his successors, that in case of failure of male issue to General Monk, the title and dukedom of Albemarle should descend to the said earl, and be continued in his family.

His said majesty did likewise pass to the said earl another warrant for the earldom of Glamorgan, it being the first title enjoyed in England by his great ancestor Fitz-Hamon'.

But enough of this somewhat frantic eulogist. He is, however, supported with most of his facts by genuine historic and even by poetic records.

In Banks' Dormant and Extinct Baronage, Granville, who was created earl of Bath, is described as having descended in a direct line as heir male from Robert Fitz-Hamo, lord of Gloucester and Glamorgan under William the Conqueror, Rufus, and Henry I, son and heir of Hamon Dentatus, earl of Corboile, lord of Thorigny and Granville in Normandy.

The most valuable evidence is to be found in the words of his creation as earl in 1661, where Charles II says of the new earl that he has his "'descent from the youngest son of the duke of Normandy as we (the king) from the eldest'".

The promise of the dukedom of Albemarle and earldom of Glamorgan is also authenticated in a similar way.

The third and last of these earls of Bath died in 1711, but some of the present greatest houses have their chief distinction by being married with the females of these Granville Sinclairs, as for example the duke of Bridgewater and his nephew George Granville Leveson-Gower, the first duke of Sutherland, the earls Granville, the dukes of Buckingham and Chandos, with others such.

Nicolas in his Extinct Peerage also goes over the same ground.

John Granville, the first earl of Bath, died, he says, in August 1701, his son Charles the second earl twelve days after his father, and the third and last of this noble, or, by Charles II's own decision, royal line, died unmarried in 1711.

There is a small literature in the library of the British Museum on these Granvilles.

Tennyson in his poem in The Nineteenth Century of March 1878, The Revenge: a Ballad of the Fleet, has revived, almost to the very words, the story of Sir Richard as told by his friend Sir Walter Raleigh. He has done little more than to cut the prose into lengths to give it the appearance of verse, and yet the inherent interest of the tale made it successful and popular.

Sir Richard fought fifteen hours with his single vessel, "The Revenge", fifty-three Spanish "armadas", as Sir Walter calls them, doing their utmost to destroy him. He wished, and tried all he could, to blow up his vessel when he had not a man able to fight longer, but being wounded he did not carry out his determination, and borne on to the Spanish admiral's ship he died admired as much by those enemies as by his nation. His ship had so shattered several of the Spanish vessels that a storm next day destroyed them.

It was to save his own men of Biddiford, Devon, who were seeking food and water at Flores, an island of the Azores, that Sir Richard imperilled "The Revenge" against the whole Spanish fleet.

The love of Cornwall and Devon men to each other, is considerable explanation of the extraordinary gallantry they showed in the Spanish naval wars of Elizabeth's reign.

In the collection of Hakluyt's Voyages, vol. iii., his writing faculty is shown by an account of his voyage for Sir Walter Raleigh to Virginia in 1585, settling that famous colony.

Raleigh, Drake, Granville, Hawkins, are names to conjure with in affairs of the sea.

There was another Sir Richard famous as a general. In 1644, when Charles I went to Cornwall and Devon, it was chiefly Greenvil who so thoroughly beat the earl of Essex out of those counties, as can be read in Rapin or any other historian of that period.

His stubborn siege of Taunton in 1645 is one of the features of the royalist successes in the Cornish, Devon, and Somerset districts, which alone fairly met and beat the parliamentarians.

But earlier than this, in 1642, Sir Bevill Granville, a member of parliament, had been distinguishing himself as a royalist in Cornwall.

Of Sir Ralph Hopton, sent by Charles with 150 horse, Rapin says, "'Hopton was well received in Cornwall, and seconded by Sir Bevil Greenvil, a Cornish gentleman, who so ordered it that the county declared for the king'".

Lord Clarendon's History of the Rebellion tells of him.

Sir William Waller, the parliamentarian general, was defeated at Lawnsdowne Hill 5th July 1643, but Sir Bevil was slain in the battle.

He was one of the great civil and military heroes of the royalists. So much was this the case that Oxford university published a volume of verses by thirteen different hands, in sorrow for his death and eulogium of his noble character.

Its title runs, "'Verses by the University of Oxford 1643 on the Death of the Most Noble and Right Valiant Sir Bevill Greenvil alias Granvil Kt., who was slain by the Rebells at the Battle on Lansdowne Hill near Bath July the 5, 1643'".

The preface of the book, which is still extant, says that such academical honours were never before given even to royalty; and undoubtedly the writers each excel the other in the graphic art of highest panegyric. There is a portrait of his line thoughtful regular manly face, his hair over his brow short, and otherwise long, after the Cavalier fashion. It was taken at the age of 39 in 1640. The inscription is, "'The magnanimous Bevill Granvil of the English, a Cornishman, and a golden-spurred knight'".

But, perhaps, after all, none of the line deserves more honour than John the son of Sir Bevil, who on the death at Lansdowne of his father, though only a boy, took his place, and fought as heroically as man or hero could. At Newbury he was all but killed, as has been noticed. Charles II's dark fortunes he followed throughout, and there is a grant of 1660, before the restoration, showing the great love between the two, both well aware of their kinsmanship.

Besides the offices described, there was a gift of property to the value of £3000 a year made to him, if the king should get his kingdom again.

It is history at one of its greatest crises how John Granville actually made Charles II king of England, after a manner which seems hereditary in the lineage, from Eudo Sinclair's management for William Rufus downwards.

Monk was perhaps less the real cause of the restoration than John, who for his services was created earl of Bath, lord Lansdowne, etc., and loaded with all kinds of additional honours and promises.

Nothing shows more the bitter state of feeling which James II induced in the noblest hearts of England, than that this John is found making himself master of Plymouth in 1688, so that the Dutch fleet may ride secure there for the purposes of the revolution under William, prince of Orange, and his wife Mary Stuart, daughter of the runaway king.

Such a change of attitude is tribute to the ability and judgment of John Granville, who evidently had not lost his head to mere royalist toryism, as the weak souls do to whatever side they go.

There is a preface addressed to this earl of Bath in one of the books, still to be seen, from which the writer of the Peerage of 1710 must have taken several of his passages; and in it there is a general of the lineage, who did various brilliant actions in Continental warfare.

Volumes could be written about these gallant Granvilles, who, though they kept this their local name of Normandy, were of the very same blood as the St.Clares of France, as has been shown in many ways.

It has not been fixed, however, that they were the only Cornwall Sinclairs; for the Complete Parochial History of Cornwall may not be wrong in making those of St.Cleer of the same branch as those of Tudwell, in Devon, and of Martock and Somerton, in Somersetshire.

Indeed, in the fourth parliament at Westminster, an. 2 and 3, Philip and Mary (1555), the member of parliament for West Loe, Co. Cornwall, was John Seyntclere or St.Clere, esquire. This may be seen in Brown Willis's Notitia Parliamentaria.

Westloe on the south coast is about ten miles from St.Cleer, which is due north from it, near Liskeard; and this John may have been the head of the Cornish family at that period.

Conclusion

If the object had been merely to get the highest proofs of distinction for the lineage, it would have been an easier and a more decisive path to have followed its Norman history; and after identifying itself, as it does to investigation, with the line, and the legitimate line, of Rollo, the ne plus ultra of most kinds of fame might have then been reached.

But it is of far more interest to watch it as it mixes with what may be called, descriptively enough, the ruck of England's nobility, and with its commoners and people.

As much as such things can be now detected, struggling against thousands of difficulties, there was hardly a house of English historic nobility which had not some connection with the Ryes, the Corboiles, the Sinclairs, the Granvilles, or whatever other variety of appellation this one lineage has in the lapse of time received.

The youngest son of the duke of Normandy was their common ancestor; the eldest son of which same duke was the ancestor of Charles II, as he and his authorities settled in a time when genealogies and successions to properties were things of the severest science.

Had fees not been partible, even to kingdoms, and had the Salique law been preserved (both solvents avoided in matters of private estate to wonderful extent), the monarch of England now would be of this lineage, as the legitimate heir to Henry I, the last male of the Norman dynasty on the throne. The Plantagenets, Tudors, and Stuarts were, on principles of just primogeniture and true male consanguinity, interlopers.

Since Henry schemed for his daughter Matilda, the crown of England has been the prize of adventurers, and not too high type even of that class.

The Fulcs or Plantagenets were a lot of Gallic robbers, not of the gallant viking, but of the common thief complexion; the Tudors were the fruit of a mesalliance of a queen of England, daughter of a French mad king, to a little brewer of Wales (and they have left sufficient proofs of their Welsh low origin by essentially weak cruel immoral Celtic tyrannical inefficiency, Elizabeth, the greatest by far of them being, in all human if not legal probability, not Celtic at all, but an energetic English London Bullen); the Stuarts were underling, provincial, and upstart, in the exact meanings of those words; but the Scandinavian Rollo line were royal time out of mind, and their conquests have been all of the royal order.

The Norse hero was in some respect even less than his ancestors.

Dudo, the chronicler, says of his agreement at St.Cler in 912, with Charles, king of France, for Normandy and Britanny, that "'Rollo put his hands into the king's hands, which never his father, grandfather, or great-grandfather did to any one'".

The Heimskringla is the Skaldic ancient authority which tells of this and other historic events.

Kingdoms distinguished themselves, like the Sicilies, by getting ruled by such manly pink of men.

Nothing better than, nothing equal to, them, has ever walked or "ganged" the globe; and their sincerity of simplicity in all matters of thorough and genuine rule, stamped them above competition as kings among the comites or peer chiefs of the peoples.

Should huxtering ever again become of second interest, and higher things call upon the best class of men to best action, there are, breathing the old spirit of valour for energetic deeds, heirs still in this kingdom to the traditions and very blood and bone of the strongest European family.

Most are hidden by local names, but some of the lineage are clear.

The extremities of the island, like its centre, were wealthy, and are not wanting yet in gallant representatives of Rollo Rich (for this is the earliest surname of all), the duke of Neustria, son of Reginald Rich, jarl of Maere, says the Heimskringla, and of Raumdahl, in Norway, and prince of the Orkneys, in Dudo of St.Quentin's words, Senex quidam in partibis Daciae.

Jonathan Duncan, B.A., paid particular attention in his List of the Norman Barons who fought at Hastings, to the localities in Normandy whence Sinclairs came. He says, "'Saint-Clair is an arrondissement of Saint-Lo. The remains of the old baronial castle are still visible near to the church'".

Around St.Lo all the blood-related families of Thorigny, Granville, Rye, had their shares of land as the Saint-Clairs increased, the lords of the arrondissement, whence the general name; though it is to be noticed that they carried this local name earlier from the Vexin, as the Corboil earls did their title from Picardy.

These relations of the reigning dukes ultimately made their home near the Norman centres of Caen and Falaise, and this fully explains their whole ante-English Neustrian history. Indeed, St.Cler in the Vexin, and Corbie or Corboile on the Somme, about where Agincourt and Cressy battles were fought, had something of foreign or of pioneering in them, and only in the region of Caen could the joy of national life be fully felt.

St.Lo grew around their castle, and the province of Coustance was largely if not altogether in the possession of this branch of the Rollo lineage, the earl of St.Cler being their head, but not their wealthiest member, at the conquest of England in 1066.

Their prevalence is suggested by Mark Antony Lower's reference in his Patronymica Britannica, which has some good paragraphs on the name.

"'Three places called St.Clair occur in the Itin. de Normandie, in the arrondissements, severally, of St.Lo, Havre, and Yvetot. The widely-spread importance of this family is shown by the fact that about twenty coats of arms are assigned to the name'".

But he knows only the Scottish branch, and of them alone there are many more coats than these.

Under "Saint Clair, Saint Clere", he writes, "'This name, usually corrupted to Sinclair, is of French origin, and springs from the great family De Sancto Claro, in France'".

He gives the right account of William of Roslin, and notes that "Richard de Sent Cler occurs in the Domesday of Norfolk".

He quotes from Father Hay's Genealogie of the Sainte Claires of Rosslyn, "'William Saintclair was second son to Walderne, earl of Sainctclair in France, whose mother was daughter to Duke Richard of Normandy, father to William the Conqueror. He was sent by his father to Scotland, to take a view of the people's good behaviour. He was able for every game, agreeable to all company, and styled the "seemly Saintclair". The report of his qualifications came to the queen's ears, who desired him of her husband because of his wisdom. The king made him her cup-bearer .... He got also of the king and queen the barony of Roslin'".

A work could be written on the Sinclairs of Normandy and of France. Even in very modern times there have been distinguished men of the lineage who, in all essential points of birth, language, and action, were entirely French. In 1820 Charles Ferdinand, the baron de St.Clair, colonel de cavalerie, figured remarkably about the assassination of the duc de Berry, *"Je suis assassine"*. He protested to the chamber that he had warned the very highest authorities, police and other, of the conspiracy; but that these, being themselves involved in it, had arrested and imprisoned him for his loyalty to his Bourbon prince. His papers are published in book form, and there are many references to his extraordinary military career, aux bords du Rhin, dans l'armee de Conde, en Angleterre, aux Antilles, en Hollande, en Egypte, en Italie, en Espagne, en Portugal, en Russie, et en Allemagne. He had seen twenty-three years' service, got eighteen wounds, and gained innumerable decorations. His enemy, M. Decazes, minister of police, afterwards count, put him into great difficulty, because he accepted the cross of the legion of honour which one of the Bourbons offered him, through the prince of Conde, two years before the twenty-five years of service formally needed were expired. The book is of historic interest as to a curiously unsafe time.

The baron does not scruple to tell M. Decazes his mind, "'He was not an upstart like him, but a descendant of the dukes of Normandy by his mother's side [as well as his father's], and of the earls of the Orkneys and the Hebrides; a descendant of John, earl of St.Clair, who in 1649 preferred to be despoiled of a condition in life the most brilliant rather than recognise Cromwell; a descendant of Henry, count of Saint Clair, who in 1689 was the only member of the British parliament who dared to make an energetic protest against the coming of William, prince of Orange, to the throne of the Stuarts; the grandson of John, Lord Sinclair, who in 1715 sacrificed immense property, and was obliged to leave his country for his strong devotion to the same cause; the son of Charles Gideon, baron de St.Clair, colonel commanding the royal Swedish regiment, who after having consecrated his life to the service of the kings of France, was sacrificed at Dijon 29th January 1793, the victim of his devotion for Louis XVI.'". The name seems to have a trick of being in at the chief events, and these extremely characteristic Frenchmen, though of the Scottish branch, are so European in their relationships to persons and history, that they may have footing wherever the lineage is discussed, and they throw some light on English doings undoubtedly.

David Sinclair, professor of mathematics in the university of Paris, was a stirring figure from 1600 till 1622. There are some Latin tracts of his extant, one of them forming sixteen quarto pages of hexameters, celebrating the coming of James I to the English throne in 1603, and finishing appropriately with an astronomical diagram of the king's horoscope. There survive also thirteen Latin pages of his criticism of Euclid and Archimedes. His skill of drawing gets him from one of his admirers the title of eruditissimus Apelles, while Le Sieur de Philethe, Disciple de Monsieur de Sainct-Clair, Conseiller et Professeur du Roy es sciences mathematiques attempts the squaring of the circle under his auspices. In 1607 David addresses Latin verses to the queen of France, Margaret of Valois, on high political ground.

Two lines of a poem by A.M. in his own praise may complete notice of this distingue:

"'Ergo te (Sanclare) manent tua debita laudis
Praemia; et ingenio debita palma tuo'".

Longfellow in Hyperion tells of some mediaeval or earlier Abraham de St.Clair who recorded the fish-sermon of St.Anthony, and Goethe, besides the male character of one of his fictions, has a literary lady of the name among his court amateur actors; but the searches would be endless of such kind.

The Franciscus de St.Clara of the Bodleian Library was only a Sinclair as alias of his real name of Davenport, the author of the famous book of the seventeenth century, Deus et Gratia.

The great Cardinal Hugo Sancto Charo of the thirteenth century, who first put the Bible into verses, and who wrote perhaps the longest and ablest commentary upon it done by a theologian, is one of the lineage, the Italian pronunciation accounting for the slight difference in the spelling of the name. To this it might be added, for problem, whether the real saint, if such have been, the St.Clare lady whom St.Francis of Assisi encouraged with success to escape from her friends for the religious life, was not a representative. Shakespeare in Measure for Measure speaks of the strict restraint

"Upon the sisterhood, the votarists of St.Clare".

The violent Protestant, Anthony Munday, in his English Roman Life, published in 1590, tells with amusing wrath of the pilgrimages which were then made to Mount Falcon "to see the body of St.Clare". As climax he says, "'There is likewise by her a glass of tears that she shed daily in remembrance of the bitter passion of our Saviour; which tears, they say, are as fresh and sweet as they were on the first day'". But there can be going too much afield in getting to Italy, France itself being enough for illustration.

One of the most interesting passages is Stanislas the king of Poland's information to Sir John Sinclair, the agriculturist, when on his European tour, that there were then three noble families of Sinclairs known to him in Sweden.

There are families still existing of the name in France (though the famous Turgots got their lands in Normandy probably by marriage), Germany, Russia, Denmark, and Norway; and much distinctive could be gathered of them, their numbers being always few compared with the distances they are spread and the deeds they some way or other come to do or to be near when done.

A Chevalier von Sinclair is one of the notable German dramatists.

To enter other field, however, now than the political and social, would bring down an avalanche of new matter, and the present purpose will not admit of such.

Delivered from all further digression or addition, the list of the arms of the different English families may close the subject.

St.Clere [Suffolk], gold background, a red lion rampant St.Cleer [Dorsetshire], blue background, a red lion rampant in a border black crusally gold.

St.Clere [Cornwall and Essex], blue background, a gold sun in its glory, on a canton red a silver lion passant St.Clere [Essex], red background, a fesse between three lions' heads erased gold.

St.Clere [Suffolk], gold background, a red lion rampant, tail forked and nowed collared silver St.Clere [Suffolk], gold background, a red lion rampant, tail forked collared silver St.Cleere, blue background, a sun in his glory.

St.Cler, gold background, a red lion rampant within a black bordure charged with eight bezants.

St.Clere, silver background, two red bars Crest, a fox current ppr.

St.Clere, blue background, a gold star of sixteen points; on a red canton a silver lion passan St.Clere, gold background, a red lion rampant, tail forked collared of the field.

St.Clere, gold background, a red lion rampant within a black bordure St.Clere, gold background, a lion ramp, within a black bordure charged with cross crosslets of the field.

St.Clere, silver background, a black cross engrailed voided of the field.

St.Clere, blue background, on a silver chevron between three gold suns, three black mullets pierced St.Clere, blue background, three gold suns, two and one.

St.Clere [Devon], per pale gold and blue the sun in his beams counter-changed. (Hulls of Lackbeare).

St.Clere, blue background, three suns within a bordure engrailed gold.

St.Clere, red background, a fesse between three silver boars' heads St.Clere, blue background, a gold sun in its glory.

St.Clere [Sussex], blue background, gold sun in splendour (viscounts Gage).

St.Clere, per pale gold and blue a sun counterchanged.

St.Clere, gold background, a red lion rampant collared silver St.Clere gold background, St.Cleere, silver a black saltire Seyncle [Essex], red background, a fesse between three lions' heads erased gold.

Seyncler, red background, a fesse between three lions' heads erased silver Sonclere gold background, St.Clere [Devonshire], per pale gold and blue three suns counterchanged.

Sonnclere, blue background, on a silver chevron between three gold suns, three red mullets pierced Sonneclere, per pale blue and gold, three suns counterchanged.

Sinclair, silver on a cross black three crescents in fesse gold.

The secret working of English life for centuries after the Norman Conquest cannot be understood witliout full realisation of the closeness of family ties between the Norman dynasty and their chief nobles. The political usefulness and craft (learnt from violent ambitions of kin long before 1066 in Neustria) of encouraging local instead of lineage names, hid the actual nepotism which was the genuine note of those centuries as to rule. The habit has also hitherto obscured beyond recognition to historians the best class of facts by which to illustrate our national history.

A new departure, full of hope and pregnant with result, can now be made. What was fashionable with the royal and first families of the land, spread by imitation through the kingdom; and the smallest proprietors who divided their fee or fees, produced as many fresh surnames as they had sons to provide for. Extremes meet, and this system became as difficult to realise truth from, without scientific as well as fortunate enlightenment and especial study, as the exactly opposite plan of naming whole clans by the same surname. An endless series of places is nearly, at first sight, as unmanageable as a string of Johns, Donalds, Thomases, Jameses ad infinitum, all with one and the same conclusion, or without it as with the Welsh.

Stubbs in his Constitutional History, who realizes the value of Norman nerve to England more generously than any of the Oxford school of historians, of which he is a substantial member, says that nearly all the Norman nobility were of the stock of Rollo; and, with the further explanation of the necessity of hiding the family oligarchy it was, from the conquered and envious Saxons, it will be seen that there was far more of the blood of the dukes of Normandy in ruling and landed ranks than the usual writers had a dream of. The same state of things, as applied to the Sinclair branch of the ducal stock, gives the valuable inference that, under many and most varied local names, it makes up a valuable contingent of what Shakespeare writing of the English in Richard II patriotically and poetically called "this happy race of men".

www.ingramcontent.com/pod-product-compliance
Lightning Source LLC
Chambersburg PA
CBHW071234160426
43196CB00009B/1056